A Modern Guide to Sports Economics

ELGAR MODERN GUIDES

Elgar Modern Guides offer a carefully curated review of a selected topic, edited or authored by a leading scholar in the field. They survey the significant trends and issues of contemporary research for both advanced students and academic researchers.

The books provide an invaluable appraisal and stimulating guide to the current research landscape, offering state-of-the-art discussions and selective overviews covering the critical matters of interest alongside recent developments. Combining incisive insight with a rigorous and thoughtful perspective on the essential issues, the books are designed to offer an inspiring introduction and unique guide to the diversity of modern debates.

Elgar Modern Guides will become an essential go-to companion for researchers and graduate students but will also prove stimulating for a wider academic audience interested in the subject matter. They will be invaluable to anyone who wants to understand as well as simply learn.

Titles in the series include:

A Modern Guide to Public Policy
Edited by Michael Howlett and Giliberto Capano

A Modern Guide to the Economics of Happiness
Edited by Luigino Bruni, Alessandra Smerilli and Dalila De Rosa

A Modern Guide to Economic Sociology
Edited by Milan Zafirovski

A Modern Guide to National Urban Policies in Europe
Edited by Karsten Zimmermann and Valeria Fedeli

A Modern Guide to Wellbeing Research
Edited by Beverley A. Searle, Jessica Pykett and Maria Jesus Alfaro-Simmonds

A Modern Guide to Philosophy of Economics
Edited by Harold Kincaid and Don Ross

A Modern Guide to the Urban Sharing Economy
Edited by Thomas Sigler and Jonathan Corcoran

A Modern Guide to the Digitalization of Infrastructure
Edited by Juan Montero and Matthias Finger

A Modern Guide to Sports Economics
Edited by Ruud H. Koning and Stefan Kesenne

A Modern Guide to Sports Economics

Edited by

Ruud H. Koning

University of Groningen, the Netherlands

Stefan Kesenne

University of Antwerp and KU Leuven, Belgium

ELGAR MODERN GUIDES

Cheltenham, UK • Northampton, MA, USA

Published by
Edward Elgar Publishing Limited
The Lypiatts
15 Lansdown Road
Cheltenham
Glos GL50 2JA
UK

Edward Elgar Publishing, Inc.
William Pratt House
9 Dewey Court
Northampton
Massachusetts 01060
USA

A catalogue record for this book
is available from the British Library

Library of Congress Control Number: 2021945103

This book is available electronically in the **Elgar**online
Economics subject collection
http://dx.doi.org/10.4337/9781789906530

ISBN 978 1 78990 652 3 (cased)
ISBN 978 1 78990 653 0 (eBook)

Typeset by Cheshire Typesetting Ltd, Cuddington, Cheshire
Printed and bound by CPI Group (UK) Ltd, Croydon, CR0 4YY

Contents

Contributors

Wladimir Andreff, Department of Economics, University Paris 1 Panthéon-Sorbonne, France.

Robert Baade, Department of Economics and Business, Lake Forest College, USA.

Robert Baumann, Department of Economics and Accounting, College of the Holy Cross, USA.

Babatunde Buraimo, Centre for Sports Business, University of Liverpool Management School, UK.

Paul Downward, School of Sport, Exercise and Health Sciences, Loughborough University, UK.

David Forrest, Centre for Sports Business, University of Liverpool Management School, UK.

Rodney Fort, Sport Management, University of Michigan, USA.

Bernd Frick, Management Department, Paderborn University, Germany.

Jaume García, Department d'Economia i Empresa, Universitat Pompeu Fabra, Spain.

Daniel Goller, Centre for Research in Economics of Education, University of Bern, Switzerland.

Brad R. Humphreys, West Virginia University, USA.

Stefan Kesenne, Economics Department, University of Antwerp, Belgium.

Michael C. Knaus, Swiss Institute for Empirical Economic Research (SEW), University of St. Gallen, Switzerland.

Ruud H. Koning, Department of Economics, Econometrics and Finance, University of Groningen, the Netherlands.

Alex Krumer, Faculty of Business Administration and Social Sciences, Molde University College, Norway.

Michael Lechner, Swiss Institute for Empirical Economic Research (SEW), University of St. Gallen, Switzerland.

Victor Matheson, Department of Economics and Accounting, College of the Holy Cross, USA.

Ian G. McHale, Centre for Sports Business, University of Liverpool Management School, UK.

Georgios Nalbantis, Institute of Sports Science, Faculty of Economics and Social Sciences, University of Tübingen, Germany.

Gabriel Okasa, Swiss Institute for Empirical Economic Research (SEW), University of St. Gallen, Switzerland.

Jake Owen, Lancaster University Management School, UK.

Rodney J. Paul, Syracuse University, USA.

Tim Pawlowski, Institute of Sports Science, Faculty of Economics and Social Sciences, University of Tübingen, Germany.

Levi Pérez, Department of Economics, University of Oviedo, Spain.

Simona Rasciute, School of Business and Economics, Loughborough University, UK.

J. James Reade, Department of Economics, University of Reading, UK.

Nicolas Scelles, Department of Economics, Policy and International Business, Manchester Metropolitan University, UK.

Rob Simmons, Lancaster University Management School, UK.

Peter J. Sloane, Emeritus Professor, Swansea University, UK.

Lara van Steen, Department of Economics, Econometrics and Finance, University of Groningen, the Netherlands.

E. Frank Stephenson, Department of Accounting, Economics, and Finance, Berry College, USA.

María José Suárez, Departamento de Economía, Universidad de Oviedo, Spain.

Stefan Szymanski, School of Kinesiology, University of Michigan, USA.

J.D. Tena, Centre for Sports Business, University of Liverpool Management School, UK and Department of Economics and CRENoS, University of Sassari, Italy.

Pamela Wicker, Department of Sports Science, Bielefeld University, Germany.

Guy Wilkinson, Faculty of Health Sciences and Sport, University of Stirling, UK.

Jie Yang, Alberta Ministry of Labour and Immigration, Canada.

In honour of Plácido Rodríguez

1. Introduction to *A Modern Guide to Sports Economics*

Ruud H. Koning and Stefan Kesenne[*]

Sports economics is now a well-established specialization in economics, with great interest from both academics and practitioners. This book presents modern research in sports economics, and is visible proof of that interest and relevance. The field has dedicated journals such as the *Journal of Sports Economics* and the *International Journal of Sport Finance*. Other journals have devoted special issues to sports economics; see for example the *Scottish Journal of Political Economy* (2015), the *Journal of Economic Psychology* (2019, volume 75B) and *De Economist* (2021, issue 1). Sport is considered to be an ideal testing ground for economic hypotheses (the objective of the participant is usually easily established – winning, and feedback from actions is rapid), and it is also interesting and important in its own right. Fan demand, as measured by time spent watching sports in a stadium or on television, is enormous. Understanding the production process underlying a sports contest is an important part of sport consumption. Fans derive utility from discussing the quality of the teams, recent transfers, refereeing errors, individual performance, competitiveness of the contest, etc. with each other. Different aspects of these items are discussed in this book.

The first main chapter, by Fort, elaborates on the development of (European) sports economics. He examines this from an American perspective, but he also looks at the future and stresses the relevance of sports analytics and media policy. The next five chapters relate to competitive balance and attendance. Reade takes a long-term perspective when he analyses attendance patterns at professional football matches in England and Wales from 1888 onwards. Attendance is persistent, which provides support for the hypothesis that fan loyalty is an important determinant. Two chapters by Andreff and Scelles focus on outcome uncertainty fluctuation and match demand. In the first they propose measuring competitive intensity as opposed to competitive balance. In their second chapter they discuss the impact of competitive intensity on fan demand. These two chapters focus on professional football. Kesenne presents an overview of important issues regarding competitive balance in any team sports league. Causes and instruments to change competitive balance are discussed. Nalbantis and Pawlowski take a very detailed look at attendance. They moderate the relation between outcome uncertainty and attendance by pricing category and seating quality at football matches. Demand for expensive tickets is primarily driven by fans preferring the *ex ante* favorite to win, while fans buying inexpensive tickets seem to prefer a home win. Finally, Paul follows up on the importance of sports analytics as identified by Fort. He shows that new shot attempt metrics developed in the National Hockey League have significant positive effects on attendance.

Traditionally, professional sports matches are consumed by attending the match in a stadium. However, during the last 30 years a new channel has emerged. Matches are broadcast live on television. Buraimo, Forrest, McHale and Tena examine determinants of the size of television audiences for English Premier League matches. They show that, for example, championship significance is shown to be an important determinant of viewership. Does traditional gate attendance decrease because of live television broadcasting? This is the topic of the chapter by Buraimo, Owen, and Simmons. They find negative effects of live broadcasting of midweek Champions League and Premier League televised games on attendances at concurrent matches. These two chapters relate to the importance of media policy in sports as also identified by Fort.

The potential economic impact of the organization of sport events is an important topic in the sport economics literature. Three chapters focus on this topic. First, Baade, Baumann and Matheson argue that the 2014 men's football World Cup finals in Brazil increased foreign tourism by roughly 1 million, exceeding expectations. However, the 2016 Summer Olympics in the same country increased tourism by less than 100 thousand tourists, clearly indicating that the economic impact is event-specific. Tourist inflow and hotel occupancy for the 2015 women's World Cup finals in Canada is examined by Stephenson, who finds that visitors to this event displaced other tourists. Pérez assesses another potential impact of events: club teams are obliged to release players when they are invited to play for their national team. What is the effect of the Africa Cup of Nations on competitive balance in European soccer leagues? He documents a differential impact on different leagues.

Professional sport is consumed by watching athletes or teams compete, but recreational sport is produced by participation of the recreational athletes. Frick compares age-performance profiles of professional and recreational marathon runners. Competitive pressures induce elite runners to retire quite early in their career. García and Suárez take a detailed look at different dimensions of sport participation: participation, time, frequency and intensity of practice. They relate these dimensions to socio-economic factors such as education and earnings. Downward, Wicker and Rasciute explore the role of sport as physical activity for health promotion. Interestingly, they take a European rather than a national perspective.

The last six chapters focus on specific issues in sport. First, Sloane discusses labor market restrictions in the four major professional leagues in England (football, cricket, rugby league and rugby union). In an open league with promotion and relegation it is difficult for teams to achieve both financial stability and equality of playing performance. Koning and van Steen follow up on recent literature on refereeing in sports. They look at potential dismissal of red cards, and document significant variation in the probability that a red card given by a specific referee is rescinded. Interestingly, introduction of the video assistant referee (VAR) in the Dutch league in the 2018–19 season has not resulted in significantly lower rates of red cards. Is the overall result of a football match determined by 'class' or 'form'? Szymanski and Wilkinson show that in the English Premier League it is better to have more valuable players than to bank on a continued run of good results. Team dynamics is the topic of the chapter by Humphreys and Yang. Is it possible to shirk in a team when there are repeated games? In a detailed empirical study based on American football they find support for a theoretical model. Does the time between two matches between the same teams matter? Krumer uses a powerful identification strategy to answer this question, using explicit randomization based on a competition schedule. An underdog team that has done well in the first match is more likely to do well in the second match if it follows sooner rather than later. The final chapter, by Goller, Knaus, Lechner and Okasa, again relates to the sports analytics revolution. They develop a machine learning model (building on an Ordered Forest estimator) to estimate probabilities of a home win, draw and away win. The method requires a large data set; but then, big data is an important development, not least in sports!

Sports economics started as an academic field of interest in the United States in the mid-1950s. Until the turn of the century, the center was the United States, even though European academics have contributed to the development. Since then, development in sports economics in Europe has taken off, with a very important role for the series of international sports economics conferences in Gijón, Spain, which brought American and European academics together. It all started with a conference in April 2006, with the participation of famous sports economists such as Roger Noll, Rodney Fort, Robert Baade, Peter Sloane, Stefan Szymanski, Bernd Frick and Bill Gerard. After only a few years, the Gijón conferences ranked among the best and most well-known sports economics conferences in Europe. Furthermore, after each conference all papers were collected and published in beautifully edited books. These conferences were organized by Plácido Rodríguez, to whom the sports economics community is greatly indebted. To show the appreciation of all contributors to this volume, this volume is dedicated to Plácido.

Most of the work on this volume was compiled before the COVID-19 pandemic hit the world in 2020. Even though the lockdowns and suspension of sports leagues gave rise to many new questions, these are not taken into account in this book explicitly. However, current developments do touch on the relevance of the chapters relating to television demand.

NOTE

* Stefan Kesenne passed away unexpectedly on 21 June 2021, while this book was in production. We will miss a good friend, and a great scholar. RHK.

2. Sports economics at sixty-five: one American's perspective

Rodney Fort

INTRODUCTION

I am unaware of anybody who has yet to address "Sports Economics" as "a thing."[1] I've chosen to attempt that in this chapter. Sports economics received technical certification in 2015 when it was added to the *Journal of Economic Literature* (*JEL*) Classification Codes, Other Special Topics (Z), Sports Economics (Z2), with sub-codes (American Economic Association, 2020). But it existed long before that, even well before the *Journal of Sports Economics* (*JSE*) appeared in 2000. I feel the time is ripe for a retrospective, a little crystal ball gazing, and some informed encouragement.

This chapter is about sports economics as a discipline. It is only about sports economics work per se, as it turns an eye toward the future. I also assume a working knowledge of a few sports economics topics that I do not take the space to define (after all, there is Google). My hope is that one American's take on where it came from, and what it has become, may inform where it can go.

I cannot stress enough that this is just one American's perspective on sports economics. While my perspective does have international context, it is far from complete on the international dimension. The perspective is based on experience that is as broad as most, and even a bit broader than some.[2] In any event, the door is open for somebody else to have as much fun collecting their own version as I've had with this American's version.

There were important milestones along the road from "work on the economics of sports" to Sports Economics, which I think will be generally accepted and provide a framework for presentation. After the earliest work by Rottenberg (1956) and Neale (1964), the first milestone was Roger Noll's "Brookings Conference", 1971, and the resulting collection in Noll (1974). The second was Paul Sommers' "Middlebury Conference", 1991, and the collection in Sommers (1992). The third was the first of the "Western Meetings" in 1995. The fourth was the formation of the International Association of Sports Economists (IASE) in 1999, followed almost immediately by the inaugural edition of the *Journal of Sports Economics* (*JSE*) in 2000. At that point in time, the previous "work on the economics of sports" was acknowledged as Sports Economics. As I mentioned earlier, this all transpired well before the official recognition in the JEL Classification Code in 2015.

The following usually surprises people. Despite the fact that Roger Noll and Lance Davis were two of my Caltech professors, and James Quirk my official dissertation advisor, there was no sports economics in my formal training. During my graduate studies at Caltech, 1980–1983, we did microeconomics, political science, and econometrics, and my dissertation was about the behavior of prices in commodity futures markets.

But there was a tidbit on one of my qualifying examination questions, in 1982. The question began, "Suppose a league of win-maximizing owners." Then there was a list of optimization and graphical questions to address. Quirk wrote the question, and later confessed he was not much interested in the answers to the list of questions. The question actually was designed to identify students willing to question modeling assumptions: in this case, what it even meant to maximize wins and why an owner would ever want to do so in the first place.[3]

Despite no formal study of sports, my first exposure to actually applying economics to a sports question did occur at Caltech. Noll was the US Department of Justice economic expert in *Selig v. US*, ultimately decided in 1984. He hired me as data assembler/econometric technician. The Major League Baseball (MLB) salary determination model in that work became my first and, for a very long time, only working paper in sports.

During my first appointment at Washington State University, starting 1984, work on risk management, public choice, and industrial organization saw me to tenure. My mentors all counseled against any sports work unless it was formulated only as an application under a major field. They needn't have worried. There was no interest in my sports work until after 1990.

Two things happened simultaneously that invigorated "work on the economics of sports," including mine. First was the rise of general interest in player salaries. MLB free agency was the result of the Seitz decision in 1975. Shortly thereafter, technological advance put cable in a large portion of US homes. By the late 1980s, regional cable revenues were pouring in to MLB.

Of course, basic labor economics informs us that dramatic increases in player pay would follow. At this time, I first heard what I still hear to this day: "When will this sports bubble pop?" That was the first time I had to define and distinguish a bubble from a demand increase for sports writers. I've been doing it ever since.

The second invigorating force was the 1991 Middlebury Conference, which I have already labeled a milestone in the evolution from "the economics of sports" to Sports Economics. I dusted off that single lonesome working paper for the Middlebury Conference. That began my publishing in sports.

Shortly after the Middlebury Conference, Quirk contacted me to join in a book effort on sports. The result was Quirk and Fort (1992). On the heels of that publication, Quirk informed me that John Pencavel, then editor of the *Journal of Economic Literature*, had solicited a proposal for a sports paper. As it turns the corner on a quarter of a century, the resulting paper, Fort and Quirk (1995), remains my most cited journal article.

That was up through 1992. Counter to the counsel of my mentors, I've been working on nothing but sports ever since: memorable events, memorable topics, and, most important to me, memorable people. Many of the experiences related above were intermingled with the observations that follow on the historical evolution of Sports Economics.

I'll cover the following in the rest of this chapter: one American's brief history of its development.[4] Why there *should be* "Sports Economics." Crystal ball gazing about the future of sports economics.

ONE AMERICAN'S BRIEF HISTORY OF THE DEVELOPMENT OF SPORTS ECONOMICS

This section gives one American's brief history. I keep references to the bare essentials, referring the reader to the three, all-encompassing literature reviews about sports economics. Cairns et al. (1986) cover nearly every sports area up to that time, with a huge volume of papers. Fort and Quirk (1995) produced a theoretical framework for covering the literature on the American sports scene. Szymanski (2003) is an all-encompassing review, also with a sound theoretical framework for discussing issues with sports modeling to that time. In the concluding section, it is suggested that it is high time for more literature reviews, by sports economic topic.

The original contributions were in truly enviable places: Rottenberg (1956) in the *Journal of Political Economy* (*JPE*), and Neale (1964) in the *Quarterly Journal of Economics* (*QJE*). They cover some of the same ground, although Neale seems to have produced the most entertaining way of putting the basic sports economics issue: production cannot occur without cooperation among economic competitors. People are still following this lead; although, as I note later, not always very well (including yours truly).

There is a bit of a time gap to the next group of economic applications to sports, but the return appeared with wonderful placement again: El Hodiri and Quirk (1971), *JPE*; Sloane (1971), *Scottish Journal of*

Political Economy (*SJPE*); Gwartney and Haworth (1974), *JPE*; Scully (1976), *American Economic Review* (*AER*). Demmert (1973) published his book, *The Economics of Professional Team Sports.*[5] Then Noll (1974) edited the contributions to his 1971 Brookings Institution Conference on Government and the Sports Business. Books and edited collections comprised the bulk of sports economics publication for about the next 25 years.[6]

In the introduction, I listed Noll's Brookings Conference as the first milestone in the evolution of sports economics. That conference lifted "work on the economics of sports" with an important, highly publicized event. The application of economics to sports was revealed to team owners, union officers, and the press for the first time. And, in my opinion, Noll (1974) remains the solid foundation of all sports economics topics to follow.

Four of its chapters were the forerunners of later major sports economics areas: Quirk and El Hodiri on theory (the extensive, dynamic version of their 1971 *JPE* work); Noll on attendance estimation (the source of the literature on teams that price where marginal revenue is negative); Scoville on labor relations (lesson: it's all in the collective bargaining agreement); Scully on salary estimation, here applied to detecting the impact of discrimination (the "prequel" to his *AER* piece); Okner on stadiums and subsidies (is there a single area of greater attention in sports economics?); Rivkin on antitrust (and my first exposure to the politics of competition policy); and Canes on the social benefits of restrictions on team quality. I reserve extensive discussion of Canes for later in this chapter, where I point out that there remain significant investigations in this heritage collection.

The remaining chapters in Noll (1974) also generated lesser areas in sports economics: Okner on taxation and the first exposure of the special tax status for team owners and college programs; Horowitz on broadcasting and, again, the special status of sports in the eyes of the law. The paper by Davis is just plain fun, chiding MLB for just how bad it had been at taking advantage of its market power.

Gwartney and Haworth (1974) and Scully (1974) also set the stage for the rash of papers on discrimination that followed. Meaning no disrespect to any of the interim work, simply for brevity the interested reader is referred to the first ever literature review in Cairns, Jennett, and Sloane (1986). While referred to as "work on the economics of sports," the large literature in that review showed that Sports Economics was on its way.

The next milestone signaled the rise of conferences, professional societies, and annual society meetings, and the networking and growth opportunities they provided. The Middlebury Conference was the first formal gathering of sports economists since Noll's Brookings Conference 20 years earlier, in 1971. Topics were once again wide-ranging, but covering the essentials: talent distribution, arbitration, fan behavior, player pay and performance, and discrimination. Perhaps most importantly, the Middlebury Conference actually "stuck" in the sense that it started the networking required to make "the economics of sports" into Sports Economics.

The works of mine mentioned in the introduction have been lauded as part of the lifting up of sports economics. I have always championed Vrooman (1995) as well. His paper covered important areas in sports economics and provided data assessment, not in my earliest works with Quirk. For the bulk of the work through the rest of this "early modern" period, see the great review in Szymanski (2003).

But back to the legacy of the Middlebury Conference. The next milestone was the firm entrenchment of sports economics at the "Western Meetings," known now as the Western Economics Association International (WEAI) meetings. The earliest Western Meetings were organized by Lawrence Hadley and Elizabeth Gustafson, starting in 1995. The sessions have occurred at the WEAI ever since.[7]

The initial Western Meetings were attended only by Americans. That eventually changed, and the WEAI meetings have become an international affair. But there were international networking opportunities opening at about the same time. A most memorable one was the conference entitled The Regulation of the Player Market in Professional Team Sports, in Neuchâtel, Switzerland, 1997. The event was organized by Stefan Kesenne and Claude Jeanrenaud under the auspices of the International Center for Sports Studies (CIES).[8]

The next milestone came a couple of years after the start of the Western Meetings. The International Association of Sports Economists (IASE) held its first meeting in 1999 in Limoges, France. The IASE was intentionally international, with founding French and American presidents Wladimir Andreff and Paul Staudohar. The IASE by-laws also required the presidency to rotate between an American and a European. The IASE is the first time I recall the words "Sports Economists" actually being used in any official capacity.

Immediately after the IASE meeting in Limoges came the next milestone, etching sports economics into academic stone. The inaugural volume of the *Journal of Sports Economics* appeared in 2000. Founding editors were Leo Kahane and Todd Idson. Now, not only was there an association of Sports Economists, but they also now had a Sports Economics journal. And both are necessary but not sufficient conditions for a true field in economics (covered in the next section of this chapter).

If you have annual meetings, society conferences, and a journal, next a true discipline needs an undergraduate textbook. In 2000 Downward and Dawson published the forerunner of their current *Sports Economics* textbook, now with Dejonghe (2015). My textbook by the same name appeared a couple of years later. Voila! In my reading of history, Sports Economics became "a thing" in the early 2000s. Enough work and important developments in sports economics occurred to lead to the third "big" literature review in Szymanski (2003).

And the opportunities for networking also continued. In 2004, the conference entitled Rottenberg's Golden Anniversary was held in Gijón, Spain. Organized by Plácido Rodríguez, Stefan Kesenne, and Jaume Garcia, the point of this first Gijón Meeting was to link Rottenberg's earliest ideas to ongoing and proposed work into the future. The hosts published the edited conference proceedings (Rodríguez et al., 2006). The Gijón Meetings became pretty much an annual affair.

While that is the end of the milestones, developments in sports economics have continued. Travel budgets were never large in general in the US and shrank, interest areas bloomed, and competition over the presentation of ideas got to the point where two more academic societies were created. The North American Association of Sports Economists (NAASE) was formed in 2007 and forged a formal journal relationship with the *JSE*. It was only a year or two before NAASE sessions spread from the Western Meetings to the Eastern Meetings (Eastern Economic Association) and the Southern Meetings (Southern Economic Association).

Not far behind, the European Sports Economics Association (ESEA) formed in 2010. The European Meetings are held at different locations annually all across Europe. The ESEA forged its own formal journal affiliation with the *International Journal of Sport Finance* (*IJSF*).

Sports Economics received official *JEL* Classification Code recognition in 2015. It has three societies (the IASE continued as well) and two society journal affiliations. Sports economics sessions proliferate in general, very large US regional economics association meetings. And I haven't really spent time on it, but the topic has proliferated among undergraduate curricula around the world with textbooks from major education publishers. And that's one American's take on the history of Sports Economics.

WHY THERE SHOULD BE "SPORTS ECONOMICS"

Disciplines within economics seem to share similar features. A discipline has a defining characteristic that separates it from other areas of study, but work in the area can also inform the mainstream of economics. They involve a major area of human economic endeavor. Finally, they are longstanding, with a large number of practitioners.

Overwhelmingly, there should be sports economics because it satisfies these criteria. However, as the title of this section gives away, sports economics is far from being widely accepted by the parent discipline. As late as 2014, Palos-Huerta (2014) still felt compelled to subtitle his wonderful book *Beautiful game theory* with *How soccer can help economics*. It has been doing so for 65 years. In this section, I do two things: first, I make the case as stated; second, I explore incomplete acceptance by the discipline at large.

Sports are unique in one very important regard: *Cooperation among economic competitors is required to make production happen.* This is just as true of individual sports as it is of team sports, and impacts all other areas of sports. Other industries benefit from *contractual cooperation*, in the sense of the "nature of the firm" (Berle and Means, 1932; Coase, 1937). But no other industry has this "peculiar economics" noted by Rottenberg (1956) and labeled explicitly by Neale (1964).

Sports also are unique in that fans care about both absolute and relative competitive outcomes. Consumer choices among chocolates are not the result of head-to-head competition between, say, Hershey and Lindt. But fans do choose their sports time allocation and spending based on teams in a league of given absolute quality playing directly against each other, relatively. This goes all the way back to Rottenberg's (1956) "Uncertainty of Outcome Hypothesis" (UOH) and its implication for another form of cooperation by league members—the determination of the talent distribution.

While concerned with an industry of unique characteristics, sports economics nonetheless can inform the parent discipline. Keeping the unique characteristics in mind, sports economists have informed practically every area of economics—consumer behavior, consumer demand, labor talent investment, labor hiring, owner and local government investment in venues, production (both for profit and for revenue), market outcomes in the presence of market power over both labor and output, tournaments, economic games, finance and asset valuation, labor law and collective bargaining, and tax and competition policy (antitrust). And, as the history in the last section details, this has been happening for decades.

For the final criteria, sports are a major focus of society and have drawn the attention of a large number of economists over an extended time period. Pro and college sports in North America, and federation and pro sports in Europe, rank in revenues with other important industries. They also occupy far more media space than any other part of the entertainment industry. Anything that big is deserving of attention in and of itself, and for its own sake. I don't think anybody should be surprised by the gradual and then rocket trajectory of the discipline of Sports Economics detailed in the last section.

Sports Economics meets the criteria of a discipline; but I will state flatly from my own experience, and experiences relayed to me by colleagues, that the discipline at large treats sports economics like a distant relation. Indeed, the discipline at large seems stuck in time with my mentors back in 1984. While sports economics work has sporadically hit the top economics journals in the US, that work is far from generally accepted as deserving its place there along with any other work under the main headings of the *JEL* Classification Codes. Just peruse the table of contents of the major journals. Issues in health, labor, and development are pervasive; sports papers disproportionately are rare.

This treatment by the parent discipline is not unique to Sports Economics. I recommend Cherrier (2017) to all interested in the growth of disciplines in economics and how they are treated by the status quo. History appears to be against all new entrants, not just Sports Economics. But the bias is there for Sports Economics.

For one example, almost all of us are used to the standard rejection line, even for papers that are of general interest: "There is nothing wrong with your work, but it is not of interest to the general readership of this journal. You should send it to one of the sports journals." As another example, I know that colleagues' proposals for *just one* sports session have been turned down by the American Economic Association when numerous sessions are offered annually in other subdisciplines.

The hopeful sign is that there simply is strength in numbers. As noted earlier, sports sessions predominate at the Western Meetings and have spread to the Eastern Meetings and the Southern Meetings. As a result, the journals of these associations are much more amenable to sports work. The WEAI's *Economic Inquiry* has even identified its own associate editor for sports economics. Other important general outlets for sports have been the *Scottish Journal of Political Economy* and *Applied Economics*.

From this perspective, having its own *JEL* Code is a mixed blessing for Sports Economics. On the one hand, having one at least makes it easier to fill in the required title page information for most journal submissions. And I suppose some colleagues are proud that the area has finally got its own official recognition. On the other hand, in the words of *Star Wars*' inimitable Admiral Ackbar, "It's a trap." The *JSE* and the *IJSF* give biased editors in major journals an easy out for desk rejection and "referrals" to sports journals.

Sports Economics is no more a "Special Topic" than the other disciplines under that "Z" category, namely, Cultural Economics, Economic Sociology, and Economic Anthropology. Each of these appears under General Economics, Teaching (A) at Relation of Economics to Other Disciplines (A12). Indeed, "sports" as a category also appears under

Industrial Organization (L) at Sports; Gambling; Restaurants; Recreation; Tourism (L83). Many sports papers are no more "just about sports" than the foundational paper by Hotelling (1929) is just about beach popsicle stands, which also could have fit as an industry study under L83.[9]

CRYSTAL BALL GAZING ABOUT THE FUTURE OF SPORTS ECONOMICS

It was my great good fortune to befriend Gerry Scully (1941–2009) along my way. He gave the keynote at the Middlebury Conference, and much of his advice from 1991 still holds. I know he wouldn't mind that I borrow from his still relevant observations, with correct attribution.

First, do good work and do your best to relate it to the parent discipline. In researching a recent paper regarding the UOH and the demand for college sports in America, I counted 17 attendance demand studies; 13 did not even entertain a discussion of the UOH, let alone test it in their empirical work! There was only one paper on the UOH in TV viewing, but it did include the UOH in its estimation.

While it is true that the UOH is "just a hypothesis" about fan preferences, it clearly is part of what makes sports different. Given that empirical findings on its importance are mixed (Szymanski, 2003; Fort, 2006), the UOH deserves to be tested in any demand analysis. There is a mountain of data available to fill in the gaps, even just in college football let alone the other college sports.

Good work is also backward looking and addresses where it fits in the literature. Interestingly, a look backward also reveals that dissertation topics abound even from the earliest work listed earlier in the chapter. I return to and now consider the chapter in Noll's book by Canes (1974) on the social benefit of restrictions on team quality. The idea that restricting team quality might be managed in order to reduce dispersion in quality and enhance social welfare is analyzed completely. It influenced the transactions cost sports literature begun by Daly and Moore (1981), and my work with Quirk on optimal balance. But there is even more because Canes is a master at identifying the proper economic comparison.

For example, in the briefest of paragraphs, Canes (1974, p. 101) treats equally shared national TV contracts. As analysts have noted, untied to team quality as they all are, equally shared national TV contract revenues are lump sum transfers. Typically, they are disregarded in the analysis of league actions to modify competitive balance because lump sum transfers, by definition, do not affect any decision margin.

But Canes rightfully points out that the proper comparison, from the perspective of changing balance, is between the national TV centralized sale version and selling rights locally and independently by each of the league's team owners. If independent local sales were replaced by league-centralized, national sales, the return to individual team quality falls since the change in TV revenue with respect to team quality is zero under the national TV version and positive under decentralized, individual team sales. Nowhere have I seen this treated in the theoretical analysis of the distribution of league talent.

As I mentioned earlier, literature reviews that provide a theoretical framework for the coverage of a body of work appeared about every ten years in Sports Economics up to 2003. But that cycle has been dramatically exceeded since it is now 18 years since then. Perhaps it is less intimidating to choose an important topic and do that literature review. Recently, for example, Fort et al. (2016) reviewed just the work on Rottenberg's Invariance Principle.

Also, return to the parent discipline. New ways to think about sports are always happening. I wasn't able to attend the last ESEA conference. I missed the opportunity to hear Brad Humphreys talk about behavioral economics and sports. Work with behavior economics already provides provocative challenges to mainstream sports economics. And I suspect it will do so into the future.

Looking to the future. Most importantly, theoretical modeling must become more important, not less, for sports economists: We have no theory of fan behavior and digital streaming, or fan valuation of mobile/social media. We have no theory of the investment in, and valuation of, player or team intellectual property. The task also remains of expanding production and profit maximization theory to the case where sports are *inputs* rather than *outputs*. I think of what I have called the "Disneyfication" of sports as elements in large-scale real estate and entertainment complexes.

Topically, I'm enjoying the expansion of sports economics in two other areas (in addition to behavioral economics). Sports Analytics already is important for those of us that use its results to inform our specification of the "marginal product" part of marginal revenue product. But I suspect purposeful expansion of the interaction between economists and sports analytics people will prove useful for both. And here's why.

In my experience, owners don't want to hear how to win more games. They know how to win. Who doesn't, judging by the pure volume on the topic in social and traditional media? They also know the level of winning, that is, their long-run quality choice that satisfies their profit or revenue objectives. What they *are* interested in is how to win their chosen number of games *as cheaply as possible*. That's what they want from sports analytics. It seems pretty obvious that sports economists and sports analytics practitioners share a mutually beneficial, common ground.

The third area involves media policy. Once upon a time … there was only gate revenue. Radio was viewed as a threat to gate but, eventually, their complementarity became clear. Radio and gate co-exist to this day and overall revenues (gate plus media) increased. Next, over the air TV was viewed as a threat to radio and gate, but it ended up that the same complementarity existed. Over the air TV, radio, and gate co-exist to this day and, once again, overall revenues (TV, radio, and gate) increased. Next, cable TV was viewed as a threat to previous revenue sources but also ended up a complement, not a substitute. Cable, over the air, radio, and gate co-exist to this day, and overall revenues increased.

The pattern should be unmistakable. But the rise of streaming media is being treated as every other technological media innovation before it. A challenge to policy-oriented sports economists is to figure out whether streaming media actually breaks the pattern. And there is a host of market power issues involved with this new media source, just as with its predecessors. I've worked for federal regulatory agencies on the thorny questions of league-imposed viewing restrictions and the same questions seem to dominate streaming media.

For some readers, I have already crossed that line, but I could go on and on. I'll end with two questions that continue to intrigue me, one longstanding and the other only just recent. The longstanding intrigue is a strategy problem. "Tanking" in sports just means failing to try one's best. There are a number of possible explanations. The regular season may just cease to matter for either the really bad teams or for the very best teams. In either case, there is no reason to risk talent to injury or exhaustion. In games of seemingly imperceptible differences, gamblers may buy tanking services to fix matches. Perverse scheduling choices might lead participants to choose to lose a particular match in order to actually increase the chances of winning the tournament overall (a run through the loser bracket may have higher odds than playing fewer games against the best teams).

But another interesting area in sports concerns tanking as a strategy to finish low in the standings, obtaining the reward of higher draft picks. This type of tanking is like a tournament for last place. It's a commonly held belief, and there is a bit of work that concludes it is operative in US pro sports. All well and good; but let's harken back to my earlier observation that theory matters.

Of course, every hypothesis needs its null. In this case, the null is no tanking (talent conservation, or randomness). The alternative is a purposeful strategy to lose in order to get the best shot at incoming talent in the draft. It's easy to just state the comparison, but the alternative has a rationality hurdle to jump.

Rationally, it is a simple matter of arithmetic which team can finish last, next to last, and so on. The rank ordering is just (Games – Current Wins) = Remaining Possible Losses. Any owner at that point *could* force all the other owners to race for the bottom, rather than just do their best and finish in the same reverse order. But why would they? Any owner that actually did force the race would also bear the cost that they put on the others, namely, greater losses and lower revenue—that is, greater losses than needed to accomplish the same purpose. There is a direct and irrational cost to tanking for draft picks.

The second rationality point is that the cherished draft picks are far from a sure thing. Drafting can be envisioned as a risk-pooling strategy by any individual team owner. Top picks matter of course, but the uncertainty attached to incoming talent evaluation results in every owner spreading the risk across multiple rounds of the draft. It isn't a "put all your eggs in one basket" endeavor; it is pay $X millions across as many as 30 picks and get the average result of the pool. The probability that any given high pick pans out is far from one and, most draft analysts agree, closer to 0.5.

Coupled with the idea that there is a direct irrational cost and the values are not a "sure thing," then in order to tank, it's not just that losers get higher draft picks. They would have gotten them anyway. It is that the expected value of tanking (the marginal gain in talent) would have to exceed the known cost of tanking if tankers actually incur the irrational costs.

But, as I said, the idea of tanking as a tournament to the bottom for draft picks seems firmly embedded in modern sports reporting, and is even voiced by some owners/general managers about the strategies of others. And fans clearly voice repeatedly that they believe the end-strategy of some owners, where they rest their star players, is evidence of tanking for draft picks. But surely all owners/general managers (or their sports analytics group) can figure it out as it is presented here. Testing the theory, rather than the observation, requires bringing sports economics to bear.

The more recent intrigue is a problem raised by my colleague at the University of Michigan, Stefan Szymanski. Years ago, I wrote a paper about whether and how sports are different in America and Europe, a topic I revisited recently. One example that escaped me at the time was preferences for different post-season formats.

In the US, tournaments in all pro and college team sports except soccer pit the highest seeds against the lowest, and so on down the seeding. For example, in a six-team bracket, the 1st seed plays the 6th seed, the 2nd seed plays the 5th seed, and the 3rd seed plays the 4th seed. Then winners play to the end. But in Europe (and US soccer), while teams are still seeded, the match-ups are random. The 1st seed could play the 2nd seed in the very first game.

Enjoyable lunch discussions have concerned how fans in different countries would react to the opposite format and why. My colleague's current hypothesis is that American fans feel strongly that the better seeds earned that ranking and it is up to the rest of the field to show they "deserve" to beat them. European fans feel strongly the fact that higher seeds got there as a matter of historical good fortune, and that they do not deserve any further "protection" by the tournament structure.

Sorting this out informs a small but growing literature on whether "a fan is a fan is a fan." Further, this type of preference assessment will also be important for how fans value amateurism and what would happen if their cherished amateur version turned professional—or just why it is that fans take one side or the other when owners and athletes reach a bargaining impasse over player earnings. This last is especially interesting as right now sports owners attempt to reduce player pay during the coronavirus recession. Fan perceptions clearly seem to be that owners, acting like good business people, are acting to reduce losses, and greedy players are just spoiling to ruin it all for everybody.

I come to the close and conclude with two pieces of advice. First, economics is a gregarious discipline, finding its way into cooperative analysis with other disciplines in many ways. Yet, Sports Economists have yet to perfect the imperialism demonstrated by the discipline at large. This was part of my earlier observation about sports analytics, an area ripe with synergies for some sports economists. But here are two more examples of synergies.

The first is the very position that I now occupy. Trained as an economist, without any other business training, I have been Professor of *Sport Management* since 2007. My past economics graduate students also are now in *sport management* programs. And I know that sports economics is spreading throughout this "business school" approach to sports in most *sport management* programs. Clearly, the market is signaling that there are synergies in sports business areas ripe for Sports Economists.

The second example of synergies. While at Michigan I was asked to write a law review piece on concussions and the National Football League (NFL). While I know the league well, I discovered that I did not know concussions well. I turned to my Athletic Training colleague, Stephen Broglio, and the paper finally produced some sensical insights. The model we developed later assesses the dollar costs of concussions and ulnar collateral ligament (elbow) injuries to MLB owners and players. My first piece of advice is branch out, seek synergies.

My second piece of advice is to communicate the results of your research. Everything about Sports Economics is applied economics. I spin models of sports leagues. I analyze competitive balance. I have done my best to communicate the comparative statics of the imposition of labor market interventions by leagues and the empirical findings in my work.

A relevant quote is popularly attributed to Saint Jerome: "No athlete is crowned but in the sweat of his brow"—a sort of "hard work pays" ethos that also suggests that "hard work is its own reward." Quality academic work in grand journals is the equivalent of St Jerome's reference to The Sweat. But it is not what the fans pay to see. They crown the results. For Sports Economists, even the theoretical results are applications to the real world. If you seek impact in sports, learn how to communicate the lessons, not the technique. Tout the outcomes, as well as your own satisfaction in the work that got you there.

Finally, remember this fabulous quote by Nikita Khrushchev— "Economics is a subject that does not greatly respect one's wishes"—just because it is a great cautionary quote for any economist. Economic results are only what they are, not what we wish we could make them. Stick to your results.

NOTES

1. This seems especially important with the passing in 2020 of two of the discipline's major modern figures, James Quirk and John Vrooman. This chapter is dedicated to my friend and esteemed colleague Plácido Rodríguez, former President of Real Sporting de Gijón FC, recently retired as the Director of the Fundación Observatorio Económico del Deporte, and Honorary President of the International Association of Sports Economists. A tireless worker on behalf of sports economics, he organized numerous and memorable Gijón conferences and was honored with the Larry Hadley Service Award, 2018, by the North American Association of Sports Economists. *Disfruta la jubilacíon. Te lo has ganado.*
2. Some may consider the chapter a bit of a boast, but I am willing to run that risk for the purposes of this contribution. Very little of my own work is cited and I'd be glad to relate references for the uncited mentions to anybody via correspondence.
3. That question later informed some of my own work on comparing objective functions, and on assessing the implications of modeling choices and contest success functions.
4. I build upon a previous talk at University College Cork, Ireland, July 2016.
5. Demmert's book seems to be almost completely forgotten and deserves better. It was the first work devoted to explicitly empirically testing the formulations in Rottenberg. Along with Rottenberg's original specification, Demmert is the obligatory citation on sports demand.
6. From Noll's Brookings Conference to the *JSE* start in 2000, the bulk of "work on the economics of sports" appeared in books and edited volumes. Unfortunately, this early work receives neither the attention it deserves nor its rightful place in the reference section of journal articles. There were more, but I think in particular of Staudohar and Mangan (1991); Scully (1992); Fizel et al. (1996, 1999); Henricks (1997); Marburger (1997); Noll and Zimbalist (1997); and Staudohar (2000).

7. This is even true at the time of this writing during the coronavirus threat. The WEAI meetings and the sports economics sessions organized by the North American Association of Sports Economists are being held online.
8. Legal appeals of the Bosman decision of 1995 had ended and European sports directors were trying to learn US lessons on how to handle free agency. I remember the conference as a first exposure to two of the major Sports Economists in Europe, who became career-long friends, Stefan Szymanski and Stefan Kesenne.
9. Behavioral Economics is a good comparative example. It is not shuffled off to Other Special Topics (Z) or even Heterodoxy (B) at something like Behavioral Economics (B5X). Instead, because it is economics applied to various areas, it appears under Microeconomics (D) at Microeconomics: Underlying Principles (D03), under Macroeconomics (E) at Behavioral Macroeconomics (E03), and under Finance (G) at Behavioral Finance (G02). This type of inclusive categorization would work under most of the first-level codes for Sports Economics.

REFERENCES

American Economic Association. (2020). JEL classification code guide. Last accessed May 22, 2020 at https://www.aeaweb.org/jel/guide/jel.php?class=M.

Berle, A.A., and Means, G.C. (1932). *The Modern Corporation and Private Property*. New York: Harcourt, Brace, and World.

Cairns, J., Jennett, N., and Sloane, P.J. (1986). The economics of professional team sports: a survey of theory and evidence. *Journal of Economic Studies*, *13*, 1–80.

Canes, M.E. (1974). The social benefits of restrictions on team quality. In Noll, R.G. (ed.) *Government and the Sports Business*. Washington, DC: Brookings Institution, pp. 81–114.

Cherrier, B. (2017). Classifying economics: A history of the evolution of the JEL Codes. *Journal of Economic Literature*, *55*, 545–579.

Coase, R.H. (1937). The nature of the firm. *Economica*, *4*, 386–405.

Daly, G., and Moore, W.J. (1981). Externalities, property rights and the allocation of resources in major league baseball. *Economic Inquiry*, *19*, 77–95.

Demmert, H. (1973). *The Economics of Professional Team Sports*. Lexington, MA: Lexington Books.

Downward, P., Dawson, A., and Dejonghe, T. (2015). *Sports Economics: Theory, Evidence, and Policy*. Abingdon, UK: Routledge.

El Hodiri, M., and Quirk, J. (1971). An economic model of a professional sports league. *Journal of Political Economy*, *79*, 1302–1319.

Fizel, J., Gustafson, E., and Hadley, L. (eds). (1996). *Baseball Economics: Current Issues*. Westport, CT: Praeger.

Fizel, J., Gustafson, E., and Hadley, L. (eds). (1999). *Sports Economics: Current Research*. Westport, CT: Praeger.

Fort, R. (2006). Competitive balance in North American professional sports. In Fizel, J. (ed.) *Handbook of Sports Economics Research*. Armonk, NY: Sharpe, pp. 190–206.

Fort, R., and Quirk, J. (1995). Cross-subsidization, incentives, and outcomes in professional team sports leagues. *Journal of Economic Literature*, *33*, 1265–1299.

Fort, R., Maxcy, J., and Diehl, M. (2016). Uncertainty by regulation: Rottenberg's invariance principle. *Research in Economics*, *70*, 454–467.

Gwartney, J., and Haworth, C. (1974). Employer costs and discrimination: The case of baseball. *Journal of Political Economy*, *82*, 873–881.

Hendricks, W. (ed.). (1997). *Advances in the Economics of Sports, Volume 2.* Greenwich, CT: JAI.

Hotelling, H. (1929). Stability in competition. *Economic Journal*, *39*, 41–57.

Marburger, D. (ed.). (1997). *Stee-rike Four: What's Wrong with the Business of Baseball.* Westport, CT: Greenwood.

Neale, W.C. (1964). The peculiar economics of professional sports. *Quarterly Journal of Economics*, *78*, 1–14.

Noll, R.G. (ed.) (1974). *Government and the Sports Business.* Washington, DC: Brookings Institution.

Noll, R.G., and Andrew Zimbalist, A. (eds). (1997). *Sports, Jobs, and Taxes: The Economic Impact of Sports Teams and Stadiums.* Washington, DC: Brookings Institution.

Palos-Huerta, I. (2014). *Beautiful Game Theory: How Soccer Can Help Economics.* Princeton, NJ: Princeton University Press.

Quirk, J., and Fort, R. (1992). *Pay Dirt: The Business of Professional Team Sports.* Princeton, NJ: Princeton University Press.

Rodríguez, P., Kesenne, S., and Garcia, J. (eds). (2006). *Sports Economics after Fifty Years: Essays in Honour of Simon Rottenberg.* Oviedo: Oviedo University Press.

Rottenberg, S. (1956). The baseball players' labor market. *Journal of Political Economy*, *64*, 242–258.

Scully, G.W. (1976). Pay and performance in Major League Baseball. *American Economic Review*, *64*, 915–930.

Scully, G.W. (ed.). (1992). *Advances in the Economics of Sport, Volume 1.* Greenwich, CT: JAI.

Sloane, P.J. (1971). The economics of professional football: The football club as a utility maximiser. *Scottish Journal of Political Economy*, *18*, 121–146.

Sommers, P. (1992). *Diamonds are Forever: The Business of Baseball.* Washington, DC: Brookings Institution.

Staudohar, P.D. (ed.). (2000). *Diamond Mines: Baseball and Labor.* Syracuse, NY: Syracuse University Press.

Staudohar, P.D., and Mangan, J.A. (eds). (1991). *The business of professional sports.* Champaign: University of Illinois Press.

Szymanski, S. (2003). The economic design of sporting contests. *Journal of Economic Literature*, *41*, 1137–1187.

Vrooman, J. (1995). A general theory of professional sports leagues. *Southern Economic Journal*, *61*, 971–990.

3. Football attendance over the centuries

J. James Reade[*]

1. INTRODUCTION

The demand for any good is of central importance, and the demand for professional sport is no different. What is unique when it comes to professional football is the length of time over which the numbers of people expressing a willingness to pay exist. For the English Football League – the oldest professional football league in the world, and operating in England and Wales – attendance data has been recorded since the league began in 1888. Since then 135 different clubs have participated in the league, providing a vast amount of data over three centuries. Data on match outcomes back to 1888 also exists, allowing analysis of determinants of attendance over a very long period of time.

In this chapter, we analyse attendance at English Football League matches over three centuries, employing panel time series methods in order to determine the extent to which patterns of attendance have changed over the years, and have varied from club to club. Of particular interest is what we might attempt to identify as habit persistence. Have football fans become more or less persistent in their attendance patterns over the years? Do fans differ between clubs, and across regions? These kinds of questions regarding the persistence of football spectator behaviour are naturally important for the financial viability of football.

We find variation across clubs, but more significantly around the regions of England and Wales, and over time. Attendance patterns have become markedly more persistent since the 1950s, and are particularly strong in the more traditional footballing parts of the country. The more we control for various other explanatory factors (competitive balance, refined measures of team quality, local interest), the less important is a small change in league position for explaining attendance.

It is a particular honour to write a chapter on attendance demand for a book recognising the unique and manifold contributions of Plácido Rodríguez to the economics of sport, not least because as a graduate student I wrote a paper inspired by his own work looking at Spanish league attendances (Reade, 2007; see also Garcia and Rodríguez, 2002). I have been fortunate enough to attend the three most recent sports economics conferences in Gijón, Spain, where I got to know Plácido, and appreciate the great contribution these events have been making to the development of the field of sports economics.

In Section 2 the relevant previous papers investigating demand for attendance are reviewed; in Section 3 the modelling methodology adopted is set out; in Section 4 our dataset and sources are introduced; in Section 5 results from the econometric estimations are presented; and Section 6 concludes.

2. LITERATURE

Many studies considering the demand for attendance at sporting events have been conducted, and as such this review is bound to be only indicative of the range of areas covered, rather than exhaustive.

Hart et al. (1975) appears to be the first demand for attendance study, and considers Saturday afternoon attendance patterns at four top division English clubs between 1969 and 1972 (Leeds, Newcastle, Nottingham Forest and Southampton). They find that both geography and team quality teams matter significantly, although they attribute a significant proportion of variation in attendance to 'a large irrational element in the psychology of football support' (Hart et al., 1975: 27).

Another early study of English Football League attendance was carried out by Bird (1982), at an historic low-point in attendances in the early 1980s. He found that demand was income inelastic, hence that at the time football was an inferior good. He also found that demand was price inelastic.

Cairns (1987) considered structural changes in the Scottish league and their impact on attendance. He noted that changes to smaller divisions in the early 1980s increased inequality in the distribution of attendances.

Two studies by Peel and Thomas (1988, 1992) look at individual seasons within the English Football League (1981/82 and 1986/87 respectively), and in particular investigate the impact of competitive balance on attendance using bookmaker odds. In the second study they introduce a measure of core support via lagged attendance numbers at particular clubs. In both cases they find that fans prefer to see their team win rather than a highly competitive match, controlling for other factors related to the quality of a given match. This is contrary to the widely cited 'uncertainty of outcome hypothesis', a theory traced back as far as Neale (1964), that spectators prefer greater levels of uncertainty when consuming a sporting event.

Both Peel and Thomas (1996) and Szymanski (2001) consider 'natural experiments' of repeat fixtures between teams to evaluate attendance demand. Peel and Thomas (1996) consider Scottish leagues, where teams play each other twice home and twice away, creating repeat fixtures. They find further evidence contrary to the 'uncertainty of outcome' hypothesis: fans prefer to see their team win rather than an exciting game. In England, the FA Cup often provides repeat fixtures when two teams in the same division are drawn against each other, and Szymanski (2001) used this to show the impact of the decreasing competitive balance in the FA Cup relative to the league on falling attendances – a more conventional 'uncertainty of outcome' finding.

Dobson and Goddard (1996) consider the demand for attendance at football matches across the regions of England and Wales, where the Football League operates, and take advantage of time series methods to consider a long-run co-integrating relationship between attendance, ticket price, team performance and a number of more economic variables. Their time dimension is seasons rather than individual matches. They note that their price term can be removed from the long-run relationship, but that in the long term unemployment matters strongly. They suggest minimal differences across regions in terms of the loyalty of supporters, although they measure loyalty in terms of the short-run response of attendance to team performance rather than simply by the persistence in attendance patterns as might be reflected by a lagged dependent variable such as that used by Peel and Thomas (1992).

Simmons (1996) makes use of time series methods within a panel of urban-based football clubs to conduct a more conventional demand analysis, finding evidence that more casual supporters are sensitive to price changes and, more generally, that standard footballing variables such as league position do matter.

Garcia and Rodríguez (2002) investigate the demand for attendance in Spanish league football, considering a panel of match-by-match data alongside extensive price data. The main objective of the paper is to estimate demand elasticities, in particular to investigate the common finding of inelastic price demand. They appear to confirm this finding, although they note that a range of estimates result from varying the specification of the regression model.

Forrest and Simmons (2002) consider in detail the extent to which the uncertainty surrounding outcome matters. They find that there is a non-linear relationship between uncertainty of outcome and attendance, namely that demand peaks when a home team is slightly more likely than usual to win a game, tailing off either side of this. They use betting prices to do this, and look at match-by-match data. They also note the interaction between competitive balance and home advantage, noting that by increasing equality across teams the case of the home outsider facing a very strong visiting team would be lost, an occasion that they argue from their data does lead to greater attendance.

Simmons and Forrest (2006) conduct an analysis similar to that of Garcia and Rodríguez (2002) for English Football League teams around the turn of the twenty-first century, looking at match-by-match data for the 72 teams that make up the Football League. They note that capacity constraints are much less binding in the Football League compared to the Premier League (a breakaway league of the top 20 teams that were previously in the Football League), enabling them to model using conventional least squares methods of estimation.

Dobson and Goddard (1995) would appear to be the study closest to the present one, considering 94 teams over 67 seasons and finding a varied role for the price in the demand for attendance at different teams. They are unable to consider match-level data, however, as we do in this chapter.

Baimbridge et al. (1996) and Buraimo and Simmons (2008, 2015) consider the distinction between spectators watching in the stadium and watching on TV. Baimbridge et al. argue that TV coverage reduces stadium attendance, but that the financial impact of this is positive nonetheless. Buraimo and Simmons (2008) find that fans on TV prefer more balanced encounters, whereas Buraimo and Simmons (2015) find a stronger effect of quality of talent in events rather than how balanced they are.

Demand for attendance has been investigated for other popular British sports, such as cricket, despite cricket authorities releasing much less data on attendance than the football authorities. Schofield (1983) considered a new one-day league which emerged in England in the late 1960s; Hynds and Smith (1994) considered international test match cricket; Sacheti et al. (2014) also looked at international cricket; Sacheti et al. (2016) focussed on one-day international cricket, while Reade (2017) considered daily observations in the post-war era at the domestic level in England.

3. METHODOLOGY

As we consider football clubs through time, we have a panel time series setting, with both a large number of cross-section units (clubs, N) and a large number of match-level observations (T). As such, most of the concerns regarding small N or T dimensions do not apply here, and we apply standard time series analysis methods to understand the dynamics present, at a general level, in our dataset.

We run an autoregressive distributed lag (ADL) model for the log attendance at club i in match t, att_{it}, as a function of a vector of explanatory variables X_{it}. We introduce the autoregressive element, as Peel and Thomas (1992) and Dobson and Goddard (1996) do, in order to potentially capture persistence in attendance. The distributed lag element allows variables from different matches to affect attendance on a given day, and enables the calculation of long-run effects.

We regress log attendance in order to interpret coefficients in terms of elasticities and semi-elasticities, where appropriate, and the transformation also helps with the differences in scale observed in attendance in our sample. We specify P lags of both log attendance and the vector of explanatory variables:

$$att_{it} = \alpha_{0i} + \sum_{p=1}^{P} \alpha_p att_{i,t-p} + \sum_{p=0}^{P} \beta_p X_{i,t-p} + \varepsilon_{it} \qquad \varepsilon_{it} \sim N(0, \sigma^2) \quad (3.1)$$

We include a range of fixed effects, allowing that the constant term can vary across units; hence α_{0i} has an i subscript. We check for how many are required. We allow $X_{i,t-p}$ to vary across p; for example X_{it} includes various fixed effects as specified later.

Persistence in attendance patterns is captured by the lagged dependent variable coefficients, hence α_p.

In an AR(1) process, the α_1 coefficient would be interpreted as the percentage of a previous attendance that returns for the next home match: persistence in attendance patterns. With P lags the persistence is measured as $\sum_{p=1}^{P} \alpha_p$. The quality of inference into persistence depends on a number of assumptions, not least those placed on the error term, $\varepsilon_{it} \sim N(0, \sigma^2)$, holding true in the regression model. Particularly important will be the inclusion of fixed effects for years, and for clubs.

In the case where attendance is non-stationary, as would be reasonable to conclude, it is conventional to consider the transformed version of (3.1):[1]

$$\Delta att_{it} = \beta_0 \Delta X_{it} + (\alpha_1 - 1)(att_{i,t-1} - \kappa_{0i} - \kappa_k X_{i,t-1}) + \varepsilon_{it} \qquad (3.2)$$

Here, we have assumed $P = 1$ for simplicity, and $\kappa_{0i} = \frac{\alpha_{0i}}{1 - \alpha_1}$ and $\kappa_1 = (\beta_0 + \beta_1)/(1 - \alpha_1)$. The expression $att_{i,t-1} - \kappa_{0i} - \kappa_1 X_{i,t-1}$ is the long-run relationship between attendance and the explanatory variables, and $\alpha_1 - 1$ represents the speed of adjustment back to equilibrium once disturbed away from it. The coefficient κ_1 can be expressed as the infinite sum of partial adjustments of attendance of each successive time period to a change in X_{it}. As such, if we assume nothing else changes in the future, we can think of this as the long-run marginal effect.

We estimate (3.1) by ordinary least squares. Many attendance studies have estimated models of attendance using models for censored data since many stadia, particularly in more recent times, are subject to capacity constraints, and, as such, we do not observe the true variation in demand. We appeal to the small proportion of our sample that is capacity constrained, in defence of our estimation strategy, and also point out that we do not seek to interpret our results in terms of demand given our lack of price data.

The coefficients on the lagged dependent variables are fundamental to the analysis of the persistence of football attendance patterns. As such, we interact them with a range of controls in order to learn a little more about the nature of persistence. Football fans tend to believe that a great deal can be determined simply by knowledge of which team another person supports. What fans refer to as 'loyalty' we can consider to be a habit, or persistence in a pattern of attendance at a club level. Loyal supporters are those that persist with watching a team. Dobson and Goddard (1996) measure loyalty in terms of attendance response to performance measured by position, whereas Peel and Thomas (1992) measure 'core support', an obviously similar concept, by an autoregressive structure.

This loyalty notion suggests that, amongst other things, the team matters for persistence patterns, and so we test this by interacting lagged dependent variables with club fixed effects. Football supporters attach a slightly lesser degree of loyalty to their region; and indeed we might anticipate that, with the regional spread of football over the three centuries of the Football League, there are differences in attendance patterns across regions. To investigate this we interact lagged dependent variables with regional fixed effects. Anecdotal evidence seems to suggest also that attendance patterns have differed over the decades, with more alternative leisure pursuits available in more recent times. To test this we interact lagged dependent variables with a dummy variable for each decade.

The most salient explanatory variable for attendance is perceived to be league position. Although many other measures of team quality exist, and indeed are described in Section 4, league position is arguably the most simple, and most reflective. Rather than analysing various aspects of a visiting team, fans will make decisions based on whether that team is top of the league, around about the top, or worse. As a result, we focus on this in our analysis of regressions, in addition to considering fan persistence patterns.

4. DATA

We use data from the www.11v11.com website, which describes itself as the 'home of football statistics and history' and is maintained by the Association of Football Statisticians. The site contains results for all league matches that have taken place in England since 1888, as well as a number of other competitions (including European competitions). Of the 224,932 matches recorded on the website as of December 2018, 182,728 had an attendance recorded for them. From the very first day of the Football League, 8 September 1888, it is recorded that 3,000 people watched Bolton Wanderers play Derby County, 12,000 watched Everton play Accrington, and 2,500 watched Wolverhampton Wanderers face Aston Villa.

In Figure 3.1 each of those 182,728 observations is plotted, with each attendance a circle in the diagram. The dataset covers the entire history of league football, and hence the early years, pre-First World War, are a time of expansion from a low level in 1888. This would naturally have been a period of considerable expansion in the supply of observation areas at football clubs to cope with the revealed demand for football. This highlights the difficulty of identifying demand from supply in attendance data, even if some measure of ticket price is available. Given that price data is not available here, we simply focus on explaining variation in attendance, using as much data as possible to explain observed patterns. After the Second World War a steady decline is visible well into the 1980s, and

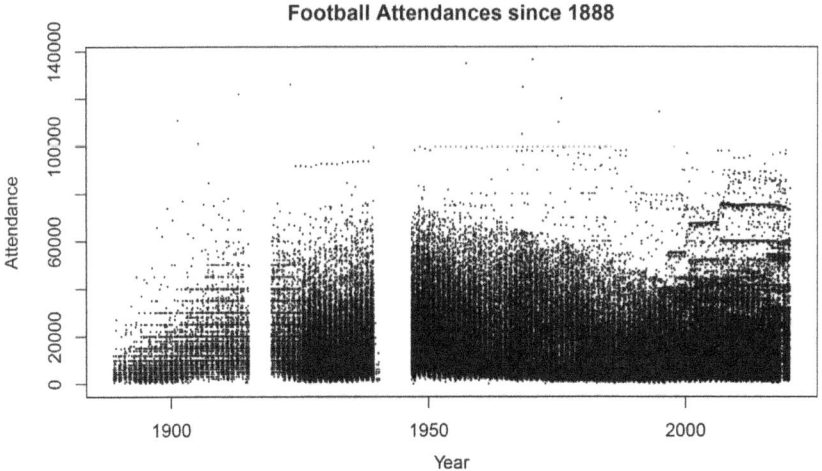

Figure 3.1   All Football League attendance through time

pick-up since the 1980s appears quite broad, albeit helped by particular growth in big attendances at a small number of constrained stadia.

When considering attendance patterns, we need to control for the level of the match as English league football has had multiple divisions since 1893, with teams separated on merit. Figure 3.2 plots the average (calendar) yearly attendance, showing that higher-level matches (black line) attract the highest attendances, with the difference being between 10,000 and 15,000. The dotted lines relate to the structure of the Football League between 1921 and 1958 as, below the top two divisions, the league was split geographically into northern and southern divisions. After 1958 there was no geographical split, and simply four divisions based on merit. The lower two divisions, geographical or otherwise, have always had considerably lower attendances than the top two divisions, making clear the need to control for the league level when explaining attendance.

We also include team fixed effects, season fixed effects and year fixed effects, to allow unobserved characteristics across each of these groupings to be reflected. League football began in the Midlands and North of England, and these areas remain traditionally strong in terms of attendance numbers. Figure 3.3 displays this regional variation, expressing the shares of total Football League attendance by region. Although by and large regional shares had settled into roughly their current levels by the end of the First World War, there is still variation through time, not least in the emergence of the East of England since that time. Because we include team

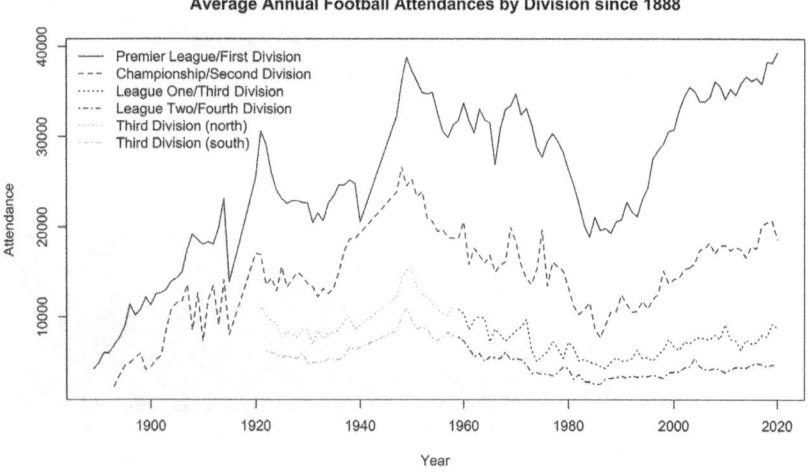

Figure 3.2   Average Football League attendance (calendar year) by division through time

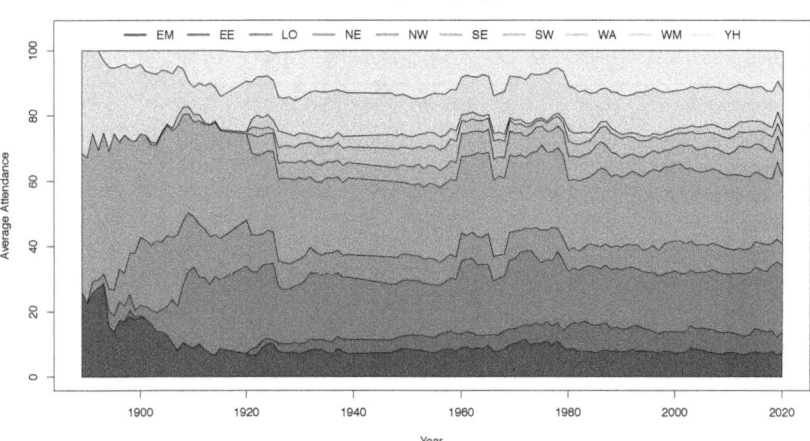

*Figure 3.3   Average Football League attendance (calendar year) by region
through time*

fixed effects, we cannot include regional fixed effects; but these team fixed effects will pick up regional patterns such as those displayed in Figure 3.3.

There are 11 NUTS1 regions throughout the entire UK, the broadest possible aggregation. These are areas such as the West Midlands and the South East. Across the Football League there are 36 NUTS2 regions, and these correspond more broadly to counties, hence Lancashire, Merseyside and Kent. There are 90 NUTS3 regions that have been represented by Football League clubs, and they represent towns, cities and, in the case of larger cities, parts of those cities. Around 14 per cent of all matches are between teams in the same NUTS1 region, almost 4 per cent in the same NUTS2 region and just 1 per cent in the same NUTS3 region.

Because the *11v11* data includes the match result for every match, we make use of this to calculate a range of explanatory variables. Table 3.1 presents descriptive statistics for the explanatory variables that are used in the model. The average attendance over the entire sample is just under 14,000, with a standard deviation almost as large, giving some indication of the extent of the variation in the variable of interest. The ranges of other variables make sense: divisions have at most contained 24 teams in Football League history, while we measure form as the total points accrued in a team's previous six matches; hence this can be at most 18.

We include measures of the quality of the home team. Football has a plethora of measures of quality, and the value of the linear regression framework is that, by including a number of them, we can determine

Table 3.1 Descriptive statistics of data

Statistic	N	Mean	Std. Dev.	Min.	Max.
Attendance	165,105	14,006.610	12,073.410	23	83,260
Log attendance	165,105	9.187	0.879	3.135	11.330
Position (home team)	196,507	12.066	6.551	1	24
Elo strength (home team)	196,507	1,074.815	141.688	637.372	1,579.160
Form (home team)	196,507	7.350	3.784	0	18
Goals scored (home team)	196,507	29.493	20.056	0	128
Position (away team)	196,507	11.662	6.558	1	24
Form (away team)	196,507	7.659	3.818	0	18
Goals scored (away team)	196,507	29.803	20.177	0	128
Elo prediction	196,507	0.494	0.142	0.065	0.931
Match balance	196,507	−0.020	0.025	−0.189	0.000
Home team in contention	196,507	0.859	0.348	0	1
Points (standard deviation)	196,507	0.021	0.013	0.000	0.750
Dynasty	196,504	26.079	133.720	1	1,940
NUTS1 region derby	196,507	0.140	0.347	0	1
NUTS2 region derby	196,507	0.037	0.190	0	1
NUTS3 region derby	196,507	0.009	0.095	0	1
Days since last match	196,368	19.237	95.688	0	16,544

which are most important. We include league position of the home team; yet this need not be the best measure of a team's within-season quality as it may be that teams have had an easier (harder) run of fixtures, which means their position is somewhat inflated (deflated). To circumvent this problem we include *Elo strengths* of the home team. Elo strengths (Elo, 1978) are an alternative method of ranking teams that takes into account the strength of opponents that have been faced (which league standings do not do as they award points regardless of the opposition for particular match outcomes). If team A has true strength at time t of $R_{A,t}$ and team B has true strength at time t of $R_{B,t}$, then the expected score for team A against team B is:

$$E_A = \frac{1}{1 + 10^{(R_{B,t} - R_{A,t})/400}} = \frac{Q_A}{Q_A + Q_B} \qquad (3.3)$$

and the expected score for team *B* against team *A* is:

$$E_B = \frac{1}{1 + 10^{(R_{A,t} - R_{B,t})/400}} = \frac{Q_B}{Q_A + Q_B} \tag{3.4}$$

where $E_A + E_B = 1$ and $Q_A = 10^{R_{A,t}/400}$ and $Q_B = 10^{R_{B,t}/400}$. Naturally, the true strengths of a team is unknown, and hence in practice one must choose a starting value for $R_{A,t}$ and allow it to be updated after each match. If the actual outcome of the match at time t for team A, $S_{A,t}$ differs from the expected outcome, then that team's score needs updating; if $S_{A,t} = E_{A,t}$, then the existing strength for each team is accurate. While we could simply treat $S_{A,t}$ as binary, scaling the match outcome between 0 and 1 (as we do) allows information on the closeness of the match to be built into the updating process. Updating in the event of $S_{A,t} \neq E_{A,t}$ is done according to the formula:

$$R_{A,t+1} = R_{A,t} + K\left(S_{A,t} - E_{A,t}\right) \tag{3.5}$$

The factor K can be varied and is conventionally set at 32. The setting of K affects both the convergence of R_A to its true value and the variation around that true value. A low K will lead to slow convergence but only small variance around that value, whereas a higher K will lead to quicker convergence but greater variance. Naturally, K can vary across different types of matches. For example, in a well-known international football variant of the Elo system, used in Reade and Akie (2013), FIFA World Cup final matches are weighted three times what international friendly matches are. We simply apply a weight of 40 to all matches.

When fans make decisions to attend or otherwise, they may do so based on simpler metrics than an Elo score. More likely, they reflect a team's recent matches, what is usually referred to as its 'form'. We include form for the home team and away team, where form is measured as the total number of points accrued in a team's most recent six league matches. This form measure averages between 7 and 8 points in our dataset, with a standard deviation of around 3.8 points. Fans may also make a decision based on how many goals a team has scored up to that point in the season, as matches with more goals are generally considered to be more entertaining. We include this for both the home and away team, and this variable averages between 29 and 30 goals, with a standard deviation of 20 goals.

How evenly matched two teams in a match are dictates the extent of the appeal of a match; the uncertainty of outcome hypothesis proposes that the greater the balance, the more interest there will be from spectators. We test this at three levels. First, we consider how evenly matched the two teams are. This is done by taking a transformation of the Elo prediction, E_A, for a match. Noting that the most equal expected score would be $E_A = 0.5$, we thus consider the negative of the squared distance from 0.5 for E_A, hence *balance* $= -(E_A - 0.5)^2$. We take the negative so that the function is inverse U-shaped, achieving a maximum of zero for a match with $E_A = 0.5$. The lowest value this measure takes in our database is −0.208, and the average value is −0.021.

Then we consider season-level indicators: the standard deviation of points in the league (which on average is 0.021), and whether the home team remains in contention (that is, whether the team can reach the top three positions in the league given the remaining points available). By this measure, almost 86 per cent of matches involve the home team in contention. Finally, we think about dynasties, where this is measured as the number of teams winning the league over the previous 25 years. On average this has been three teams, with a high of 21 and a low of one (which occurred only after the first ever season of the Football League.

Garcia and Rodríguez (2002) introduce the opportunity cost of attending matches, and we are also able to include non-football-related variables that reflect the appeal of a match. First, we add a variable for whether a match is between two teams from the same NUTS1, NUTS2 or NUTS3 region, reflecting the greater interest there usually is for matches between neighbouring teams – known as derby matches: 14 per cent of matches are between teams in the same NUTS1 region; 4 per cent between teams in the same NUTS2 region; and 1 per cent between teams of the same NUTS3 region.

We also add a variable for the number of days since the last home match to again capture opportunity cost. A shorter length of time between matches makes them (potentially) more difficult to afford, and reflects a greater burden on a potential attendee's time use. The mean value of this variable is 17.6 days, but it is heavily skewed by, for example, teams exiting the Football League and returning at a later date. The median is 14 days between matches, the standard fortnight between home matches.

We don't include any macroeconomic variables in our estimation, such as GDP levels, growth or unemployment rates. By including season fixed effects we crudely pick up the kind of impact of such variables over time.

5.   RESULTS

We present our results in steps, building up from a very basic model. This enables us to consider the impact of the additional variables we add. It is worth noting that such a basic-to-general approach runs counter to standard statistical principles; the most general model is most likely to satisfy the assumptions we place upon any statistical model, as expressed in (3.1). As such, while we do consider these small models, we do not emphasise their numerical values other than for the purposes of illustrating the bias induced by the omission of variables.

The most basic relationship to be posited, regarding attendance, is that it depends on league position. If a team is doing better, more people will attend. League position acts as a sufficient statistic as far as potential supporters are concerned. As such, we run a range of regressions of log attendance on league position, building from the most basic regression. We present these regressions as columns in Table 3.2, adding more and more variables as we read from left to right. The top panel shows the regression coefficients and, where appropriate, the fixed effects coefficients are suppressed. The panel beneath presents, where appropriate, the long-run solution coefficients as in (3.2). The bottom panel presents a small number of statistics evaluating the quality of the estimated model.

The leftmost regression simply regresses log attendance on league position, and suggests that a team gaining one league position can increase attendances by 3.6 per cent, but that equally this variation in league position is only able to explain 7.4 per cent of the variation in attendance over the years. Naturally, this is a rather meaningless number as there is nothing in the model to distinguish Manchester United from Accrington Stanley. There are many ways to include this information, and we attempt to do so in a number of informative ways.

First, we include the lag of attendance – hence a club's most recent attendance as an explanatory variable. We also include dynamic information on league position, via its lag. This regression is run over 14,000 fewer observations, reflecting that the data is somewhat patchy in places and, hence, the most recent match may not have attendance recorded. Nonetheless, there are still 151,025 observations, and the lagged dependent coefficient is 0.86, suggesting that the attendance at any given match is about 86 per cent of what it was at the previous match, plus a contribution from league position. The contribution of league position is smaller, from the contemporaneous variable at 1.4 per cent; however this does not include the lagged information. Including this enables us to consider the long-run impact of a change in position from the middle panel of the table; if a club were one position higher, attendance would be about 3.9 per cent higher, consistent with the previous estimate.

Adding dynamic information improved the model fit dramatically, as would be expected, with the adjusted R^2 coefficient increasing to 0.8 from 0.07 and the standard error of the residuals falling by more than half. In the third column we add a second lag of the log attendance and league

Table 3.2 Regression output focussing on dynamics and fixed effects

			Dependent variable			
			Log attendance			
	(1)	(2)	(3)	(4)	(5)	(6)
Constant	9.625***	1.330***	0.756***	2.014***	2.562***	3.170***
	(0.004)	(0.011)	(0.011)	(0.017)	(0.055)	(0.079)
Log attendance (lag)		0.864***	0.486***	0.414***	0.370***	0.280***
		(0.001)	(0.002)	(0.002)	(0.002)	(0.002)
Log attendance (second lag)			0.438***	0.364***	0.319***	0.228***
			(0.002)	(0.002)	(0.002)	(0.002)
Position	−0.036***	−0.014***	−0.013***	−0.015***	−0.014***	−0.015***
	(0.0003)	(0.0003)	(0.0003)	(0.0003)	(0.0003)	(0.0003)
Position (lag)		0.009***	0.005***	0.004***	0.004***	0.002***
		(0.0003)	(0.0004)	(0.0003)	(0.0003)	(0.0003)
Position (second lag)			0.005***	0.004***	0.004***	0.002***
			(0.0003)	(0.0003)	(0.0003)	(0.0003)
κ_0		9.779	9.916	9.069	8.220	6.451
κ_1		−0.039	−0.041	−0.031	−0.020	−0.021
Observations	165,105	151,099	143,959	143,959	143,959	143,959
Adjusted R^2	0.074	0.802	0.851	0.861	0.867	0.879
Residual std. error	0.846	0.393	0.342	0.330	0.323	0.308
	(df = 165103)	(df = 151095)	(df = 143953)	(df = 143941)	(df = 143812)	(df = 143693)
F statistic	13,108.590***	203,876.700***	163,910.700***	52,340.820***	6,421.143***	3,944.707***
	(df = 1; 165103)	(df = 3; 151095)	(df = 5; 143953)	(df = 17; 143941)	(df = 146; 143812)	(df = 265; 143693)
Division fixed effects	N	N	N	Y	Y	Y
Team fixed effects	N	N	N	N	Y	Y
Season fixed effects	N	N	N	N	N	Y

Note: * p < 0.1; ** p < 0.05; *** p < 0.01.

position variable to create a second-order autoregressive distributed lag model. The second lag is important, especially for attendance, suggesting that the persistence through time of football attendances is more complex than simply reflecting the most recent match.[2] Taking the sum of the two lagged dependent variables as the total persistence, the total effect is about the same (92 per cent) but is distributed over the two most recent matches. About 7,000 observations are lost by adding an extra lag, although again model fit improves and the impact of league position remains similar from the bottom panel, at 4.1 per cent.

In the third, fourth and fifth columns, fixed effects are added. Figure 3.2 displays the importance of controlling for the division of the Football League that a club was competing in, and so we add in divisional fixed effects. These fixed effects have a further time dimension as they relate to various league restructurings.[3] The persistence of attendance falls, with both the first and second lag coefficients markedly smaller and their total effect at about 78 per cent. The long-term impact of a change in position falls too, from 4.1 per cent to 3.1 per cent once we consider only changes within division. Naturally, movements up divisions lead to larger crowds.

In the fourth column, we control for club-specific effects by adding team fixed effects. This addition further reduces the persistence of attendance to 69 per cent, suggesting that with a simpler regression specification attendance patterns attributable to club-specific characteristics were wrongly being attributed to persistence. Adding in club-specific fixed effects reduces the long-run impact of a change in position to 2 per cent.

In the final column, we allow for time-specific fixed effects; we include a fixed effect for each season of the Football League's existence. Consideration of both Figures 3.1 and 3.2 shows clear secular patterns throughout the Football League's existence, with initial growth, post-war peaks, a trough in the 1980s and subsequent recovery. This addition reduces persistence yet further to 51 per cent, makes little difference to the impact of position on attendance and does affect the constant term, κ_0, by accounting for secular patterns in attendance levels over the centuries.

In sum then, adding these fixed effects, along with the club and division fixed effects, almost halves the effect of persistence. Much of what may have been attributable to habits and loyalty can better be explained by considering the division, the club and the period of time that a given match took place in. While unmeasurable club-specific and time-specific trends undoubtedly exist, it is important where possible to separate the unmeasurable from the measurable; and one benefit of sport-related data is the ability to measure what is often considered to be unmeasurable in other economic contexts. As such, we add a number of control variables, although each of these variables is of interest in its own right when thinking about determinants of attendances.

The first column of Table 3.3 presents the baseline model. The first six rows are the constant, lagged dependent variables and distributed lags of league position, as in Table 3.2. Persistence remains at about 50 per cent, as it was in the final column of Table 3.2. In the next three rows are other measures related to the quality of the home team; their Elo strength, their form and the number of goals the team has scored. The Elo strength variable has a mean of 1077.2, and hence is much larger than form, with an average value of 7.4; and, as such, the impact of Elo is proportionately greater, as well as being much more precisely measured. The impact of goals scored is negative, suggesting that, once form and the intrinsic strength of the team as measured by position and Elo strength, the impact of goals is negative and probably indicative of a weaker side that also concedes more goals.

The following four rows provide a measure of the visiting (away) team in a match via their relative Elo strength (from the Elo prediction), their position, form and goals scored. The negative coefficient on the visiting team position implies that the stronger the visiting team, the larger the attendance – with each position higher increasing attendance by 0.7 per cent. Form and goals scored by the visiting side prior to the match have negative coefficients also, indicating that spectators would like to watch the home team play out-of-form visiting sides that don't score too many goals, after controlling for their league position. The Elo prediction has a negative coefficient, which suggests that the more likely the home team is to win (the larger the prediction variable), the less likely fans are to attend (after controlling for all other variables included).

The next four rows relate to measures of competitive balance. There is no impact of dynasties, as measured by the number of different winners of the league over the previous 25 years. The standard deviation of points in the league table, which is higher in the case of less competitive leagues, has the anticipated effect: a less competitive league lowers attendances at matches within it. The third level of uncertainty is match level, and we capture this by both the balance implied by the Elo ranking and a dummy variable for whether the home team remains in contention to finish in the league's top three positions. If the home team is still in contention, attendances are higher by between 2.5 and 3 per cent, while the more balanced a match is, the lower the attendance. This is a pattern noted elsewhere; not least in Buraimo and Simmons (2008), where fans in the stadium are found to prefer their team to win, whereas fans watching on TV would prefer a more evenly matched event.

The following three rows are non-football-related variables: we have dummies for NUTS1, NUTS2 and NUTS3 region-specific matches

Table 3.3 Regression results interacting persistence with other factors (fixed effects for seasons, clubs, regions and divisions included)

	Dependent variable			
	Log attendance			
	(1)	(2)	(3)	(4)
Constant	4.854*** (0.210)	6.595*** (0.786)	11.183*** (1.285)	8.233*** (0.678)
Log attendance (first lag)	0.273*** (0.002)	−0.053 (0.069)	0.293*** (0.006)	0.242*** (0.091)
Log attendance (second lag)	0.224*** (0.002)	0.192*** (0.065)	0.222*** (0.006)	0.434*** (0.095)
Position (home team)	−0.011*** (0.0003)	−0.010*** (0.0003)	−0.011*** (0.0003)	−0.010*** (0.0003)
Position (home team, first lag)	0.003*** (0.0003)	0.003*** (0.0003)	0.003*** (0.0003)	0.003*** (0.0003)
Position (home team, second lag)	0.002*** (0.0003)	0.002*** (0.0003)	0.002*** (0.0003)	0.002*** (0.0003)
Elo strength (home team)	0.001*** (0.00002)	0.001*** (0.00002)	0.001*** (0.00002)	0.001*** (0.00002)
Goals scored (home team)	−0.001*** (0.0001)	−0.001*** (0.0001)	−0.001*** (0.0001)	−0.001*** (0.0001)
Form (home team)	0.005*** (0.0003)	0.005*** (0.0003)	0.005*** (0.0003)	0.005*** (0.0003)
Elo prediction	−0.498*** (0.013)	−0.524*** (0.013)	−0.498*** (0.013)	−0.500*** (0.013)

Table 3.3 (continued)

	Dependent variable			
	Log attendance			
	(1)	(2)	(3)	(4)
Position (away team)	-0.006***	-0.006***	-0.006***	-0.006***
	(0.0002)	(0.0002)	(0.0002)	(0.0002)
Form (away team)	-0.006***	-0.005***	-0.006***	-0.006***
	(0.0003)	(0.0003)	(0.0003)	(0.0003)
Goals scored (away team)	-0.0004***	-0.001***	-0.0004***	-0.0004***
	(0.0001)	(0.0001)	(0.0001)	(0.0001)
Dynasties	0.00000	0.00000	0.00000	0.00001
	(0.00001)	(0.00001)	(0.00001)	(0.00001)
Match balance	-0.931***	-0.893***	-0.931***	-0.953***
	(0.031)	(0.031)	(0.031)	(0.031)
In contention (home team)	0.024***	0.029***	0.024***	0.024***
	(0.003)	(0.003)	(0.003)	(0.003)
League points standard deviation	-0.279***	-0.365***	-0.273***	-0.243***
	(0.072)	(0.071)	(0.072)	(0.071)
NUTS1 derby	0.112***	0.111***	0.113***	0.112***
	(0.003)	(0.003)	(0.003)	(0.003)
NUTS2 derby	0.176***	0.175***	0.176***	0.176***
	(0.005)	(0.005)	(0.005)	(0.005)

NUTS3 derby	0.136***	0.135***	0.136***	0.135***
	(0.009)	(0.009)	(0.009)	(0.009)
Days since last home game	0.0002***	0.0001***	0.0002***	0.0001***
	(0.00001)	(0.00001)	(0.00001)	(0.00001)
κ_0	5.239	6.125	5.504	2.942
κ_1	−0.011	−0.006	−0.012	−0.017
Observations	143,956	143,956	143,956	143,956
Adjusted R^2	0.895	0.897	0.895	0.898
Residual std. error	0.286	0.284	0.286	0.283
	(df = 143677)	(df = 143639)	(df = 143659)	(df = 143425)
Persistence with	N/A	Decade	Region	Club
F test	N/A	64.884***	23.671***	14.26***
	N/A	(df = 38; 143639)	(df = 18; 143659)	(df = 252; 143425)

Note: * p < 0.1; ** p < 0.05; *** p < 0.01.

(derbies). A game between clubs in the same NUTS1 region has about 11 per cent greater attendance; games between clubs in the same NUTS2 areas have a further 18 per cent larger attendances; and matches between teams within NUTS3 areas have another 14 per cent more spectators in attendance.

Finally, each extra day between matches increases the attendance by 0.02 per cent, reflecting that matches with only a few days' gap will attract fewer spectators than if there has been a longer period of time since the last match. This indirectly reflects the budget constraints of supporters.

Adding these control variables reduces the long-run impact of position on league position further, to just 1.1 per cent.

The second, third and fourth columns in Table 3.3 interact the lagged dependent variable with the fixed effects for secular trends (inserting only decade indicators rather than a fixed effect for each year), regional effects and club effects. The bottom two rows display which fixed effects are interacted, and report an F test for the significance of those fixed effect interactions. In all three cases, the null that they are zero is rejected.

From the second column, persistence has changed over the decades. The variation is perhaps best expressed graphically, and the sum of the autoregressive parameters related to each decade is presented in the top panel of Figure 3.4. Recorded persistence increased distinctly between the 1950s and the 1970s, which corresponds to the period of the most precipitous decline in attendances from Figure 3.1. This greater persistence in attendance patterns has continued at this higher level of 0.55 since the 1970s.

A staple of football supporter interactions is the notion that some supporters are more loyal than others. Loyalty is the idea that fans are persistent in attending regardless of how their team is performing. In the third column of Table 3.3 we consider whether there are regional disparities in persistence, and hence 'loyalty'. We plot the differences across regions in the middle panel of Figure 3.4. Supporters in Wales are the most 'loyal', followed by those in the East Midlands, Yorkshire and the Humber, and the North West. Persistence is lowest in London, the South West and the East of England.

The final column of Table 3.3 interacts club fixed effects with teams. This is the bottom panel in Figure 3.4, but with 130 clubs it is not possible to distinguish each team. A number of the outliers are teams with very few observations, relatively (those with short stays in the Football League). The significant majority of observations are within a range of 0.4 to 0.6, and as such are statistically indistinguishable from each other.[4]

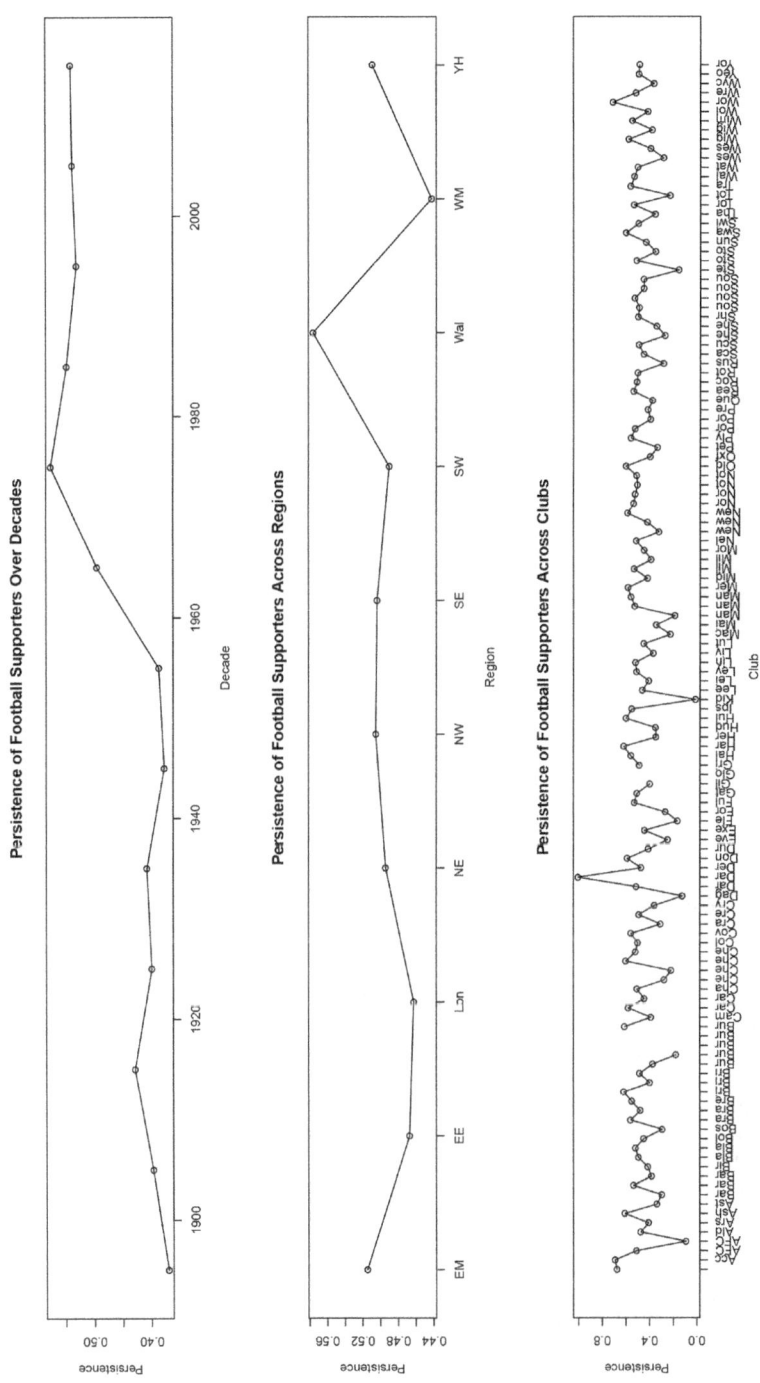

Figure 3.4   Variation in persistence of attendance patterns across decades and regions in the Football League

41

6. CONCLUSIONS

Attendance patterns across three centuries are considered in this chapter, using almost 200,000 match-level observations on over 100 Football League clubs. In the absence of price data, focus is instead placed on the persistence of attendance patterns. Adequate controlling for variation attributable to the quality of the teams involved in the match, as well as other factors such as those related to competitive balance, we find a smaller but nonetheless significant persistence effect that has varied over time, and which also varies across regions and teams.

NOTES

*   Thanks to Carl Singleton for helpful comments on a draft of this chapter.
1.   It is worth noting that the transformation remains valid statistically even if the data series are stationary in their levels.
2.   In addition, unreported though important, the second lag removes all autocorrelation from the residuals of the estimated model.
3.   The second, third and fourth tiers were added gradually, with a geographical third tier after the First World War, which became simply a third and fourth tier in 1959. In 1992 the FA Premier League was created, a breakaway from the Football League; and in 2005 another renaming saw the division beneath the Premier League become the Championship.
4.   According to this measure, the following teams have the most loyal fanbases – Accrington Stanley, Hartlepool, Brighton, Bury, Chester and Oldham; and the following have the least loyal – Dagenham and Redbridge, Stevenage, Fleetwood, Burton, Manchester City, Cheltenham, Macclesfield Town, Tottenham Hotspur and Everton.

REFERENCES

Baimbridge, M., S. Cameron, and P.M. Dawson. Satellite television and the demand for football: a whole new ball game? *Scottish Journal of Political Economy*, 43: 317–333, 1996.
Bird, P.J.W.N. The demand for league football. *Applied Economics*, 14(6): 637–649, 1982.
Buraimo, B. and R. Simmons. Do sports fans really value uncertainty of outcome? Evidence from the English Premier League. *International Journal of Sport Finance*, 3(3): 146, 2008.
Buraimo, B. and R. Simmons. Uncertainty of outcome or star quality? Television audience demand for English Premier League football. *International Journal of the Economics of Business*, 22(3): 449–469, 2015.
Cairns, J.A. Evaluating changes in league structure: the reorganization of the Scottish Football League. *Applied Economics*, 19(2): 259–275, 1987.
Dobson, S.M. and J.A. Goddard. The demand for professional league football in England and Wales, 1925–92. *The Statistician*, 44(2): 259–277, 1995.

Dobson, S.M. and J.A. Goddard. The demand for football in the regions of England and Wales. *Regional Studies*, 30(5): 443–453, 1996.

Elo, A.E. *The Rating of Chessplayers, Past and Present*, volume 3. Batsford, London, 1978.

Forrest, D. and R. Simmons. Outcome uncertainty and attendance demand in sport: the case of English soccer. *Journal of the Royal Statistical Society: Series D (The Statistician)*, 51(2): 229–241, 2002.

Garcia, J. and P. Rodríguez. The determinants of football match attendance revisited: empirical evidence from the Spanish football league. *Journal of Sports Economics*, 3(1): 18–38, 2002.

Hart, R.A., J. Hutton, and T. Sharot. A statistical analysis of Association football attendances. *Applied Statistics*, 24(1): 17–27, 1975.

Hynds, M. and I. Smith. The demand for Test match cricket. *Applied Economics Letters*, 1(7): 103–106, 1994.

Neale, W.C. The peculiar economics of professional sports. *Quarterly Journal of Economics*, 78(1): 1–14, 1964.

Peel, D.A. and D.A. Thomas. Outcome uncertainty and the demand for football: an analysis of match attendances in the English football league. *Scottish Journal of Political Economy*, 35(3): 242–249, 1988.

Peel, D.A. and D.A. Thomas. The demand for football: some evidence on outcome uncertainty. *Empirical Economics*, 17(2): 323–331, 1992.

Peel, D.A. and D.A. Thomas. Attendance demand: an investigation of repeat fixtures. *Applied Economics Letters*, 3(6): 391–394, 1996.

Reade, J.J. Modelling and forecasting football attendances. *Oxonomics*, 2(1–2): 27–32, 2007.

Reade, J.J. Daily demand: Leicestershire cricket in the post-war era. Discussion paper, University of Reading Department of Economics, 2017.

Reade, J.J. and S. Akie. Using forecasting to detect corruption in international football. Working Papers 2013-005, George Washington University, Department of Economics, H.O. Stekler Research Program on Forecasting, 2013.

Sacheti, A., I. Gregory-Smith, and D. Paton. Uncertainty of outcome or strengths of teams: an economic analysis of attendance demand for international cricket. *Applied Economics*, 46(17): 2034–2046, 2014.

Sacheti, A., D. Paton, and I. Gregory-Smith. An economic analysis of attendance demand for One Day International cricket. *Economic Record*, 92(296): 121–136, 2016.

Schofield, J.A. The demand for cricket: the case of the John Player League. *Applied Economics*, 15(3): 283–296, 1983.

Simmons, R. The demand for English league football: a club-level analysis. *Applied Economics*, 28(2): 139–155, 1996.

Simmons, R. and D. Forrest. New issues in attendance demand: the case of the English Football League. *Journal of Sports Economics*, 7(3): 247–263, 2006.

Szymanski, S. Income inequality, competitive balance and the attractiveness of team sports: some evidence and a natural experiment from English soccer. *Economic Journal*, 111(469): 69–84, 2001.

4. Outcome uncertainty fluctuation and match demand: a plea for a competitive intensity metrics

Wladimir Andreff and Nicolas Scelles

This chapter evidences the limitations of competitive balance as a metrics capturing outcome uncertainty fluctuation with a view to explaining match demand (Section 1), before developing the competitive intensity approach as a potentially valid alternative (Section 2).

1. OUTCOME UNCERTAINTY FLUCTUATION, TIME HORIZON AND STAKEHOLDERS

Outcome uncertainty (OU) emerged as a core concept after the first article published in sports economics (Rottenberg, 1956), with a basic argument contending that consumer demand for a sports contest is higher the more uncertain its outcome is expected to be. A given level of competitive balance (CB) translates into a degree of uncertainty about the sport contest's outcome. An abundance of literature devoted to the OU hypothesis has developed in empirically testing the relationship between CB and demand for sports, initially understood as stadium attendance (see e.g. García and Rodríguez, 2002, 2009).

A first question remained unheeded for years, and started to be investigated only during the past two decades: Does OU pertain to a rather stable or a very much fluctuating dimension of a sports contest? If it is fluctuating, which time horizon is appropriate to check it? Then, following Szymanski (2003), one can distinguish between game uncertainty (or short-term CB), seasonal uncertainty (mid-term CB) and championship inter-seasonal uncertainty (long-term CB). However, in most studies analysing the impact of game uncertainty on stadium attendance the results were opposite to the OU hypothesis: fans do prefer their favourite team to have a higher chance of winning (Pawlowski and Nalbantis, 2019). As regards seasonal uncertainty, the few existing studies are supportive of a positive relationship between CB and attendance, while empirical evidence is sparse and ambiguous on inter-seasonal CB.

A second question is: Who are the consumers of sports contests? Until the mid-1990s, when team sports were drawing a major part of their revenue from spectators – gate receipts, match-day revenues (Andreff and Staudohar, 2000) – the response was without doubt those demanding entrance tickets and filling the stadia. However demand for sports contests has increasingly diversified between fans eager to see their favourite team winning, couch potatoes and casual spectators more sensitive to CB (Simmons, 1996; Buraimo and Simmons, 2008), and season-ticket holders who attend all games they paid for, whatever the expected outcome.

Since the mid-1990s a major share of team sports' revenue has derived from the media (e.g. TV broadcasting rights), so the most significant consumer is quite often the mass of TV viewers. Buraimo (2008) found that there is a demand for televised games that is distinct from the fans' demand for attending games in stadia. Consequently, more recent studies have tested the OU hypothesis in analysing the impact of game uncertainty on TV viewing figures and have exhibited ambiguous results (Nalbantis and Pawlowski, 2016). Finally, OU is of concern for punters who bet on a game's outcome and may either attend it live or watch it on TV or online (laptop, tablet, smartphone). The demand for online viewing is on the rise since it is partly linked with the skyrocketing growth of online betting, which is no longer confined to bets on the final outcome of a game. Another demand, though underground, emanates from those who attempt to deliberately lower the OU, i.e. match fixers (Andreff, 2019).

As a consequence of consumer diversification, sports gambling and in particular online in-play betting, the CB approach does not cover all the dimensions of OU that are of interest to all stakeholders. For instance, with new technologies bookmakers learned routinely to offer odds during a match by developing statistical algorithms to automate odds-setting; odds are updated with every significant event in the match (Forrest, 2018). Those involved in online in-play betting (and match fixers as well) are looking for information about intra-match OU fluctuation. This is one concern for which a competitive intensity (CI) approach is a must.

Neale (1964) suggested, in addition to CB, a league standing effect as a major determinant of sports contest attendance. Jennett (1984) then elaborated on a calculation, fixture after fixture, of the number of required wins compared to the number of remaining matches in a model of 'championship significance'. Eventually, following the same train of thought, Kringstad and Gerrard (2004) introduced the competitive intensity concept (see Section 2). Let us just note here that any CB index is calculated in such a way as to capture the OU at the end (or *ex ante* at the beginning) of a game – that is, when a game is completed; seasonal CB is calculated at the end of a season of all games played. Therefore a CB index does not provide any information about intra-match OU or intra-seasonal OU.[1] This is why the CI concept and its different metrics have developed during the past decade and are the focus of the rest of this chapter.

As is shown in Section 2, some teams are in contention for a sporting prize only over a certain number of minutes in a match (they are no longer in contention at the end of the match), and this is what a CI index is all about. From the standpoint of online in-play betting, intra-match CI is much more interesting than any kind of CB information. Moreover, we can think about CI indexes that could vary at any second of a match – not only when teams are in contention – since an online in-play punter may change his/her wager at any time up to the last second of a match. This opens avenues for further research with a view to conceiving a kind of 'instant competitive intensity' notion and finding an appropriate index for it. Table 4.1 summarises what kind of stakeholders may be concerned with/interested in different CB and CI indexes over different OU time horizons.

2.   DIGGING DEEPER INTO THE COMPETITIVE INTENSITY APPROACH

2.1   From Competitive Balance to Competitive Intensity

Analysis of competitive balance (ACB) and uncertainty of outcome hypothesis (UOH) literatures are complementary in helping us obtain an overall view about CB. But is it relevant to only talk about CB? In the European leagues, there is a promotion/relegation system (opened leagues), and so there are sporting prizes at the bottom of the league ranking, unlike in American leagues. An unbalanced championship can be potentially more interesting than a more balanced one if each team has a sporting prize to defend, as in the first system, whereas the second may offer fewer sporting prizes.

These elements highlight a key weakness with CB: it does not consider the different sporting prizes existing in a national league (Kringstad and Gerrard, 2004), e.g. championship, qualification to continental competitions, fighting against relegation in open leagues or playoffs in closed leagues. Kringstad and Gerrard (2004, p. 117) wrote that "The relationship between competitive balance and uncertainty of outcome can [...] be shown in a general function: UO = CB + u, where UO is uncertainty of outcome, CB is the competitive balance and u is other factors affecting uncertainty of outcome." This indicates that UO does not solely depend

Table 4.1   *Competitive balance and intensity: time horizon and
stakeholders*

Outcome uncertainty	Attractiveness index	Metrics	Stakeholders
Game uncertainty	Short-term CB	Win probabilities, fixed betting odds, Theil measure	Casual spectators, TV viewers, punters
Seasonal uncertainty	Mid-term CB	Points, league ranking	Fans, season ticket holders, team managers, sponsors
Inter-seasonal uncertainty: static	Static long-term CB: performance difference over time	Noll–Scully index, Herfindahl–Hirschman index, Gini coefficient, concentration ratio	Fans, team managers, team owners, sponsors, TV channels
Inter-seasonal uncertainty: dynamic	Dynamic long-term CB: dynasty domination	Rank correlation between successive seasons' rankings	Fans, team managers, team owners, sponsors, TV channels
Intra-match uncertainty	Intra-match CI	Time with a possible fluctuation in the next minutes for reaching a sporting prize	Fans, punters, team managers
Intra-seasonal uncertainty	Intra-championship CI	Points needed for reaching different sporting prizes	Fans, casual spectators, season ticket holders, TV viewers, team managers
Instant intra-match uncertainty	Instant intra-match CI (to be conceived)	Fluctuating intra-play betting odds	Online in-play punters, match fixers

Note: CB: competitive balance; CI: competitive intensity.

on CB. Sloane (2006) went further when he noted that CB becomes unimportant if there is no chance of a sporting success – no sports prizes to be competed for. In European leagues, sports prizes and CB have to be analysed bearing in mind the need for domestic teams fighting for success in continental competitions. Beyond being an objective per se, success in continental competitions leads to more places in these competitions due to a better UEFA ranking and, as such, more sporting prizes in the national league. Nevertheless, the need for strong domestic teams may require that they have a better sporting level than others. In other words, competition in the national league should not be too balanced. This questions whether CB is the most appropriate concept to capture the attractiveness of a competition.

Based on the elements above, it may be argued that, in European leagues, there is a need for CB between teams in contention for the different sporting prizes rather than an overall CB. Thus, there is a need for a concept including both sporting prizes and CB. Kringstad and Gerrard (2004, 2005a, 2005b,[2] 2007a, 2007b) suggested such a concept through competitive intensity (CI). They considered that, apart from the degree of equality between teams, audiences are also interested in the prizes distributed. Kringstad and Gerrard (2004, p. 120) referred to Jennett (1984) as having introduced earlier the idea behind CI, although he did not use this terminology:

> The basic idea behind competitive intensity is related to the match significance introduced by Jennett (1984). Jennett uses match significance on two outcomes, the championship race and the fight for avoiding relegation. Gerrard (2004) uses the expression contest significance relating the significance of a sporting contest to the tournament outcome, and is affected by the structure of the tournament. Competitive intensity will capture these conditions, reflecting the number of prizes, their importance, and the intensity around each prize.

Although Kringstad and Gerrard initiated the concept of CI, they abandoned it in 2007 (Andreff and Scelles, 2015). Scelles' PhD and subsequent research (2009, 2010) are based on this concept of CI as developed below.

2.2 Competitive Intensity Metrics

2.2.1 Pioneering metrics by Kringstad and Gerrard

Although Kringstad and Gerrard introduced the concept of CI, they did not provide a measure for it. They ended their chapter by stating that "The challenge will be to find proper measures for competitive intensity. A suggestion is that it has to take into account all prizes/outcomes of a league, computing the level of uncertainty of each of them, and finally weight them on basis of their relevance" (Kringstad and Gerrard, 2004, p. 128). They applied it in a subsequent paper (Kringstad and Gerrard, 2005a). According to them, there is an assumption that the sporting prizes at the top of the ranking are more attractive than the 'prize' of avoiding relegation. In line with this, they proposed specific weightings for the European national football championships, with 1 for the title, $1/1.5^2$ for direct entry to the UEFA Champions League, $1/1.75^2$ for entry to the Champions League qualifying rounds, $1/2^2$ for entry to the UEFA Cup (now UEFA Europa League) and $1/3^2$ for relegation. Based on this, the authors suggested the following formula to measure end-of-season competitive intensity: $CI_{end-of-season} = \Sigma w_i P_i$, where w_i is the weight of prize i and P_i the intensity of prize interval i. Kringstad and Gerrard (2005a) set the prize interval at 10 points and suggest measuring P_i as the sum of the proportional gap between the points of the prize-winning (losing) team and the points of each team in the prize interval: $P_i = \Sigma (1 - \frac{Gap}{10})$. For example, if the first four teams have, respectively, 75, 72, 67 and 64 points, the intensity of the prize for the title is: $P_1 = \left[1 - \dfrac{75-72}{10}\right] + \left[1 - \dfrac{75-67}{10}\right] = 0.9$ (4th is

not taken into account for P_1 because the gap with the 1st is more than 10 points).

Kringstad (2005) adapted this measure to calculate within-season CI in the Norwegian football league over the 1995–2004 period. The formula became: $CI_{within} = x_t \Sigma w_{it} P_{it}$, where x_t is the time weighting of stage t of the season, w_{it} the weight of prize i at stage t of the season and P_{it} the intensity of prize interval I at stage t of the season. Kringstad (2005) indicated that the prize interval remained in general set at 10 points (less at the start and end of the season). He also specified that w_{it} was treated as a binary variable to allow for varying significance of different prizes throughout the season. More exactly, Kringstad (2005, pp. 165–166) noted that:

> The championship prize is assumed to be significant during the whole season, whereas UEFA's Champions League qualification is assumed to be significant only in the second half of the season, and entry to the UEFA Cup/Royal League only in the last quarter. Relegation significance is divided into three parts – the last place is significant from the second quarter onwards, the second-last place for the second half and the third-last place in the last quarter of the season.

With a within-season measure, Kringstad (2005) introduced a dynamic dimension that is relevant to capture the essence of CI and provide an indicator for which the impact may be tested on fan demand for each individual game. Nevertheless, similar to Kringstad and Gerrard (2005a), the formula relied on arbitrary choices, which may explain why both studies did not end with publication in peer-reviewed journals.

Kringstad and Gerrard (2007a) selected two different indicators depending on whether the leagues are North American (closed) or European (open). For the American leagues, the authors used the classic Herfindahl index to analyse the distribution between the participants in playoffs: $H = 100 * \Sigma s_i^2 / (1/N)$, where s_i is club i's share of participations in playoffs, and $i = 1,2,…,N$, where N is the number of clubs in the league. For a perfectly balanced league (each club with a share of participations in playoffs equal to $1/N$), the index takes a value of 100. A rise in the index means a decline in competitive balance. For the five major European football leagues, they chose the relegation rate for the teams recently promoted as a measure capturing the sporting equilibrium between the latter and teams already in the league. Consequently, Kringstad and Gerrard (2007a) relied on original measures with regard to the pre-existing ones by privileging the access to key places: qualification for playoffs or relegation. Nevertheless, they were closer to competitive balance than competitive intensity. In their chapter published the same year, Kringstad and Gerrard (2007b) referred to CI but measured only CB. We could not find more recent research from (either of) these two authors relying on CI. In his PhD thesis, Kringstad underlined the importance of CI but used only CB measures, ending his text as follows: "Future research should therefore go beyond competitive balance and focus more on the competitive intensity of professional sports leagues" (Kringstad, 2008, p. 301).

At that time, Nicolas Scelles was conducting his PhD thesis on CI under the supervision of Prof. Christophe Durand (from 2006 to 2009). This document and his first articles and communications on CI were in French (from 2007 to 2010). His first research on CI in English was a presentation at the European Sport Economics Association (ESEA) conference in Cologne (Germany) in October 2010 (Scelles and Durand, 2010). It was a summary of his thesis, providing an overview on how to measure CI, the latter being considered at two levels: intra-championship and intra-match. For each level, there are two indicators: uncertainty and fluctuations. Measuring the latter is quite straightforward:

- Intra-championship fluctuations (ICF) correspond to the average per gameweek of teams with fluctuations on positions with sporting prizes over the whole season.
- Intra-match fluctuations (IMF) correspond to the average per game of fluctuations in the state of the score (e.g. home team leading/draw/away team leading).

Further details are required for uncertainty indicators, both at intra-championship (ICU) and intra-match (IMU) levels.

2.2.2   A methodology for estimating intra-championship uncertainty

This method for estimating intra-championship uncertainty (ICU) relies on four steps (Scelles et al., 2011), illustrated here with the example of the 2018–19 English Premier League (EPL) season:

1. **Identify the different sporting prizes.** In the 2018–19 EPL, there were six sporting prizes: 1) championship (1st); 2) qualification for the Champions League (2nd, 3rd and 4th); 3) qualification for the Europa League group stage (5th); 4) potential qualification for the Europa League group stage or second qualifying round (6th); 5) potential qualification for the Europa League second qualifying round (7th); and 6) fighting against relegation (18th, 19th and 20th). The 6th position was confirmed as at least qualifying for the Europa League second qualifying round on 2 March 2019. Indeed, Manchester City earned a berth in the Europa League second qualifying round as winner of the 2018–19 English Football League (EFL) Cup on 24 February 2019. As the club was then in the first five positions in the EPL, its berth would pass to the best team not already qualified for the Champions League or the Europa League (then the 6th ranked team). On 2 March 2019 the club was sure it would not finish lower than 6th in the EPL, meaning that the 6th team was guaranteed at least this berth.

2. **Define when considering that a team is in contention for a prize.** Scelles, Desbordes et al. (2011) consider it to be the case when a team can change its situation within the next two games. In the 2018–19 EPL season, this was when a team needed no more than 6 points (two wins) to change its situation. However, goal differences and, if needed, goals scored have also to be taken into account. The differences between the two teams under consideration should not exceed a goal difference of 8 goals and, if the difference in goal differences is 8 goals, a difference of goals scored equal to 8. A team winning its next two games 4–2 should have exactly the same number of points, goal difference and goals scored as a team losing its next two games 2–0. For example, at the end of the 26th gameweek (11 February 2019), West Ham (10th, 33 points, goal difference −7, 32 goals scored) was considered in contention for the 7th position despite the gap with Wolverhampton (7th, 39 points, +1, 34 goals scored). It is also necessary to take into account that teams may not have played the same number of games; for example one team may have played one more game than another. In this case, the temporal horizon is extended to three games (ten for differences in goal differences and goals scored) if this is the best ranked team that played one more game, maintained to two games otherwise.

3. **Define when calculating ICU.** It does not make sense to do it during the first gameweeks, when all teams are close to each other and there is still plenty of time. It makes more sense during the last gameweeks, when more is at stake. Based on this, eight times are chosen: at a third, half, two-thirds, five, four, three, two and one game from the end of the season. In the 2018–19 EPL season, this means that the eight times

chosen were at the end of the 13th, 19th, 26th, 33rd, 34th, 35th, 36th and 37th gameweeks.

4. **Define how to calculate ICU.** It is done through the percentage of teams in contention for prizes at the eight times chosen above. An illustration is provided below, based on the EPL table in Table 4.2.

⇨ **ICU = mean of the eight percentages of teams in contention.**

Table 4.2 shows the 2018–19 EPL table at the end of the 26th gameweek. Manchester City, Liverpool and Tottenham were in contention for the championship; Manchester United, Arsenal and Chelsea for qualification for the Champions League; Wolverhampton, Watford, Everton and West Ham for potential qualification for the Europa League second qualifying round; and Crystal Palace, Brighton, Burnley, Newcastle, Cardiff and Southampton were fighting to avoid relegation. The four other teams were considered not in contention: Bournemouth (gap equal to 6 points with Bournemouth but difference in goal differences equals to 11, so exceeding 8), plus Leicester, Fulham and Huddersfield. This means that ICU was equal to 16/20 = 80% at the end of the 26th gameweek in the 2018–19 EPL season. By repeating this calculation for the seven other times then calculating the mean, ICU for the 2018–19 EPL is obtained.

2.2.3   A methodology for estimating intra-match uncertainty
This method of estimating intra-match uncertainty (IMU) relies on three steps (Scelles, Durand et al., 2011):

1. **Identify the maximum score spread allowing a fluctuation:** 1 goal in football, 3 points in basketball, 7 points in rugby (try converted), etc.
2. **Define when considering that a fluctuation is possible in the very next minutes:** *The* next change of score in sports like football and rugby where there is on average less than one change every 3 minutes; the next or the following *two* changes of score in sports like basketball (difference of no more than 6 points between teams in this sport) where there are in average more than two changes every 3 minutes.
3. **Define how to calculate IMU:** This is the percentage of game-time with a score spread of no more than the spread allowing a fluctuation in the very next minutes.

⇨ **IMU = average game-time with a fluctuation possible in the very next minutes/game duration.**

Table 4.2   2018–19 English Premier League table at the end of the 26th gameweek

Position and Team	Games played	Points	Goal difference
1. Manchester City	27	65	+54
2. Liverpool	26	65	+44
3. Tottenham	26	60	+29
4. Manchester United	26	51	+17
5. Arsenal	26	50	+16 (53 for)
6. Chelsea	26	50	+16 (45 for)
7. Wolverhampton	26	39	+1
8. Watford	26	37	0
9. Everton	27	33	−3
10. West Ham	26	33	−7
11. Bournemouth	26	33	−10
12. Leicester	26	32	−3
13. Crystal Palace	26	27	−7
14. Brighton	26	27	−11
15. Burnley	26	27	−18
16. Newcastle	26	25	−12
17. Cardiff	26	25	−23
18. Southampton	26	24	−16
19. Fulham	26	17	−33
20. Huddersfield	26	11	−34

Source: footstats.co.uk.

Figure 4.1 provides the evolution of the spread in the score and intra-match uncertainty in a rugby game. The spread in the score is more than 7 points from the 16th to the 31st minute than from the 38th minute to the end, meaning 57 minutes without IMU – so 23 minutes with IMU since there are 80 minutes in a rugby game. This means that IMU = 23/80 = 28.75% in this game. By averaging the minutes with IMU in the different games played over a season then dividing by the game duration (80 minutes), IMU for the whole season is obtained.

CONCLUSION

This chapter has developed the competitive intensity approach as a potentially valid alternative to competitive balance as a metrics capturing outcome uncertainty fluctuation with a view to explaining match demand.

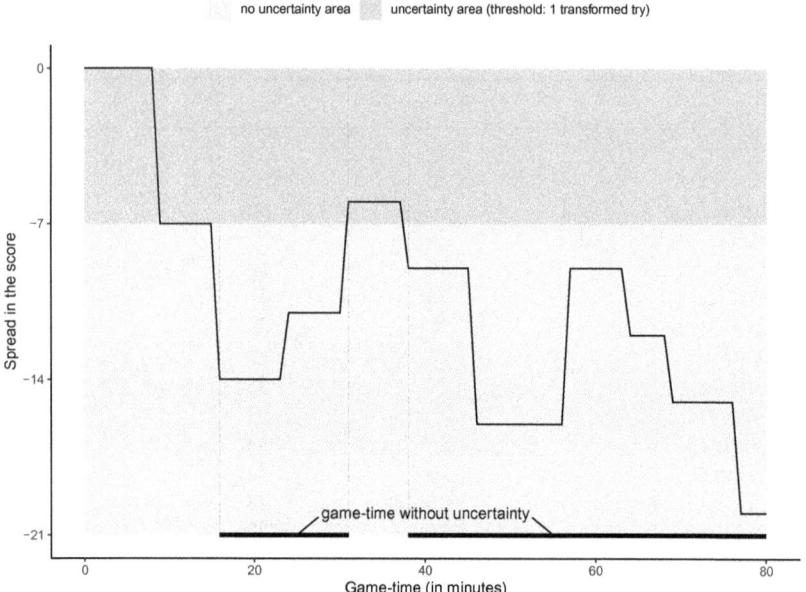

Figure 4.1   Evolution of the spread in score and intra-match uncertainty in a rugby game

The next chapter goes further on whether the competitive intensity approach is indeed a valid alternative.

NOTES

1. Except in the case of a multiple prizes sport contest or if we assume the existence of several competitions within a single league (Owen, 2014); but this assumption paves the way to the competitive intensity approach.
2. In the abstract corresponding to this conference presentation, Morten Kringstad is mentioned as sole author. However, his PhD thesis, Kringstad (2008), refers to Prof. Bill Gerrard (his PhD supervisor) as co-author. Later in text we refer to Kringstad (2005) rather than Kringstad and Gerrard (2005b) because we rely on the abstract.

REFERENCES

Andreff, W. (2019), *An Economic Roadmap to the Dark Side of Sport*. Cham: Palgrave Macmillan.
Andreff, W., and Scelles, N. (2015), Walter C. Neale 50 Years After: Beyond Competitive Balance, the League Standing Effect Tested with French Football Data, *Journal of Sports Economics*, 16(8), 819–34.

Andreff, W., and Staudohar, P. (2000), The Evolving European Model of Professional Sports Finance, *Journal of Sports Economics*, 1(3), 257–76.

Buraimo, B. (2008), Stadium Attendance and Television Audience Demand in English League Football, *Managerial and Decision Economics*, 29(6), 513–23.

Buraimo, B., and Simmons, R. (2008), Do Sports Fans Really Value Uncertainty of Outcome? Evidence from the English Premier League, *International Journal of Sport Finance*, 3(3), 146–55.

Forrest, D. (2018), Match-fixing, in: M. Breuer and D. Forrest, eds, *The Palgrave Handbook on the Economics of Manipulation in Professional Sports*, Cham: Palgrave Macmillan, pp. 91–114.

García, J., and Rodríguez, P. (2002), The Determinants of Football Match Attendance Revisited: Empirical Evidence from the Spanish Football League, *Journal of Sports Economics*, 3(1), 18–38.

García, J., and Rodríguez, P. (2009), Sports Attendance: A Survey of the Literature 1973–2007, *Rivista di Diritto ed Economa dello Sport*, 5(2), 111–51.

Gerrard, B. (2004), Still Up for Grabs? Maintaining the Sporting and Financial Viability of European Club Soccer, in: J. Fizel and R. Fort, eds, *International Sports Economics Comparisons*, Westport, CT: Praeger, pp. 39–59.

Jennett, N. (1984), Attendances, Uncertainty of Outcome and Policy in the Scottish Football League, *Scottish Journal of Political Economy*, 31(2), 176–98.

Kringstad, M. (2008), *Competitive Balance in Complex Professional Sports Leagues*, PhD thesis, Leeds University Business School, UK. http://etheses.whiterose. ac.uk/681/1/uk_bl_ethos_493299.pdf.

Kringstad, M., and Gerrard, B. (2004), The Concepts of Competitive Balance and Uncertainty of Outcome, in: G.T. Papanikos, ed., *The Economics and Management of Mega Athletic Events: Olympic Games, Professional Sports and Other Essays*, Athens, Greece: ATINER, pp. 115–30.

Kringstad, M., and Gerrard, B. (2005a), Theory and Evidence on Competitive Intensity in European Soccer, *2005 International Association of Sports Economists (IASE) Conference Paper*, 18–19 July, Ottawa, Canada.

Kringstad, M., and Gerrard, B. (2005b), Competitive Intensity in European Football, *Communication to the 13th European Association for Sport Management Conference*, 7–10 September, Newcastle, UK.

Kringstad, M., and Gerrard, B. (2007a), Competitive Balance in a Modern League Structure, *Communication Abstract to the 2007 North American Society for Sport Management (NASSM) Conference*, 30 May–2 June, Ft. Lauderdale, FL, 26–27.

Kringstad, M., and Gerrard, B. (2007b), Beyond Competitive Balance, in: M.M. Parent and T. Slack, eds, *International Perspectives on the Management of Sport*, Amsterdam: Elsevier, pp. 149–72.

Nalbantis, G., and Pawlowski, T. (2016), *The Demand for International Football Telecasts in the United States*, Cham: Palgrave Macmillan.

Neale, W.C. (1964), The Peculiar Economics of Professional Sports: A Contribution to the Theory of the Firm in Sporting Competition and in Market Competition, *Quarterly Journal of Economics*, 78(1), 1–14.

Owen, D. (2014), Measurement of Competitive Balance and Uncertainty of Outcome, in: J. Goddard and P. Sloane, eds, *Handbook on the Economics of Professional Football*, Cheltenham, UK and Northampton, MA, USA: Edward Elgar Publishing, pp. 41–59.

56 *A modern guide to sports economics*

Pawlowski, T., and Nalbantis, G. (2019), Competitive Balance Measurement and Relevance, in: P. Downward, B. Frick, B.R. Humphreys, T. Pawlowski, J.E. Ruseski, and B.P. Soebbing, eds, *The SAGE Handbook of Sports Economics*, London: Sage, pp. 154–62.

Rottenberg, S. (1956), The Baseball Players' Labor Market, *Journal of Political Economy*, 64(3), 242–58.

Scelles, N. (2009), *L'incertitude du résultat, facteur clé de succès du spectacle sportif professionnel: L'intensité compétitive des ligues: Entre impacts mesurés et effets perçus* [Uncertainty of Outcome, Key Success Factor of Professional Sport Spectacle: Competitive Intensity of Leagues: Between Measured Impacts and Perceived Effects], PhD thesis, University of Caen, France.

Scelles, N. (2010), *La glorieuse incertitude du sport. L'intensité compétitive des ligues professionnelles: Entre impacts mesurés et effets perçus* [The Glorious Uncertainty of Sport. Competitive Intensity of Professional Leagues: Between Measured Impacts and Perceived Effects], Sarrebruck, Germany: Éditions Universitaires Européennes.

Scelles, N., Desbordes, M., and Durand, C. (2011), Marketing in Sport Leagues: Optimising the Product Design. Intra-championship Competitive Intensity in French Football Ligue 1 and Basketball Pro A, *International Journal of Sport Management and Marketing*, 9(1/2), 13–28.

Scelles, N., and Durand, C. (2010), Competitive Intensity of Professional Sports Leagues: Between Measured and Perceived Realities, *2nd European Conference in Sport Economics*, 5–6 October, Cologne, Germany.

Scelles, N., Durand, C., Bah, S.T., and Rioult, F. (2011), Intra-match Competitive Intensity in French Football Ligue 1 and Rugby Top 14, *International Journal of Sport Management and Marketing*, 9(3/4), 154–69.

Simmons, R. (1996), The Demand for English League Football: A Club-Level Analysis, *Applied Economics*, 28(2), 139–55.

Sloane, P.J. (2006), Rottenberg and the Economics of Sports After 50 years: An Evaluation, in: P. Rodríguez, S. Kesenne, and J. García, eds, *Sports Economics After Fifty Years: Essays in Honour of Simon Rottenberg*, Oviedo, Spain: Ediciones de la Universidad de Oviedo, pp. 211–26.

Szymanski, S. (2003), The Economic Design of Sporting Contests, *Journal of Economic Literature*, 41(4), 1137–87.

5. Competitive intensity: sporting rules generating it and impact on fan demand

Nicolas Scelles and Wladimir Andreff

This chapter develops the lines of the nascent literature on competitive intensity (CI), introduced in the previous chapter. These lines are similar to those identified for the literature on competitive balance (CB). According to Fort and Maxcy (2003), there are two such lines of literature on CB:

1. The evolution of CB over time or as a result of the introduction, disappearance or change in redistribution mechanisms (Analysis of Competitive Balance, ACB).
2. The impact on fans (Uncertainty of Outcome Hypothesis, UOH).

Consistent with Fort and Maxcy for CB, this chapter identifies the sporting rules supposed to generate CI and analyses their efficiency (Section 1) before discussing the impact of CI on fan demand (Section 2).

1. THOSE SPORTING RULES SUPPOSED TO GENERATE COMPETITIVE INTENSITY AND THEIR EFFICIENCY

When developing the competitive intensity approach, the previous chapter distinguished two levels of uncertainty: intra-championship uncertainty (ICU) and intra-match uncertainty (IMU). The sporting rules favouring both uncertainties are described below.

1.1 Sporting Rules Favouring Intra-Championship Uncertainty

Scelles, Desbordes and Durand (2011) identify three main sporting rules supposed to generate ICU:

- *Many prizes on offer.* Playoffs/playdowns with an incentive to reach the best possible position – e.g. home advantage/home advantage for the return game in the next round(s) – may help extend the number of sporting prizes.
- *A low percentage of positions without a prize.* A limited number of teams may help prevent a large number of positions without a sporting prize.
- *A limited number of gameweeks.* Indeed, more gameweeks means a greater likelihood of large differences between teams in the table.

The league must also not be too imbalanced, e.g. the 1st ranked team being far better than the 2nd ranked team, or teams in relegation places being too weak.

Scelles, Desbordes et al. (2011) find *some evidence that these rules are efficient in generating ICU* by looking at two French leagues – the men's basketball Pro A and football Ligue 1 – over the 2004–2009 period. The authors note that both leagues had a fairly similar number of gameweeks (34 in Pro A vs. 38 in Ligue 1); but the Pro A had more sporting prizes towards the end of the season (due to the different positions leading to a qualification in playoffs and their different consequences (13 sporting prizes vs. 7 in Ligue 1) and a lower percentage of positions without sporting prize (22 per cent vs. 50–60 per cent in Ligue 1). Despite a lower CB, Pro A had a better ICU than Ligue 1 over the 2004–2009 period (85.8 vs. 76.0 per cent).

Scelles, Durand and Rioult (2013) also find some evidence that the rules supposed to generate ICU are efficient in doing so for five North American men's leagues – MLB (Major League Baseball), MLS (Major League Soccer), NBA (the National Basketball Association), NFL (the National Football League) and NHL (the National Hockey League) – over the 2004–2010 period. They note that the MLS (32 gameweeks) and NFL (only 17 gameweeks) had a far lower number of gameweeks than the NBA, NHL (82 gameweeks for both) and MLB, the latter having the highest number of gameweeks (162). MLB also had the highest percentage of positions without sporting prizes (73 per cent), with the NFL having also a higher percentage than the other three leagues (62.5 vs. 47 per cent). Based on these elements, the expectation would be that, if all five leagues had similar levels of competitive balance, MLS and the NFL would have the best ICU, ahead of the NBA and the NHL, while MLB would have the lowest ICU. Results confirm this expectation to some extent, with MLS having the best ICU (85.1 per cent) ahead of the NFL, the NHL (respectively 69.1 and 66.9 per cent, so quite similar), the NBA (52.3 per cent) and MLB (31.0 per cent). Scelles, Durand and Rioult (2013) explain that MLS had a better ICU than the NFL, and the NHL an ICU almost the same as the NFL and better than the NBA, due to their respective CB. Indeed, over the 2004–2010 period, the authors find that MLS had the best CB, ahead of the NHL (and MLB), while the NFL and the NBA had the lowest CB.

1.2 Bonus and Intra-Match Uncertainty

In the previous chapter, IMU is illustrated in rugby without considering the existence of the bonus system in league games. In rugby, the bonus system involves both an offensive and a defensive bonus. The most common form of the offensive bonus corresponds to one additional point in the league table for each team scoring at least four tries in a game. The defensive bonus corresponds to one additional point in the league table for each team losing by no more than seven points in a game. The consequence of these two bonuses is that there is IMU as long as at least one team has scored three tries, whatever the score (offensive bonus) and/or the score spread between both teams does not exceed 14 points instead of seven without a bonus.

As an illustration, Figure 5.1 adapts Figure 4.1 in the previous chapter, with the bonus now taken into account. It can be seen that the uncertainty area extends from a difference of seven to 14 points. Besides, even when the difference is more than 14 points, there can still be IMU if at least one team has scored three tries, which is the case for the away team from the 46th to the 77th minutes. In the example, the game-time without uncertainty moves from 57 to 3 minutes, i.e. the game-time with IMU moves from 23 to 77 minutes. As such, IMU = 71 / 80 = 96.25% (instead of 28.75 per cent).

Scelles, Durand et al. (2011) find *some evidence that the bonus has a positive impact on IMU* in the French men's rugby Top 14. In this league, the bonus system was implemented in 2004. The authors calculate that IMU was between 60 and 65 per cent over the 2001–2004 period, before rising to between 85 and 90 per cent over the 2004–2007 period. It even increased to between 90 and 95 per cent in 2007–2008, when the offensive bonus was allocated to a team scoring at least three tries more than its opponent, instead of any team scoring at least four tries. To illustrate why the new offensive bonus was even more efficient in generating IMU than the previous one, consider the situation where one team has scored four tries and the other one try, the former team and even the defensive bonus being not within reach of the latter team in terms of score spread. With the previous bonus, there is no IMU since the best team is sure to get the offensive bonus while the other team is too far from it and the defensive bonus. With the new bonus, the best team would end up with the offensive

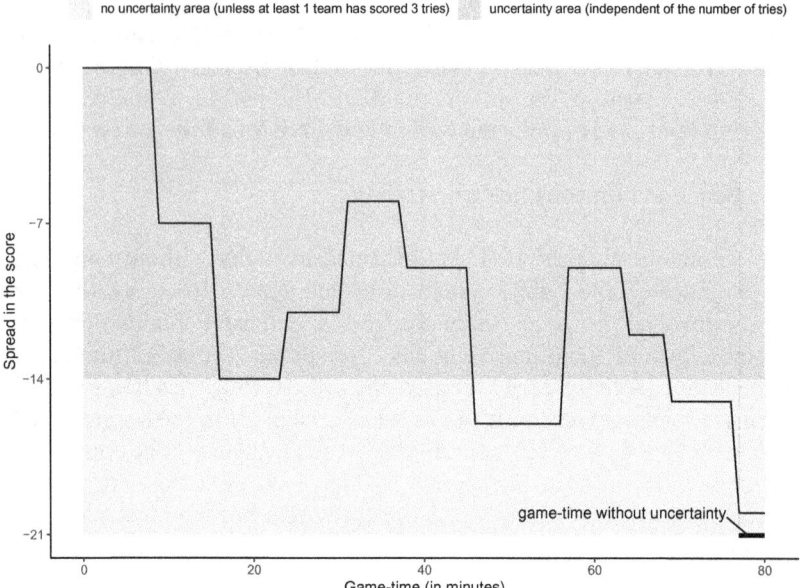

Figure 5.1   Evolution of the spread in score and intra-match uncertainty in a rugby game with bonus taken into account

bonus if the score does not change (since it has scored three more tries than its opponent), but there is still IMU since a try by the other team would mean a difference of only two tries between the teams, so no longer an offensive bonus for the best team.

2.   THE IMPACT OF COMPETITIVE INTENSITY ON FAN DEMAND

The previous section underlined the importance of sporting prizes in view of generating CI. This section establishes whether such sporting prizes and the subsequent CI affect fan demand, first for stadium attendance (Section 2.1) and then for TV audience (2.2), before comparing the results obtained for both types of fan demand (2.3).

2.1   Impact on Stadium Attendance

This subsection relies on four articles: Scelles et al. (2013a, 2013b, 2016) and Andreff and Scelles (2015). These studies explain stadium attendance in the French men's football Ligue 1 over the 2008–2011 period (n = 1135 matches) with the same 25 variables as well as CB and CI, the last two being different across the four articles. The variables – largely inspired by García and Rodríguez (2002) – are as follows:

- 4 socioeconomic variables (population, inhabitants' income, unemployment and youth);
- 2 proxies of expected match quality (home and away team budgets);
- 16 variables capturing incentives to attend a match (home and away team position, day and time, etc.);
- 3 dummies related to the 'season effect' (2008–2009, 2009–2010 and 2010–2011); dummy = 1 or 0 depending on whether the condition is met, e.g. 1 for 2008–2009 if the game was played during that season, 0 otherwise.

These variables are not commented on here since they are not the main focus of interest. It is just worth noting that the 'season effect' indicates a lower stadium attendance over time. This could have been the consequence of the economic crisis from 2008, with its effects on consumption from 2009. The different variables for CB and CI are presented below.

In Scelles et al. (2013a), there is one variable for CB and one variable for CI. CB is measured by the point difference between teams before a match. CI is measured by the point difference for the home team with the closest competitor with a different situation (sporting prize) before a match. The results show that CB before a match is not significant, while CI before a match has a significant positive impact on stadium attendance. It must be noted that CB before a match is a specific level of CB and the indicator chosen is a specific measure of CB before a match. As such, it would be wrong to conclude that CB is not relevant at all in explaining stadium attendance. On the contrary, we can think that CI needs CB within different groups of teams (those fighting for the championship, those fighting for qualification in European competitions, those fighting against relegation). Last, the same results are obtained for CI whether or not we include the positions potentially qualifying for European competitions (5th and 6th in French Ligue 1).

Scelles et al. (2013b) use the same variable as Scelles et al. (2013a) for CB (still not significant) but new measures for CI. These new measures correspond to a dummy equal to 1 for a possibility of change in the home team's situation (sporting prize) as a consequence of the next game (Model 1), the next two games (Model 2) ... up to the next eight games (Model 8). Almost all dummies are significant across the eight models, but only at the 10 per cent level for the next game and not for the next two games when relying on 'sure' positions only (rather than 'sure' and 'potentially qualifying' positions). An additional test is made with a distinction, in a single model, between dummies corresponding to a possibility of change as a consequence of the next game, the next 2nd game … up to the next 8th game. A significant positive impact is found for the first five dummies vs. a significant negative impact for the last three dummies. In the model with 'sure' positions only, the first three dummies are significant at the 1 per cent level, the fourth at the 10 per cent level and the fifth at the 5 per cent level. In the model with 'sure' and 'potentially qualifying' positions, the first two dummies are significant at the 1 per cent level, the third and fourth at the 5 per cent level and the fifth at the 10 per cent level. Results are more logical in the second model, consistent with the idea that 'potentially qualifying' positions have to be taken into account.

Andreff and Scelles (2015) use new measures for both CB and CI. CB is based on betting odds. CI is measured by the point difference for the home team with the closest competitor with a different situation (sporting prize) before a match, as in Scelles et al. (2013a), but also two new measures corresponding to positive and negative changes in the situation in the table during the last two matches. CB is not significant; the point difference for CI has a significant positive impact as in Scelles et al. (2013a), while both positive and negative changes have no significant impact. When excluding the variable home team position, positive change becomes significantly positive while negative change remains not significant, meaning that overall changes have a positive impact on fan attendance. As such, Neale's (1964) 'league standing effect' is confirmed empirically, although Andreff and Scelles' (2015) focus is on changes in relation to sporting prizes rather than any position.

Scelles et al. (2016) use the same measure as Andreff and Scelles (2015) for CB but new measures for CI. These new measures correspond to dummies for the different sporting prizes:

1. Winning the league (1st).
2. Direct entry to the UEFA Champions League (2nd).
3. Entry to the UEFA Champions League qualifying round (3rd).
4. Direct entry to the UEFA Europa League (4th and potentially 5th).
5. Entry to the UEFA Europa League qualifying round (potentially 5th or 6th).
6. Potential direct entry to the UEFA Europa League (5th).
7. Potential entry to the UEFA Europa League qualifying round (6th).
8. Double prize (home team in contention for sporting prizes at both the top and bottom of the table).
9. Relegation (18th, 19th and 20th).

If a team is in contention for several prizes among the first seven ('top prizes'), only the prize associated with the best ranking is taken into account.

It is necessary to define the temporal horizon. Scelles et al. (2013b) suggest that the most appropriate horizons are the next match and the subsequent two matches, but also find a significant impact for the next three and four matches. Thus, the first three horizons are chosen (three models), with the fourth horizon being controlled for in the third model through two variables: top prizes and relegation for the next fourth match. In addition, so as to limit the number of observations with a "double prize" (difficult to interpret), the following rule is applied for the second and third horizons: if one match (two matches) is sufficient for the top (bottom) prize vs. two (three) for the bottom (top) prize, the prize is considered a top (bottom) prize. For example, for the second horizon, if a team is two points behind the 6th and four points ahead of the 18th, it is considered in contention for the 6th position.

Results reported for the different sporting prizes (other than relegation) are those without incorporating home team position. All prizes have a significant positive impact in at least one model:

- In the three models for prizes 1, 2, 5, 7, 8 and 9.
- In two models for prizes 3 and 4.
- In one model for prize 6.

Top prizes for the next fourth match is not significant, while there is a significant impact of relegation for the next fourth match but only at the 10 per cent level. This is partially consistent with the hypothesis that the horizon of the next fourth match is too large to maintain public interest. Additional tests in the article are supportive of the next match and the next second match being better horizons than the next third match to capture CI.

To sum up, all sporting prizes are significant in explaining stadium attendance in a European national men's football league (the French Ligue 1). Of course, there is a need to extend into other countries before generalising the results to European men's football. Bond and Addesa (2020) test the determinants of stadium attendance in the Italian men's football league (Serie A) over the 2012–2015 period, including dummies similar to Scelles et al. (2016). They find similar results, except for the Europa League. The significant impact of relegation in both Scelles et al. (2016) and Bond and Addesa (2020) provides an argument for open leagues, as opposed to authors suggesting that a closed European Super League would be a better option (Hoehn and Szymanski, 1999; Szymanski, 2007; Vrooman, 2007) ... including Scelles (2017)!

2.2   Impact on TV Audience

Scelles (2017) adapt a model from Buraimo and Simmons (2015). While the latter apply their model to TV audiences in the English Premier League (EPL) over the 2000–2008 period, the former applies a revised model to the 2013–2014 EPL season. The main variables of interest are star quality and contention. Star quality is measured through the sum of the two teams' relative wages. In Buraimo and Simmons (2015), contention is measured through dummies for league champion, European qualification and relegation. Dummies equal 1 if a team can earn a prize as a consequence of winning all its remaining games while others draw them (on average). In Scelles (2017), measures from contention are derived from Scelles et al. (2013b, 2016), with a distinction between Champions League, Europa League and potential Europa League for European qualification.

Scelles' (2017) results show a significant positive impact of star quality (consistent with Buraimo and Simmons, 2015), championship and Champions League contention (while Buraimo and Simmons (2015) find no significant impact for champion and European qualification contention) and no significant impact of Europa League, potential Europa League and relegation contention (consistent with Buraimo and Simmons for the latter). As such, it is concluded that the EPL should encourage both star quality and CB so that all teams would be in contention for the title or qualification in the Champions League. Nevertheless, this is not realistic given the differences in revenue generation between English teams. Thus, it is suggested that the best way to achieve both star quality and CB is through a European Super League.

As for the results found by Scelles et al. (2016) for stadium attendance, there is a need to study other countries before generalising the results to European men's football. Bond and Addesa (2019) look at the determinants of TV demand for the Italian Serie A over the 2012–2015 period, including CI variables inspired by Scelles (2017), while adding a *nofight* variable in order to account for matches where the home team is not in contention for any prize. They find a negative impact for the latter variable and a positive impact for all other variables except for Europa League playoffs (qualifying round). In particular, they find a positive impact for relegation, in contrast with Scelles (2017). Nevertheless, they note that the coefficients of the CI variables are small and significantly lower than the star quality coefficients. This may be interpreted as the need to encourage teams with high star quality (which should indirectly generate CB if all teams have such high star quality). It is suggested here (not by the authors) that the best way to achieve such high star quality is again through a European Super League.

2.3 Synthesis on Stadium Attendance vs. TV Audience in European Men's Football: A Need for Further Research

Scelles et al. (2016) find a significant positive impact of all sporting prizes on stadium attendance in Ligue 1, while Scelles (2017) finds a positive impact of the very top prizes (championship and Champions League) only on TV audience in the EPL. Although care is needed before generalising these results to European men's football, as demonstrated by the comparisons with Italian football for stadium attendance (Bond and Addesa, 2020) and TV audience (Bond and Addesa, 2019), it may be the case that stadium attendees are mainly interested in the home team, while TV viewers are mainly interested in the best teams. A European Super League would then be an economic vs. a social choice: putting the best teams together with a high potential in terms of TV audience (economic), with detrimental consequences for other teams (vs. social); or preserving the European model in its historical form (social), despite the potential additional revenue coming from a change for the best teams (vs. economic). A warning should be highlighted in that a European Super League may be unsustainable. Indeed, it may lead to fewer economic resources for football academies, with players in the future not as well trained as currently. In the long term, this would affect the quality of players in the European Super League, potentially leading to less fan interest. Besides, some of the richest continental clubs would become less prestigious as they would become 'losers' among the richest continental clubs instead of 'winners' among domestic clubs.

Beyond the case against a European Super League developed here, there is also a need to observe further whether fans across the world value continental competitions more than domestic competitions. Consistent with the need for a broader understanding of fan demand for domestic competitions, Scelles and Brocard (2019) note that more studies are required on smaller men's football leagues (Pawlowski and Nalbantis, 2015), other sports and women's sports, including women's football (Valenti et al., 2018). With regard to continental competitions, studies on fan demand in the UEFA men's Champions League (and other men's continental competitions) including CI would be welcome. To the best of the authors' knowledge, there is little in the literature as yet.[1] By contrast, Valenti et al. (2020) test the impact of CI on stadium attendance in the

UEFA women's Champions League over the 2009–2018 period. They measure CI as the possibility of score reversals after the first leg game and find a significant positive impact of such possibility (negative impact of goal difference in absolute value after the first leg, including the away goal rule) on stadium attendance. They also find a significant positive impact of the 'superclub' effect (teams from the 'big five' countries that are integral to men's clubs).

Valenti et al.'s (2020) results for stadium attendance in women's football at the European level are consistent with those of Scelles (2017) for TV audience in men's football at the English level. Indeed, they suggest the need for star quality and CB in European women's football. Nevertheless, rather than implementing a European Super League in women's football, the authors stress the need to develop further participation. Indeed, based on the positive relationship between available playing talent and CB highlighted by authors such as Schmidt and Berri (2003), Berri et al. (2005) and Flores et al. (2010), "this is expected to narrow the gap between players' performances and therefore encourage contests that are more balanced" (Valenti et al., 2020, p. 518). To some extent, this has been confirmed in men's football by Scelles et al. (2020), although these authors acknowledge the importance of a country/league's economic development to attract foreign players performing well (and retain the best domestic players) beyond participation/available playing talent in football in the country. The fact that Valenti et al. (2020) reach a different conclusion than Scelles (2017), despite results in the same vein, illustrates a requirement to adapt the conclusions to the specific case under investigation, underlining again the risks associated with generalising results and the need for further research on the impact of CI on fan demand across different contexts and sports, as well as over different periods since fans' preferences may change over time.

3.   CONCLUSION

This chapter confirms that the competitive intensity approach is a valid alternative (or at least complement) to competitive balance after the previous chapter suggested that it could be the case. It first identifies a number of sporting rules that are efficient in generating competitive intensity, both at the intra-championship level (many sporting prizes, low percentage of positions without a sporting prize, limited number of gameweeks, competitive balance) and the intra-match level (offensive and defensive bonuses). This identification would become less meaningful if there is no positive impact of competitive intensity on fan demand. The second part of the chapter evidences the existence of such a positive impact of competitive intensity on fan demand, both on stadium attendance and TV audience. Indeed, previous literature has found such evidence in men's football, more specifically in the French Ligue 1 and the Italian Serie A for stadium attendance, in the English Premier League and again in Serie A for TV audience. A positive impact of competitive intensity on stadium attendance has also been found in the UEFA women's Champions League. Although the chapter confirms that the competitive intensity approach is a valid alternative to competitive balance, it also calls for further research on this approach with a number of directions that would strengthen its understanding.

NOTE

1. Scelles and Durand (2010) deal with (intra-match) CI in the UEFA men's Champions League over the 1955–2008 period, but they do not test its impact on fan demand despite referring to the latter in their title.

REFERENCES

Andreff, W., and Scelles, N. (2015), Walter C. Neale 50 Years After: Beyond Competitive Balance, the League Standing Effect Tested With French Football Data, *Journal of Sports Economics*, 16(8), 819–34.

Berri, D.J., Brook, S.L., Frick, B., Fenn, A.J., and Vicente-Majoral, R. (2005), The Short Supply of Tall People: Competitive Imbalance and the National Basketball Association, *Journal of Economic Issues*, 29(4), 1–12.

Bond, A.J., and Addesa, F. (2019), TV Demand for the Italian Serie A: Star Power or Competitive Intensity?, *Economics Bulletin*, 39(3), 2110–16.

Bond, A.J., and Addesa, F. (2020), Competitive Intensity, Fans' Expectations, and Match-day Tickets Sold in the Italian Football Serie A, 2012–2015, *Journal of Sports Economics*, 21(1), 20–43.

Buraimo, B., and Simmons, R. (2015), Uncertainty of Outcome or Star Quality? Television Audience Demand for English Premier League Football, *International Journal of the Economics of Business*, 22(3), 449–69.

Flores, R., Forrest, D., and Tena, J.D. (2010), Impact on Competitive Balance from Allowing Foreign Players in a Sports League: Evidence from European Soccer, *Kyklos*, 63(4), 546–57.

Fort, R., and Maxcy, J. (2003), Competitive Balance in Sports Leagues: An Introduction, *Journal of Sports Economics*, 4(2), 154–60.

García, J., and Rodríguez, P. (2002), The Determinants of Football Match Attendance Revisited: Empirical Evidence from the Spanish Football League, *Journal of Sports Economics*, 3(1), 18–38.

Hoehn, T., and Szymanski, S. (1999), The Americanization of European Football, *Economic Policy*, 14(28), 202–40.

Neale, W.C. (1964), The Peculiar Economics of Professional Sports: A Contribution to the Theory of the Firm in Sporting Competition and in Market Competition. *Quarterly Journal of Economics*, 78, 1–14.

Pawlowski, T., and Nalbantis, G. (2015), Competition Format, Championship Uncertainty and Stadium Attendance in European Football: A Small League Perspective, *Applied Economics*, 47(38), 4128–39.

Scelles, N. (2017), Star Quality and Competitive Balance? Television Audience Demand for English Premier League Football Reconsidered, *Applied Economics Letters*, 24(19), 1399–402.

Scelles, N., and Brocard, J.F. (2019), European Sports Leagues: Origins and Features, in: P. Downward, B. Frick, B.R. Humphreys, T. Pawlowski, J.E. Ruseski, and B.P. Soebbing, eds, *The SAGE Handbook of Sports Economics*, London: Sage, pp. 135–43.

Scelles, N., Desbordes, M., and Durand, C. (2011), Marketing in Sport Leagues: Optimising the Product Design. Intra-championship Competitive Intensity in French Football Ligue 1 and Basketball Pro A, *International Journal of Sport Management and Marketing*, 9(1/2), 13–28.

Scelles, N., and Durand, C. (2010), Incertitude du résultat et demande du public: L'intensité compétitive intra-match comme variable clé. Le cas de la Ligue des champions de l'UEFA (1955/2008) [Uncertainty of Outcome and Fan Demand: Intra-match Competitive Intensity as Key Variable. The Case of the UEFA Champions League (1955/2008)], *Science et Motricité*, 71, 65–70.

Scelles, N., Durand, C., Bah, S.T., and Rioult, F. (2011), Intra-match Competitive Intensity in French Football Ligue 1 and Rugby Top 14, *International Journal of Sport Management and Marketing*, 9(3/4), 154–69.

Scelles, N., Durand, C., Bonnal, L., Goyeau, D., and Andreff, W. (2013a), Competitive Balance Versus Competitive Intensity before a Match: Is One of These Two Concepts More Relevant in Explaining Attendance? The Case of the French Football Ligue 1 over the Period 2008–2011, *Applied Economics*, 45(29), 4184–92.

Scelles, N., Durand, C., Bonnal, L., Goyeau, D., and Andreff, W. (2013b), My Team Is in Contention? Nice, I Go to the Stadium! Competitive Intensity in the French Football Ligue 1, *Economics Bulletin*, 33(3), 2365–78.

Scelles, N., Durand, C., Bonnal, L., Goyeau, D., and Andreff, W. (2016), Do All Sporting Prizes Have a Significant Positive Impact on Attendance in a European National Football League? Competitive Intensity in the French Ligue 1. *Ekonomicheskaya Politika/Economic Policy*, 11(3), 82–107. In Russian, English version at https://mpra.ub.uni-muenchen.de/73844.

Scelles, N., Durand, C., and Rioult, F. (2013), Intra-Match and Intra-Championship Competitive Intensity across American Sports Leagues, Presentation to the Colloquium 'Sport Management'/ISC Paris, 13–14 June, Paris.

Scelles, N., François, A., and Dermit-Richard, N. (2020), Determinants of Competitive Balance across Countries: Insights from European Men's Football First Tiers, 2006–2018. *Managing Sport and Leisure*, doi: 10.1080/23750472.2020.1784036.

Schmidt, M.B., and Berri, D.J. (2003), On the Evolution of Competitive Balance: The Impact of Increasing Global Search, *Economic Inquiry*, 41(4), 692–704.

Szymanski, S. (2007), The Champions League and the Coase Theorem, *Scottish Journal of Political Economy*, 54(3), 355–73.

Valenti, M., Scelles, N., and Morrow, S. (2018), Women's Football Studies: An Integrative Review, *Sport, Business and Management: An International Journal*, 8(5), 511–28.

Valenti, M., Scelles, N., and Morrow, S. (2020), The Determinants of Stadium Attendance in Elite Women's Football: Evidence from the UEFA Women's Champions League, *Sport Management Review*, 23(3), 509–20.

Vrooman, J. (2007), Theory of the Beautiful Game: The Unification of European Football, *Scottish Journal of Political Economy*, 54(3), 314–54.

6. Uncertainty of outcome and competitive balance: impact, causes and cures

Stefan Kesenne

1. INTRODUCTION

There are few variables that show up more often in the literature on sports economics than competitive balance (CB); but, at the same time, few other variables generate more discussion and disagreement among sports economists.

What exactly is meant by CB? The concept is ill defined both theoretically and empirically (see Kringstad and Gerrard, 2007). As indicated by Sanderson (2002), CB turns out to have many dimensions, and each dimension should be considered in one way or another. However, in this contribution, as in most approaches of CB, we refer to deviation in performances of teams, caused mainly by budget differences among teams, and the deviations in playing talent teams can afford to pay.

The well-known peculiarity of the team sports industry is its inverted joint product (see Neale, 1964). Joint production occurs when one production process generates two or more outputs. In sports the opposite is the case: two or more independent production processes are necessary to generate one single output. At least two teams are needed to play a game or organise a league championship. Because sport is basically about competition, and not just a show, the competitors should be more or less of the same strength. The more balanced the competition, the higher is the uncertainty of outcome (UO). If playing strengths of teams are too far apart, there is no UO and a basic characteristic of sport is lost, causing a loss of public interest. A professional sport can only survive if spectators are willing to spend money to watch the games.

In this contribution, different levels of UO are presented in Section 2, as well as the most common ways they can be measured. Section 3 discusses the Uncertainty of Outcome Hypothesis (UOH). In Section 4 the optimal UO or CB in a league will be analysed theoretically. Section 5 presents the most important factors affecting CB. In Section 6, some important policy measures to improve CB are analysed.

2.   UNCERTAINTY OF OUTCOME

In professional team sports, UO is generally approached at three different levels: match uncertainty, within-season uncertainty, and between-season or long-term uncertainty.

The most obvious notion of uncertainty is the UO of an individual match. If a very strong and talented team is meeting a very weak team, there will be little UO. Nevertheless, the outcome of an individual match is very unpredictable because it all happens in an hour or two, and many different factors, which are beyond control, can affect the outcome. These factors are mostly cancelled out during the length of a season championship or over a period of several seasons. One important factor affecting the outcome is home advantage, but in most championships each team plays all other teams twice, home and away. Other factors are the incidence of injuries as well as dubious refereeing decisions; a top player of a strong team can get injured, or the referee makes a mistake in one particular match. But, then again, no team is free of player injuries, and no referee is free of mistakes during a full season.

Match uncertainty in its most simple way is measured by the square of the difference between the winning percentages (w), or the positions in the rankings (r), of teams x and y:

$$UO_m = (w_x - w_y)^2 \text{ or } (r_x - r_y)^2 \qquad (6.1)$$

If UO_m is close to zero, there is a high degree of match UO; the larger UO_m, the more predictable or certain the outcome of the game will be.

Within-season uncertainty refers to the uncertainty about the winner of the league in one particular season. Many different measures have been proposed in the literature, but the best-known measures start from the standard deviation (SD) of the winning percentages of all teams in the league. The smaller the standard deviation is, the higher the within-season UO. Many sports economists have used the concept of an idealised standard deviation of winning percentages. If all teams are of equal strength, the standard deviation of the winning percentages would be $\sigma = 0.5/\sqrt{n}$, where *n* is the number of games that each team plays in one season. An index of UO that has been used by many researchers is the ratio between the actual standard deviation and the idealised standard deviation, $\frac{SD}{0.5/\sqrt{n}}$, which is known as the Noll-Scully ratio (see Noll, 1988). Nevertheless, there are a few shortcomings and problems with this index. Not only can it not be applied if games allow ties, as in soccer, it can also (in some applications) be smaller than one, whereas, theoretically, its minimum value should be one.

A related but more elegant measure has been proposed by Goossens (2006), which is the ratio of the actual SD and the SD in case of perfect imbalance or perfect predictability of outcome. This index, called the National Measure of Seasonal Imbalance (NAMSI), lies between zero and one. The closer to zero, the higher is seasonal uncertainty. The advantage of this index is that comparisons can be made between leagues with a different number of teams and games; it is also applicable in championships allowing ties.

Between-season or long-term UO considers more than one championship in order to find out if the same teams always top the final ranking. One way to do this is by simply counting the number of different teams in the top three positions of the final ranking over a number of years. The higher this number of teams, the higher is the between-season UO. If one team always wins the championship, or only three or four different teams (often called dynasties) have made it to the top positions over a period of, say, ten years, the between-season UO is very low.

An interesting measure, proposed by Humphreys (2002), combines the within-season and the between-season UO in one single indicator, called the Competitive Balance Ratio (CBR). The CBR is the ratio of two average variations:

$$CBR = \frac{\bar{\sigma}_T}{\bar{\sigma}_N} \text{ where } \bar{\sigma}_T = \frac{\sum_i^N \sigma_{Ti}}{N} \text{ and } \bar{\sigma}_N = \frac{\sum_t^T \sigma_{Nt}}{T} \qquad (6.2)$$

with σ_{Ti} being the standard deviation of team i's winning percentages over a number of seasons, and T and σ_{Nt} the standard deviation of the within-season winning percentages in season t. The CBR scales the average time variation in winning percentages for teams in the league by the average variation in winning percentages across seasons.

3. COMPETITIVE BALANCE AND PUBLIC INTEREST

An important issue in the discussion about CB is the uncertainty of outcome hypothesis (UOH), which states that supporters and spectators prefer a more equal CB in a league. However, the empirical evidence regarding the UOH is not very convincing. Some researchers find a significant impact of CB on attendance, while others don't (see Borland and Macdonald, 2003; García and Rodríguez, 2002). It has also been observed that spectators care more about absolute quality in a league than relative quality (see Canes, 1974; Bruggink and Eaton, 1996: Marburger, 1997; Szymanski, 2003). Moreover, it turns out that there is a difference between the preferences of diehard supporters of a specific team and more neutral spectators, who just want to see a high-quality and thrilling game. This deviation has also been observed between stadium spectators and television viewers, who are more neutral spectators rather than diehard supporters of one team (see Buraimo and Simmons, 2009).

The response of spectators to within- and between-season UO is also different. If the public does not seem to care too much about within-season UO, they don't like to see the same teams (dynasties) on top year after year (see Krautmann and Hadley, 2004). Recently, it has been shown that dynasties in national soccer leagues in Europe significantly reduce stadium attendances (see Kesenne, 2020).

In a novel and interesting theoretical and empirical approach by Coates, Humphreys and Zhou (2012), the UOH is rejected, based on reference-dependent preferences of spectators and loss aversion. The assumption is that the utility of a home-team win is higher if spectators expected a loss than if they expected a win. The utility of a home-team loss is lower if

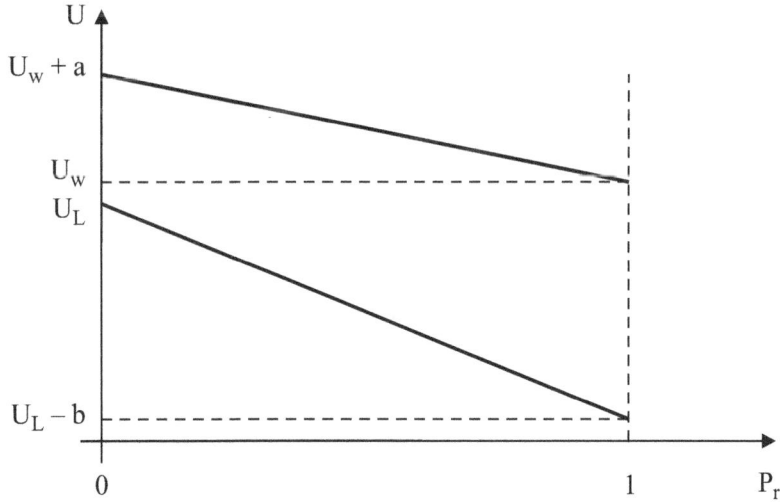

Figure 6.1   Reference dependent preferences and loss aversion

spectators expected a win than if they expected a loss. This is illustrated in Figure 6.1.

The expectation of a win (P_r) is indicated on the horizontal axis, and the utility of a win or a loss (U) on the vertical axis. The utility of a win depends on the expectation of a win (the reference) and is higher ($U_x + a$) if a loss was expected ($P_r = 0$).

The utility of a loss is lower ($U_L - b$) if a win was expected ($P_r = 1$). Furthermore, assuming loss aversion, b > a, or the slope of the lower curve is steeper than the slope of the higher curve.

From these assumptions, the following quadratic equation can be derived for the expected utility:

$$E(U) = (b-a)p^2 + [(U_w - U_L) - (b-a)]p + U_L \qquad (6.3)$$

Furthermore, $A = \gamma p^2 + \theta p + \varepsilon$, where A is game attendance and p is some measure of the probability that the home team wins a specific game. The estimation results of this equation with $\gamma > 0$ (or b > a) and $\theta < 0$ (or $U_w - U_L < b - a$) are consistent with loss aversion and the presence of reference-dependent preferences. The empirical evidence from Major League Baseball (MLB) supports this model, and so supports loss aversion and rejects the UOH.

4.   OPTIMAL COMPETITIVE BALANCE

Can the optimal CB be derived theoretically in one way or another? In deriving the optimal CB theoretically, one has to start from the optimal winning percentages of all teams in the league. Based on these winning percentages, which are different for each team, the social optimum can be derived based on a specific welfare function.

4.1   The Optimal Winning Percentage of a Team

Among the most important variables, affecting attendance, are the size of the market and the winning percentage of the team. The absolute quality of the league and the ticket prices are assumed to be exogenously given in this analysis. Teams with a high drawing potential, in large markets or densely populated areas, attract more spectators than teams with a limited drawing potential in small towns. But the empirical research also shows that spectators prefer a winning home team and that they turn away from a losing home team. However, if some degree of uncertainty of outcome is necessary in sports, the question is whether an optimal competitive balance can be derived, taking into account the interest of all supporters and spectators.

In order to analyse this, we start from a simplified two-team league with one large-market team x and one small-market team y, so $m_x > m_y$. The utility function of the supporters of both teams, with a given market size, depends on the team's winning percentage (w) and on the uncertainty of outcome (uo) in the league, which is measured in its most simple way by

$$uo = w_x w_y \qquad (6.4)$$

This indicator is zero if $w_i = 0$ *or if* $w_i = 1$, and it reaches its highest value of 0.25 if $w_i = 0.5$. Assuming that the utility function of a team's supporters can be approached by the weighted product of the winning percentage and the uncertainty of outcome, this can be written for a two-team league as:

$$U_x = w_x^{1-\alpha} uo^{\alpha} = w_x w_y^{\alpha} \qquad \textit{with } 0 \leq \alpha \leq 1$$

$$U_y = w_y^{1-\beta} uo^{\beta} = w_y w_x^{\beta} \qquad \textit{with } 0 \leq \beta \leq 1$$

$$(6.5)$$

The weights α and β are assumed to be different in the two teams because it is reasonable to assume that the supporters of a strong large-market team value winning and competitive balance differently than the supporters of a weak small-market team.

Based on these utility functions, we can derive the optimal winning percentage for both teams from the first-order conditions:

$$\frac{\partial U_x}{\partial w_x} = w_y^{\alpha} - \alpha w_x w_y^{\alpha-1} = 0 \qquad or \qquad w_y^{\alpha-1}(w_y - \alpha w_x) = 0$$

$$\frac{\partial U_y}{\partial w_y} = w_x^{\beta} - \beta w_y w_x^{\beta-1} = 0 \qquad or \qquad w_x^{\beta-1}(w_x - \beta w_y) = 0$$

$$(6.6)$$

Because $w_y^{\alpha-1}$ *and* $w_x^{\beta-1}$ are both different from zero, we can derive that the optimal competitive balance for the supporters of both teams is:

$$w_x / w_y = 1 / \alpha$$
$$w_y / w_x = 1 / \beta$$
$$(6.7)$$

The more the supporters value winning (that is, the smaller α *and* β), the higher the optimal winning percentage of their home team will be. If the weights of winning and UO are the same (that is, $\alpha = \beta = 0.5$), the optimal winning percentage the supporters prefer for their home team can be found as:

$$\frac{w_x}{w_y} = 2 \ or \ w_x^* = 2/3 = 0.67$$

$$\frac{w_y}{w_x} = 2 \ or \ w_y^* = 2/3 = 0.67 \tag{6.8}$$

It is obvious that both teams prefer a winning percentage that is between 0 and 1, and larger than 0.5, but this is impossible because the sum of the winning percentages in a two-team league has to equal 1.

4.2   The Optimal Uncertainty of Outcome in a League

The optimal UO in a league can be approached theoretically by specifying a social welfare function that takes account of the preferences of all spectators. Given that, in a two-team league, the large-market team x has more supporters than the small-market team y, the welfare function could be the weighted product of the utilities of the supporters of the large and small team:

$$W = U_x^{m_x} U_y^{m_y} U_n^{m_n} = U_x^m U_y U_n^n \tag{6.9}$$

where the weight m equals the ratio of the market sizes; and, because a large-market team has more supporters than a small-market team, so $m = \dfrac{m_x}{m_y} > 1$. We have also included a third utility function – that of the more neutral TV-spectators, which is:

$$U_n = uo = w_x w_y \tag{6.10}$$

Assuming that neutral spectators are not die-hard supporters of one of the teams, the winning percentage does not matter, and the utility of the neutral supporters is only determined by the uncertainty of outcome. Its weight in the welfare function is given by the parameter n, which equals the ratio of the number of neutral (television) spectators m_n and the number of supporters of the small-market team (m_y). So, we can derive that:

$$W = U_x^m U_y U_n^n = (w_x w_y^\alpha)^m (w_y w_x^\beta)(w_x w_y)^n = w_x^{m+\beta+n} w_y^{\alpha m+n+1} \tag{6.11}$$

The first-order condition for the optimal winning percentage of the large team x, $(\frac{\partial W}{\partial w_x} = 0)$, can, after some rearrangement, be written as:

$$w_y^{\alpha m+n} w_x^{m+\beta+n-1}[(m+\beta+n)w_y - (\alpha m+n+1)w_x] = 0 \tag{6.12}$$

Because the product before the parentheses is non-zero, the expression between the parentheses has to equal zero. So, we can find that the optimal competitive balance is:

$$\frac{w_x}{w_y} = \frac{m + \beta + n}{\alpha m + 1 + n} \qquad (6.13)$$

Based on these simple utility and welfare functions, we can derive that the optimal competitive balance depends on the preferences of the supporters of the large- and the small-market team, on the relative size of the markets of the two clubs, and on the number of neutral spectators (the importance of televised sport). We can also derive from the optimal CB:

$$\frac{\partial(w_x / w_y)}{\partial m} > 0 \quad and \quad \frac{\partial(w_x / w_y)}{\partial \beta} > 0 \quad and \quad \frac{\partial(w_x / w_y)}{\partial \alpha} < 0 \quad (6.14)$$

The larger the market of a team, the higher will be the optimal winning percentage of that team. The more supporters value a winning team, the higher the optimal winning percentage of that team.

   Also, it comes as no surprise that if $m = 1$ *and* $\alpha = \beta$, for whatever value of n – that is, the relative size of the group of neutral supporters – we find that both teams should have the same winning percentage:

$$\frac{w_x}{w_y} = \frac{1 + \alpha + n}{\alpha + 1 + n} = 1 \qquad (6.15)$$

More interesting is the result that even a very large difference in market size or drawing potential does not justify strong, large-team dominance in the league. Indeed:

$$\lim_{m \to \infty} \frac{w_x}{w_y} = \lim_{m \to \infty} \frac{m + \beta + n}{\alpha m + 1 + n} = 1 / \alpha \qquad (6.16)$$

So, if $\alpha = 0.5$ (that is, the supporters of the large-market team value winning and uncertainty of outcome equally), whatever the difference between the market sizes of the teams in a league, and whatever the preferences of the small-market team supporters, the optimal competitive balance should always stay below 2, which implies that on no account should the optimal winning percentage of a large-market team be larger than $w_x = 0.67$.

   Only if the supporters of the large-market team show a strong preference for winning, relative to uncertainty of outcome, can the optimal competition be very unbalanced. Large differences in preferences for winning between the supporters of two teams with the same market size do not strongly affect the optimal competitive balance. Again, the winning percentage of the large-market team should not be larger than $w_x = 0.67$. Furthermore, we can also derive from the optimal CB that:

$$\frac{\partial(w_x / w_y)}{\partial n} = \frac{(\alpha m + 1 + n) - (m + \beta + n)}{(\alpha m + 1 + n)^2} < 0 \; for \; w_x > w_y \qquad (6.17)$$

It follows that the larger the group of neutral television spectators becomes, the more balanced the competition should be from a welfare economic perspective.

Empirically, attempts have been made to estimate the optimal UO of a team. Surprisingly, or maybe not, the optimal value of 0.67 that was derived above, based on a very simple theoretical model, has also been found based on extensive empirical research by Rascher and Solmes (2007).

5. DETERMINING FACTORS OF COMPETITIVE BALANCE

In most applications, the CB is simply based on the distribution of talent among teams in a league. If a few large teams in big cities have budgets that are large enough to hire all the best players, the competition will probably be very unbalanced. In its most simple approach of a two-team league, the CB – defined as the ratio of the winning percentages (w_x/w_y) – is determined by the ratio of the playing talent (t_x/t_y). However, it is obvious that the quality of the coach, team spirit and motivation, and the effort that players are willing to make, or simply luck, will also affect the teams' winning percentages and the CB. If the players of team y are willing to make more effort (indicated by the index e_y) and the players of team x are not, $w_x/w_y = t_x/e_y t_y < t_x/t_y$. So team y with less talent can beat the more talented team x (see Kesenne, 2007).

The CB in a league is also affected by the objectives of team owners. If teams are profit-maximisers, which is the usual assumption in most North American major leagues, the CB is more balanced than in a league where all teams are win-maximisers, which is the assumption in European football (soccer) (see Sloane, 1971; Kesenne, 1996, 2000).

Starting from the following team revenue functions in a two-team league:

$$R_i = m_i w_i - 0.5 m_i w_i^2 \; for \; i: x, y \; with \; w_x = \frac{t_x}{t_x + t_y}$$
$$and \; w_y = \frac{t_y}{t_x + t_y} \qquad (6.18)$$

The CB at the Nash equilibrium with a given unit cost of talent c can then be found from the reaction functions under profit-maximisation:

$$(m_x - m_x w_x)w_y = c(t_x + t_y) \quad \text{or} \quad \frac{t_x^\pi}{t_y^\pi} = \frac{w_x}{w_y} = \sqrt{\frac{m_x}{m_y}} \quad (6.19)$$
$$(m_y - m_y w_y)w_x = c(t_x + t_y)$$

If teams are win-maximisers under the breakeven constraint, the CB in a Nash equilibrium model can be derived from equalising the reaction functions:

$$m_x - 0.5m_x w_x = c(t_x + t_y) = m_y - 0.5m_y w_y \quad \text{or} \quad \frac{t_x^w}{t_y^w} = \frac{2m_x - m_y}{2m_y - m_x} \quad (6.20)$$

It is clear that the CB is more unequal in the win-maximisation than in the profit-maximisation scenario:

$$\frac{t_x^w}{t_y^w} = \frac{2m_x - m_y}{2m_y - m_x} > \frac{t_x^\pi}{t_y^\pi} = \sqrt{\frac{m_x}{m_y}} \quad (6.21)$$

The CB in a league will also be different if team owners, in their strategy, take the strategies of their opponents into account. This is not the case in a closed league where the supply of talent is fixed and internalised, as in the North American major leagues. The market demand for talent, which is given by the horizontal sum of all teams' demand curves and the fixed supply of talent, determines the market-clearing unit cost of each team's hiring of talent. In this scenario, the competitive balance is more unbalanced compared with a league where the supply of talent is flexible and talent can be hired from other leagues, as in European soccer. This deviation can be approached by comparing the player–market equilibrium in a fixed-supply Walras equilibrium with the flexible- or fixed-supply model under the Nash conjecture (see Szymanski, 2004; Szymanski and Kesenne, 2004). In the fixed-supply Walras model, where $\dfrac{\partial w_x}{\partial t_x} = \dfrac{\partial w_y}{\partial t_y} = 1$, the CB is found where the marginal revenue of a win is the same for both teams, and total league revenue is at its maximum level, that is: $\dfrac{\partial R_x}{\partial w_x} = \dfrac{\partial R_y}{\partial w_y}$.

Under the Nash conjecture in the Nash-equilibrium model, the CB is more balanced, and total league revenue is not maximised. It follows that the Nash equilibrium is inefficient.

In a two-team league, with $w_x = \dfrac{t_x}{t_x + t_y}$ and $w_y = \dfrac{t_y}{t_x + t_y}$, the Nash equilibrium can be written as:

$$\frac{\partial R_x}{\partial w_x}\frac{\partial w_x}{\partial t_x} = \frac{\partial R_y}{\partial w_y}\frac{\partial w_y}{\partial t_y} \text{ with } \frac{\partial w_x}{\partial t_x} = \frac{t_y}{(t_x + t_y)^2}$$

$$\text{and } \frac{\partial w_y}{\partial t_y} = \frac{t_x}{(t_x + t_y)^2} \tag{6.22}$$

or

$$\frac{\dfrac{\partial R_x}{\partial w_x}}{\dfrac{\partial R_y}{\partial w_y}} = \frac{\dfrac{\partial w_y}{\partial t_y}}{\dfrac{\partial w_x}{\partial t_x}} = \frac{t_x}{t_y} \tag{6.23}$$

If $t_x > t_y$, the marginal revenue of winning is higher in the large-market team than in the small-market team. In order to reach equality between the marginal revenues of winning, the winning percentage of the stronger team has to go up because club revenue is concave in winning percentage. In other words, the distribution of talent is too balanced to reach maximum league revenue and meet supporters' preferences (see Szymanski and Leach, 2005).

The CB in a league also depends on the number of teams in the league. In an open league with promotion and relegation, it is always the weakest team that is relegated to a lower division. In a closed league, the team losing its licence is probably a poorly performing team. It follows that the sum of the win percentages of the teams will be lower in a contracted league. Furthermore, based on the standard deviation of the winning percentages, the within-season uncertainty of outcome will be lower the larger the size of the league. This can be seen in Table 6.1, which presents a numerical example of winning percentages in six-team league compared with a four-team league. Assuming that the relative strength of the teams is given by: A>B>C>D>E>F, and that there is a 50 per cent chance that the stronger team beats the next one in the row and a 100 per cent chance that it wins against the weaker teams, the theoretical winning percentages in a six-team league are calculated in the first row of Table 6.1. If the league is reduced to four teams, with the two weakest teams (E and F) leaving

Table 6.1   League contraction, numerical example

League size	Winning percentages						Sum	SD
	A	B	C	D	E	F		
6 teams	0.90	0.80	0.60	0.40	0.20	0.10	3	0.32
4 teams	0.83	0.67	0.33	0.17			2	0.30

or relegated, the adjusted winning percentages are given in the second row. The standard deviation, as a simple indicator of the within-season competitive balance, is lower in the contracted league. So, the contracted league is more balanced. However, as observed by Noll (2003), the pennant race in the contracted league is not as close, which makes the competition less balanced.

The preferences of spectators also affect the CB in a league. If only the relative quality matters, the CB in a Nash equilibrium model *was* derived above as:

$$\frac{w_x^{\pi}}{w_y^{\pi}} = \sqrt{\frac{m_x}{m_y}} \qquad (6.24)$$

If spectators value not only the relative quality (or CB) but also the absolute quality of the league, the competition turns out to be more unbalanced. If the absolute quality is approached by the sum of all talent in a two-team league ($t_x + t_y$), club revenue is:

$$R_i = m_i w_i - 0.5 m_i w_i^2 + \varepsilon_i (t_x + t_y) \ \text{ for all } i = x, y \text{ with } \varepsilon_x > \varepsilon_y \qquad (6.25)$$

Solving the reaction equations under profit-maximisation, and assuming that the effect of absolute quality on revenue is larger in the large-market club than in the small-market club, we can derive that:

$$m_x w_y^2 - m_y w_x^2 = (\varepsilon_y - \varepsilon_x)(t_x + t_y) < 0 \quad \text{so} \quad m_x w_y^2 < m_y w_x^2$$

$$\text{and} \quad \frac{w_x^{\pi}}{w_y^{\pi}} > \sqrt{\frac{m_x}{m_y}} \qquad (6.26)$$

The CB is more unequal in the model where also absolute quality affects team revenue.

6.   POLICIES TO IMPROVE COMPETITIVE BALANCE

The issue of the previous section raises the important question of how league administrators can improve the CB in a league. Several policies have been put forward to improve CB. One is the limitation of player mobility by a reservation or retain-and-transfer system; but this limitation on end-of-contract players was abolished in Europe by the famous Bosman verdict of the European Court of Justice in 1995, and 20 years earlier in the North American major leagues. The abolition was supported by economic research showing that these systems do not change the CB in a league if teams are profit-maximisers. This finding is known as the Invariance Proposition (see Rottenberg, 1956).

If teams are win-maximisers, a transfer system might improve the CB because small teams will use the transfer fees received from selling a talented player to hire another talent. But this positive impact will be extremely small or non-existent because teams in small towns do not have many talented players who can be sold. Also, a player who is sold to a large team will be a top player, whereas the players a small team can buy with the resulting transfer fee will be average at best, which weakens the small team (see Kesenne, 2014).

Another important policy measure is generally known as 'revenue sharing'. Its impact on CB is complicated because it depends, among other factors, on teams' objectives, talent-supply condition and specifics of the sharing arrangement. Things are further complicated by the fact that research findings, based on a simplified two-team league, do not generally apply to an n-team league. In this overview, we only present the best-known results from the literature.

The Invariance Proposition applies to the simple gate-revenue sharing arrangement in a two-team, fixed-supply Walras-equilibrium model under profit-maximisation (see Quirk and Fort, 1992).

If R_x is the season revenue of the large-market club, R_y the season revenue of the small-market club, and an asterisk indicates the after-sharing values and μ is the share parameter, the after-sharing revenues (indicated by an asterisk) in this simple gate-sharing system can be written as:

$$\begin{aligned} R_x^* &= \mu R_x + (1-\mu)R_y \\ R_y^* &= \mu R_y + (1-\mu)R_x \end{aligned} \text{ with } 0.5 \leq \mu < 1 \qquad (6.27)$$

Because the demand curve for talent of a profit-maximising team is given by the marginal revenue curve (MR), the clubs' demand curves for talent can be written as:

$$\begin{aligned} MR_x^* &= \mu MR_x - (1-\mu)MR_y \quad because \ \frac{\partial t_y}{\partial t_x} = -1 \\ MR_y^* &= \mu MR_y - (1-\mu)MR_x \quad because \ \frac{\partial t_x}{\partial t_y} = -1 \end{aligned} \qquad (6.28)$$

The switch from a positive sign to a negative sign by taking the first derivative is due to the fact that, given the constant supply of talent, one talent more in one team implies one talent less in the other team. If the new market equilibrium is found where $MR_x^* = c_\pi^* = MR_y^*$, it can easily be derived that if $MR_x^* = MR_y^*$ also $MR_x = MR_y$. It follows that revenue-sharing does not change the distribution of talent or the CB in the league.

However, the same simple gate-sharing arrangement in a win-maximisation league will improve the CB because the after-sharing revenue of the small-budget club will be higher than its pre-sharing revenue, and the opposite holds for the large-budget club, i.e.

$$R_y^* = \mu R_y + (1-\mu)R_x > R_y$$
$$R_x^* = \mu R_x + (1-\mu)R_y < R_x \tag{6.29}$$

Because a win-maximising team under the breakeven constraint will spend its whole budget on talent, after its compensation of capital, it is obvious that the small club's demand for talent goes up and the large club's demand goes down. The result is a more equal distribution of talent and a more balanced competition, all else being equal (see Kesenne, 1996, 2000).

As distinct from the previous result, it can be shown that, in a flexible-supply Nash equilibrium model, revenue sharing worsens the competitive balance under the profit-maximisation hypothesis. This can be shown using a model with simplified revenue functions and only the product of market size and winning percentage as explanatory variables. Assume that the revenue function of the large-market team is $R_x = \alpha w_x$ with $\alpha = m_x/m_y > 1$, and the revenue function of the small-market club is $R_x = w_y$. These revenue functions are linear in win percentage, but concave in talent. With a constant marginal cost of talent, the Nash equilibrium can then be found at the point of intersection of the reaction curves, i.e. $\dfrac{\alpha t_y}{(t_x + t_y)^2} = \dfrac{t_x}{(t_x + t_y)^2}$,

so the competitive balance is $\dfrac{t_x}{t_y} = \alpha > 1$. The large-market club is more talented than the small-market club. If revenues are shared (an asterisk indicating the after-sharing values), revenues are:

$$R_x^* = \mu \alpha w_x + (1-\mu)w_y$$
$$R_y^* = \mu w_y + (1-\mu)\alpha w_x \tag{6.30}$$

The new Nash equilibrium is then found, where

$$\frac{\partial R_x^*}{\partial t_x} = \frac{\mu \alpha t_y - (1-\mu)t_y}{(t_x + t_y)^2} = \frac{\partial R_y^*}{\partial t_y} = \frac{\mu t_x - (1-\mu)\alpha t_x}{(t_x + t_y)^2} \tag{6.31}$$

The competitive balance $\dfrac{t_x^*}{t_y^*} = \dfrac{\mu \alpha + \mu - 1}{\mu \alpha + \mu - \alpha} > \alpha$ indicates that revenue sharing worsens the competitive balance (see Szymanski and Kesenne, 2004).

Then again, an alternative sharing system improves the CB in the Nash equilibrium model (see Szymanski, 2003). The impact of revenue sharing on CB is positive if each team contributes the same amount to a pool and the collected money is redistributed in accordance with the winning percentages of the teams. Starting again with the simplified two-team model above, a pool v is created with an equal contribution $v/2$ by both teams. Each team receives a share of that pool in accordance with its winning percentage, i.e. $w_x v$ and $w_y v$. If an asterisk indicates again the after-sharing values, we find that:

$$R_x^* = \alpha w_x - v / 2 + w_x v$$
$$R_y^* = w_y - v / 2 + w_y v \qquad (6.32)$$

The Nash equilibrium can then be found at the point of intersection of the reaction functions, $\dfrac{(\alpha + v)t_y}{(t_x + t_y)^2} = c = \dfrac{(1 + v)t_x}{(t_x + t_y)^2}$, so the after-sharing competitive balance is $\dfrac{t_x^*}{t_y^*} = \dfrac{\alpha + v}{1 + v} < \alpha$.

An important paper by Feess and Stähler (2009) starts from revenue functions of n heterogeneous profit-maximising teams that include, besides relative and absolute quality, the competitive balance itself as an explanatory variable. Starting from the Nash equilibrium model, they derived that revenue sharing always improves the competitive balance if profit-maximising teams differ only with respect to the impact of absolute quality on revenue, and revenue sharing worsens competitive balance only if teams' relative quality plays a role in revenue. One can add to their conclusion that, under win-maximisation conditions, in both the Walras and the Nash equilibrium revenue sharing improves the competitive balance, because teams spend their entire available budget on playing talent, regardless of their opponents' strategy.

If the impact of revenue sharing on competitive balance is not very clear, it has been shown that a *salary cap* improves the competitive balance. After the abolition of the reserve clause in the North American major leagues in the mid-seventies, player salaries rose dramatically, and club-owner profits took a nosedive. In reaction to this profit squeeze, league administrators and club owners looked for an alternative regulation system to guarantee a reasonable profit rate. One of these alternatives is generally known as a salary cap. In their well-known review article on cross-subsidisation, Fort and Quirk (1995) conclude that a salary cap is the only cross-subsidisation scheme currently in use that can be expected to improve the competitive balance. Furthermore, a salary cap improves the competitive balance in both a profit-maximisation and a win-maximisation league. The typical

North American salary cap, which is in fact a payroll cap, is calculated as a percentage (α) of average club revenue in the league during the previous season:

$$cap = \alpha \frac{\sum_{i}^{n} R_{i,-1}}{n} \quad with \ \alpha < 1 \tag{6.33}$$

A team is not allowed to pay more on player salaries than the value of the cap – which holds for all teams, large or small. The percentage is fixed in collective bargaining agreements between club owners and player associations. Obviously, players prefer a higher percentage as their revenue share, and owners want a lower percentage.

In a competitive player labour market imposing a payroll cap means that:

$$c \cdot t \leq cap \quad \text{so that} \quad c \leq \frac{cap}{t} \tag{6.34}$$

This implies that, graphically, the cap line is a simple hyperbolic function that can easily be presented for a two-club model as in Figure 6.2, where x is again the large-market club and y is the small-market club. We assume that the salary cap is not effective for the small-market club because it cannot afford to pay the amount of the cap.

If the payroll cap is not a floor, it does not affect the demand for talent of the low-budget club. As can be seen, the low-budget club's demand curve stays below the cap line. The high-budget club's demand curve, which is above the cap line, has to stay below the hyperbolic function (cap_x). Obviously, the high-budget team will try to get as close as possible to its profit-maximising demand for talent. As a result, the hyperbole becomes its new demand curve for talent. The new market equilibrium is now found at E_c^π, the intersection of the marginal revenue curve of the low-budget club MR_y and the hyperbolic cap_x. The result is a more equal distribution of talent t_c^π and a lower salary level $c_{c'}^\pi$.

Algebraically, starting from a well-behaved quadratic revenue function, it can be derived, by equalising $MR_y = \dfrac{cap}{t_x}$, that $t_x = \sqrt{\dfrac{cap}{m_y}}$.

The talent of club x is positively affected by the value of the cap and negatively affected by the market size of the opponent club y.

Also in a win-maximisation league, a salary cap improves the CB. In Figure 6.2, the MR-curves can simply be replaced by the AR-curves. One of main problems with salary caps is enforcement, because there are many ways to compensate players besides their regular salary. Vrooman (1995) argues that it is a myth that the salary cap improves CB. The salary cap is just a collusive attempt to control total player cost and exploit players.

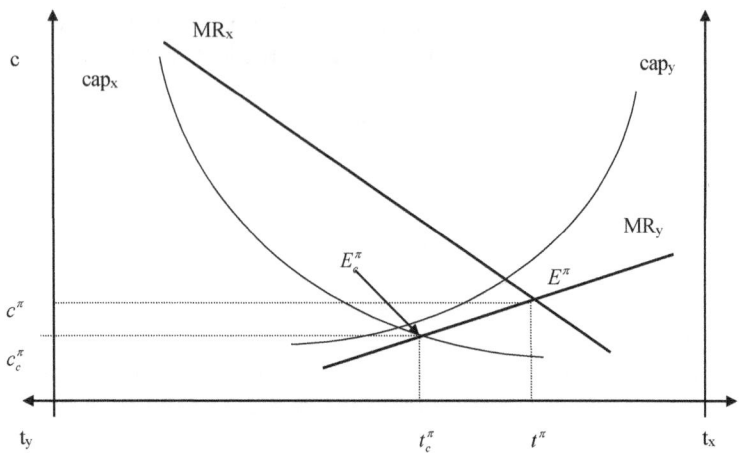

Figure 6.2   Salary or payroll cap

A different type of salary or payroll cap was proposed by the so-called G-14, an association of the most successful football clubs in Europe. The G-14 no longer exists, replaced by the European Club Association (ECA). This proposal was only a gentleman's agreement on a team's maximum wage–turnover ratio: $\frac{ct_i}{R_i}$.

An important difference with the North American salary cap is that the maximum amount a team can spend on player salaries is different for every team, whereas it was the same for every team under the North American cap. It follows also that the impact on competitive balance will be different. As shown by Kesenne (2003), the G-14 cap would worsen the competitive balance in a profit-maximisation league. Also, in a win-maximisation league the competitive balance will become more unequal if low-budget teams have a higher wage turnover ratio than large-budget teams. For the same reason, the breakeven requirement in UEFA's *Financial Fair Play* regulation (UEFA, 2010) can also be expected to worsen the competitive balance (see Peeters and Symansky, 2014).

7.   CONCLUSION

From this overview of a number of issues concerning competitive balance in professional team sports, it is clear that it has many dimensions. In an attempt to derive the optimal competitive balance, one can find that a very unequal distribution of talent is certainly not optimal. We can also conclude that the impact of competitive balance on attendance is unclear;

only long-term competitive balance seems to have an effect on spectator interest. Considering different league policies to improve the competitive balance, the impact of revenue sharing in a profit-maximisation league is complex, whereas revenue sharing in a win-maximisation league simply improves the competitive balance. Although its main objective is to increase profits by lowering player salaries, the North American salary or payroll cap can also improve the competitive balance under profit- and win-maximisation, but a cap on the teams' wage turnover rate clearly worsens the competitive balance.

REFERENCES

Borland, J. and R. Macdonald (2003), 'Demand for Sport', *Oxford Review of Economic Policy*, 19 (4), 478–503.

Bosman verdict (1995), European Court of Justice, Luxembourg.

Bruggink, T. and J. Eaton (1996), 'Rebuilding Attendance in Major League Baseball'. In: J. Fizel, E. Gustafson and L. Hadley, eds, *Baseball Economics: Current Research*. Westport: Greenwood.

Buraimo, B. and R. Simmons (2009), 'A Tale of Two Audiences: Spectators, Television Viewers and Outcome Uncertainty in Spanish Football', *Journal of Economics and Business*, 61, 326–38.

Canes, M. (1974), 'The Social Benefits of Restrictions on Team Quality'. In: R. Noll, ed., *Government and the Sports Business*. Washington, DC: Brookings Institution.

Coates, D., B. Humphreys and L. Zhou (2012), 'Outcome Uncertainty, Reference-Dependent Preferences and Live Game Attendance'. Department of Economics paper, UMBC, Baltimore.

Feess, E., and F. Stähler (2009), 'Revenue Sharing in Professional Sports Leagues', *Scottish Journal of Political Economy*, 56 (2), 255–65.

Fort, R. and J. Quirk (1995), 'Cross-Subsidization, Incentives and Outcomes in Professional Team Sports Leagues', *Journal of Economic Literature*, 33 (3), 1265–99.

García, J. and P. Rodríguez (2002), 'The Determinants of Football Match Attendance Revisited: Empirical Evidence from the Spanish Football League', *Journal of Sports Economics*, 3 (1), 18–38.

Goossens, K. (2006), 'National Measure of Seasonal Imbalance for Team Sports'. Discussion paper, Economics Department, University of Antwerp.

Humphreys, B. (2002), 'Alternative Measures of Competitive Balance', *Journal of Sports Economics*, 3 (2), 133–48.

Kesenne, S. (1996), 'League Management in Professional Team Sports with Win Maximizing Clubs', *European Journal for Sports Management*, 2 (2), 14–22.

Kesenne, S. (2000), 'Revenue Sharing and Competitive Balance in Professional Team Sports', *Journal of Sports Economics*, 1 (1), 56–65.

Kesenne, S. (2003), 'The Salary Cap Proposal of the G-14 in European Football', *European Sports Management Quarterly*, 3 (2), 120–28.

Kesenne, S. (2007), 'Does a Win Bonus Help to Increase Profits or Wins in Professional Team Sports?' *International Journal of Sport Finance*, 2 (3), 142–49.

Kesenne, S. (2014), *The Economic Theory of Professional Team Sports: An Analytical Treatment* (2nd revised edition). Cheltenham, UK and Northampton, MA, USA: Edward Elgar Publishing.

Kesenne, S. (2020), 'Do Spectators Like Dynasties?' In: P. Rodríguez, S. Kesenne and B. Humphreys, eds, *Outcome Uncertainty in Sporting Events: Winning, Losing and Competitive Balance*. Cheltenham, UK and Northampton, MA, USA: Edward Elgar Publishing, pp. 135–40.

Krautmann, A. and L. Hadley (2004), 'Of Dynasties and Dogs'. Paper presented at the IASE conference in Athens, Greece.

Kringstad, M. and B. Gerrard (2007), 'Beyond Competitive Balance'. In: M. Parent and T. Slack, eds, *International Perspectives on the Management of Sport*. San Diego: Elsevier, pp. 149–172.

Marburger, D. (1997), 'Gate Revenue Sharing and Luxury Taxes in Professional Sports', *Contemporary Economic Policy*, 15 (April), 114–23.

Neale, W. (1964), 'The Peculiar Economics of Professional Sports', *Quarterly Journal of Economics*, 78 (1), 1–14.

Noll, R. (1988), 'Professional Basketball', *Stanford University Studies in Industrial Economics*, 144.

Noll, R. (2003), 'The Economics of Baseball Contraction', *Journal of Sports Economics*, 4 (4), 367–88.

Peeters, T. and S. Szymanski (2014), 'Financial Fair Play in European Football', *Economic Policy*, 29 (78), 343–90.

Quirk, J. and R. Fort (1992), *Pay Dirt: The Business of Professional Team Sports*. Princeton: Princeton University Press.

Rascher, D. and J. Solmes (2007), 'Do Fans Want Close Contests?' *International Journal of Sport Finance*, 2, 130–42.

Rottenberg, S. (1956), 'The Baseball Players' Labor Market', *Journal of Political Economy*, 64 (3), 242–58.

Sanderson, A. (2002), 'The Many Dimensions of Competitive Balance', *Journal of Sports Economics*, 3 (2), 204–28.

Sloane, P. (1971), 'The Economics of Professional Football: The Football Club as a Utility Maximiser', *Scottish Journal of Political Economy*, 17 (2), 121–46.

Szymanski, S. (2003), 'The Economic Design of Sporting Contests', *Journal of Economic Literature*, 41 (4), 1137–87.

Szymanski, S. (2004), 'Professional Team Sports Are a Game: The Walrasian Fixed-Supply Conjecture Model, Contest-Nash Equilibrium, and the Invariance Principle', *Journal of Sports Economics*, 5 (2), 111–26.

Szymanski, S. and S. Kesenne (2004), 'Competitive balance And Gate Revenue Sharing in Team Sports', *Journal of Industrial Economics*, 51 (4), 513–25.

Szymanski, S. and S. Leach (2005), 'Tilting the Playing Field: Why a Sports League Planner Would Choose Less, Not More, Competitive Balance?' Working paper, Tanaka Business School, Imperial College, London.

UEFA (2010), *Club Licensing and Financial Fair Play Regulations, Edition 2010*. Nyon, Switzerland: UEFA.

Vrooman, J. (1995), 'A General Theory of Professional Sports Leagues', *Southern Economic Journal*, 61 (4), 971–90.

7. Game uncertainty and the demand for quality seating: a pilot case study*

Georgios Nalbantis and Tim Pawlowski[1]

INTRODUCTION

Six decades after the publication of the seminal works by Rottenberg (1956) and Neale (1964), the Uncertainty of Outcome Hypothesis (UOH) still constitutes one of the most extensively researched topics in the sports economics literature.[2] Until late in the first decade of the 2000s, an important stimulus for the related research was the fact that the UOH facilitates a competitive balance argument to justify restrictive market practices such as salary caps and revenue-sharing devices (Vrooman, 2009; Kesenne, 2000; Fort and Quirk, 1995). However, over the last few years, the lack of clear evidence on its empirical relevance has been the primary motivation for the vast majority of scholars. In this regard, several studies have tried to demystify the reasons that demand rises as the certainty of a home (or away) team's winning rises.

In one strand of the literature, the authors have suggested a potential divergence between the way in which economists measure uncertainty about the outcome of a competition and the way fans perceive it (Pawlowski et al., 2018; Budzinski and Pawlowski, 2017; Pawlowski and Budzinski, 2013). However, recent evidence suggests that "objective" measures derived from betting odds are highly correlated with "subjective" measures based on fan perceptions (Pawlowski et al., 2018).

Another strand follows the concept of reference-dependent preferences (Humphreys and Zhou, 2015; Coates et al., 2014). In the proposed framework, the authors distinguish between consumption utility and gain–loss utility as generated by deviations between the actual game outcome and fans' expectations *ex ante* (i.e., reference points). The UOH is confirmed when the marginal utility of experiencing an unexpected win exceeds the marginal utility of an unexpected loss. Otherwise, a u-shaped relationship between the home-win probability and demand arises, suggesting that fans exhibit loss aversion and derive more utility from seeing upsets. In fact, in some follow-up studies, scholars have reported that fans' preferences for game uncertainty are dominated by loss aversion (e.g., Besters et al., 2019; Humphreys and Pérez, 2019).

Parallel to the aforementioned strands, other scholars have focused on the moderating conditions under which the UOH might hold. For instance, motivated by the finding that risk and uncertainty preferences may vary based on cultural background (Vieider et al., 2015), Nalbantis and Pawlowski (2019) explored the UOH in a cross-country setting, i.e. the United States' demand for European professional football (soccer). They confirmed that the u-shaped relationship between game uncertainty and demand still holds in this setting. Other scholars have examined whether the relationship of interest may depend on the affective disposition of consumers towards teams. Initial evidence in this regard suggests that "neutral" spectators of North American sports might value game uncertainty (Tainsky et al., 2014). Likewise, Schreyer et al.'s (2016) analysis of season ticket holders' (no-)show behavior in European professional football supports the UOH for this particular consumer group. In other studies, however, the authors have found no moderating effects based on supporter status (i.e., home, away, or "neutral" fans) (Nalbantis and Pawlowski, 2019; Pawlowski et al., 2018).

In this pilot case study, we build upon the aforementioned studies and complement the literature by providing some insights on whether the impact of game uncertainty is moderated by pricing category/seating quality. This appears to be a largely neglected issue by the literature so far, mainly due to a lack of disaggregated data.[3]

The rationale behind this exercise is that clubs offer potential spectators a choice between distinct "products" that differ in terms of price (e.g., cheap seats behind the goals, expensive seats in the main stands) and characteristics (e.g., quality of view), and thus target different types of consumer (Dobson and Goddard, 1992).[4] Building upon Coates et al.'s (2014) work, we see two plausible channels for a moderating effect. *First*, one could argue that the consequences of attending a game with an outcome that differs from the reference point may differ based on the costs of attending. *Second*, as noted by Coates et al., fans weigh the expected utility from attending a game against a reservation utility. The level of reservation utility may vary depending (amongst other things) on their identification/involvement with the team. Therefore, it seems plausible to assume that fans who buy inexpensive tickets (most likely dedicated supporters of the club) have a rather low reservation utility, and may thus attend games regardless of whether the outcomes are certain. On the other hand, fans who buy expensive tickets (most likely casual spectators and neutral fans) may have a relatively high reservation utility. As such, they may be interested in watching either a clear home team win or an upset.

SETTING AND EMPIRICAL DESIGN

To test whether the impact of game uncertainty differs based on pricing category/seating quality, we utilized a unique dataset that contains attendance data per seating location for 34 home games of a German Bundesliga club, VfB Stuttgart.[5] In the 1st Bundesliga's all-time table (1963–64 to 2018–19), VfB Stuttgart is among the top five most successful clubs in the league. The club became the 1st Bundesliga champion for the fifth time in 2006–07; however, its performance has been unstable for the last ten years, being relegated twice to the 2nd Bundesliga (2015–16; 2018–19).

As to its popularity, VfB Stuttgart is among the top ten football clubs in Germany with regard to the number of registered members (70,000 as of July 2019). In the last decade the club realized an average attendance of about 50,000 spectators and an average capacity utilization of more than 80 percent. The club plays in the Mercedes-Benz Arena (capacity 60,449), whose most recent renovations took place in 2011 when the stadium became a football-only arena. The stadium includes executive suites for about 1,000 guests, and offers about 2,500 business seats as well as about 400 exclusive spots for attendees with special needs and those accompanying them. According to German Bundesliga regulations, the club must provide a designated space for at least 1,000 visiting fans but can host up to 6,000 fans (10 percent of the total stadium capacity), with an average of about 4,000 away fans per game.[6]

Concerning ticketing policy, the club categorizes matches into A-games and B-games based (amongst other things) on the opponent's popularity. Admission to A-games costs an extra €1.5 (standing stand) to €8 (main stand) compared to B-games. For all games, and regardless of the opponent, the club implements six different pricing categories (see Table 7.1), with tickets usually available for purchase at least four weeks prior to each game. For each of these categories the club offers discounts for club members (about €2), for special groups such as pensioners (between €3 and €6), and for children aged 13 or below (between €7 and €10), while special prices are offered to parents attending with one or more child in this age category. Individuals with special needs can buy tickets for €7, while accompanying persons attend for free.

Data

Our data contains information on the number of tickets sold (including season tickets) two days before each of the club's home games for a total of 183 blocks of the stadium (excluding blocks for guest fans, business seats and executive suites). We manually assigned each block to the six pricing categories implemented by the club and derived an aggregated game-level attendance per pricing category. The data includes a total of 34 VfB Stuttgart home games, spanning two Bundesliga seasons (2nd Bundesliga: 2016–17; 1st Bundesliga: 2017–18). This translates to 204 game-pricing category observations. Table 7.1 shows the average attendance per pricing category.

Since, our demand variable is based on attendance figures two days prior to each home game, we compared it with actual game attendance reported by the club (Figure 7.1).[7] The average of our demand measure was 46,032 (excluding blocks for guests, business seats and executive suites), while the average reported figure by the club was 53,543. Since the correlation between both figures is very high (r = 0.94), we argue that our dependent variable is a valid demand proxy.

Econometric Specification

We regressed the natural logarithm of attendance per pricing category and game based on variables capturing game uncertainty based on margin-corrected betting odds (source: football-data.co.uk). *First*, we estimated the home-win probability and its squared term (Peel and Thomas, 1988) to test whether an *inverse* u-shaped relationship would arise: that is, whether attendance would be maximized in games where VfB Stuttgart was

Table 7.1   Average attendance per pricing category

Pricing category	Mean	SD	Min.	Max.	> Cap 99%
Cat 1 (€14.50 to €16.00)	7,869.059	105.800	7,770	8,268	0.059
Cat 2 (€22.00 to €27.00)	14,520.470	1,533.725	10,029	15,670	0.206
Cat 3 (€27.00 to €32.00)	4,245.118	876.345	2,083	4,836	0.206
Cat 4 (€34.00 to €39.50)	7,448.471	1,876.180	3,519	9,864	0.029
Cat 5 (€44.50 to €50.50)	7,894.559	2,211.010	3,590	10,620	0.118
Cat 6 (€55.50 to €63.50)	3,893.353	565.283	2,263	4,584	0.118

Notes: Prices correspond to full prices; the lowest price per category for B-games, the highest for A-games.

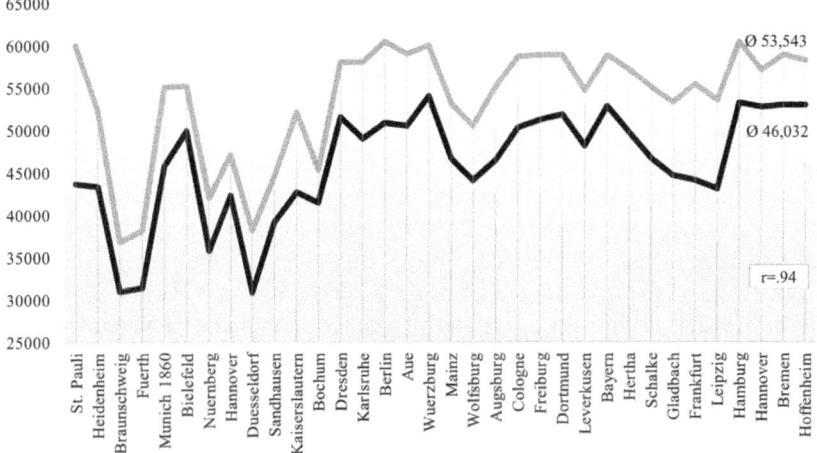

Notes: Black line denotes sample attendance; gray line actual attendance.
Sample attendance was calculated by aggregating all tickets sold per pricing category two
days before each game; actual attendance represents the actual number of attendees per
game (collected from transfermarkt.de).
VfB Stuttgart's opponents are listed in chronological order, starting with the first home
game of the season (2nd Bundesliga: vs. St. Pauli; 1st Bundesliga: vs. Mainz).

Figure 7.1   Comparison between sample and actual attendance

anticipated to share a similar win probability with its opponents. *Second,*
we implemented the Theil (1967) measure, which uses information on
home win, away win, and draw probabilities (p_i):

$$\text{Theil} = \sum_{i=1}^{3} \frac{p_i}{\sum_{i=1}^{3} p_i} \; \log\left(\frac{\sum_{i=1}^{3} p_i}{p_i} \right) \qquad (7.1)$$

An increase in the Theil index denotes an (*a priori*) increased uncertainty
of the match's outcome. As such, for the UOH to hold, the index should
be positively associated with attendance, indicating fans' preference for (*a
priori*) predicted close games.

To examine possible moderating effects on the impact of the aforementioned measures, we discriminated between inexpensive and expensive tickets following Nalbantis et al.'s (2017) study. They surveyed VfB
Stuttgart fans and found that the average maximum willingness-to-pay for
a ticket was about €25. We used this value to discriminate between "inexpensive" tickets (i.e., pricing categories 1 and 2) and "expensive" tickets

(all other pricing categories). We interacted this dummy variable with the uncertainty measures.

Our models also include control variables that are frequently associated with attendance demand (see García and Rodríguez, 2009; Borland and McDonald, 2003).[8] Considering the impact of weather, we included variables denoting whether there was precipitation on matchday as well as the maximum temperature during that day. We expected weather conditions to affect attendance behavior even though our dependent variable was measured two days before each game. Rather accurate weather predictions are currently readily available for several days in advance. We expected rain to have either no impact or a positive impact on demand. The reasons are threefold: (i) the state of Baden-Württemberg (whose capital is Stuttgart) is one of the rainiest regions in the country, which factor might shape the fans' habits (Ge et al., 2020); (ii) the stadium's roof protects all stands from rain; (iii) rainy days limit other outdoor leisure activities (Pawlowski and Anders, 2012). Concerning temperature, we expected a positive relationship with attendance, since warmer days can create more comfortable conditions for the fans (Welki and Zlatoper, 1994).

Furthermore, we controlled for the number of home games, expecting that fans' interest would rise as the season progressed.[9] We also took into account whether each game took place at the weekend, as we expected demand to be lower during the week (Knowles et al., 1992). Since VfB Stuttgart participated in two different divisions during our examination period, we controlled for whether the games were played in the 1st Bundesliga. To capture the performance of VfB Stuttgart, we used the club's league ranking prior to each game (García and Rodríguez, 2002).[10] Since, however, the club was expected to perform well in the 2nd Bundesliga and avoid relegation in the 1st Bundesliga, we interacted the performance variable with the Bundesliga variable to capture possible differences. We expected VfB Stuttgart fans to be more sensitive to good performances in the 2nd Bundesliga than in the 1st Bundesliga. Finally, we included a variable denoting whether the opposing team had been promoted from a lower league to control for a "newcomer effect" (Pawlowski and Nalbantis, 2015). Table 7.2 shows all variable descriptions and descriptive statistics.

We estimated our first set of demand models with fixed effects regressions, with the panel dimension being the six pricing categories. Due to (right) censoring issues arising from sellouts and crowd segregation, as reported in Table 7.1, we further implemented Tobit models with individual cut-off points (Tobin, 1958) and pricing category unconditional fixed effects. For both model specifications, we employed robust standard errors clustered at the pricing category level.[11]

Table 7.2   Variable descriptions and descriptive statistics

Variable	Variable description	Mean	Std. Dev.	Min.	Max.
ATT	Attendance per price category two days before game	7,645.172	3,763.524	2,083	15,670
log(ATT)	Natural logarithm of attendance variable	8.823	0.493	7.642	9.660
Hwin	Probability of home win derived from betting odds	47.129	12.506	10.060	69.164
Theil	Theil index based on all outcome probabilities	1.014	0.079	0.783	1.094
Inexpensive	Pricing category 1 and 2 (1 if "yes")	0.333	0.473	0	1
Temperature	Maximum temperature on matchday (°C)	13.412	7.868	2	30
Precipitation	Precipitation on matchday (1 if "yes")	0.471	0.500	0	1
Matchday	Number of matchday for each home game	18	9.771	1	34
Weekend	Game played on Saturday or Sunday (1 if "yes")	0.618	0.487	0	1
1st Bundesliga	Game played in 1st Bundesliga (1 if "yes")	0.500	0.501	0	1
Ranking VfB	Ranking of VfB Stuttgart before game	7.294	5.477	1	16
Promoted	Opponent promoted from a lower league (1 if "yes")	0.118	0.323	0	1

Note: Total number of game-pricing category observations 204.

Sources: Betting odds data retrieved from football-data.co.uk; weather data from freemeteo.de.

RESULTS

Table 7.3 provides estimates of the fixed effects (FE) regressions and the Tobit models. All models were consistent with regard to the impact of the game uncertainty measures. The estimates for home-win probability and its squared term were statistically significant, indicating a u-shaped relationship between the expected home-win probability and attendance (see Figure 7.2). Likewise, the Theil index estimates were statistically significant with a negative sign, indicating that demand decreases with increasing game uncertainty. Overall, these findings contradict the UOH and are in line with findings reported in the empirical literature (e.g., Coates et al., 2014; Pawlowski et al., 2018), suggesting fans' preference for games involving an *ex ante* favorite.

The signs of all uncertainty measures remained the same when interacted with the dummy variable of "inexpensive tickets." Interestingly, however, the interaction term denoted differences with regard to their impact. Figure 7.3 depicts the two-way interaction, and provides the predicted demand for the expensive and inexpensive ticket categories with regard to both game uncertainty measures. Overall, the demand for inexpensive tickets was higher than for expensive ones. Moreover, the demand for expensive rather than inexpensive tickets seems to drive the u-shaped relationship between game uncertainty and attendance. Likewise, the demand for expensive tickets seems to drive the negative effect of the Theil index.

These findings correspond with some plausible effects of the control variables. We found that an increase in temperature was associated with an increase in attendance. Likewise, games that took place during rainy days had higher attendance. In contrast to our expectations, the demand for games at the weekend was not statistically different from the demand during the week. However, as the season progressed, demand for VfB Stuttgart games increased. In general, attendance was higher in 1st Bundesliga games than in 2nd Bundesliga games. Concerning the impact of performance, as anticipated, we found that an increase in ranking in the 2nd Bundesliga (i.e., a deterioration in performance) decreased attendance, while VfB Stuttgart's performance in the 1st Bundesliga seemed to have no significant statistical association with increased demand. The interaction of both indicates that a deterioration in performance leads to a higher demand for VfB Stuttgart games in the 1st Bundesliga than in the 2nd Bundesliga. Finally, in line with our predictions, games involving an opponent that had been promoted from a lower league were associated with a higher demand for tickets.

To assess the robustness of our findings, we ran two different tests.[12] *First*, we estimated Tobit models for each price category. To improve the

Table 7.3 Regression estimates

	FE Regression		Tobit		
Hwin	-0.014** (0.004)		-0.023*** (0.006)	-0.031*** (0.002)	
Hwin SQ	0.0005** (0.0002)		0.0002*** (0.0001)	0.0004*** (0.00003)	
Theil		-0.595** (0.178)	-0.947*** (0.257)		-1.062*** (0.183)
Inexpensive				0.141 (0.127)	0.333*** (0.052)
Inexpensive#Hwin				0.024*** (0.004)	
Inexpensive#Hwin SQ				-0.0002*** (0.00002)	
Inexpensive#Theil					0.367*** (0.053)
Temperature	0.006** (0.002)	0.007** (0.002)	0.008*** (0.002)	0.008*** (0.002)	0.008*** (0.002)
Precipitation	0.068** (0.020)	0.069** (0.021)	0.060*** (0.019)	0.060*** (0.021)	0.065*** (0.020)
Weekend	0.004 (0.010)	0.002 (0.011)	0.003 (0.011)	0.003 (0.011)	-0.001 (0.011)
Matchday	0.004** (0.002)	0.004** (0.002)	0.005*** (0.002)	0.005*** (0.002)	0.005*** (0.002)

Table 7.3 (continued)

	FE Regression		Tobit		Tobit	
1st Bundesliga	0.059*	0.052	0.123	0.129	0.122	0.130
	(0.027)	(0.037)	(0.081)	(0.091)	(0.086)	(0.090)
Ranking VfB	−0.040**	−0.040**	−0.038***	−0.039***	−0.038***	−0.039***
	(0.013)	(0.014)	(0.012)	(0.013)	(0.013)	(0.013)
1st Bundesliga #Ranking VfB	0.044**	0.044**	0.041***	0.041***	0.041***	0.041***
	(0.012)	(0.012)	(0.011)	(0.011)	(0.010)	(0.011)
Promoted	0.057**	0.060**	0.077***	0.076***	0.077***	0.075***
	(0.020)	(0.018)	(0.024)	(0.022)	(0.024)	(0.022)
Pricing category FEs	yes	yes	yes	yes	yes	yes
Constant	8.834***	9.205***	9.089***	9.665***	8.577***	9.077***
	(0.062)	(0.132)	(0.076)	(0.201)	(0.121)	(0.134)
N_{total}	204	204	204	204	204	204
$N_{censored}$			25	25	25	25
AIC	−1,369.217	−1,377.763	−70.044	−71.845	−75.793	−72.787
BIC	−1,203.311	−1,211.857	−53.454	−55.255	−59.203	−56.197

Notes: The dependent variable is the natural logarithm of game attendance per pricing category (see Table 7.2 for variable descriptions). Results with individual cut-off points at 99% of pricing category capacity utilization. Robust standard errors clustered at price-category-level in parentheses.
Significance levels: *** p ≤ 0.01, ** p ≤ 0.05, * p ≤ 0.1.
AIC = Akaike information criterion; BIC = Bayesian information criterion.

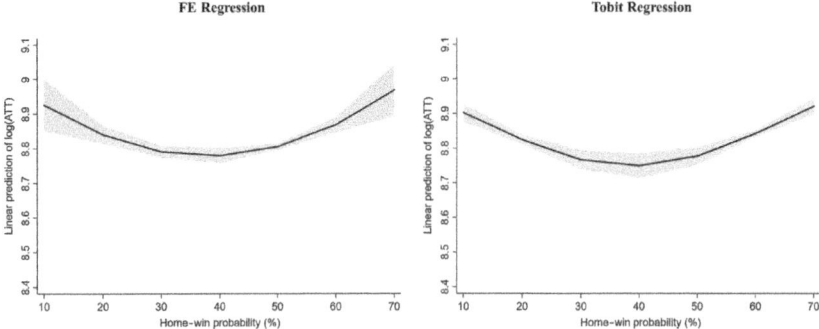

Notes: Gray shaded areas denote the 95% confidence interval.
Predictions were calculated based on models presented on Table 7.3.
The dependent variable is the natural logarithm of attendance; 204 game-pricing category observations.

Figure 7.2   Predictive margins for home-win probability (95% CIs)

accuracy of these models, we used bootstrap standard errors with 4,999 replications (Efron and Tibshirani, 1986). Overall, these models support our main finding on the moderating effect of ticket pricing category/ seating quality (Figure 7.4). Since, however, these models only contained 34 observations, we were unable to use the same set of control variables given the low degree of freedom (1:10 rule; see VanVoorhis and Morgan, 2007).

Second we gathered information on the total number of season tickets sold per price category in the seasons under consideration and removed these tickets from each respective category. The regression estimates of the Tobit models excluding season tickets show that our main findings with regard to the overall impact of the uncertainty measures remain (Figure 7.5). Moreover, they confirm that, in contrast to inexpensive ticket categories, the impact of home-win probability on the demand for expensive tickets is u-shaped (Figure 7.6). Finally, the exclusion of season tickets did not affect the attested impact of the control variables.

CONCLUSION AND DISCUSSION

This chapter contributes to the literature by exploring, for the first time, the moderating role of pricing category/seating quality in the game uncertainty–demand relationship. We found that fans' preference for games involving *any ex ante* favorite is primarily driven by the demand for

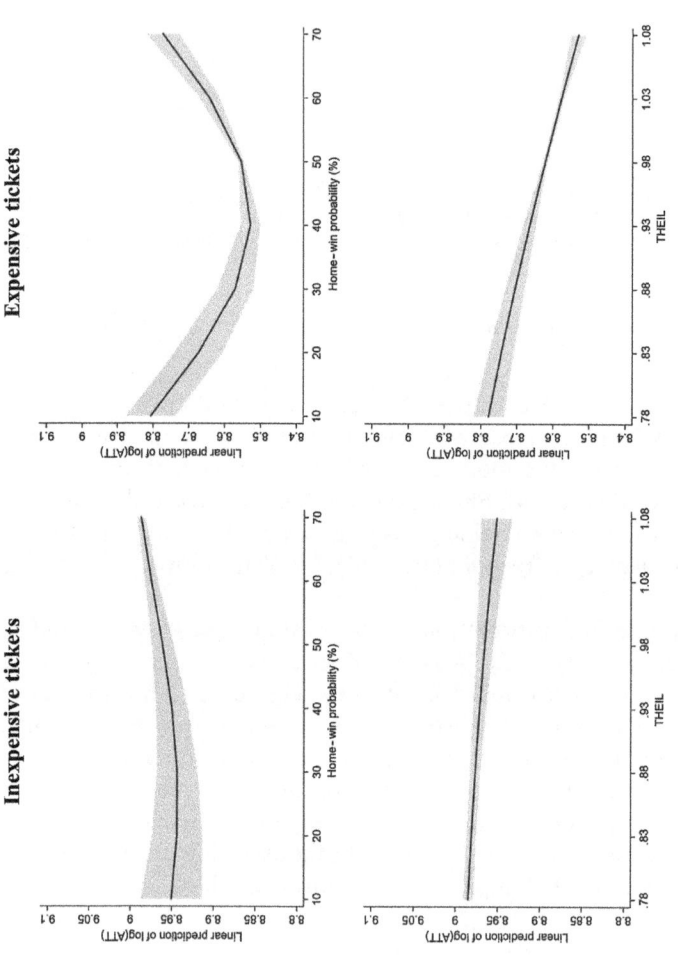

Notes: Gray shaded areas denote the 95% confidence interval.
Predictions were calculated based on models including the two-way interactions presented in Table 7.3.
The dependent variable is the natural logarithm of attendance; 204 game-pricing category observations.

Figure 7.3 *Inexpensive vs. expensive tickets: predictive margins for home-win probability and Theil index (95% CIs)*

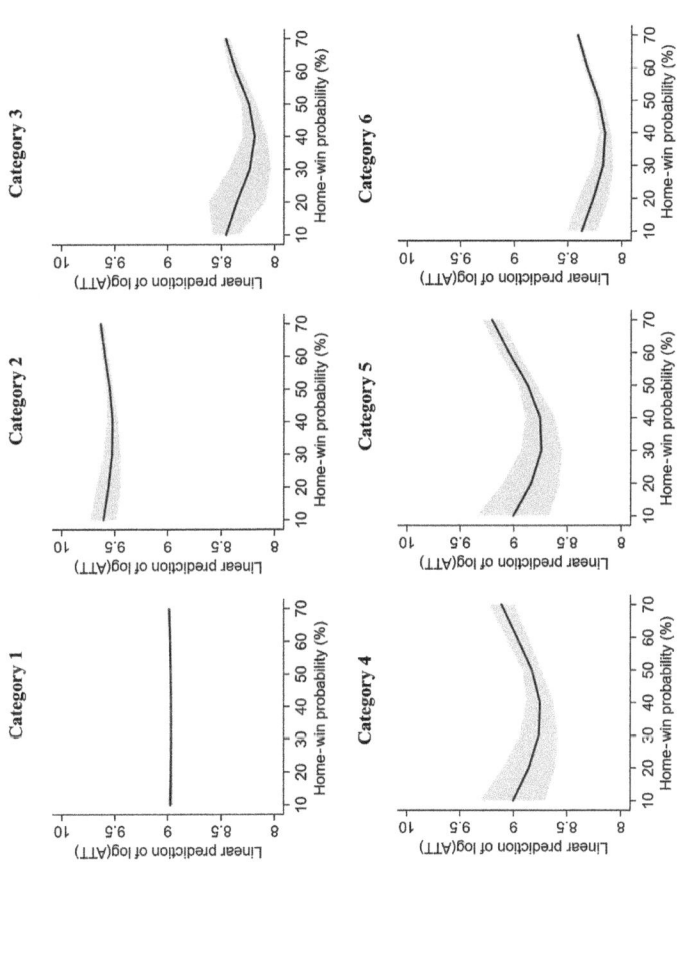

Notes: Gray shaded areas denote the 95% confidence interval.
Predictions were calculated based on models per price category.
The dependent variable is the natural logarithm of attendance; 34 observations per price category.

Figure 7.4 Predictive margins for home-win probability (95% CIs) per price category

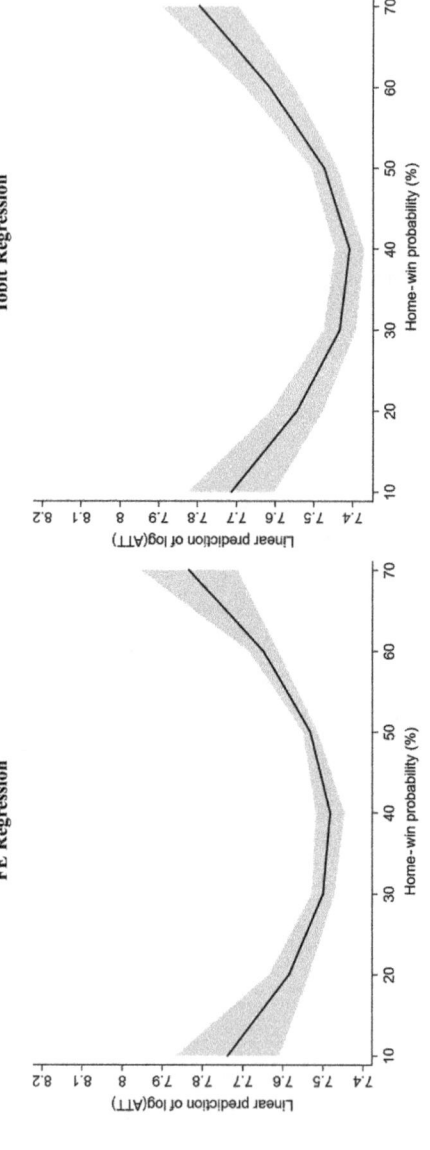

Notes: Gray shaded areas denote the 95% confidence interval.
Predictions were calculated based on models excluding season tickets.
The dependent variable is the natural logarithm of attendance; 204 game-pricing category observations.

Figure 7.5 Predictive margins for home-win probability (95% CIs), excluding season tickets

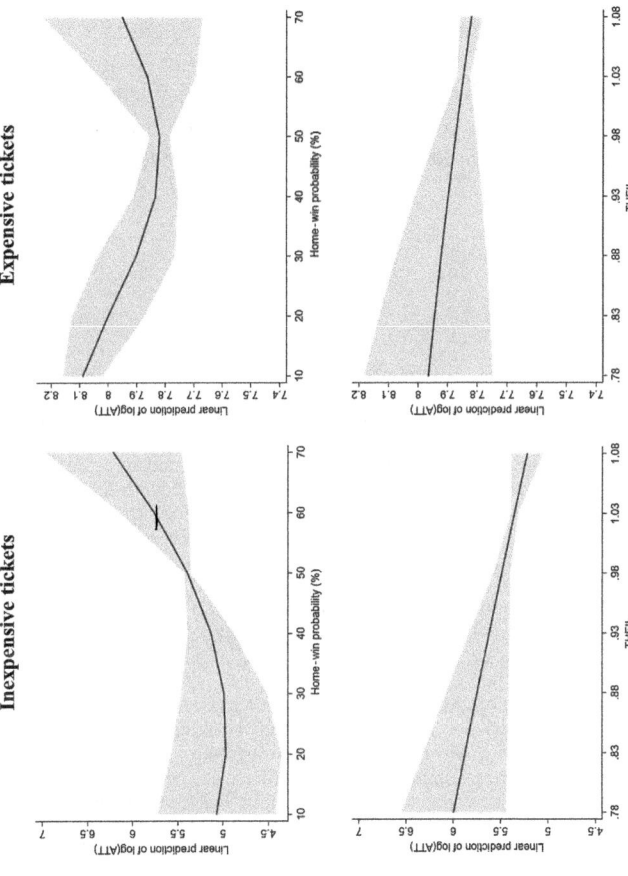

Notes: Gray shaded areas denote the 95% confidence interval.
Predictions were calculated based on models including two-way interactions and excluding season tickets.
The dependent variable is the natural logarithm of attendance; 204 game-pricing category observations.

Figure 7.6   *Inexpensive vs. expensive tickets (excluding season tickets): predictive margins for home-win probability and Theil index (95% CIs)*

expensive tickets, whereas fans buying inexpensive tickets seem to prefer a home win.

Overall, these findings are in line with those reported in previous literature (e.g., Schreyer et al., 2016), suggesting that fan attendance behavior patterns in the same club might differ. However, with the data available, we are unable to further unravel the channels driving these differences. In this regard, surveys collecting data about home fans' perceptions of the expected game outcome (similar to Pawlowski et al., 2018) and their degree of identification with the club, as well as the prices paid for tickets, might be insightful. A further caveat of the present study is the lack of information about the (no-)show behavior of season ticket holders per pricing category. Testing whether this might affect our findings and/or whether our general findings hold for other clubs and sports is a task for future research.

NOTES

*   We gratefully acknowledge that the data used in this manuscript was provided by VfB Stuttgart as well as Aramark Restaurations GmbH (the company provides, amongst others, catering services for several Bundesliga stadia). Special credit is due to Alexander Kästle and Torsten Reissig, who gave us access to the data and guided us through the data preparation. A previous version of this manuscript was presented at the XIII Gijón Conference of Sports Economics. We would like to thank all participants for their valuable comments and suggestions. Any remaining errors and omissions are ours alone.
1.   Tim Pawlowski is also affiliated with the LEAD Graduate School and Research Network.
2.   For recent reviews on the impact of game uncertainty on stadium attendance, see Coates et al. (2014) and Pawlowski (2013). For reviews on the impact of game uncertainty on TV demand, see Nalbantis and Pawlowski (2016) and Schreyer et al. (2018). Pawlowski and Nalbantis (2019) provide a recent review on the impact of policy interventions and regulations on competitive balance.
3.   The only study that touched on this issue is by Nalbantis et al. (2017), who examined whether perceptions of suspense of a single game affect the choice of quality seating. However, their study relies on survey data and willingness-to-pay statements.
4.   Since ancient times, different seating locations in stadia (such as the Colosseum in Rome) have frequently been associated with social standing (Bale, 1993) or even with the spectators' political ideologies (Guschwan, 2016a). Many have argued that committed fans, including young and working-class spectators, predominately occupy the seats behind the goals and buy affordable tickets, while casual fans and neutral spectators mostly occupy the main stands and buy more expensive tickets (Guschwan, 2016b).
5.   VfB = Verein für Bewegungsspiele [literally, club for motion games].
6.   The average of away fans was calculated for 24 (out of 34) of VfB Stuttgart's home games during the seasons 2016–17 and 2017–18. Data was collected from various online sources. No data was available for ten games.
7.   Our figures also cover attendees with special needs. As elaborated before, the club offers these individuals an exclusive stand as well as special prices. Since, however, there is almost no variation in the data for this category (standard deviation is about seven individuals), we decided not to report this as a separate category.

8. For a discussion on the historical development of the attendance literature see Rodríguez (2019).
9. In line with previous findings (e.g., Pawlowski and Nalbantis, 2015; Pawlowski and Anders, 2012), we checked whether the impact of matchday on demand is u-shaped by including a second-order term of matchday in our estimations. The results, however, indicate just a linear relationship.
10. Unfortunately, it is not possible to control for opponent performance. The variance inflation factors indicate that multicollinearity is present when including variables capturing the opponent's performance in the last five games or in the opponent's ranking.
11. We are reporting models utilizing a capacity (right-censoring) limit of 99 percent as a robustness check; however, we ran models with alternative cut-off points. Moreover, we ran Tobit models without the pricing category unconditional fixed effects, Tobit models with random effects, and multilevel mixed effects Tobit models. All models yielded similar results. They are available on request.
12. We report only the graphical depiction of the impact of game uncertainty measures. Regression estimates are available on request.

REFERENCES

Bale, J. (1993). The spatial development of the modern stadium. *International Review for the Sociology of Sport, 28*(2–3), 121–133.

Besters, L.M., van Ours, J.C., and van Tuijl, M.A. (2019). How outcome uncertainty, loss aversion and team quality affect stadium attendance in Dutch professional football. *Journal of Economic Psychology, 72*, 117–127.

Borland, J., and MacDonald, R. (2003). Demand for sport. *Oxford Review of Economic Policy, 19*(4), 478–502.

Budzinski, O., and Pawlowski, T. (2017). The behavioural economics of competitive balance: Theories, findings and implications. *International Journal of Sport Finance, 12*(2), 109–122.

Coates, D., Humphreys, B.R., and Zhou, L. (2014). Reference-dependent preferences, loss aversion, and live game attendance. *Economic Inquiry, 52*(3), 959–973.

Dobson, S.M., and Goddard, J.A. (1992). The demand for standing and seated viewing accommodation in the English Football League. *Applied Economics, 24*(10), 1155–1163.

Efron, B., and Tibshirani, R. (1986). Bootstrap methods for standard errors, confidence intervals, and other measures of statistical accuracy. *Statistical Science, 1*(1), 54–75.

Fort, R., and Quirk, J. (1995). Cross-subsidization, incentives, and outcomes in professional team sports leagues. *Journal of Economic Literature, 33*(3), 1265–1299.

García, J., and Rodríguez, P. (2002). The determinants of football match attendance revisited: Empirical evidence from the Spanish football league. *Journal of Sports Economics, 3*(1), 18–38.

García, J., and Rodríguez, P. (2009). Sports attendance: A survey of the literature 1973–2007. *Rivista di Diritto ed Economia dello Sport, 5*(2), 111–151.

Ge, Q., Humphreys, B.R., and Zhou, K. (2020). Are fair weather fans affected by weather? Rainfall, habit formation, and live game attendance. *Journal of Sports Economics, 21*(3), 304–322.

Guschwan, M. (2016a). Performance in the stands. *Soccer and Society*, *17*(3), 290–316.

Guschwan, M. (2016b). Fan politics: Dissent and control at the stadium. *Soccer and Society*, *17*(3), 388–402.

Humphreys, B.R., and Pérez, L. (2019). Loss aversion, upset preference, and sports television viewing audience size. *Journal of Behavioral and Experimental Economics*, *78*, 61–67.

Humphreys, B.R., and Zhou, L. (2015). The Louis-Schmeling paradox and the league standing effect reconsidered. *Journal of Sports Economics*, *16*(8), 835–852.

Kesenne, S. (2000). The impact of salary caps in professional team sports. *Scottish Journal of Political Economy*, *47*(4), 422–430.

Knowles, G., Sherony, K., and Haupert, M. (1992). The demand for major league baseball: A test of the uncertainty of outcome hypothesis. *American Economist*, *36*(2), 72–80.

Nalbantis, G., and Pawlowski, T. (2016). *The Demand for International Football Telecasts in the United States*. Cham: Palgrave Macmillan.

Nalbantis, G., and Pawlowski, T. (2019). U.S. demand for European soccer telecasts: A between-country test of the uncertainty of outcome hypothesis. *Journal of Sports Economics*, *20*(6), 797–818.

Nalbantis, G., Pawlowski, T., and Coates, D. (2017). The fans' perception of competitive balance and its impact on willingness-to-pay for a single game. *Journal of Sports Economics*, *18*(5), 479–505.

Neale, W.C. (1964). The peculiar economics of professional sports: A contribution to the theory of the firm in sporting competition and in market competition. *Quarterly Journal of Economics*, *78*(1), 1–14.

Pawlowski, T. (2013). Testing the uncertainty of outcome hypothesis is European professional football: A stated preference approach. *Journal of Sports Economics*, *14*(4), 341–367.

Pawlowski, T., and Anders, C. (2012). Stadium attendance in German professional football: The (un)importance of uncertainty of outcome reconsidered. *Applied Economics Letters*, *19*(16), 1553–1556.

Pawlowski, T., and Budzinski, O. (2013). The (monetary) value of competitive balance for sport consumers: A stated preference approach to European professional football. *International Journal of Sport Finance*, *8*(2), 112–123.

Pawlowski, T., and Nalbantis, G. (2015). Competition format, championship uncertainty and stadium attendance in European football: A small league perspective. *Applied Economics*, *47*(38), 4128–4139.

Pawlowski, T., and Nalbantis, G. (2019). Competitive balance: Measurement and relevance. In Downward, P., Frick, B., Humphreys, B.R., Pawlowski, T., Ruseski, J.E., and Soebbing, B.P. (eds), *The SAGE Handbook of Sports Economics* (pp. 154–162). London: Sage.

Pawlowski, T., Nalbantis, G., and Coates, D. (2018). Perceived game uncertainty, suspense and the demand for sport. *Economic Inquiry*, *56*(1), 173–192.

Peel, D.A., and Thomas, D.A. (1988). Outcome uncertainty and the demand for football. *Scottish Journal of Political Economy*, *35*(2), 242–249.

Rodríguez, P. (2019). Economics of attendance. In Downward, P., Frick, B., Humphreys, B.R., Pawlowski, T., Ruseski, J.E., and Soebbing, B.P. (eds), *The SAGE Handbook of Sports Economics* (pp. 163–170). London: Sage.

Rottenberg, S. (1956). The baseball player's labour market. *Journal of Political Economy*, *64*(3), 242–258.

Schreyer, D., Schmidt, S.L., and Torgler, B. (2016). Against all odds? Exploring the role of game outcome uncertainty in season ticket holders' stadium attendance demand. *Journal of Economic Psychology*, *56*, 192–217.

Schreyer, D., Schmidt, S.L., and Torgler, B. (2018). Game outcome uncertainty and television audience demand: New evidence from German football. *German Economic Review*, *19*(2), 140–161.

Tainsky, S., Xu, J., and Zhou, Y. (2014). Qualifying the game uncertainty effect: A game level analysis of NFL postseason broadcast ratings. *Journal of Sports Economics*, *15*(3), 219–236.

Theil, H. (1967). *Economics and Information Theory*. Amsterdam: North-Holland.

Tobin, J. (1958). Estimation of relationships for limited dependent variables. *Econometrica*, *26*(1), 24–36.

VanVoorhis, C.W., and Morgan, B.L. (2007). Understanding power and rules of thumb for determining sample sizes. *Tutorials in Quantitative Methods for Psychology*, *3*(2), 43–50.

Vieider, F.M., Lefebvre, M., Bouchouicha, R., Chmura, T., Hakimov, R., Krawczyk, M., and Martinsson, P. (2015). Common components of risk and uncertainty attitudes across contexts and domains: Evidence from 30 countries. *Journal of the European Economic Association*, *13*(3), 421–452.

Vrooman, J. (2009). Theory of the perfect game: Competitive balance in monopoly sports leagues. *Review of Industrial Organization*, *34*(1), 5–44.

Welki, A.M., and Zlatoper, T.J. (1994). US professional football: The demand for game-day attendance in 1991. *Managerial and Decision Economics*, *15*(5), 489–495.

8. Fan response to the analytics revolution in hockey: possession metrics and NHL attendance

Rodney J. Paul

After the "Moneyball" revolution in baseball, where advanced statistics and analytics were used in player personnel and coaching decisions, other sports followed in its footsteps. Although decidedly more difficult than baseball, with its highly individualized matchups, the other sports began to find better ways to measure player performance and incorporate this information into draft, free agency, and on-field decisions. One of the last sports to officially enter the analytics revolution in sports was ice hockey. This could be due to a variety of reasons that stem from the speed and within-game changes being difficult to measure and model, to resistance in the ranks of front office personnel; but, whatever the underlying reasons, hockey appeared slow to adapt.

This pattern officially changed in the summer of 2015. Independent public hockey researchers and those that developed analytical systems at lower levels of hockey were hired by National Hockey League (NHL) teams. The biggest initial name was Kyle Dubas, who was hired by the Maple Leafs in the hockey hotbed of Toronto, Canada. Others who had developed a following on their advanced hockey statistics websites – such as Sunny Mehta, Tyler Dellow, and Tim Barnes – were also hired in the same short period of time by the New Jersey Devils, the Edmonton Oilers, and the Washington Capitals. The following season, John Chayka of the Arizona Coyotes became the youngest general manager in NHL history, based upon his background and use of analytics in hockey.

The hiring of these hockey analytics pioneers was met with much fanfare, both positive and negative, and media outlets for hockey began to explain the basic concepts of hockey analytics to its fanbase. The advent of advanced statistics and analytics in professional hockey mostly centered on the concept of possession. Possession of the puck is deemed to be highly desirable as the team that possesses the puck has a chance to score while simultaneously denying their opponent a chance to score.

While current technology promises to revolutionize the concept of possession through the use of cameras, wearables, and tracking devices, current collective bargaining rules between the NHL and its Players' Association do not allow this technology to be used in-game. Therefore, when researchers in hockey analytics wanted to be able to track possession, they needed a proxy. This proxy became different forms of shot attempt metrics.

One key hockey possession statistic is named Corsi. A Corsi stat, whether for or against, is a proxy for possession based upon shot attempts. Specifically, Corsi consists of three parts: Shots on Goal, Missed Shots, and Blocked Shots. Shots on Goal is a well-known traditional metric that a team is given credit for if a shot attempt gets through to the net and has a chance to go into the goal. Missed shots are attempted shots that are taken on the ice, get through toward the net, but do not qualify as a shot on goal. Missed shots could be wide of the net, above the crossbar, or shots that hit the post or crossbar. Blocked shots are shots that are blocked by the opposing team before making it to the net. The sum of these three metrics is combined to form Corsi statistics.

The main possession statistic alternative to Corsi is called Fenwick. Fenwick is similar to Corsi in that it sums Shots on Goal and Missed Shots, but it does not include Blocked Shots in its computation. The rationale behind the omission of blocked shots is that avoiding an opposing player attempting (or not attempting) to block a shot is a skill. Therefore, proponents of Fenwick prefer possession to only be measured by shots that make it toward the net and are either on goal or wide/above/hit the posts or crossbar. In many cases, Corsi and Fenwick are both presented on analytics websites or are included in hockey possession research.

Although Corsi and Fenwick were and still are commonly used in the hockey statistics community, the NHL decided against using these names in their official website computations. NHL.com enhanced statistics refer to Corsi as Shot Attempts (SAT), while it refers to Fenwick as Unblocked Shots (USAT). These statistics are available on a 5-vs-5 basis (most commonly used for research purposes on possession, or any other on-ice situation (in addition to being computed when leading, trailing, game is close, etc.).

Empirical models of hockey performance using Corsi and Fenwick have been shown to be better than models using goals as a predictor of future goals (i.e. Likens, 2011; Desjardins, 2009). Therefore, these models have become popular in the sport as a way to evaluate players and team performance. These possession-based models served as the foundation for the development of other performance measures in the sport, such as expected goals (i.e. Macdonald, 2012).

In this research, we approach the analytics revolution and the adoption of possession statistics from a different perspective: that of the fans. Although the use of possession statistics is highly debated on social media and in other sources, one way to objectively observe if fans appreciate teams that play more of a possession-style game is to directly test their interest in terms of attendance. If shot attempts, the statistic currently used to measure possession, are valued by fans beyond their ability to help teams win games, this should be seen at the gate. We test the null hypothesis that possession statistics have no effect on attendance through various regression model specifications using the natural log of attendance as the dependent variable and controlling for factors such as team success, outcome uncertainty, expected scoring, fighting, day of the week, season progression, special events, etc. We specifically compare the results of using Corsi and Fenwick figures to the simple inclusion of shots on goal and goals to separate the individual components of the possession metrics.

This chapter is arranged as follows. Section 1 contains a background literature review of studies of hockey attendance. Section 2 presents and describes the regression model and its results. The final section discusses the results and presents the conclusions of the empirical findings related to possession statistics and attendance at NHL games.

1.   LITERATURE REVIEW

A key element of past studies of hockey attendance relates to outcome uncertainty. The level of individual game competition between two teams is likely a possible determinant of fan interest. The Uncertainty of Outcome Hypothesis (UOH) was first hypothesized by Rottenberg (1956). In his classic paper, Rottenberg stated that fans would prefer to attend games where teams were evenly matched. Coates and Humphreys (2012) rejected the UOH for the NHL. An alternative hypothesis has been suggested in the literature by Coates et al. (2014) that incorporates reference-dependent preferences and loss aversion. They suggest that fans prefer to see the home team win, would prefer not to see the home team upset, but do like to see the home team possibly earn an upset. Paul et al. (2019) recently found no evidence of preference for outcome uncertainty, in any statistically significant form, for junior hockey in Canada and the United States (the Canadian Hockey League). Mixed results were also found for how outcome uncertainty relates to hockey attendance in Russia, Finland, and Sweden (Paul et al., 2016).

While outcome uncertainty focuses on individual game situations, typically using betting market prices as proxies for perceived closeness between teams, the concept is closely related to season-to-season studies of attendance that include estimates for competitive balance (CB). Competitive balance is the concept of how evenly balanced a particular sports league is within a season and across seasons. There are different forms of within-season competitive balance measures that have been offered in the literature. One measure is the idealized standard deviation of win percentage (i.e. Scully, 1989; Quirk and Fort, 1997). Other proposed measures include the CB Ratio statistic (Humphreys, 2002) and the use of Herfindahl indices related to championships (i.e. Gerrard, 2004). Another competitive balance measure that has been suggested is the Hope Statistic (Kaplan et al., 2011; O'Reilly et al., 2008). This measure uses statistics related to how far from a playoff spot a team finished (and has finished over a span of different seasons) to estimate "hope" for a franchise to turn into contenders for playoff spots and championships in the coming season. A combination of outcome uncertainty on a game-by-game basis and competitive balance, over a season or multiple seasons, is likely a key factor entering the minds of sports fans when they choose to attend games.

A frequent issue that has been studied as it relates to hockey attendance is the role of in-game fighting. This factor was previously studied for NHL attendance by Jones (1984), Jones et al. (1993, 1996), and Paul (2003). In these studies, fighting was shown to have a positive and significant effect on attendance. Although there were differences in magnitude as it relates to the country where NHL games were played, the impact of fighting on attendance was seen in both Canadian and American cities. During the time frames studied in these articles, more fighting led to more fans in attendance at games.

Although fighting is subject to only a five-minute penalty in the NHL and in the minors and Canadian Juniors in North America, in most European leagues fighting is not allowed. Fighting in most European leagues results in immediate ejection from the game and can lead to player suspensions. Although fighting is not allowed in the Deutsche Eishockey Liga (DEL) in Germany, penalty minutes, a proxy for physical play, were found to have a positive and significant effect on attendance in this league (Coates et al., 2012). However, physical play (using penalty minutes as a proxy) was not found to significantly impact attendance in Finland's elite SM-Liiga (Coates et al., 2012). Fighting was not shown to have a statistically significant impact on attendance in junior hockey in the Quebec Major Junior Hockey League (Paul and Weinbach, 2011). In a more recent study of Canadian junior hockey (the Canadian Hockey League), however, fighting was shown to have a positive and significant effect on attendance at these games (Paul et al., 2019). Rockerbie (2012) found that fans prefer more physical games, as attendance in the NHL was found to respond positively to hits. Burdekin and Morton (2015) found rewards to the play of "enforcers" in the NHL, as salaries of this class of player were found to be positively influenced by penalty minutes.

Fighting and physicality may play a role in attendance in some leagues, but studies have also investigated whether fighting tends to contribute to game outcome success. Leard and Doyle (2011) studied fighting, determining winners and losers of individual fights in the NHL, and did not find a statistically significant relationship between winning fights and winning games. Coates et al. (2012) found a negative relationship between fighting and team success in the NHL.

In terms of the North American minor hockey leagues, fighting has been shown to increase attendance in the American Hockey League (AHL) (Paul et al., 2013), the ECHL (formerly the East Coast Hockey League) (Paul et al., 2015), and the Southern Professional Hockey League (SPHL) (Paul, 2018). In all three leagues, fighting was shown to have a positive and significant effect on attendance. Other factors that were found to influence attendance in these studies of minor league hockey were promotional activities or giveaways and city demographic factors.

2.   REGRESSION MODEL AND RESULTS

The aim of this study is to test the role of possession statistics on attendance, beyond any impact they might have on team success. If possession statistics, proxied by various metrics related to different types of shot attempts and outcomes, are something that fans enjoy, then these figures should lead to higher attendance figures at home games for teams that exhibit these on-ice characteristics. To test this null hypothesis, regression models are used across a variety of specifications that incorporate different forms of possession statistics.

The dependent variable in all the regression models is the natural log of game attendance for all regular-season games for the seasons 2015–16 to 2018–19. These figures were gathered from box scores of NHL games and from the public hockey analytics website Natural Stat Trick (www.naturalstattrick.com). The independent variables in the model include control variables for day of the week, game number, game setting, team success, fighting, and outcome uncertainty – in addition to the variables of interest that relate to possession statistics.

Days of the week were included as dummy variables in the model to account for different opportunity costs of time that are likely to occur on different days of the week. Weekend games are likely to be more popular than weekday games due to this attribute. We would expect Friday, Saturday, and Sunday games to have a positive and significant effect on attendance. *Ex ante*, the weekdays are expected to be similar, but Wednesday could be an interesting day of the week due to a typical lighter slate for NHL games coupled with the national TV game of the week for the NHL broadcast on NBC Sports Network. The reference category for the day of the week is Wednesday, with all results compared to this day.

The game number for the home team is included as a linear trend in the model. This variable is included in the model to account for season progression and games becoming possibly more meaningful as the end of the season and playoffs approach. This variable will also account for interest in hockey possibly being lower during the early months of the season due to competition from sports such as college and professional football, which exhibit very high popularity across the United States.

Two dummy variables were constructed to account for special games that occur on team schedules. The first is a dummy for the home opener. After a long off-season, hope often springs eternal for fans. This, coupled with various festivities to start the season, typically leads to large crowds for the first home game of the season. A dummy for whether the game is played outdoors is also included in the regression model to account for the special cases where NHL teams play outdoors in larger stadiums (that typically house football or baseball). These games are a major spectacle each season (even with more of their type being added to the schedule by the NHL) and typically see much higher attendance than other games due to increased capacity. Both the home opener and outdoor game dummy variables are expected to have positive and significant effects on attendance.

Team performance variables are also included in the model to account for the role of team success and fighting. Team success is measured by the variable points-per-game (PPG), which is calculated as a running average throughout the season. In the NHL, teams receive two points for a win, one point for an overtime or shootout loss, and zero points for a regulation loss. Points-per-game adds the game result, in points, over time divided by the number of games played. For each individual game, it is the points-per-game average of the home team entering that game. It is expected to have a positive and significant effect on attendance as fans prefer winning teams.

The other team performance variable is fights-per-game (FPG). Fight statistics were gathered from www.hockeyfights.com and were computed as a running average throughout the season. The number of fights-per-game, on average, that the team has compiled going into a game is the variable in the model. Previous research has shown that fighting has been popular with fans, leading to increases in attendance in the NHL and other leagues. However, the league has put policies in place to limit fighting (i.e. the "instigator rule" where if one fighter is deemed as instigator, he gets an additional penalty and could be subject to suspension), teams have carried fewer fighters on their rosters (opting for more skilled players on the 4th line of teams on-ice rather than "tough guys"), and fan attitudes toward fighting could be changing. Given the recent sample in this study, the inclusion of this figure allows for investigation of how fans currently view the role of fighting in the game.

Outcome uncertainty is also included in the regression model. Outcome uncertainty is calculated from NHL game odds, which were gathered from www.covers.com. Odds were converted to win probabilities, and the win probability figures (both win probability and win probability squared) are included in the model to determine how fans view uncertainty of outcome. If fans prefer outcome uncertainty, the win probability terms should be positive and significant, while the win probability squared terms should be negative and statistically significant. If fans do not prefer outcome uncertainty, but instead prefer the home team to easily win, both the win probability and its square should have positive and significant effects on attendance. If fans have loss aversion coupled with a desire to see upsets, as described by Coates et al. (2014), then instead of the traditional concave relationship hypothesized by Rottenberg (1956), there could be a convex relationship where the win probability is negative and significant but the win probability squared variable is positive and significant.

The key variables of interest in this study, possession statistics, are included in a variety of ways across different model specifications. The possession statistics measured for NHL games include statistics based upon Corsi (shots on goal, missed shots, and blocked shots), Fenwick (shots on goal and missed shots), Shots on Goal, and Goals Scored. Since they are the default on the NHL statistical websites (both official and unofficial) and the most commonly quoted, we use the possession statistics as calculated during 5-on-5 play: even strength for both teams 5-on-5 accounts for the five skaters on the ice for each team (goalies are not counted in these measures, so 5-on-5 is the most common situation in the game).

These variables are included individually in regression models in different ways. The first method creates a moving average of each count statistic entering the game. These statistics are calculated from the point of view of the home team. The second method is a comparison between what the home team averages per game for that statistic compared to what they give up, expressed as a percentage. The last method used the sum of that statistic, for and against, from the perspective of the home team to give an overall number of events in a game (taken and given up by the home team). Results using Corsi, Fenwick, Shots on Goal, and Goals are all included in different model specifications as they relate to the moving average of the count statistics. In terms of percentages and sums of these variables, the results for the possession statistics (Corsi and Fenwick) are run in separate regression models.

To illustrate what is meant by the above breakdown of specifications, consider the possession statistic Corsi. In the first method, average Corsi For (CF) from the perspective of the home team going into that game is included in the regression model. The second method uses Corsi For Percentage (CF%), which is Corsi For divided by Corsi For plus Corsi Against (CA). The last method is the average of the sum of Corsi For and Corsi Against. The first method tests if fans prefer teams that possess the puck more, as measured by Corsi. The second method tests if fans prefer teams that have a greater percentage of possession (shot attempts) than they give up to the opponent. The last method tests whether fans prefer more overall possession (shot attempts) as it sums both what the home team generates and what it gives up. The last metric is more about overall excitement in the game as using the sum measures overall shot attempts. Although the above example is for Corsi, the same logic is used for the other possession metric, Fenwick.

Since each possession metric is included separately in each regression model, there will be nine different model specifications presented. Table 8.1 includes model specifications I–V, which are the results without possession metrics, and then each of the possession, shot, and goal metrics included individually as an average of the count of that statistic entering the game. Tables 8.2 and 8.3 present model specifications I–V and VI–IX, where each

Table 8.1   *Summary stats for key variables related to NHL attendance and possession metrics*

Variable	Mean	Median	Standard Deviation
Attendance	17,464.51	18,032.00	3,047.40
Win Probability	0.56	0.56	0.09
Total	5.56	5.5	0.44
FPG	0.23	0.21	0.14
CF	53.70	54.78	6.67
FF	40.13	40.82	4.99
SF	28.98	29.59	3.60
GF	2.56	2.57	0.60
CF%	50.05	49.86	2.98
FF%	55.64	54.83	2.76
CA	53.58	55.16	6.30
FA	40.13	41.04	4.86

Table 8.2   *Regression model results I–V: dependent variable natural log of attendance*

Variable	I	II	III	IV	V
Intercept	9.5418***	9.5526***	9.5560***	9.5519***	9.5134***
	(57.0351)	(57.2011)	(57.1882)	(57.2696)	(55.8290)
Sunday	0.0149***	0.0149***	0.0149***	0.0150***	0.0150***
	(2.7450)	(2.7426)	(2.7494)	(2.7513)	(2.7444)
Monday	−0.0085	−0.0085	−0.0085	−0.0085	−0.0084
	(−1.4493)	(−1.4611)	(−1.4681)	(−1.4519)	(−1.4325)
Tuesday	−0.0101**	−0.0102**	−0.0102**	−0.0101**	−0.0100**
	(−2.0790)	(2.1005)	(−2.0100)	(−2.0823)	(−2.0514)
Thursday	0.0005	0.0003	0.0003	0.0040	0.0006
	(0.1027)	(0.0618)	(0.0703)	(0.0850)	(0.1217)
Friday	0.0341***	0.0342***	0.0342***	0.0342***	0.0340***
	(6.2348)	(6.2747)	(6.2744)	(6.2800)	(6.2164)
Saturday	0.0411***	0.0409***	0.0409***	0.0410***	0.0414***
	(9.4904)	(9.5136)	(9.5152)	(9.5216)	(9.4368)
Game	0.0006***	0.0006***	0.0006***	0.0006***	0.0006***
Number	(12.9113)	(12.3978)	(12.6105)	(12.7359)	(12.9045)
Home Opener	0.0761***	0.0824***	0.0814***	0.0770***	0.0780***
	(7.4518)	(7.9422)	(7.7067)	(7.8326)	(7.0827)
Outdoor	0.9730***	0.9728***	0.9729***	0.9728***	0.9729***
	(11.5398)	(11.5222)	(11.5375)	(11.5449)	(11.5232)
PPG	0.0293***	0.0321***	0.0313***	0.0298***	0.0352***
	(4.1273)	(4.4940)	(4.3729)	(4.2466)	(3.7504)
FPG	−0.0183	−0.0170	−0.0174	−0.0186*	−0.0171
	(−1.5470)	(−1.5205)	(−1.5626)	(−1.6759)	(−1.5573)
Win	0.1716	0.1512	0.1519	0.1656	0.1782
Probability	(1.3206)	(1.2449)	(1.2468)	(1.2767)	(1.3646)
Win	−0.1596	−0.1561	−0.1560	−0.1575	−0.1647
Probability^2	(−1.4417)	(−1.4139)	(−1.4101)	(−1.4242)	(−1.4811)
Total	0.0377	0.0144	0.0187	0.0248	0.0484
	(0.6659)	(0.2530)	(0.3265)	(0.4383)	(0.8396)
Total^2	−0.0035	−0.0017	−0.0020	−0.0025	−0.0043
	(−0.7044)	(−0.3327)	(−0.3998)	(−0.5042)	(−0.8527)
CF		0.0012***			
		(2.6134)			
FF			0.0012*		
			(1.8750)		
SF				0.0011	
				(1.4744)	

Table 8.2   (continued)

Variable	I	II	III	IV	V
GF					−0.0053
					(−1.2876)
R-squared	0.7967	0.7973	0.7971	0.7969	0.7969

Note: Asterisks denote statistical significance at the following levels: 10% (*), 5% (**), and 1% (***).

Table 8.3   Regression model results VI–IX: dependent variable natural log of attendance

Variable	VI	VII	VIII	IX
Intercept	9.4452***	9.6040***	9.5570***	9.5449***
	(54.9091)	(49.5860)	(57.3906)	(57.1736)
Sunday	0.0149***	0.0150***	0.0149***	0.0150***
	(2.7269)	(2.7485)	(2.7491)	(2.7448)
Monday	−0.0084	−0.0085	−0.0085	−0.0085
	(−1.4400)	(−1.4566)	(−1.4580)	(−1.4519)
Tuesday	−0.0102**	−0.0101**	−0.0101**	−0.0101**
	(−2.2947)	(−2.0843)	(−2.0876)	(−2.0804)
Thursday	0.0003	0.0005	0.0004	0.0005
	(0.0711)	(0.0965)	(0.0882)	(0.9207)
Friday	0.0341***	0.0341***	0.03411***	0.0341***
	(6.2222)	(6.2514)	(6.2647)	(6.2396)
Saturday	0.0411***	0.0411***	0.0410***	0.0411***
	(9.4417)	(9.4912)	(9.5072)	(9.4703)
Game Number	0.0006***	0.0006***	0.0006***	0.0006***
	(12.9455)	(12.5830)	(12.3890)	(12.6707)
Home Opener	0.0756***	0.0783***	0.0802***	0.0769***
	(7.3593)	(6.7865)	(7.1496)	(6.4665)
Outdoor	0.9734***	0.9729***	0.9728***	0.9730***
	(11.5381)	(11.5387)	(11.5307)	(11.5373)
PPG	0.0316***	0.0295***	0.0299***	0.0294***
	(4.3835)	(4.1629)	(4.2121)	(4.1362)
FPG	−0.0155	−0.0187	−0.0187*	−0.0184*
	(−1.4241)	(−1.4825)	(−1.6844)	(−1.6538)
Win Probability	0.1717	0.1679	0.1651	0.1704
	(1.3243)	(1.2911)	(1.2725)	(1.3106)
Win Probability^2	−0.1657	−0.1568	−0.1544	−0.1587
	(−1.4986)	(−1.4155)	(−1.3967)	(−1.4324)

Table 8.3　(continued)

Variable	VI	VII	VIII	IX
Total	0.0425	0.0300	0.0208	0.0347
	(0.7501)	(0.5218)	(0.3621)	(0.6022)
Total^2	−0.0039	−0.0029	−0.0022	−0.0033
	(−0.7826)	(−0.5739)	(−0.4285)	(−0.6472)
CF%	0.0016**			
	(2.5511)			
FF%		−0.0007		
		(−0.5833)		
CF+CA			−0.0022	
			(−0.4285)	
FF+FA				0.0001
				(0.2045)
R-squared	0.7972	0.7968	0.7969	0.7968

Note: Asterisks denote statistical significance at the following levels: 10% (*), 5% (**), and 1% (***).

possession metric (Corsi and Fenwick) is included as a percentage in terms of for versus against, and the summed possession metrics are presented. The null hypothesis of each specification, as it relates to possession statistics, is that consumers do not consider possession in NHL hockey beyond its implications for winning games versus the alternative hypothesis that possession statistics are valued by fans as it relates to attending games. The regressions are run as fixed effects models using White cross-section standard errors and covariances to account for heteroskedasticity in the sample. Summary statistics are presented in Table 8.1. Tables 8.2 and 8.3 present the regression results for the models described above.

To cover the regression model results shown in Tables 8.2 and 8.3, the general results across all model specifications will be discussed first, followed by the specifics related to the hockey possession statistics and their impact on attendance. In relation to days of the week, weekends were found to be the most popular days to attend NHL games, with the highest attendance seen on Saturday, followed by Friday, and then Sunday. Each weekend day was found to be statistically significant at the 1 percent level. Tuesday was also found to have statistically significant results. It was found to have a negative and statistically effect on attendance at the 5 percent level compared to the reference category day of Wednesday across the different model specifications. Therefore, Tuesday was the lowest attended day for NHL games in this sample.

The game number of the season for each team was found to have a positive and significant effect on attendance at the 1 percent level. This linear trend representing the progression of the regular season represents the growing excitement as the season continues toward the playoffs. Games played later in the season take on additional importance in the minds of fans, as the possibility of making the playoffs, securing home ice advantage, or increasing playoff positioning makes attending later season games more popular than early season games.

The home opener dummy for the first home game of the season was found to have a positive and significant effect on attendance at the start of the season, and the fanfare associated with opening night tended to attract large home crowds. Another situation where crowds were much larger was outdoor games as this dummy variable was found to be positive and statistically significant at the 1 percent level. Outdoor games were played at different venues than other home games (typically at the city's football or baseball stadium), with much larger capacities than typical home games.

In terms of team performance, team point-per-game (PPG) average was found to have a positive and significant effect on attendance at the 1 percent level. Teams that won more often were found to have more fans attending games than teams that did not. Team success was found to be a huge driver of attendance for National Hockey League games. Fights-per-game (FPG), on the other hand, were either found to not have a statistically significant effect on attendance or had a negative and statistically significant effect on attendance at the 10 percent level, depending upon model specification. With a decreased emphasis on fighting in the league, fans do not appear to positively react to the number of fights a team has throughout the season. This result is different than in previous results and leagues, which could signify a change in consumer attitudes as it relates to fighting in the sport at its highest levels.

In this sample of games, outcome uncertainty was found to have its typical non-linear relationship with attendance, but the results were statistically insignificant. Using the odds on the game from the betting market, the win probability and its square were not found to be individually or jointly significant as it relates to attendance. This stands in contrast with previous studies and could stem from this model including team success (points-per-game) and the possession-related statistics. The impact of outcome uncertainty may be much easier seen in longer data samples. Another possible rationale for this result is the relative balance across teams in the NHL during this time frame as much parity was seen throughout the league. An alternative model specification where the win probability itself was included in the model (not in a quadratic form) was also found to have statistically insignificant results.

The betting market total on the game, a proxy for expected scoring, was also found to have statistically insignificant effects on attendance. The total and the total squared were found to have positive and negative signs respectively, but neither was statistically significant at any generally accepted level. In addition, alternative model specifications only using the total (not entered into the model as a quadratic) or individual dummy variables representing various thresholds of totals (i.e. 5, 5.5, 6, etc.) were also found to be statistically insignificant in this sample. Expected scoring does not appear to play a noticeable role in fan attendance. This could be due to the relative slight differences in scoring across NHL games during this sample (and in general).

The variables of interest of this study, NHL possession statistics, are discussed across model specification, by table, as to their impact on attendance in the following paragraphs. The model specifications for the role of possession statistics on attendance in Table 8.1 were per-game count statistic averages from the perspective of the home team. The first regression model presented did not include any possession-related statistics and is used as a benchmark for comparison. In terms of the other regression model results presented in Table 8.2, different results were found across the possession-related metrics. In model II, the average of home team Corsi For entering the game was found to have a positive and significant effect on attendance at the 1 percent level. Teams with a greater average number of Corsi events (Shots on Goal, Missed Shots, and Shots Blocked) were found to have higher attendance figures. These in-game events likely lead to more excitement in the game, and fans rewarded teams that created these events more frequently in games. The other relatively new possession statistic, Fenwick For (FF), was also found to have positive and significant effects on attendance, but only at the 10 percent level of statistical significance. With the key difference in Corsi and Fenwick being the inclusion of Blocked Shots in the metrics (Corsi includes blocked shots, while Fenwick does not), it appears fans react more strongly to all possible offensive chances generated by puck possession, including shots that get blocked on the way to the net.

Regression models IV and V illustrate the key insights about possession metrics, their impact on the game and fan reaction to these events. Regression model IV included shots on goal and model V used goals. These are subsets of the Corsi and Fenwick possession statistics as shots on goal and goals themselves are included in both Corsi and Fenwick. However, when including just shots on goal, a long-reported statistic in the NHL, the results show a positive but statistically insignificant effect on attendance. The same is shown in model V using goals. Therefore, it appears that fans do respond favorably to teams that possess the puck more and generate more chances, even if these shot attempts miss the net or are blocked on the way to the net.

From Table 8.3, the only statistically significant result shown for the possession-related statistics is in model VI, where the Corsi For Percentage was included. As the home team generated a higher percentage of overall shot attempts (shots on goal, missed shots, and blocked shots) compared to its opponent, attendance at games increased. Fans not only appear to enjoy the home team having higher possession figures, but also that they limit those given to the opposition. The Fenwick For Percentage results were not shown to be statistically significant, which reveals that the blocked shot component of possession included in Corsi is a key driving factor of fan interest, which is explored further in the conclusion. Regression models VIII and XI used the sum of Corsi For and Against average and the Fenwick For and Against average to ascertain if fans enjoy more possession-related events overall in a game (not dependent upon which team has the shot attempts generated by possession). These variables were not found to be statistically significant in either model. It therefore appears that home team possession, particularly as measured by Corsi, is a significant driver of attendance compared to the other measures tried in the different models presented.

3.   DISCUSSION AND CONCLUSION

The "Summer of Analytics" brought about change in terms of player evaluation and roster construction as it related to advanced metrics in the National Hockey League. Although successful teams had been using key "possession" statistics for years in terms of the acquisition and use of talent, the public adoption of key statistics that had been relegated to the world of fringe websites and discussions at analytics conferences was brought to the fore. Organizations, some in major hockey markets like Toronto, openly adopted the use of possession-style advanced statistics and touted their use through front office signings. Individuals, meanwhile, created new hockey statistics and had their own analytics companies, such as John Chayka, who became the youngest General Manager in National Hockey League history through his devotion to and use of analytics.

When these front office moves swept through the league, it also brought mainstream recognition to the statistics that were being used in the hockey analytics community. The main National Hockey League website (www.nhl.com) added advanced statistics to its pages, and hockey coverage on television, radio, and the internet began to discuss these statistics in earnest. Although the NHL decided against using the names the analytics community had assigned to these statistics (opting instead for Shot Attempts and Unblocked Shot Attempts), it now passed along the possession stats that were the focus of the hockey analytics community, Corsi and Fenwick.

Corsi and Fenwick statistics are called possession statistics as they serve as a proxy for control of the puck leading to offensive shot-on-goal attempts. The analytics community had long suggested that possession was a better measure of future success compared to simple goal or shots on goal measures. Goals scored, from an offensive point of view, not only encompass individual player and line mate skill and execution but also depends upon defensive and goaltender abilities. Shots on goal are also dictated by offensive skill and execution as well as the opponent's defensive abilities, but require a shot to have a chance to enter the net for a goal to count in its measure. Fenwick adds to this count of shot attempts by adding shots that miss the net, and Corsi adds shots that miss the net in addition to shots that were blocked by defenders on the way to the net. The difference between the blocked shots statistics stems from a debate in the analytics community over whether avoiding having a shot blocked is skill or luck. If the belief is that getting the puck on net without being blocked is a skill the offensive skater possesses, then this line of reasoning leads to Fenwick being its preferred measure. If not, Corsi is typically preferred by that camp in the analytics community. In either case, research revealed that these statistics are more predictive for the future than goals or shots on goal, and possession statistics began popular usage across the NHL.

Beyond the use of possession-related metrics by the front office, scouts, and coaches, possession statistics also became more generally accepted with respect to fans of the game. With these statistics easily available, and many teams and announcers incorporating them into broadcasts of the games and pre- and post-game analysis on team websites, fans now became familiar with these terms.

This study considered a different angle on the use and expansion of coverage of possession statistics in the NHL by expanding it to fan preferences. Beyond any advantage that possession statistics earned a team in winning games, the research question presented was whether fans preferred to attend games for teams that have greater possession numbers and/or a higher percentage of possession statistics than their opponents. To attempt to answer this question, a series of regression models were specified that analyzed the natural log of game-by-game attendance, controlling for factors such as day of the week, season progression, special games (opening night and outdoor games), team success, outcome uncertainty, and expected scoring. Added to these independent variables were a series of possession-based metrics, one at a time, over different regression model specifications.

Beyond the role of winning games, which was found to have a large positive and significant effect on attendance at the 1 percent level across the different model specifications, Corsi-related statistics were found to have a positive and significant effect on fan attendance at NHL games. A running average of Corsi For entering a given game, from the perspective of the home team, was found to have a positive effect on attendance and was significant at the 1 percent level. In addition, the Corsi For Percentage (running average of Corsi For divided by the running averages of Corsi For and Corsi Against) was also found to have a positive and significant effect on attendance at the 5 percent level. Therefore, beyond any effects Corsi statistics have on winning hockey games, fans appear to enjoy watching teams that accumulate more shot attempts (shots on goal, missed shots, and blocked shots) and have a higher percentage of these statistics than their opponent.

The results for Fenwick statistics, which excludes blocked shots in its measure compared to Corsi, revealed a positive and significant effect at the 10 percent level on attendance, but it was not found to be statistically significant in terms of its percentage compared to the opponent. This could be due to the blocking of opponents' shots being viewed as a positive by fans, which could mitigate its impact when measured this way. The results using Fenwick statistics were less significant than with Corsi, meaning that shots that were blocked on the way to the net as a result of offensive possession were still viewed as a desirable attribute when watching a hockey game.

Other regression model specifications – such as the use of Shots on Goal, Goals, and the sum of the possession metrics for home and away teams (Corsi and Fenwick) – did not reveal statistically significant results. This illustrates two points. First, it is not only the goals or shots on goal that fans appreciate when attending hockey games, but also possession in the offensive zone that leads to shot attempts. Second, the home team generating a greater number of shot attempts through possession and, to a lesser extent, having a higher percentage than their opponent appears to be a desirable attribute from the point of view of fans. Therefore, possession statistics appear to not only matter in terms of the way front office staff, scouts, and coaching staff obtain and utilize talent on the ice to help win games; the style of play, where more shot attempts are made by the home team, also has a small but statistically significant effect at the arena in terms of fan attendance.

REFERENCES

Burdekin, Richard C.K., and Matthew G. Morton. 2015. Blood Money: Violence for Hire in the National Hockey League. *International Journal of Sport Finance*, 10: 328–56.

Coates, Dennis, and Brad Humphreys. 2012. Game Attendance and Competitive Balance in the National Hockey League. *Journal of Sports Economics* 13: 364–77.

Coates, Dennis, Marcel Battre, and Christian Deutscher. 2012. Does Violence in Professional Ice Hockey Pay? Cross Country Evidence from Three Leagues. *Sports Economics: Management and Policy* 4: 47–63.

Coates, Dennis, Brad Humphreys, and Li Zhou. 2014. Reference-Dependent Preferences, Loss Aversion, and Live Game Attendance. *Economic Inquiry* 52: 959–73.

Desjardins, G. 2009. What Is a Corsi Number? http://www.arcticicehockey.com/2009/10/8/1076788/frequently-asked-questions-3-what, Accessed May 12, 2020.

Gerrard, Bill. 2004. Still Up for Grabs? Maintaining the Sporting and Financial Viability of European Club Soccer. In *International Sports Economics Comparisons*. Edited by R. Fort and J. Fizel. Westport, CT: Praeger.

Humphreys, Brad R. 2002. Alternative Measures of Competitive Balance in Sports Leagues. *Journal of Sports Economics* 3: 133–48.

Jones, J. Colin H. 1984. Winners, Losers, and Hosers: Demand and Survival in the National Hockey League. *Atlantic Economic Journal* 12: 54–63.

Jones, J. Colin H., Donald G. Ferguson, and Kenneth G. Stewart. 1993. Blood Sports and Cherry Pie: Some Economics of Violence in the National Hockey League. *American Journal of Economics and Sociology* 52: 87–101.

Jones, J. Colin H., Kenneth G. Stewart, and R. Sunderman. 1996. From the Arena into the Streets: Hockey Violence, Economic Incentives, and Public Policy. *American Journal of Economics and Sociology* 55: 231–49.

Kaplan, Alan, John Nadeau, and Norm O'Reilly. 2011. The Hope Statistic as an Alternative Measure of Competitive Balance. *International Journal of Sport Finance* 6: 170–84.

Leard, Benjamin, and Joanne Doyle. 2011. The Effect of Home Advantage, Momentum, and Fighting on Winning in the National Hockey League. *Journal of Sports Economics* 12: 538–60.

Likens, J. 2011. Shots, Fenwick, and Corsi. http://objectivenhl.blogspot.com/2011/02/shots-fenwick-and-corsi.html. Accessed May 12, 2020.

Macdonald, Brian. 2012. An Expected Goals Model for Evaluating NHL Teams and Players. MIT Sloan Sports Analytics Conference. http://www.sloansportsconference.com/wp-content/uploads/2012/02/NHL-Expected-Goals-Brian-Macdonald.pdf. Accessed May 12, 2020.

O'Reilly, Norm, Alan Kaplan, Ryan Rahinel, and John Nadeau. 2008. If You Can't Win, Why Should I Buy a Ticket? Hope, Fan Welfare, and Competitive Balance. *International Journal of Sport Finance* 3: 106–18.

Paul, Rodney J. 2003. Variations in NHL Attendance: The Impact of Violence, Scoring, and Regional Rivalries. *American Journal of Economics and Sociology* 62: 345–64.

Paul, Rodney J. 2018. The Role of Team Success, Fighting, and Other Factors in Southern Professional Hockey League Attendance. *Southern Business and Economic Journal* 41(1): 2–13.

Paul, Rodney J., and Andrew P. Weinbach. 2011. Determinants of Attendance in the Quebec Major Junior Hockey League. *Atlantic Economic Journal* 39: 303–11.

Paul, Rodney J., Andrew P. Weinbach, and Daniel Robbins. 2013. American Hockey League Attendance: A Study of Fan Preferences for Fighting, Team Performance, and Promotions. *International Journal of Sport Finance* 7: 21–38.

Paul, Rodney J., Andrew P. Weinbach, and Daniel Robbins. 2015. Fighting, Winning, Promotions, and Attendance in the ECHL. *Sport, Business, and Management: An International Journal* 5: 139–56.

Paul, Rodney J., Andrew P. Weinbach, and Nick Riccardi. 2019. Attendance in the Canadian Hockey League: The Impact of Winning, Fighting, Uncertainty of Outcome, and Weather on Junior Hockey Attendance. *International Journal of Financial Studies* 7(1): 12–22.

Paul, Rodney J., Colby Conetta, and Jeremy Losak. 2016. Betting Market Prices, Outcome Uncertainty, and Hockey Attendance in Russia, Sweden, and Finland. *Managerial Finance*, 42(9): 852–865.

Quirk, James, and Rodney D. Fort. 1997. *Pay Dirt: The Business of Professional Team Sports*. Princeton: Princeton University Press.

Rockerbie, Duane W. 2012. The Demand for Violence in Hockey. In *The Oxford Handbook of Sports Economics*. Edited by L. Kahane and S. Shmanske. New York: Oxford University Press, vol. 1, pp. 159–76.

Rottenberg, Simon. 1956. The Baseball Players' Labor Market. *Journal of Political Economy* 64: 242–58.

Scully, Gerald W. 1989. *The Business of Major League Baseball*. Chicago: University of Chicago Press.

9. Television audience demand for football: disaggregation by gender, age and socio-economic status

**Babatunde Buraimo, David Forrest,
Ian G. McHale and J.D. Tena**

1. INTRODUCTION

The first journal paper to report a modelling exercise on the size of television audiences for football (Forrest et al., 2005) stimulated a large successor literature: 29 such papers on football (as well as several more on other sports) were identified in a review by Van Reeth (2020), who noted that most had been published only since 2015. Typically they were motivated in part by the increasing dependence of elite leagues on revenue derived from the sale of television rights. In the latest year for which data were available at the time of writing, the proportion of clubs' total revenue accounted for by broadcasting in Europe's 'big five' leagues ranged from 39 per cent (Germany) to 59 per cent (England) (Deloitte, 2019). When these figures are compared with the proportions earned from matchday income (11–17 per cent across the 'big five'), the shift of emphasis in the academic literature from studying stadium demand to studying television demand is clearly validated: it is of obvious importance to the sport to understand what appeals to the audience in the market that supplies the bulk of revenue.[1]

While two studies (Alavy et al., 2010; Buraimo et al., 2020) have broadened the scope of the relevant literature by attempting to model how audience size varies within a match as events on the field unfold, most contributions follow the precedent of Forrest et al. (2005) by regressing the TV audience figure for the whole match on covariates describing game characteristics, typically including measures of the quality of the two teams, *ex ante* outcome uncertainty and match significance, as well as controls for time of day, week and season, and, sometimes, club fixed effects.

This template is also adopted in the present chapter, but with innovations. First, we will argue that the covariates typically included in prior papers fail adequately to capture the conceptual factors (in particular team quality and match significance) hypothesised to influence demand. We propose instead to employ metrics suggested by developments in sports analytics which appear not yet to have been taken on board by sports economists. Using the measures we devised improved model fit and led to modified conclusions. Second, we apply our models to sub-sets of the audience defined by gender, age and socio-economic status. To date, little attention has been paid to investigating separate segments of the audience for televised football, although Schreyer et al. (2016) explore differences between male and female preferences for match outcome uncertainty in German domestic competitions; and Bergmann and Schreyer (2019) distinguish between age groups in their modelling of demand for 174 televised national team matches in Germany. We are not aware of any studies defining audiences by socio-economic status. Yet examining market segments is potentially important to the extent that part of the business model of broadcasters is to deliver viewers to advertisers. Some viewers are worth more than others; for example young males are harder to reach through television, and a higher proportion of this group in the audience may ultimately increase the value of the television contract.

We will also address a problem raised by Van Reeth (2020) but typically not discussed or even acknowledged in the literature. Audience estimates are expensive to procure, and it is understandable that most academic users will access only the most basic information available, namely estimated 'number of viewers'. We know that this is the figure used as the dependent variable in some well-known studies, and suspect that it is also the dependent variable in others (where the papers do not even specify or discuss what it represents).

In Europe, agencies producing these estimates of 'number of viewers' register viewership in their household samples every minute and then extrapolate to the level of the whole population.[2] Their headline audience size for a given programme is then simply the mean of all these minute-by-minute estimates. This is potentially a problem in the context of the broadcast of a football match because the programme will nearly always be longer than the match itself. Typically the programme will also include pre-match 'build-up' and post-match reaction and analysis; but the duration of these segments may vary substantially across matches. For example, in the data set we employed for this chapter, the mean duration of the post-match segment for weekend matches was 25 minutes; but the standard deviation was 21 minutes and, on one occasion, the programme ended only after 79 minutes had passed since the final whistle. Audience size during programmes is known to be appreciably higher while the match is in progress, and so including pre- and post-match content in the measurement will pull down the estimate of the average audience by a greater proportionate amount where the programme has been longer. This will introduce 'noise' into the data, making estimation less precise. Worse, it may lead to biased coefficient estimates if the length of the programme is correlated with covariates. Such correlation is plausible: for example broadcasters may schedule longer coverage for a fixture with high 'match significance' or for a game featuring popular clubs. Our preference would have been to isolate viewing figures only for the match itself but we were unable to obtain minute-by-minute viewing data disaggregated to the level of the demographic group. Instead we take account of the problem by introducing a set of additional covariates capturing the duration of segments of the football programme outside the match itself.

The broadcasting data for our study, focused on the English Premier League (EPL), were sourced from the Broadcasters' Audience Research Board (BARB), which supplies the broadcasting and advertising industries in the United Kingdom with audience size estimates for every programme shown on domestic television. Data are collected by 'peoplemeters' placed in a representative panel of more than 5,000 households, including some 12,000 individuals.[3] Peoplemeters are connected to televisions and other devices in each home and detect which channel is being received in any room; members and guests of the household use handsets to register their entry to and exit from the room. Audience size for a match is therefore based on counts of how many individuals are present in a room where the programme is playing. But, of course, not everyone may be actively following the match. Thus, although we will include models for the youngest demographic group (children as young as four are counted), we advise that a particularly strong degree of scepticism should be attached to figures for the bottom age band since it seems plausible that the youngest children included in the count may be particularly likely to be engaged in some other activity than viewing the game, for example play.

We analyse audience data from 790 EPL matches staged between seasons 2013–14 and 2018–19 inclusive.[4] The television coverage was provided by one of two broadcasters, the long-established Sky Sports or the newer BT Sport, whose first season showing EPL games coincided with the first year of our data set. Both are subscription services. Sky Sports customers can also watch matches allocated to BT Sport but only through an add-on, chargeable package. Over the data period, 154 matches were contracted to be broadcast in the first three seasons and 168 in the last three.

Our model, to be estimated by ordinary least squares, was:

log (audience) = f(quality of the teams, match significance, match outcome uncertainty, club dummies, season dummies, time of week dummies, duration of pre- and post-match programme segments, broadcaster).

2. SPECIFICATION OF COVARIATES

2.1 Quality of the Teams

Forrest et al. (2005) proxied the quality of players involved in a match by the total of the published wage bills, for that season, of the two competing clubs (normalised according to the divisional average for the season). This choice has been mimicked in some more recent studies – such as Caruso et al. (2019), which modelled viewership for Italian matches – and was justified by an assumption that labour markets for talent will be sufficiently efficient for relative wages to reflect relative marginal productivity. However, the approach may be regarded as potentially greatly flawed. First, published wage bills not only include remuneration for non-playing staff but also cover different squad sizes: superfluous players increase the wage bill but do not appear on the field, and so do not raise the amount of talent to be viewed by the television audience. Second, some of the best-paid players may be unavailable to play because of injury or suspension, or participation in, say, the African Cup of Nations. Third, wages are set at the time a player signed his contract, and some of these contracts may have been struck several years before, such that current wages may not capture a player's true ability now. For example, some hirings may have proved disappointing; and some older players may have been signed with the club anticipating a downward age-related trajectory of performance (but with wages smoothed out over the contract duration). Fourth, each club's wage bill is invariant through a season and unresponsive to fresh information being revealed about player and team quality. Further, wage bills for larger market clubs will be expected to be persistently higher than for small market clubs, and this will make it problematic to include club fixed effects in the specification (because relative wage bills may broadly correlate with the power of the club's brand name).

Other studies have employed alternative proxies for quality. For example, Schreyer et al. (2016) used the sum of the 'transfer values' of players in the match. Some researchers have attempted to capture quality through a performance metric for the club rather than sum across players; for example, Cox (2018) uses goals scored and conceded in recent fixtures. This has the disadvantage of failing to account for differences in team composition between recent fixtures and the present fixture. Here we retain a focus on individual players. Specifically, we sum the 'player ratings' (as evaluated immediately before the match) of the 11 starting players for a team in order to capture 'team strength'; and then our quality measure is the *average team strength* of the two teams in the match.

Our approach draws on the strong strand of literature in sports analytics that deals with player ratings. There is no one 'correct' method. However, 'plus–minus' ratings have been used and adapted to several team sports, including football. At its simplest level, a plus–minus rating estimates the change in performance of a team when a player plays, compared to when he does not. In football, performance is typically measured using goals. But this presents complications: football is a low-scoring sport, and there is often little or no change in performance in terms of goals (when no goals are scored). Further, there are complications arising from there being fewer within-match changes in team line-ups than is observed in ice hockey and basketball, other sports to which the plus-minus method has been applied. Nevertheless, statistical methods can now cope with, and allow for, the highly correlated covariates that result from players playing on the same team for a high proportion of the time the team is playing. Kharrat et al. (2019) present a new plus-minus rating for rating footballers which measures performance using the expected points in a match, where expected points at any time point, t, in a match is calculated as:

$$E_t (points) = 3 \times \Pr_{(t)} (win) + 1 \times Pr_{(t)} (draw) \qquad (9.1)$$

This metric has the advantage that it is continually evolving with time (unlike scoreline). Kharrat et al. (2019) provide details of this approach, based on how a player influences expected points for a team whilst allowing for the strength of his team mates and opposition players as well as home advantage. The model used in our analysis is fitted to all games in the preceding 12 months, up to but not including the match in question. More recent matches count more in estimating the ratings, and the speed of the decay is chosen to maximise the predictive performance of a simple ordered logistic regression model for match result (out-of-sample). Thus the ratings update for each player after every game.

2.2 Match Significance

Similar to other European top divisions, the EPL features three levels of prize awarded at the end of the season. The premier prize is the championship itself, and is awarded to the first-placed club in the final table. Both the champion and the following few clubs in the finishing order earn the next prizes of interest, the right to participate in one of UEFA's pan-European competitions in the following season. The more important of these tournaments is the Champions League, and currently the top four clubs in the EPL are allocated places – a valuable prize for clubs because the tournament is highly lucrative for those taking part, but also perhaps for fans since their team may then play at the top table with other European teams. Finally, there are negative prizes on offer for the clubs with the weakest performance levels over the season: the bottom three are demoted to the English Football League (EFL), with catastrophic loss of revenue and prestige.

It is reasonable to suppose that interest in viewing a match will be influenced by whether and to what extent its outcome is relevant to which clubs will qualify for these very important prizes. Indeed the organisation of fixtures into a league itself demonstrates that the sport regards interest in the competition as stimulating demand above what it would be if each match were a self-contained contest. Hence 'match significance' variables have an obvious place in a television demand model. However, none of the literature to date has succeeded in finding an adequate measure to correspond to the concept.

A few papers (such as Pérez et al., 2017 and Cox, 2018) do not include a match significance variable in their specification, but instead rely on month dummies to subsume any impact from how important a game is, arguing that elevated demand late in the football year is attributable in part at least to this being when it is obvious that particular matches may be crucial to clubs' fates. Where an attempt to capture match significance is made, the proxies appear always to be remarkably ad hoc. Forrest et al. (2005) included a series of dummies to represent matches in the second half of the season involving clubs currently occupying places of interest in the standings (e.g. relegation places). Buraimo and Simmons (2015) have 'contention' dummies – for championship, European qualification and relegation – to represent games in the second half of the season where at least one of the clubs still has an interest in that prize. For example, a club is deemed to be still in contention for the league title if it would exceed the points total of the clubs ahead of it in the event that it were to win all of its remaining matches while other clubs averaged one point per match over the rest of the season. Scelles (2017) offers a variant on this theme, replacing the idea of 'contention' with 'competitive intensity', which focuses on the possibility of a club being top of the league (or in a European or relegation place) after one, two or three subsequent rounds of matches.

All the resulting covariates from these authors prove to be patchy in terms of statistical significance; but, in any case, the results are inherently fragile because of the weaknesses of the measures employed. These measures do not take into account how probable it is that the hypothetical prize will be won (for example, a mid-table team might technically be 'in contention' in January according to the authors' algorithm, but it would scarcely be likely to win all remaining fixtures while all teams ahead of it could only draw) or how different each remaining match will be in terms of its likely decisiveness (for example, a more plausible measure might give greater weight to a fixture between two rivals for the same prize). Further, all these measures are necessarily applied only to the second half of the season (since all clubs would be in contention for all prizes at the beginning), whereas potential viewers might correctly view some early season contests as very significant indeed. For example, a game between the two strongest clubs would probably be considered potentially very important for the outcome of the championship even if held in September. Overall it seems probable that the measures proposed in previous papers will fail to identify some of the most significant matches as at all important while characterising other matches as significant even where neither club has anything but the remotest chance of finishing anywhere else than mid-table. These weaknesses matter because league design and policy on revenue sharing should be informed by how much interest viewers have in the 'leagues within leagues', which could be gauged from results from models with better specified match significance variables.

Here, we calculate the significance of a given match to a club with respect to any given prize as the absolute change in the probability of securing the prize if the team wins the match compared with if the team loses the match. This is calculated for both teams in the match, and the overall significance of the match, with respect to the prize, is the sum of the two teams' match significances. We do this for each of the three outcomes of interest: championship, top-four place, and relegation. Thus, a match between two sides vying for the title will have high match significance for the championship but low match significance for relegation.

To calculate the probabilities of each position in the league table for a club at the end of the season, the match outcome forecasting model presented in Boshnakov et al. (2017) is first used to estimate the probability of each outcome in a single match. Once these outcome probabilities for all remaining matches in the season have been calculated, the results of these remaining matches are simulated and the final finishing positions of the teams recorded under two alternatives: the match in question is won by the subject club or the match in question is lost by the subject club. This process is repeated 100,000 times and the probabilities of winning the title, finishing in the top four places and of being relegated are recorded and used to calculate our measures of match significance. For example, the match significance of a particular game for the championship is:

match significance

$$= |\Pr(HT \text{ wins title}|HT \text{ wins game}) - \Pr(HT \text{ wins title}|HT \text{ loses game})| + $$
$$|\Pr(AT \text{ wins title}|AT \text{ wins game}) - \Pr(AT \text{ wins title}|AT \text{ loses game})|$$

where *HT* and *AT* reference the home and away team respectively. The match significance for the top four and for relegation is calculated in a similar manner (for 'relegation significance', we take the absolute value of the change in probability as a win which would lower the probability of relegation).

The match outcome forecasting model employed is based on estimating the strengths of the competing teams implied by bookmaker odds. We backward engineer the estimated team strengths assuming the bookmaker has used a double Poisson model to generate odds. From the home win, draw, away win (1X2) market and the over-under 2.5 goals markets (for each match week) we can estimate the implied team strengths from the bookmaker's model. We then use the estimated strengths to generate outcome probabilities for matches (and do so for all matches remaining to be played in the season).

2.3   Outcome Uncertainty

Many of the prior papers focus on match 'outcome uncertainty', even to the extent of including the phrase in their title. Forrest et al. (2005) measured uncertainty by the current difference in points-per-game between the two clubs, with an adjustment to allow for home advantage. The paper reported that greater outcome uncertainty predicted higher audience size; but, while the relevant coefficient estimate was statistically significant, the effect size was very limited. Later authors have proxied outcome uncertainty based on points-per-game or the difference in talent levels between the teams or the difference in win probabilities implied by betting odds.[5] Generally they have obtained very inconsistent results. For the EPL, Buraimo and Simmons (2015) found no role for outcome uncertainty after 2002, but detected strengthening responsiveness over time to their player quality variable (based on the combined wage bills of the clubs). From analysis of a similar time period, and still in the EPL, Cox (2018) claimed support for the outcome uncertainty hypothesis using an odds-based measure; but the evidence was weak (a single coefficient estimate which was significant only at the 10 per cent level). Caruso et al. (2019) claimed support for the outcome uncertainty hypothesis from estimation of a model of Italian audiences for Serie A matches, though their results are hard to interpret given that they include betting-market-probability-difference, wage-bill-difference and points-per-game-difference between the teams, none adjusted for home advantage and all included in the same model (and with contrasting signs).

The inconsistency in results across these and other studies could reflect that tastes indeed vary across space and time but might instead be explained by inappropriate definitions of covariates. For example, authors using absolute difference in wage budgets make the implicit assumption that the prospectively closest contests would be between clubs that spend the same amount; but this assumption is ill-founded because it ignores the strong home advantage in football. Again, in the absence of a match-significance metric, a low value for points-per-game-difference may signal a 'significant' fixture between two rivals for the same league prize. In this case, the coefficient estimate would not readily be interpretable as measuring a pure outcome uncertainty effect.

Here we will use the absolute difference in bookmaker implied probabilities of a win for either team as our measure of *ex ante* outcome uncertainty. We extracted odds offered by William Hill from the archive at football-data. co.uk. These were expressed in decimal-odds format, and the inverse of the decimal-odds gave us the 'bookmaker probability' of each outcome (home win, draw, away win). Finally, since the sum of the three bookmaker probabilities always exceeds 1, to allow the betting provider its commission, each bookmaker probability was then multiplied by a constant such that the three 'implied probabilities' for any match summed to 1.

Using a measure of outcome uncertainty based on betting market odds has the advantage that, always supposing markets are 'efficient', they should reflect all information relevant to how close a match is expected to be. This information will include factors such as player suspensions or short recovery time from the last fixture for one of the teams, which are not captured by variables derived from league tables.

2.4   Other Variables

A full list of variables included in our models, together with brief definitions and summary statistics, is presented as Table 9.1. Here we note only a couple of points where additional comment seems appropriate.

Forrest et al. (2005) included in their model dummy variables set equal to 1 to signify matches involving what they identified as the two clubs with the highest drawing power in English football, Liverpool and Manchester United. Similarly, Pérez et al. (2017) specified variables to indicate matches featuring Barcelona or Real Madrid; their access to regional audience data from Spain indicated these two as the only clubs with national drawing power. Here we choose a specification with a full set of club fixed effects because, even though we too found two clubs with far more drawing power than the rest, there were still significant differences between the others. Including a full set of fixed effects was feasible because, in contrast to, say, combined wage bill, our measure of player quality shows sufficient variation within seasons to prevent undue correlation with the club dummies. In our results, the effects of the presence of each club in the televised match are measured relative to AFC Bournemouth. This club was chosen as reference

Table 9.1 Summary statistics

Variable	Description	N	mean	sd	min	max
total audience size		790	829,682	380,248	171,500	2,432,500
audience size, men		790	593,720	261,813	130,900	1,671,200
audience size, women		790	236,634	121,884	35,200	761,300
audience size, group AB		790	209,991	106,492	17,200	635,400
audience size, group C1		790	248,453	114,783	41,800	809,900
audience size, group C2		790	204,360	100,785	38,400	558,300
audience size, group DE		790	167,551	77,524	21,700	493,400
audience size, age 4–15		790	51,232	31,577	1,500	195,400
audience size, age 16–24		790	61,151	36,479	7,600	200,400
audience size, age 25–34		790	106,278	60,024	5,000	376,200
audience size, age 35–44		790	117,580	60,835	11,900	417,100
audience size, age 45–54		790	158,711	83,348	22,000	508,000
audience size, age 55–64		790	140,409	62,401	13,400	342,800
audience size, age 65+		790	194,988	74,678	42,000	498,300
average team strength	described in text	790	0.013	0.012	−0.02	0.05
abs. diff. in probs.	absolute difference in adjusted home and away win probabilities	790	0.341	0.217	0.00	0.89
derby match	dummy variable = 1 for matches involving local rivals	790	0.114	0.318	0.00	1.00
match significance, championship	described in text	790	0.063	0.101	0.00	1.00
match significance, top 4	described in text	790	0.136	0.133	0.00	0.92
match significance, relegation	described in text	790	0.090	0.125	0.00	1.60
Pre-match duration (weekday)	lead-in minutes prior to kick-off × weekday	790	10.67	21.796	0.00	91.00

Table 9.1 (continued)

Variable	Description	N	mean	sd	min	max
pre-match duration (weekend)	lead-in minutes prior to kick-off × weekend	790	28.62	21.344	0.00	90.00
post-match duration (weekday)	post-match minutes after final whistle × weekday	790	10.62	21.938	0.00	82.00
post-match duration (weekend)	post-match minutes after final whistle × weekend	790	24.93	20.989	0.00	79.00
BT Sport	dummy variable = 1 if broadcaster is BT Sport	790	0.257	0.437	0.00	1.00
Christmas	dummy variable = 1 if broadcast is between December 26 and New Year's Day Bank Holiday inclusive	790	0.059	0.237	0.00	1.00
weekday	dummy variable = 1 if day is Monday to Friday inclusive (but = 0 if Christmas = 1)	790	0.213	0.409	0.00	1.00
October	dummy variable = 1 if month is October	790	0.095	0.293	0.00	1.00
November	dummy variable = 1 if month is November	790	0.094	0.292	0.00	1.00
December	dummy variable = 1 if month is December	790	0.148	0.355	0.00	1.00
January	dummy variable = 1 if month is January	790	0.111	0.315	0.00	1.00
February	dummy variable = 1 if month is February	790	0.108	0.310	0.00	1.00
March	dummy variable = 1 if month is March	790	0.108	0.310	0.00	1.00
April	dummy variable = 1 if month is April	790	0.163	0.370	0.00	1.00
May	dummy variable = 1 if month is May	790	0.086	0.281	0.00	1.00
2014–15	dummy variable = 1 if season is 2014–15	790	0.172	0.378	0.00	1.00
2015–16	dummy variable = 1 if season is 2015–16	790	0.171	0.377	0.00	1.00
2016–17	dummy variable = 1 if season is 2016–17	790	0.189	0.391	0.00	1.00
2017–18	dummy variable = 1 if season is 2017–18	790	0.190	0.392	0.00	1.00
2018–19	dummy variable = 1 if season is 2018–19	790	0.187	0.390	0.00	1.00

simply because it was first in alphabetical order. However, it should be noted that it is one of the smallest market clubs to have played in the EPL, having won promotion to it for the first time in 2015, and therefore our expectation was that most of the club dummies would attract a positive coefficient estimate.

Including a dummy variable to indicate where a match was shown on a different channel from most games has obvious justification. But we also include dummies where BT Sport is interacted with a season. This series of interaction terms was added to the specification because BT Sport was a new broadcaster of the EPL at the start of our data period, and we anticipated that its degree of market penetration might increase across seasons as its offering became better known to prospective subscribers.

3.   RESULTS AND CONCLUSIONS

Tables 9.2, 9.3 and 9.4 report results estimated for different market segments, delineated first by gender (this table also presents results for 'total audience'), then by age, and finally by socio-economic status (SES). SES is recorded in BARB data following conventions used by the UK Office for National Statistics. It is defined according to the occupation (or last occupation) of the household member responsible for the property (paying rent or mortgage). If the latter responsibility is shared, the individual with the highest income (from any source) is designated as the 'household reference member'. The AB group covers professional and higher administrative and managerial occupations. Group C1 refers broadly to individuals in junior managerial or supervisory roles, and also in clerical jobs. Skilled manual workers are assigned to Group C2. Finally, group DE contains semi-skilled and unskilled manual workers, those in the 'lowest grade jobs' and the long-term unemployed.

We organise our conclusions around the covariates of interest.

Duration of programme   For most groups, not accounting for the varying length of the pre-kick-off part of the television programme will significantly distort relative audience size across matches. For example, in the case of weekend matches, if this lasts one standard deviation longer than the mean, the expected total audience as recorded in the official data falls by 13.4 per cent. By contrast, the length of post-match programming is almost uniformly non-significant, implying that, while there may be an initial fall-off in the several minutes following the end of the game, a high proportion of those then remaining will stay to the end of the transmission.

Table 9.2 Regression results by gender. Dependent variable: log (audience size)

	Total audience		Men		Women	
average team strength	3.358**	(2.57)	3.400***	(2.67)	3.162**	(2.10)
abs. diff. in probs.	−0.014	(0.30)	−0.028	(0.64)	−0.008	(0.15)
derby match	0.058**	(2.11)	0.062**	(2.37)	0.041	(1.21)
match significance, championship	0.663***	(5.99)	0.646***	(6.04)	0.700***	(5.25)
match significance, top 4	0.165	(1.61)	0.151	(1.52)	0.223*	(1.91)
match significance, relegation	0.332***	(3.77)	0.325***	(3.77)	0.284***	(2.59)
Arsenal	0.372***	(7.68)	0.348***	(7.34)	0.437***	(7.47)
Aston Villa	0.107**	(2.02)	0.097*	(1.89)	0.140**	(2.17)
Brighton and Hove Albion	0.019	(0.25)	0.012	(0.15)	0.021	(0.23)
Burnley	0.014	(0.27)	0.009	(0.17)	0.058	(0.82)
Cardiff City	−0.052	(0.69)	−0.065	(0.92)	−0.001	(0.01)
Chelsea	0.330***	(6.43)	0.301***	(6.04)	0.407***	(6.59)
Crystal Palace	0.085*	(1.87)	0.075*	(1.69)	0.110*	(1.94)
Everton	0.231***	(5.05)	0.210***	(4.67)	0.283***	(5.17)
Fulham	−0.087	(0.79)	−0.088	(0.83)	−0.073	(0.58)
Huddersfield Town	0.094	(1.38)	0.063	(0.97)	0.170**	(1.99)
Hull City	0.039	(0.54)	0.013	(0.18)	0.123	(1.53)
Leicester City	0.182***	(3.32)	0.159***	(2.93)	0.260***	(4.07)
Liverpool	0.552***	(11.18)	0.522***	(10.73)	0.637***	(10.79)
Manchester City	0.238***	(4.66)	0.223***	(4.44)	0.279***	(4.59)
Manchester United	0.555***	(10.71)	0.522***	(10.32)	0.638***	(10.26)
Middlesbrough	0.017	(0.20)	0.021	(0.27)	0.020	(0.18)
Newcastle United	0.224***	(4.69)	0.202***	(4.38)	0.297***	(5.02)
Norwich City	0.048	(0.70)	0.030	(0.46)	0.118	(1.44)

	(1)		(2)		(3)	
Queens Park Rangers	0.154**	(2.30)	0.125*	(1.90)	0.247***	(3.02)
Southampton	0.159***	(3.20)	0.147***	(3.02)	0.190***	(3.12)
Stoke City	0.008	(0.12)	0.010	(0.16)	0.028	(0.40)
Sunderland	0.135**	(2.35)	0.123**	(2.17)	0.184***	(2.73)
Swansea City	0.019	(0.30)	0.009	(0.15)	0.050	(0.69)
Tottenham Hotspur	0.296***	(5.73)	0.275***	(5.39)	0.351***	(5.74)
Watford	0.088*	(1.84)	0.073	(1.55)	0.125**	(2.17)
West Bromwich Albion	−0.001	(0.02)	−0.012	(0.24)	0.027	(0.42)
West Ham United	0.134***	(2.77)	0.124***	(2.60)	0.161***	(2.81)
Wolverhampton Wanderers	0.022	(0.19)	0.015	(0.13)	0.038	(0.30)
pre-match duration (weekday)	−0.004**	(2.30)	−0.004**	(2.35)	−0.004**	(2.11)
pre-match duration (weekend)	−0.006***	(8.05)	−0.006***	(7.64)	−0.008***	(8.18)
post-match duration (weekday)	−0.000	(0.19)	0.000	(0.31)	−0.002	(1.00)
post-match duration (weekend)	−0.001	(1.50)	−0.001	(1.62)	−0.001	(1.07)
BT Sport	−0.809***	(16.01)	−0.773***	(16.57)	−0.903***	(13.39)
BT Sport × 2014–15	0.151**	(2.44)	0.144**	(2.47)	0.165**	(2.06)
BT Sport × 2015–16	0.275***	(4.28)	0.288***	(4.70)	0.222***	(2.68)
BT Sport × 2016–17	0.282***	(4.47)	0.272***	(4.60)	0.302***	(3.59)
BT Sport × 2017–18	0.322***	(4.90)	0.321***	(5.26)	0.298***	(3.43)
BT Sport × 2018–19	0.222***	(3.40)	0.198***	(3.21)	0.283***	(3.33)
Christmas	0.059*	(1.67)	0.005	(0.14)	0.193***	(4.56)
weekday	−0.206**	(2.41)	−0.252***	(2.97)	−0.073	(0.76)
October	0.012	(0.31)	0.004	(0.09)	0.045	(1.00)
November	0.103***	(3.02)	0.093***	(2.83)	0.145***	(3.39)
December	0.132***	(4.19)	0.116***	(3.81)	0.183***	(4.75)
January	0.205***	(6.36)	0.186***	(5.96)	0.257***	(6.67)
February	0.134***	(4.24)	0.115***	(3.78)	0.183***	(4.64)
March	0.052	(1.38)	0.032	(0.87)	0.109**	(2.42)

Table 9.2   (continued)

	Total audience		Men		Women	
April	0.043	(1.40)	0.020	(0.69)	0.101***	(2.62)
May	−0.120**	(2.41)	−0.148***	(3.10)	−0.046	(0.78)
2014–15	−0.093**	(2.43)	−0.082**	(2.25)	−0.128***	(2.78)
2015–16	−0.182***	(4.42)	−0.161***	(4.03)	−0.242***	(5.09)
2016–17	−0.309***	(8.11)	−0.273***	(7.45)	−0.407***	(8.99)
2017–18	−0.283***	(6.95)	−0.251***	(6.45)	−0.338***	(6.91)
2018–19	−0.206***	(4.95)	−0.168***	(4.18)	−0.313***	(6.29)
constant	13.469***	(137.46)	13.163***	(136.84)	12.123***	(103.29)
observations	790		790		790	
R^2	0.762		0.758		0.746	
adjusted-R^2	0.743		0.738		0.726	

Note: Absolute t statistics in parentheses; * $p < 0.1$, ** $p < 0.05$, *** $p < 0.01$.

Table 9.3 Regression results by age group. Dependent variable: log (audience size)

	4–15		16–24		25–34		35–44		45–54		55–64		65+	
average team strength	5.184**	(2.15)	2.493	(1.28)	2.869*	(1.73)	1.644	(0.89)	4.069**	(2.37)	4.197***	(3.05)	3.167**	(2.30)
abs. diff. in probs.	0.093	(1.09)	0.011	(0.16)	0.070	(1.03)	-0.021	(0.33)	-0.016	(0.27)	-0.019	(0.36)	-0.056	(1.24)
derby match	0.139**	(2.55)	-0.006	(0.14)	0.083**	(2.25)	0.076**	(2.18)	0.081**	(2.37)	0.014	(0.47)	0.026	(0.97)
match significance, championship	0.644***	(3.63)	0.718***	(4.37)	0.571***	(4.00)	0.745***	(5.52)	0.830***	(5.71)	0.681***	(5.17)	0.508***	(4.51)
match significance, top 4	0.387***	(2.60)	0.262*	(1.95)	0.050	(0.41)	0.168	(1.40)	0.231**	(2.01)	0.175	(1.47)	0.137	(1.27)
match significance, relegation	0.165	(0.90)	0.325**	(2.06)	0.302**	(2.48)	0.200	(1.29)	0.389***	(3.49)	0.445***	(4.57)	0.281***	(3.25)
Arsenal	0.432***	(3.85)	0.602***	(7.68)	0.397***	(4.91)	0.456***	(6.81)	0.376***	(5.81)	0.373***	(6.58)	0.268***	(5.40)
Aston Villa	0.229*	(1.94)	0.308***	(3.72)	0.086	(0.97)	0.102	(1.55)	0.083	(1.06)	0.095	(1.54)	0.092*	(1.70)
Brighton and Hove Albion	0.145	(1.10)	-0.029	(0.24)	-0.058	(0.49)	0.056	(0.55)	-0.019	(0.21)	0.001	(0.01)	0.051	(0.67)
Burnley	0.018	(0.13)	0.142	(1.56)	-0.009	(0.10)	0.001	(0.01)	-0.024	(0.33)	0.021	(0.33)	0.044	(0.84)
Cardiff City	0.066	(0.37)	0.005	(0.04)	-0.096	(0.60)	-0.008	(0.08)	-0.071	(0.60)	-0.060	(0.78)	-0.057	(0.82)
Chelsea	0.383***	(3.48)	0.538***	(6.63)	0.392***	(4.70)	0.394***	(5.77)	0.339***	(4.95)	0.330***	(5.52)	0.221***	(4.28)
Crystal Palace	0.169	(1.62)	0.123*	(1.72)	0.048	(0.59)	0.120*	(1.86)	0.117*	(1.75)	0.048	(0.84)	0.067	(1.38)
Everton	0.324***	(3.07)	0.299***	(3.95)	0.195***	(2.59)	0.359***	(5.80)	0.240***	(3.95)	0.206***	(3.93)	0.162***	(3.36)
Fulham	0.144	(0.83)	0.041	(0.35)	-0.297*	(1.94)	-0.059	(0.55)	-0.080	(0.59)	-0.085	(0.54)	-0.104	(0.95)
Huddersfield Town	0.013	(0.06)	0.149	(1.29)	-0.102	(0.81)	0.089	(0.85)	0.139*	(1.69)	0.140*	(1.78)	0.083	(1.18)
Hull City	0.132	(0.99)	0.197*	(1.88)	-0.083	(0.71)	0.151*	(1.78)	-0.003	(0.03)	0.002	(0.02)	0.063	(0.93)
Leicester City	0.242**	(2.23)	0.244***	(2.94)	0.200**	(2.31)	0.147*	(1.97)	0.226***	(3.19)	0.171***	(2.64)	0.178***	(3.06)
Liverpool	0.891***	(8.25)	0.773***	(9.65)	0.611***	(7.41)	0.719***	(10.98)	0.586***	(8.93)	0.443***	(7.58)	0.375***	(7.42)
Manchester City	0.339***	(3.07)	0.440***	(5.29)	0.265***	(3.25)	0.299***	(4.32)	0.201***	(2.90)	0.187***	(3.16)	0.198***	(3.89)
Manchester United	0.700***	(6.34)	0.834***	(10.46)	0.676***	(8.19)	0.626***	(8.90)	0.561***	(8.24)	0.509***	(8.49)	0.408***	(7.78)
Middlesbrough	0.062	(0.33)	0.126	(1.06)	0.050	(0.34)	0.035	(0.33)	-0.000	(0.00)	0.025	(0.28)	-0.004	(0.05)
Newcastle United	0.265**	(2.34)	0.288***	(3.67)	0.250***	(3.11)	0.246***	(3.66)	0.204***	(3.13)	0.237***	(4.37)	0.220***	(4.68)
Norwich City	0.222*	(1.69)	0.080	(0.66)	-0.019	(0.17)	-0.019	(0.17)	0.049	(0.54)	0.048	(0.59)	0.085	(1.16)
Queens Park Rangers	0.250*	(1.94)	0.347***	(2.97)	0.160*	(1.74)	0.187*	(1.83)	0.187**	(2.24)	0.110	(1.46)	0.109	(1.42)

Table 9.3 (continued)

	4-15		16-24		25-34		35-44		45-54		55-64		65+	
Southampton	0.271**	(2.46)	0.217***	(2.66)	0.155*	(1.83)	0.170**	(2.37)	0.111*	(1.74)	0.165***	(2.81)	0.163***	(3.37)
Stoke City	0.056	(0.44)	0.125	(1.56)	-0.016	(0.18)	0.041	(0.45)	-0.040	(0.48)	0.025	(0.39)	-0.002	(0.03)
Sunderland	0.305***	(2.71)	0.226**	(2.22)	-0.029	(0.33)	0.165**	(2.12)	0.184**	(2.35)	0.133**	(2.00)	0.144***	(2.61)
Swansea City	0.078	(0.68)	0.089	(0.97)	-0.057	(0.61)	-0.005	(0.06)	0.054	(0.69)	0.042	(0.56)	0.016	(0.25)
Tottenham Hotspur	0.349***	(3.16)	0.425***	(5.05)	0.387***	(4.62)	0.387***	(5.50)	0.246***	(3.53)	0.291***	(4.82)	0.227***	(4.30)
Watford	0.209*	(1.92)	0.067	(0.77)	0.050	(0.55)	0.180***	(2.74)	0.063	(0.94)	0.097*	(1.73)	0.048	(0.89)
West Bromwich Albion	0.045	(0.39)	-0.011	(0.13)	-0.019	(0.22)	0.001	(0.02)	0.012	(0.17)	-0.004	(0.07)	-0.005	(0.10)
West Ham United	0.261**	(2.40)	0.174**	(2.29)	0.074	(0.91)	0.182***	(2.73)	0.140***	(2.15)	0.156***	(2.83)	0.100**	(1.97)
Wolverhampton Wanderers	0.116	(0.71)	-0.040	(0.25)	-0.090	(0.60)	0.181	(1.40)	-0.019	(0.13)	0.098	(0.73)	-0.037	(0.30)
pre-match duration (weekday)	-0.006*	(1.72)	-0.008***	(3.52)	-0.003*	(1.74)	-0.003	(1.39)	-0.003*	(1.66)	-0.005**	(2.52)	-0.003*	(1.68)
pre-match duration (weekend)	-0.007***	(6.57)	-0.007***	(7.10)	-0.006***	(6.21)	-0.006***	(5.88)	-0.007***	(6.73)	-0.008***	(8.57)	-0.006***	(6.95)
post-match duration (weekday)	0.002	(0.67)	0.002	(1.15)	-0.001	(0.69)	0.000	(0.05)	-0.002	(1.13)	0.002	(0.92)	-0.000	(0.25)
post-match duration (weekend)	-0.001	(0.74)	-0.002**	(2.33)	-0.001	(1.39)	-0.000	(0.15)	-0.000	(0.49)	-0.001*	(1.90)	-0.001*	(1.77)
BT Sport	-0.607***	(6.94)	-0.767***	(7.21)	-0.938***	(11.90)	-0.786***	(13.58)	-0.749***	(10.34)	-0.940***	(14.14)	-0.855***	(17.87)
BT Sport × 2014-15	0.143	(1.27)	0.170	(1.40)	0.077	(0.80)	0.145*	(1.85)	0.047	(0.52)	0.204**	(2.50)	0.287***	(4.90)
BT Sport × 2015-16	0.269**	(2.36)	0.313**	(2.35)	0.293***	(2.99)	0.265***	(3.24)	0.180**	(2.03)	0.237***	(2.83)	0.401***	(6.22)
BT Sport × 2016-17	0.051	(0.45)	0.195	(1.53)	0.336***	(3.36)	0.321***	(4.17)	0.075	(0.81)	0.481***	(5.76)	0.378***	(6.02)
BT Sport × 2017-18	0.021	(0.13)	0.199	(1.61)	0.221*	(1.93)	0.215**	(2.47)	0.145	(1.63)	0.506***	(6.16)	0.486***	(7.63)
BT Sport × 2018-19	-0.157	(1.23)	0.057	(0.45)	0.097	(0.91)	0.050	(0.62)	0.060	(0.64)	0.508***	(5.88)	0.432***	(6.45)
Christmas	0.003	(0.04)	0.116*	(1.81)	0.090*	(1.67)	0.035	(0.78)	0.103**	(2.19)	0.069*	(1.66)	0.007	(0.19)
weekday	-0.520***	(3.53)	-0.135	(1.15)	-0.082	(0.72)	-0.112	(1.05)	-0.113	(1.07)	-0.330***	(3.31)	-0.245***	(2.65)
October	-0.071	(1.08)	-0.175***	(3.09)	-0.004	(0.07)	0.059	(1.15)	-0.075	(1.46)	0.063	(1.47)	0.088*	(2.13)
November	0.065	(0.92)	-0.081	(1.43)	0.055	(0.97)	0.069	(1.50)	0.056	(1.18)	0.155***	(3.65)	0.213***	(6.02)

	(1)	(2)	(3)	(4)	(5)	(6)	(7)
December	0.175*** (2.74)	−0.001 (0.02)	0.053 (1.05)	0.113** (2.49)	0.074* (1.76)	0.196*** (4.81)	0.214*** (6.62)
January	0.195*** (3.32)	0.024 (0.44)	0.150*** (2.96)	0.192*** (4.18)	0.172*** (4.16)	0.253*** (6.24)	0.288*** (8.60)
February	0.151** (2.37)	0.009 (0.18)	0.071 (1.27)	0.119** (2.51)	0.079* (1.90)	0.173*** (4.19)	0.208*** (6.39)
March	−0.033 (0.50)	−0.136** (2.56)	−0.012 (0.22)	0.035 (0.73)	0.011 (0.22)	0.097** (1.97)	0.166*** (4.48)
April	−0.096 (1.62)	−0.049 (0.94)	−0.004 (0.07)	−0.050 (1.08)	−0.015 (0.35)	0.108*** (2.80)	0.150*** (4.82)
May	−0.227*** (2.74)	−0.297*** (4.23)	−0.213*** (3.40)	−0.164** (2.40)	−0.170*** (2.70)	−0.055 (1.00)	0.002 (0.05)
2014–15	−0.184*** (3.12)	−0.240*** (4.22)	−0.122** (2.47)	−0.154*** (3.00)	−0.148*** (2.92)	0.062 (1.54)	−0.041 (1.11)
2015–16	−0.307*** (5.50)	−0.461*** (8.05)	−0.330*** (6.75)	−0.266*** (4.78)	−0.230*** (4.33)	−0.051 (1.14)	0.006 (0.14)
2016–17	−0.410*** (7.16)	−0.574*** (9.79)	−0.477*** (9.84)	−0.376*** (7.51)	−0.436*** (8.55)	−0.207*** (4.75)	−0.058 (1.57)
2017–18	−0.447*** (6.86)	−0.361*** (6.20)	−0.633*** (11.78)	−0.319*** (5.94)	−0.435*** (8.10)	−0.109** (2.35)	0.003 (0.07)
2018–19	−0.347*** (5.67)	−0.311*** (5.25)	−0.428*** (8.46)	−0.273*** (5.18)	−0.296*** (5.52)	−0.090* (1.89)	0.008 (0.18)
constant	10.516*** (50.97)	10.870*** (70.66)	11.561*** (70.91)	11.410*** (85.11)	11.888*** (90.69)	11.606*** (99.88)	11.905*** (119.90)
observations	790	790	790	790	790	790	790
R^2	0.647	0.683	0.733	0.692	0.713	0.696	0.658
adjusted-R^2	0.6180	0.6576	0.7119	0.6668	0.6901	0.6711	0.6299

Note: Absolute t statistics in parentheses; * $p < 0.1$, ** $p < 0.05$, *** $p < 0.01$.

143

Table 9.4 Regression results by socio-economic classification. Dependent variable: log (audience size)

	AB		C1		C2		DE	
average team strength	5.324***	(3.29)	3.234**	(2.35)	2.918*	(1.88)	1.782	(1.19)
abs. diff. in probs.	-0.025	(0.43)	-0.004	(0.08)	-0.053	(0.96)	-0.015	(0.30)
derby match	0.070**	(2.09)	0.063**	(2.09)	0.060*	(1.67)	0.025	(0.89)
match significance, championship	0.686***	(4.73)	0.625***	(5.45)	0.772***	(5.61)	0.580***	(5.14)
match significance, top 4	0.149	(1.14)	0.163	(1.44)	0.254**	(2.16)	0.125	(1.32)
match significance, relegation	0.470***	(4.20)	0.319***	(3.42)	0.248*	(1.94)	0.262***	(2.83)
Arsenal	0.465***	(7.44)	0.401***	(7.12)	0.250***	(3.76)	0.371***	(7.31)
Aston Villa	0.120	(1.63)	0.148**	(2.40)	0.119*	(1.69)	0.014	(0.22)
Brighton and Hove Albion	-0.033	(0.31)	0.056	(0.64)	-0.007	(0.08)	0.022	(0.24)
Burnley	-0.038	(0.58)	0.095	(1.55)	-0.000	(0.01)	0.018	(0.30)
Cardiff City	-0.064	(0.66)	-0.156**	(2.10)	-0.044	(0.38)	0.069	(0.81)
Chelsea	0.359***	(5.65)	0.372***	(6.18)	0.242***	(3.55)	0.337***	(6.55)
Crystal Palace	0.106*	(1.84)	0.069	(1.26)	0.082	(1.25)	0.083	(1.63)
Everton	0.303***	(5.32)	0.218***	(4.07)	0.187***	(3.00)	0.202***	(4.11)
Fulham	-0.228	(1.48)	-0.004	(0.04)	-0.076	(0.64)	-0.076	(0.64)
Huddersfield Town	0.120	(1.45)	0.037	(0.45)	0.095	(1.07)	0.139**	(2.01)
Hull City	0.077	(0.82)	0.084	(1.10)	-0.002	(0.02)	-0.010	(0.14)
Leicester City	0.212***	(3.02)	0.230***	(3.67)	0.117*	(1.76)	0.180***	(3.18)
Liverpool	0.589***	(9.31)	0.572***	(9.89)	0.508***	(7.61)	0.548***	(10.87)
Manchester City	0.224***	(3.47)	0.276***	(4.71)	0.166**	(2.43)	0.285***	(5.34)
Manchester United	0.580***	(8.69)	0.539***	(8.88)	0.531***	(7.73)	0.578***	(10.99)
Middlesbrough	-0.076	(0.65)	0.099	(0.94)	-0.010	(0.09)	-0.011	(0.11)
Newcastle United	0.196***	(3.16)	0.265***	(4.80)	0.242***	(3.80)	0.183***	(3.59)
Norwich City	-0.023	(0.24)	0.124	(1.49)	0.075	(0.89)	-0.015	(0.21)
Queens Park Rangers	0.102	(0.94)	0.201**	(2.55)	0.181**	(2.02)	0.127	(1.51)

Variable	(1)	(2)	(3)	(4)
Southampton	0.179*** (2.73)	0.200*** (3.58)	0.110 (1.60)	0.120** (2.27)
Stoke City	-0.039 (0.54)	0.051 (0.74)	0.053 (0.69)	-0.050 (0.67)
Sunderland	0.165** (2.29)	0.162** (2.46)	0.121 (1.58)	0.097 (1.48)
Swansea City	0.013 (0.16)	0.015 (0.21)	0.001 (0.01)	0.047 (0.73)
Tottenham Hotspur	0.299*** (4.47)	0.312*** (5.16)	0.234*** (3.54)	0.344*** (6.46)
Watford	0.046 (0.74)	0.077 (1.33)	0.158** (2.33)	0.064 (1.18)
West Bromwich Albion	-0.031 (0.46)	0.017 (0.27)	-0.007 (0.11)	0.004 (0.07)
West Ham United	0.113* (1.89)	0.203*** (3.73)	0.109* (1.66)	0.076 (1.43)
Wolverhampton Wanderers	0.022 (0.17)	0.050 (0.42)	0.045 (0.38)	-0.049 (0.39)
pre-match duration (weekday)	-0.005** (2.45)	-0.004* (1.86)	-0.004** (2.18)	-0.002 (1.45)
pre-match duration (weekend)	-0.008*** (8.32)	-0.007*** (8.25)	-0.006*** (6.55)	-0.005*** (5.38)
post-match duration (weekday)	0.001 (0.41)	-0.000 (0.28)	-0.000 (0.34)	-0.001 (0.35)
post-match duration (weekend)	-0.001 (1.22)	-0.000 (0.47)	-0.002** (2.49)	-0.001 (1.11)
BT Sport	-0.902*** (9.64)	-0.867*** (13.39)	-0.756*** (12.21)	-0.743*** (13.46)
BT Sport × 2014–15	0.156 (1.42)	0.117 (1.51)	0.143* (1.78)	0.222*** (3.12)
BT Sport × 2015–16	0.361*** (3.47)	0.361*** (4.43)	0.185** (2.32)	0.213*** (2.95)
BT Sport × 2016–17	0.426*** (3.95)	0.352*** (4.34)	0.210** (2.54)	0.121* (1.68)
BT Sport × 2017–18	0.447*** (4.16)	0.380*** (4.55)	0.246*** (2.97)	0.172** (2.39)
BT Sport × 2018–19	0.537*** (4.95)	0.244*** (3.09)	0.059 (0.71)	0.045 (0.62)
Christmas	0.047 (1.07)	0.115*** (3.04)	0.019 (0.39)	0.031 (0.71)
weekday	-0.205** (2.11)	-0.152 (1.55)	-0.262** (2.50)	-0.203** (2.35)
October	-0.029 (0.59)	0.020 (0.46)	0.043 (0.85)	0.016 (0.35)
November	0.194*** (4.40)	0.082** (1.97)	0.095** (2.14)	0.061 (1.54)
December	0.196*** (5.17)	0.109*** (2.83)	0.134*** (3.18)	0.105*** (2.78)
January	0.273*** (6.67)	0.152*** (3.91)	0.212*** (4.99)	0.199*** (5.14)
February	0.167*** (3.93)	0.121*** (3.16)	0.118*** (2.83)	0.142*** (3.88)
March	0.075 (1.47)	0.007 (0.16)	0.080 (1.63)	0.051 (1.26)
April	0.037 (0.94)	0.027 (0.75)	0.101** (2.50)	0.009 (0.25)

Table 9.4 (continued)

	AB		C1		C2		DE	
May	-0.110^*	(1.80)	-0.109^{**}	(2.01)	-0.124^{**}	(2.08)	-0.151^{***}	(2.72)
2014-15	0.020	(0.39)	-0.161^{***}	(3.72)	-0.107^{***}	(2.34)	-0.147^{***}	(3.61)
2015-16	-0.144^{***}	(2.70)	-0.292^{***}	(6.47)	-0.072	(1.52)	-0.239^{***}	(5.85)
2016-17	-0.337^{***}	(6.72)	-0.292^{***}	(6.56)	-0.347^{***}	(7.61)	-0.295^{***}	(7.83)
2017-18	-0.196^{***}	(3.75)	-0.250^{***}	(5.45)	-0.359^{***}	(7.00)	-0.350^{***}	(8.46)
2018-19	-0.274^{***}	(4.96)	-0.198^{***}	(4.33)	-0.199^{***}	(4.07)	-0.180^{***}	(4.30)
constant	11.985^{***}	(97.77)	12.243^{***}	(107.05)	12.165^{***}	(91.13)	11.886^{***}	(114.07)
observations	790		790		790		790	
R^2	0.702		0.729		0.699		0.725	
adjusted-R^2	0.678		0.707		0.675		0.703	

Note: Absolute t statistics in parentheses; * p < 0.1, ** p < 0.05, *** p < 0.01.

Quality of players At the aggregate level, matches which feature stronger players are predicted to draw a larger audience (a relationship not evident when we experimented with combined wages as an alternative measure). However, the effect size appears rather modest. Even for a match where our index of quality increases from the mean to two standard deviations above the mean, expected total audience size increases by only 8.4 per cent. On the other hand, this result conceals significant differences between audience segments. The highest status socio-economic group appears to be particularly sensitive to quality, whereas households in the manual worker categories respond to quality barely at all. Similarly, older adults are shown to be much more discerning than younger adults. However, coefficient estimates on dummies representing the 'big' clubs are appreciably higher for younger than for older adults, which hints that the young may in fact be more inclined to use brand names as a proxy for quality.

Outcome uncertainty Our measure of outcome uncertainty is decisively non-significant in both the model for total audience and in the models for all 13 audience segments included in the analysis. Nor did outcome uncertainty appear as relevant when, in unreported experiments, we entered the difference in win-probabilities as a quadratic. Nor did experimenting with regression splines reveal variation in outcome uncertainty to matter in any range of the outcome uncertainty variable. An alternative variable, based on the difference between the quality level of the two sets of players, was equally lacking in explanatory power. Hence our results support the conclusion of Buraimo and Simmons (2015): that the television audience for EPL matches seems to be responsive to what they termed 'star quality' (albeit they measured quality differently from us) but has ceased to have a taste for outcome uncertainty, if it ever had such a preference. Our finding adds to the weight of literature on both stadium and television demand indicating that empirical evidence to support the very strong emphasis on outcome uncertainty in sports economics is in fact scarce. The implication is that one might not wish to make too strongly the case for permitting revenue sharing on the ground that the audience demands competitive balance.

Match significance Interest in the outcome of the league championship is intense. A match with the highest significance observed in our data set would be expected to attract an aggregate audience size 94 per cent higher than one with no implications at all for the prizes to be awarded at the end of the season. There is little difference across the 13 audience segments in the enthusiasm shown for such matches. So clearly it is strongly in the interests of the league that there should be a closely fought battle for the title so that 'significant' fixtures continue to be on offer until very late in the season. Interest in matches relevant for relegation is also very strong, but here there is some gradation in terms of SES.[6] Audience size in households classified as lower status show a proportionately lower response to matches with implications for relegation. However, they also respond less to player quality (and also to variables such as 'derby match'), and we suspect that these results reflect simply that viewers in lower-status households are less selective in their viewing: perhaps many, having paid their subscription, will watch regardless. Regarding the intermediate prize of European qualification, coefficient estimates are positive across the board but seldom statistically significant, implying that commentators' heavy promotion of the competition for Champions League places may not be always reflective of the underlying degree of public interest.

Clubs   Which clubs appear in the match has a very strong impact on audience size, generally a little more so among women than among men (i.e. women appear to be more selective in this dimension). Across both genders and all age and SES groups, Liverpool and Manchester United remain by some distance the strongest brands in English football. Either of these appearing in a televised match increases expected audience size by 74 per cent compared with the (low) baseline represented by Bournemouth, holding constant all the other covariates, such as player quality. But even making a comparison with the club with next greatest drawing power, replacing Arsenal for one of the 'big two', would increase expected audience size by 20 per cent. It follows that these two clubs would be far the greatest beneficiaries of any change in the direction of clubs selling their broadcasting rights individually rather than collectively. Their ability compared with any other club to reach a national fan base was demonstrated in a study by Feehan et al. (2003) of distances travelled by supporters to attend different EPL stadia and, from the results here, evidently continues till now in respect of 'armchair fans'. The enduring power of brands is underlined by the fact that these two were not dominant clubs in this period. Manchester United's final league position varied between 2nd and 7th, and Liverpool's between 2nd and 8th. By contrast, Manchester City won the championship in three of the six seasons but still exhibited lower brand power than, say, Tottenham, and only about the same as Everton. This appears to suggest that playing success builds brand loyalty only slowly. Another implication of the pattern of coefficient estimates is that total audiences over the season may be somewhat sensitive to which clubs make up the division. For example, Sunderland is a relatively large market club which was relegated during our data period, and AFC Bournemouth a small market club which was promoted for the first time. According to our results, replacing Sunderland with Bournemouth in any fixture with given characteristics would shrink the audience size by about one-third. Repeated several times over a season, the impact on achieved number of viewers will be non-trivial.

Christmas Jürgen Klopp, current coach of Liverpool, is one of many foreign managers who have viewed as absurd the English tradition of scheduling several fixtures during the Christmas holiday period. Not only does this create injury risk for players, but Klopp also declared it as bad for relationships as it leads to men spending too much time watching television rather than interacting with their partners.[7] However, our results show a strong commercial pay-off to concentrating matches in this period. A weekday match (always in the evening) attracts a 19 per cent smaller aggregate audience than a weekend match (always in the afternoon) according to our estimates, the negative effect entirely attributable to men and especially significant for the youngest and oldest age groups.[8] Shifting a hypothetical fixture from midweek to the Christmas period would almost wholly recover this lost audience, with females actually more likely to view during Christmas than at a weekend (whether with or without their partners we cannot say). The same is true of SES group C1. Together, our findings confirm that aggregate audience size over the season, and therefore the expected value of the television rights, would be significantly diminished were the EPL to follow other European leagues by shutting down for Christmas and moving those rounds of matches to midweek slots during the rest of the season.

Broadcaster In the first year of our data set, BT Sport was a new entrant to EPL broadcasting; and so it is perhaps unsurprising that, according to our model, its showing a match with given characteristics would have more than halved the audience compared with it appearing on the well-established Sky platform. The interaction terms involving BT Sport show that this differential shrank over subsequent seasons, as BT Sport gained greater market penetration, but remained large even in the last year. In fact, there was a clear pattern that the differential noticeably narrowed for the highest SES group, whereas it barely changed at all for the lowest. It is plausible that this is a price effect. BT pitches its price much higher than Sky Sports. Butler and Massey (2019) report that, per-match, in 2015–16 a BT subscription cost 2.6 times as much as a Sky subscription.[9] Affordability is likely to be an issue for the lowest social group.

NOTES

1. According to information in past issues of the Deloitte *Annual Review of Football Finance*, broadcasting income for clubs in the English Premier League (EPL) overtook matchday income in the 2000–01 season, when the shares of revenue were 38.5 and 31.5 per cent respectively.
2. Individuals who are recorded as having viewed for only a very short duration are not included in the count. For example, in the United Kingdom, an individual must be present for at least three consecutive minutes to be counted.
3. Because information is collected only in households, estimates of audience size relate only to household viewing, thus excluding audiences in communal residences, such as prisons, and in social spaces, such as pubs.
4. For 2013–14, we had access to data only from mid-season, so approximately half of televised matches in the first year are absent from our analysis. Also, we chose to exclude matches from the last day of each season. Uniquely, in order not to disadvantage any clubs, those ten fixtures are played concurrently. In the rest of the season, every televised match is played at a time when no other EPL game is in progress. Finally, we excluded televised matches from the first three rounds of fixtures in each season from 2014–15 on as information from these was required for calibration of our match significance variable, described below.
5. Another measure of outcome uncertainty related to gambling markets was proposed and employed in Pérez et al. (2017). They drew on match forecasts made by entrants to the Spanish football pools game, an idea based on the 'wisdom of crowds'.
6. A caveat is that a large proportionate effect from the significance of a match for relegation may still deliver a modest number of additional viewers. The most relegation-relevant matches typically feature small market clubs with low team quality, factors which will make the base level of audience size relatively low.
7. BBC interview, available as video at https://www.bbc.co.uk/sport/football/50986483.
8. Midweek matches usually run until nearly 10.00pm, and so may be past the bedtime of many in the 4–15 age band.
9. A private communication from Dr Butler informed us that the differential now is of a similar magnitude.

REFERENCES

Alavy, K., Gaskell, A., Leach, S., and Szymanski, S. (2010). On the edge of your seat: Demand for football on television and the uncertainty of outcome hypothesis. *International Journal of Sport Finance*, 5(2), 75–95.
Bergmann, A., and Schreyer, D. (2019). Factors that shape the demand for international football games across different age groups. *International Journal of Sport Finance*, 14(1), 13–23.
Boshnakov, G., Kharrat, T., and McHale, I.G. (2017). A bivariate Weibull count model for forecasting association football scores. *International Journal of Forecasting*, 33(2), 458–466.
Buraimo, B., and Simmons, R. (2015). Uncertainty of outcome or star quality? Television audience demand for English Premier League football. *International Journal of the Economics of Business*, 22(3), 449–469.
Buraimo, B., Forrest, D., McHale, I.G., and Tena, J.D. (2020). Unscripted drama: Soccer audience response to suspense, surprise and shock. *Economic Inquiry*, 58(2), 881–896.

Butler, R., and Massey, P. (2019). Has competition in the market for subscription sports broadcasting benefited consumers? The case of the English Premier League. *Journal of Sports Economics, 20*(4), 603–624.

Caruso, R., Addesa, F., and De Domizio, M. (2019). The determinants of the TV demand for soccer: Empirical evidence on Italian Serie A for the period 2008–2015. *Journal of Sports Economics, 20*(1), 25–49.

Cox, A. (2018). Spectator demand, uncertainty of results, and public interest: Evidence from the English Premier League. *Journal of Sports Economics, 19*(1), 3–30.

Deloitte LLP (2019). *World in Motion: Annual Review of Football Finance, 2019.*   https://www2.deloitte.com/content/dam/Deloitte/uk/Documents/sports-business-group/deloitte-uk-annual-review-of-football-finance-2019.pdf.

Feehan, P., Forrest, D., and Simmons, R. (2003) Premier league soccer: Normal or inferior good? *European Sport Management Quarterly, 3*(1), 31–45.

Forrest, D., Simmons, R., and Buraimo, B. (2005). Outcome uncertainty and the couch potato audience. *Scottish Journal of Political Economy, 52*(4), 641–661.

Kharrat, T., McHale, I.G., and López Peña, J. (2019). Plus–minus player ratings for soccer. *European Journal of Operational Research, 283*(2), 726–736.

Pérez, L., Puente, V., and Rodríguez, P. (2017). Factors determining TV soccer viewing: Does uncertainty of outcome really matter? *International Journal of Sport Finance, 12*(2), 124–139.

Scelles, N. (2017). Star quality and competitive balance? Television audience demand for English Premier League football reconsidered. *Applied Economics Letters, 24*(19), 199–203.

Schreyer, D., Schmidt, S.L., and Torgler, B. (2016). Game outcome uncertainty and television audience demand: New evidence from German football. *German Economic Review, 19*(2), 140–161.

Van Reeth, D. (2020). Pitfalls in understanding reported TV Audiences for live sports broadcasts. Unpublished manuscript.

10. Does live broadcasting displace gate attendances? Evidence from the English Football League

Babatunde Buraimo, Jake Owen and Rob Simmons*

INTRODUCTION

This chapter investigates the potential threat to gate attendances from live television broadcasting. We will focus on impacts of live broadcasting on gate attendances at English Football League games. The English Football League (EFL) has three divisions comprising 72 professional clubs below the English Premier League (EPL), each with promotion and relegation transitions.[1] The three divisions have undergone many branding changes over time, so we will refer to these as Tier 2, Tier 3 and Tier 4 to indicate their status.

Although the effects of live broadcasting on lower division attendances have been studied before (Buraimo et al., 2009; Forrest and Simmons, 2006; Wallrafen et al., 2019, 2020), there is now an extra reason to revisit this topic. In September 2018, live streaming of Football League matches took place alongside competing live transmissions of midweek UEFA Champions League games. Fans of Football League teams then faced three viewing alternatives: watch their favoured team by live stream, watch a Champions League game via BT Sport or attend the League game regardless. With two viewing alternatives rather than just one, the impact of live broadcasting on gate attendance for Football League teams could be substantial (Baker, 2018).

As football recovers from the Covid-19 crisis, initially without any fans in attendance at games, live streaming offers a service to fans. Once fans are permitted to attend, we expect live streaming of at least some Football League games to persist. In this chapter, we estimate the impact of midweek live broadcasts of Champions League games on attendances at concurrent Football League games. This will establish a lower bound for estimates of overall impact from the forms of live broadcasting that become available.

Since we do not observe a sizeable number of concurrent Football League and Premier League games, where some of the latter are televised we draw lessons from impacts of televised coverage of UEFA Champions League games and English Premier League games on Football League games played in midweek.

We find negative effects of live broadcasting of midweek Champions League and Premier League televised games on attendances at concurrent Football League games, where these effects vary by division. New results are: (1) that adverse effects on attendances from Champions League broadcasts are much greater than from Premier League midweek scheduling; and (2) that the adverse attendance effects from Champions League coverage are greater for the bottom division of the league, Tier 4, relative to Tiers 2 and 3. There is a clear ranking of adverse effects between tiers.

The chapter is structured as follows. First, we outline the context of English lower division football over our sample period. We then review related literature on broadcasting effects on gate attendance. We present our model and data, followed by econometric results with discussion. We conclude with a set of policy recommendations.

INDUSTRY CONTEXT

In each of the three divisions of the English Football League, there are 24 teams who play each other home and away, making for 46 league games in a season. In addition, Football League clubs compete in three domestic cup competitions: the FA Cup, the Football League Cup and a competition specifically for Tier 3 and 4 teams, currently the Checkatrade Trophy. The requirement to play at least 50 games, and possibly as many as 60 depending on progress in the cup competitions, means that some games must be played during weekdays. To this end, the English Football League organises rounds of midweek fixtures throughout the season. The overwhelming majority of midweek games are on Tuesdays, but some games take place on Wednesday evenings. We have data on attendances at all Football League games between the 2000/01 and 2017/18 seasons taken from Sky Football Yearbooks. Our starting season is determined by the availability of betting odds data used to obtain our measure of home win probability.

Figure 10.1 shows attendance time-series plots over our sample period, by tier. The peaks and troughs will reflect compositional changes as larger or smaller teams enter and exit a given tier. On average, clubs in each tier were able to withstand the financial crisis and associated recession of 2008–09 with no discernible downturn. Whilst Tier 2 shows a modest rising

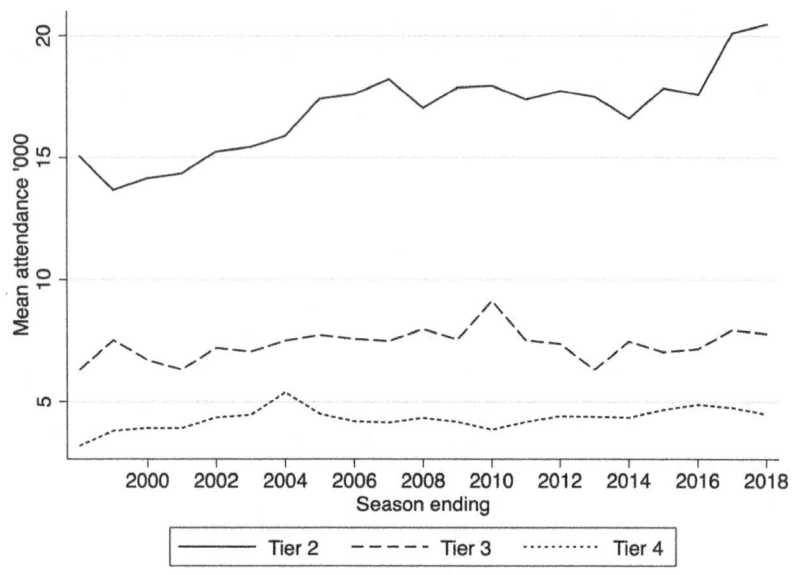

Figure 10.1   Attendance time-series plots for EFL Tiers 2–4, 2000–2018

trend, Tiers 3 and 4 exhibit stationary attendances, and stagnant revenues are a source of concern for clubs in these divisions. Given the reliance of clubs in Tiers 3 and 4 on matchday revenues, this pattern reinforces the problem of growing disparity in financial resources between clubs at the bottom of the Football League and those near the top that aspire to Premier League status.

The only mechanisms available to redistribute revenues in Tiers 2 to 4 are some sharing of (limited) broadcast revenues and some sharing of gate revenues in cup competitions. The Premier League offers ad hoc 'solidarity payments' to the English Football League designed to sustain the financial integrity of English professional football as a whole. Expenditures on payroll are formally limited by a Football League salary cap where violations can incur point penalties. Insolvency, i.e. 'going into administration' in British terminology, leads to an automatic 12-point penalty (Szymanski, 2017).

Table 10.1 shows the numbers of league games that clash with Champions League games broadcast at the same time. These numbers are substantial. The data are organised by broadcast regime as identity of broadcasters varied through the sample period. Table 10.2 shows which broadcasters had rights to show Champions League games within our sample period.

Table 10.1   Number of Football League midweek games that clash with Champions League broadcasts

Period	Tier 2	Tier 3	Tier 4
2000/01–2002/03	224	206	203
2003/04–2008/09	448	290	267
2009/10–2011/12	251	180	173
2012/13–2014/15	238	220	196
2015/16–2017/18	242	213	185

Table 10.2   UK Champions League broadcast regime

Period	Tuesday	Wednesday
1999/00–2002/03	ITV	ITV
2003/04–2008/09	ITV/Sky	Sky
2009/10–2011/12	Sky	ITV/Sky
2012/13–2014/15	ITV/Sky	Sky
2015/16–2017/18	BT	BT

ITV is a free-to-air terrestrial broadcaster, while Sky and BT are subscription cable providers. Between 2003 and 2015, ITV and Sky shared coverage of Champions League games, with ITV awarded first choice of games. Naturally, the television companies promoted coverage of British teams. In a typical season, four English teams and one Scottish team (usually Celtic) qualified for the group stages played between September and December. Some of these teams would then qualify for the knockout phases played between February and May, again midweek. Champions League broadcast rights are negotiated every three years, with rights allocated by auction. Currently, BT is the sole UK rights holder for Champions League broadcasts, having outbid ITV and Sky in the 2015 and 2018 rounds. We shall examine the effects of Champions League broadcasts on Football League midweek attendances, broken down by broadcast regime as shown in Table 10.2.

Buraimo et al. (2006) and Szymanski (2017) have shown that Football League clubs have greater risk of insolvency than Premier League clubs. Szymanski shows that club insolvencies are due to sequences of random shocks that drive clubs into a vicious circle of poor on-field performances, relegation, reduced revenues and related inability to hire and retain good players. Clubs in Tiers 3 and 4 of English football have very little live television coverage, and hence rely on matchday and commercial revenues for financial sustainability. These clubs do benefit from a broadcast deal between the Football League and Sky TV, but the sums involved are smaller than for the Premier League. Income from the broadcast deal is distributed amongst all Football League clubs, but the major share goes to Tier 2 clubs. Tier 2 has at least one game per week broadcast live, while Sky broadcasts around 20 Tier 2 and 3 games in total per season. Hence in 2018/19, when Sunderland was relegated to Tier 2 in a second consecutive demotion, the club received an estimated £1.5m from the Football League broadcast deal, compared to £7m in the previous season in Tier 1. In 2016/17 Sunderland's television revenue in the Premier League was £93m. This illustrates the dramatic reduction in broadcast income as a consequence of relegation in English football (Hunter, 2018).

LITERATURE REVIEW

Many papers have analysed the impacts of broadcasting on gate attendances, and a selection is summarised in Table 10.3. We exclude North American sports for brevity. The consensus from these studies is that the broadcasting impacts are either zero or modestly negative. Only two European studies found positive effects on attendance from live broadcasts: Kringstad et al. (2018) for Norwegian football and Storm et al. (2018) for Danish handball. Where negative effects are found, redistribution of TV revenues more than compensates for revenue losses at the gate (Cox, 2012, 2018; Forrest et al., 2004). In the English Premier League in particular, the compensation to clubs comes in the form of a 'facility fee', which is a direct lump-sum payment for each team participating in a broadcast match, home or away.

The papers closest to ours are Forrest and Simmons (2006) on English Football League and Wallrafen et al. (2019) on German semi-professional football. Each of these finds substantial negative effects on attendances from concurrent higher status games and from live television broadcasts. Forrest and Simmons (2006) have just three seasons of data and one broadcast regime while we have 18 seasons and some important variations in broadcast regime, including removal of the terrestrial broadcaster and arrival of a new entrant to the sports broadcasting market for the Champions League (BT). The Champions League has grown over our sample period in audience interest and revenue opportunities from broadcasting and commercial sponsorships.

Table 10.3 *Literature on effects of live broadcasting on gate attendance*

Study	League and period	Effect on attendance
Allan and Roy (2008)	Scottish Premier League (SPL) 2002/03	30% reduction in attendance of casual home fans
Allan (2004)	English Premier League (EPL); Aston Villa, 1995/96 to 2000/01	7.75% reduction
Baimbridge et al. (1995)	English Rugby League 1993/94	Significant reduction
Baimbridge et al. (1996)	EPL, 1993/94	16% reduction in attendance from live broadcasting on Monday night
Buraimo (2008)	EPL, 1997/98 to 2003/04	Significant negative effects from ITV coverage of Champions League (19%) and Sky coverage of Premier League (4%)
Buraimo and Simmons (2008)	EPL, 2000/01 to 2005/06	5% reduction from Sky Sunday coverage; 10% reduction from Sky Monday
Buraimo and Simmons (2009)	Spain La Liga 2003/04 to 2005/06	21% reduction from public TV on weekdays; 3% reduction ($t = 1.88$) from public TV at weekends; zero effect from subscription channels
Buraimo et al. (2009)	English Football League (EFL), Tier 2, 1997/98 to 2003/04	24% reduction from ITV live coverage of Tier 2; 5% reduction from Sky coverage of Tier 2; 5% reduction from ITV coverage of Champions League
Carmichael et al. (1999)	English Rugby League, 1994/95	Significant reduction
Cox (2012)	EPL, 2004/05 to 2007/08	Models revenue not attendance. Significant reductions in gate revenues from Sky live broadcasts. Impacts greater for worst performing teams. Impacts more than offset by Sky facility fee
Cox (2018)	EPL, 2004–2012	1–2% reduction in attendances from live Sky broadcasts; statistically significant

Table 10.3 *(continued)*

Study	League and period	Effect on attendance
Forrest and Simmons (2006)	EFL, 1999/2000 to 2001/02	Tier 3 had 24% reduction from concurrent Champions League broadcasts; Tier 4 had 18% reduction; small/zero effects for Tier 2
Forrest et al. (2004)	EPL, 1992/93 to 2000/01	Small effects; extra broadcast fees more than offset gate revenue losses
García and Rodríguez (2002)	Spain La Liga, 1992/93 to 1995/96	3% reduction for private subscription channels; 5% reduction for public channels
Kringstad et al. (2018)	Norwegian football, 2005 to 2011	Positive effect from broadcasting domestic games; negative effect from concurrently televised games in large European leagues
Storm et al. (2018)	Danish handball, 2011/12/ to 2015/16	Positive effects from own-league games broadcast on TV; 10% negative effect from rival leagues on same channel as shows handball
Wallrafen et al. (2019)	German 4th tier (semi-pro), 2012/13 to 2015/16	19% reduction from concurrent Bundesliga 1 and 2 games; 14% reduction from concurrent Champions League games
Wallrafen et al. (2020)	German 3rd tier, 2015/16 to 2017/18	Negative and significant effects on gate attendance when selection of 3rd tier games for broadcast is explicitly modelled

MODEL AND DATA

Our dependent variable is log attendance. We have panel data by clubs, tiers and seasons, and we utilise all league games between 2000/01 and 2017/18 for which betting odds are available. Sample sizes of games are 9,553 for Tier 2, 9,500 for Tier 3 and 8,131 for Tier 4. Our focus is on impacts of television coverage of Champions League games on midweek gate attendances. Hence our model is:

Log attendance = f (*Control variables, TV variables*) + home team fixed effects + season fixed effects + error term.

Our choice of control variables reflects the literature summarised above, and follows Borland and Macdonald (2003) (see Buraimo et al., 2018 for a recent application). Each team has a core group of loyal supporters which nevertheless can vary in size through demographics, relocation and response to team fortunes. The variations in core support can be summarised as changes in *habit* (Borland and Lye, 1992). Between-season variations in home fan support are captured by the log of average home attendance in the previous season (*last season home attendance*). The propensity of away fans to travel to attend games is also driven by habit, to some extent. Greater long-term attractiveness and reputation of away teams might also induce home fans to attend games (Czarnitzki and Stadtmann, 2002). These factors are controlled for by the log of average away team's attendance at home in the previous season (*last season away attendance*).

The characteristics and status of the home and away teams are controlled for using a set of *contest variables*. We have dummy variables for whether or not the home team was newly promoted (*promoted*) and whether or not the home team was newly relegated (*relegated*). Current league standings of the respective teams in a match are represented by *home points per game* and *away points per game*. The first game of each season has to be removed to accommodate these variables. A large number of papers has modelled outcome uncertainty surrounding sports fixtures using probability of home win and its square, where the probability is derived from betting odds (see, for example, Buraimo and Simmons, 2009, on Spain; Cox, 2018, on the English Premier League; Martins and Cro, 2018, on Portuguese football; Peel and Thomas, 1992, on the English Football League; and Sung and Mills, 2018, on US Major League Soccer). A positive coefficient on home win probability and negative coefficient on the squared term would indicate evidence in support of the outcome uncertainty hypothesis. Conversely, a negative coefficient on home win probability and positive coefficient on the squared would provide evidence consistent with the loss aversion hypothesis taken from cumulative prospect theory and proposed by Coates et al. (2014) and Humphreys and Zhou (2015). To accommodate either hypothesis, we include *home win probability* and *home win probability squared* as control variables. Our home win probability was derived from bookmaker William Hill and supplied by www.football-data.co.uk. Some 561 matches had no betting odds information and so these were dropped from the analysis. Probabilities were scaled by bookmaker overround.[2] The final control characteristic to include is a dummy variable for matches of local rivalry (*Derby*).

We lack information on matchday ticket prices so cannot include these in a variable. We follow standard practice and use home team fixed effects to capture unobserved variation in attendances across teams, where ticket prices are part of the unobserved heterogeneity in the data. We can include a proxy measure for travel costs, however, by using distance and its square (*distance* and *distance squared*). We predict a positive coefficient on the former and a negative coefficient on the latter, in line with attendance demand literature (Buraimo et al., 2009; Forrest and Simmons, 2006).

Scheduling matters for team attendances, and we include dummy variables for *weekday*; for the Christmas holiday period (December 26 to January 2, denoted by *Christmas break*); and for the movable Easter period (*Easter*). It is common for the Football League to schedule three games over the Christmas holiday and two games over the Easter break, with a full set of games scheduled for Easter Monday. Boxing Day (December 26) has the highest attendances of any date in the League schedule despite a lack of public transport across the UK on that day. We include a full set of month dummies to capture attendance variations through the season.

Turning to our focus variables, we have six main dummy variables for television coverage. These are: *Champions League 2000–03, Champions League 2003–09, Champions League 2009–12, Champions League 2012–15, Champions League 2015–18* and *Premier League weekday*. The Champions League dummies can be expanded further by splitting up day of week into Tuesday and Wednesday and by separation of broadcaster (ITV versus Sky, in particular). We will report estimates for these more finely tuned dummy variables below.

Table 10.4 shows descriptive statistics for our continuous variables. As is to be expected, mean attendances decline through the tiers. The minimum attendance of 849 in Tier 2 was for a televised game, Rotherham versus Wimbledon, shown on ITV Digital – for which commentators noted that travel cost per potential fan was less than average per-game TV rights fee at the time for that broadcaster. The maximum attendance refers to

Table 10.4   Descriptive statistics

Variable	Mean	Standard deviation	Minimum	Maximum
Attendance, Tier 2	17,350	6,892	849	52,301
Attendance, Tier 3	7,412	4,613	1,396	38.256
Attendance, Tier 4	4,414	2,578	893	28.343
Home points per game	1.35	0.456	0	3
Away points per game	1.37	0.460	0	3
Home win probability	0.432	0.097	0.085	0.787
Distance, Tier 2	110.1	60.0	0	334.4
Distance, Tier 3	111.9	61.8	3.1	322.1
Distance, Tier 4	117.7	64.8	5.4	322.1

Newcastle United, relegated from the Premier League but still sustaining large support. The zero distance refers to a ground-share between Crystal Palace and Wimbledon. Descriptive data for distances are similar through tiers; but we should note that England's radial transport network, converging on London, means that cross-country travel between extreme locations in Britain (e.g. Carlisle to Plymouth, Swansea to Norwich) is very costly in time. Several Tier 3 and 4 teams are in remote, small-town locations (e.g. Yeovil and Forest Green Rovers).

Table 10.5 shows a breakdown of mean attendances by broadcasting regime. We see that, for Tier 2, weekday games without TV competition draw slightly higher crowds, on average, than weekend games. Across the board, midweek Premier League games have average attendances only slightly below weekday games without TV competition. The rising trend in Tier 2 attendances shown in Figure 10.1 carries over to midweek games scheduled against Champions League games. However, there are

Table 10.5   Mean attendances by broadcast regime

Group	Tier 2	Tier 3	Tier 4
Weekend	17,555	7,630	4,512
Weekday without TV	17,619	7,364	4,354
Champions League 2000–2003	14,417	5,818	3,726
Champions League 2003–2009	16,011	6,631	3,700
Champions League 2009–2012	16,256	7,477	3,491
Champions League 2012–2015	15,859	5,845	3,891
Champions League 2015–2018	17,951	6,788	3,836
Premier League weekday	17,374	7,300	4,511

attendance reductions from weekday games without TV coverage up to 2015. For Tiers 3 and 4, there are systematically reduced attendances from midweek averages for games competing with Champions League matches. Games concurrent with midweek Premier League fixtures show little difference compared to games without TV competition. Of course, these are just comparisons of means, and we need to control for confounding factors by regression analysis for more meaningful inferences.

Estimation is by Ordinary Least Squares (OLS) with home team and season fixed effects. There were no sell-out games in our sample means, and so we do not require the Tobit estimator for censoring. Estimation is performed separately by tier and standard errors are clustered by home team.

RESULTS

Our regression estimates are shown in Table 10.6. The coefficients on control variables are not of primary interest but nevertheless yield some insights. In all tiers, larger previous season average home attendance is associated with bigger crowds in the current season, *ceteris paribus*. This suggests a role for habit persistence, and we also find that this effect is reduced as one moves down the tiers. We attribute this result to greater loyalty amongst home fans of Tier 2 teams, in line with Forrest and Simmons (2006). Larger previous season away team attendance is also associated with greater home team attendance, with stronger effects for Tiers 3 and 4 relative to Tier 2. Teams that were promoted to Tiers 2 and 3 generate larger crowds than those which were not, reflecting positive dynamics of a successful, winning team emerging from a lower division. Conversely, teams relegated to Tier 2 from the Premier League deliver lower attendance than those which were not demoted, although this assumes last season home attendance is taken as constant.

Improvements in League standings for both home and away teams yield greater attendances, with stronger sensitivities in Tiers 3 and 4 compared to Tier 2. The coefficients on home win probability and its square are negative and positive respectively, with turning points within the sample for all tiers. This result is in line with other studies of European football attendance (Buraimo and Simmons, 2008, 2009; Martins and Cro, 2018) and is contrary to the conventional uncertainty of outcome hypothesis. Our estimated pattern of coefficients on home win probability is consistent with the loss aversion hypothesis set out by Coates et al. (2014) and Humphreys and Zhou (2015).

Longer distances between home and away teams are associated with lower attendances, with the effect diminishing over distance. The turning point is at the extremes of distribution of distances in each tier. The Christmas and Easter holiday periods have larger attendances *ceteris paribus*, considerably so for Christmas. Month dummies (not reported for brevity) show greater attendances in March, April and May relative to August, which is likely to reflect fan interest in end-of-season resolution of contests for promotion and relegation. Each tier has a playoff competition for one promotion place to the tier above, and this helps sustain fan interest and attendance as the season draws to a close in early May (Bojke, 2008). Midweek games have lower attendances than weekend matches, in line with expectations.

The broadcasting regime dummy variables are our focus of attention. In each regime, Champions League games were broadcast on Tuesday and Wednesday evenings. Four English teams appeared in the group stages, and typically at least one of these would progress in February to the knockout phase. Our sample period contains three English winners of the Champions League and six English runners-up. The vast majority of fixture clashes with Champions League games for Football League teams were on Tuesdays.

In the period 2003 to 2015, Champions League telecasts were shared between ITV and Sky TV, with the former, terrestrial broadcaster awarded first pick on games shown. Over 2009 to 2012, ITV switched its coverage from Tuesday to Wednesday, and then reverted to Tuesday in 2012.[3] F-tests of coefficient equality of coefficients for split dummy variables (for example, ITV Tuesday equal to Sky Wednesday in the 2009–12 period) show: a) that ITV coefficients are equal to Sky coefficients; and b) that Tuesday coefficients are equal to Wednesday coefficients. It might be expected that adverse effects of Champions League broadcasts would be greater when a terrestrial company is the provider, due to much greater audience reach. This turns out not to be the case: cable TV effects are not systematically lower than adverse effects from terrestrial TV broadcasts. We note the growth of provision of cable TV broadcasts (Sky and BT) in pubs and social clubs over our sample period, which might well have countered the effect of larger audience reach of free-to-air ITV.

F-tests reject coefficient equality for Tuesday and Wednesday coefficients for the 2000–03 and 2015–18 periods when one provider had exclusive Champions League coverage (ITV and BT). However, we have small sample sizes of Wednesday games in these two periods and so the F-tests have low power. Hence, we combine the Tuesday and Wednesday dummy variables into a single variable as shown in Table 10.6.

We convert the coefficients on the dummy variables for Champions League broadcast regimes and Premier League midweek games from

Table 10.6   Regression estimates; dependent variable is log attendance

	Tier 2 coefficients	Tier 3 coefficients	Tier 4 coefficients
Control variables			
Last season home attendance	0.654*** (8.56)	0.474*** (3.66)	0.438*** (9.12)
Last season away attendance	0.086*** (12.55)	0.145*** (23.57)	0.146*** (18.39)
Promoted	0.155*** (9.58)	0.091*** (6.13)	
Relegated	−0.089*** (2.90)	−0.047 (1.06)	−0.035* (1.95)
Home points per game	0.081*** (7.10)	0.109*** (10.77)	0.112*** (10.24)
Away points per game	0.059*** (9.63)	0.088*** (8.94)	0.101*** (11.35)
Home win probability	−0.763** (2.21)	−0.493** (2.33)	−0.912*** (3.59)
Home win probability squared	1.182*** (3.29)	0.981*** (4.30)	1.663*** (5.78)
Distance	−0.002*** (11.40)	−0.003*** (9.79)	−0.004*** (11.91)
Distance squared (000s)	0.006*** (9.54)	0.007*** (7.08)	0.009*** (7.98)
Weekday	−0.046*** (7.33)	−0.069*** (7.35)	−0.057*** (5.98)
Christmas break	0.119*** (15.32)	0.140*** (13.64)	0.189*** (14.07)
Easter	0.016* (1.85)	0.031** (2.45)	0.061*** (4.54)
TV variables			
Champions League 2000–2003	−0.026** (2.02)	−0.076*** (4.79)	−0.105*** (5.51)
Champions League 2003–2009	−0.047*** (5.45)	−0.073*** (5.44)	−0.122*** (7.14)
Champions League 2009–2012	−0.047*** (6.08)	−0.104*** (6.76)	−0.165*** (6.42)
Champions League 2012–2015	−0.066*** (6.07)	−0.144*** (7.78)	−0.147*** (7.97)
Champions League 2015–2018	−0.054*** (5.20)	−0.095*** (4.48)	−0.150*** (7.56)
Premier League weekday	−0.021** (2.41)	−0.023** (2.22)	−0.037*** (2.76)
R^2 within	0.49	0.44	0.43
R^2 overall	0.84	0.78	0.71
N	9553	9522	8131

Note: t-statistics in parentheses with standard errors clustered by home team; estimates contain home team and season fixed effects and month dummies. *, ** and *** denote significance at 10%, 5% and 1% respectively.

Table 10.7   Negative impacts of Champions League broadcasts on midweek league attendances, %

TV variable	Tier 2	Tier 3	Tier 4
Champions League 2000–2003	2.57	7.32	9.97
Champions League 2003–2009	4.59	7.04	11.49
Champions League 2009–2012	4.59	9.88	15.21
Champions League 2012–2015	6.39	13.41	13.67
Champions League 2015–2018	5.26	9.06	13.93
Premier League weekday	2.08	2.27	3.63

Table 10.6 into percentage impacts using the formula $\exp(\beta) - 1$ and these are shown in Table 10.7.

All coefficients on broadcast type are negative and statistically significant at 5 per cent or less. Impacts are over and above those from midweek scheduling, captured by the weekday dummy. There are several striking results. The impacts of concurrent Premier League weekday games are negative but fairly modest, and considerably less than for concurrent Champions League broadcasts. This is in sharp contrast to Wallrafen et al. (2019), who found larger impacts from concurrent Bundesliga 1 and 2 games on Tier 4 attendances in Germany, relative to concurrent Champions League games. Our reversal of Wallrafen et al.'s result is possibly related to selection of midweek televised Premier League games. Up to 2019, only one Premier League game was selected for broadcast on each of Tuesday and Wednesday from a given midweek round of fixtures.[4] The most attractive Premier League games tend to be reserved for Saturday and Sunday afternoon telecasts.

The second key finding is that there is a clear ranking of adverse effects of Champions League broadcasts on midweek Football League gate attendances, with Tier 4 having a larger response than Tier 3 which has a greater effect than Tier 2. Tier 2 displacement effects from Champions League broadcasts are stable at around 2–6 per cent. Tiers 3 and 4 show much larger effects of between 7 and 15 per cent, though not as high as the impacts reported in the much earlier study by Forrest and Simmons (2006), who found a 24 per cent reduction for Tier 3 over 1999 to 2002. Our findings suggest that Tier 4 clubs are especially vulnerable to audience substitution towards Champions League games away from gate attendance with magnitudes of 10 to 15 per cent throughout our sample period. Moreover, while the most recent BT Champions League broadcast era shows smaller midweek attendance reductions for Tier 3 (9 per cent from 13 per cent), the adverse effects were sustained at 14 per cent for Tier 4 teams on average over 2015 to 2018. This is of great concern for Tier 4 clubs, which are more reliant than those in higher tiers on matchday income as a component of total revenues.

To see the potential adverse effects of midweek attendance reductions on club revenues, we perform a simple simulation exercise, shown in Table 10.8. Ticket prices were taken from the BBC's Football Fan Survey 2017 and the simulations refer to the 2016/17 season, with BT as sole Champions League broadcaster.

Since Tier 2 clubs have much larger attendances and revenues than Tier 3 and 4 clubs, the revenue losses from concurrent broadcasts are substantial in this tier. Unlike the Premier League, 19 out of the 24 Tier 2 clubs had net losses in 2015/16, and 15 out of 23 clubs that published accounts had wage bill to turnover ratios of 100 per cent or more (Conn, 2018). In most cases, losses were covered by wealthy owners and investors. These parlous financial statements had already prompted the Football League to impose a Financial Fair Play policy in all tiers, similar to that applied in UEFA competitions and termed the Salary Cost Management Protocol, with violations punishable by transfer embargoes and points penalties.

Hence, revenue losses from television broadcasting of concurrent League games could amplify the effects on club balance sheets from exogenous shocks, and conceivably propel a vulnerable club into insolvency (Szymanski, 2017). As offsets, Figure 10.1 shows a slightly rising attendance trend for Tier 2, and recently the Football League has negotiated more lucrative broadcast contracts, both domestically and through sales of overseas rights.[5] However, clubs in Tier 3 and 4 derive few benefits from these positive developments.

In absolute terms, Tier 2 clubs suffer more than Tier 3 and 4 clubs from concurrent broadcasting of Champions League and Premier League games in midweek. But, in proportionate terms, Tier 4 teams lose out by more than Tier 3 teams.

Over the 2015/16 to 2018/19 seasons, the Football League offered each Tier 3 club £677,000 and each Tier 4 club £472,000 as flat-rate sums from the sale of broadcast rights. In addition, each home and away team in a televised game received £30,000 and £10,000 respectively. Around 20 Tier 3 and Tier 4 games are televised live each season. There is no prize money component of payments from broadcast revenues in the Football League, in stark contrast to the established Premier League practice of a linear schedule of payments according to final League placings.[6] Similarly, the Premier League made payments of £645,000 per Tier 3 club and £430,000 per Tier 4 club. The latter represent what the Premier League terms 'solidarity payments'. These are made in recognition of a need to preserve a financially viable professional league structure of 92 teams from which

Table 10.8   *Seasonal revenue losses from concurrent Champions League and Premier League midweek games, 2016/17*

	Tier 2	Tier 3	Tier 4
Midweek attendance	20,000	7,800	4,400
Loss of fans/CL clash	1,052	707	612
Ticket price (£)	28	22	20
Loss of revenue/CL clash (£)	29,500	15,550	12,240
Number of CL clashes	3	3	2
Loss of revenue from CL clashes (£)	88,500	46,650	24,480
Loss of fans/PL clash	416	177	160
Loss of revenue/PL clash (£)	11,650	3,890	3,200
Number of PL clashes	2	1	1
Loss of revenue from PL clashes (£)	23,300	3,890	3,200
Overall loss of revenue from TV scheduling (£)	111,800	50,540	27,680

promoted teams can compete in financial and playing resources with incumbent teams.[7] More broadly, there is some implicit recognition by the Premier League that it might be imposing negative externalities on the Football League.[8] Our computations make explicit the cost of one form of externality, Premier League midweek scheduling of its matches, and that cost is rather small. We should stress, though, that the revenue losses in Table 10.8 are lower bounds as they cover ticket sales only and exclude matchday revenues from catering, parking and other services. The much larger negative externality comes from elite Premier League clubs playing in the UEFA Champions League. At present, there is no form of compensation for Tier 2 to 4 teams for the negative externality revealed by our regression estimates in Table 10.7 and by the estimated revenue losses in Table 10.8.

POLICY RECOMMENDATIONS AND CONCLUSIONS

The policy implications following these results should be of interest to decision takers within the industry. At one level, if market forces are to prevail, football clubs in the lower levels of English football will have to adapt to the changing landscape of football broadcasting. In such an instance, football clubs will need to make their stadium offering compelling enough so that fans will be willing to consume the live stadium experience. Clearly, a means of doing so is to improve the quality of players. Such an approach is costly, and it is debatable as to whether clubs can recoup this increase in costs. If market forces were to prevail, it is likely that football clubs, particularly those in Tiers 3 and 4, would suffer declines in attendances and revenue, and may be forced to reconsider their presence within the market. Some might even shift status from being fully professional to semi-professional, similar to Tier 5 of English football.

Such an outcome is not ideal for the Football League. There is a prevailing view that a degree of solidarity in professional football is desirable. In English football, such solidarity is evident not only via the subsidy to all clubs in the lower tiers, but also via institutional arrangements. For example, games played between 2.45 and 5.15 are ineligible for live broadcast transmission under a League blackout policy. This benefits Premier League clubs whose matches are scheduled at that time; but it is also argued to help sustain gate attendances at all those clubs in Tiers 2, 3 and 4 that play the bulk of their matches during this time slot. The increased pressure to televise more Premier League games has meant that other days and times (e.g. Friday and Saturday evenings) have been used for live broadcasting. Despite economists' objections that the blackout policy is a restraint of trade, reduces consumer surplus and removes potential revenue opportunities from broadcasting (Noll, 2007), the Saturday 3pm slot remains protected by League rules, although the blackout policy was suspended during the Covid-19 pandemic as crowds were not permitted inside stadia in any tier.

UEFA, the rights owner of the Champions League, is in a delicate position in that, whilst it is a commercial rights owner looking to exploit the rights value for its competitions, it is also a governing body responsible for the well-being of European football within member countries. In this regard, the League organisers have two main options. The first is to allocate revenue from these competitions to the lower levels of football where there is evidence of a substitution effect if there is agreement that the continued survival of these lower level tiers are beneficial to football as a whole. Losses in gate revenues attributable to live broadcasting can be offset by appropriate redistribution of broadcast income. The second option for League organisers is to consider institutional arrangements, including changes in fixture schedules, which reduce the substitution effect. This latter option is more difficult since there are pressures to expand the live broadcasting of football, especially through streaming.

Based on our econometric results, we propose a revision of the formulae for redistributing broadcast income to lower division clubs in the English Football League. The gap in solidarity payments from Premier League to English Football League clubs between Tier 4 clubs and Tier 2 should be narrowed, and further narrowed between Tier 4 and Tier 3 clubs. The distribution of payments could be made more equal. Such a policy would compensate for the negative externalities imposed on Tier 3 and 4 clubs by English Premier League clubs playing in UEFA Champions League matches, concurrent with Football League matches. Additionally, the size of the solidarity payment could be increased.

Further consideration in future research should be given to the impact of live streaming on Football League attendances. So far, literature offers a broad consensus that live television broadcasts do adversely affect gate attendances at the game being televised. Evidence from the Premier League (Cox, 2012, 2018; Forrest et al., 2004) suggests these effects are modest, however, and revenue redistribution can more than offset any losses in matchday revenues. Our own analysis found small effects of concurrent Premier League games on midweek Football League attendances of the order of 2 to 3 per cent. We predict that similar results will apply for the impact of live streaming on Football League attendances, but research will be needed to test this conjecture as data emerge.

In the 2020/21 season, both the Premier League and the English Football League had games played in stadia without any fans present ('behind closed doors') due to Government-imposed restrictions relating to the Covid-19 pandemic. According to BBC Sport (2020), the chairman of the English Football League, Rick Parry, predicted a £200m deficit for Football League clubs as at September 2020, with associated high risk of insolvency, especially as many Football League clubs were financially fragile even before the pandemic (Szymanski, 2017).

As football generally emerges from the global Covid-19 pandemic, we can only speculate on possible impacts on future English Football League attendances and revenues. Our empirical results show only modest reductions in gate attendances from concurrent Premier League games broadcast live in midweek. To the extent that the Premier League might expand live broadcasting to recover revenues lost during the Covid-19 pandemic, the effects on English Football League clubs from lost gate receipts due to concurrent Premier League telecasts need not be large.

The greater problems facing English Football League clubs are the losses of gate revenues as the competition is suspended and further losses as games revert to being played in closed stadia without paying spectators. There are several policy responses to this bleak scenario:

- Expand live streaming of Football League games, currently available for midweek games played concurrently with Champions League games.
- More flexible scheduling where Football League games are played at times not occupied by Premier League fixtures. This is the approach

taken in Germany by Bundesliga 2 and lower divisions, where time slots are taken where Bundesliga 1 games are not being played, e.g. Friday early evening, Saturday early afternoon and Monday night where the latter Bundesliga 2 game is broadcast live. Midweek Football League games could be scheduled away from concurrent live broadcasts of high profile Champions League games featuring English clubs.

● Revision of the Premier League's 'solidarity' policy of direct subsidy to the Football League. Specifically, there is an apparent anomaly that in the 2019/20 season six former Premier League clubs in the English Championship received a total of £240m parachute payments derived from sale of domestic broadcast rights while the remaining 18 clubs in Tier 2 received a total of £81m in financial subsidy from the Premier League. Financial support for Tiers 3 and 4 was considerably less (Szymanski, 2017).

In policy discussion on the future of English Football League club revenues and finances, we suggest that the evidence presented in this chapter on the impacts of live broadcasting from rival competitions should be seriously considered.

NOTES

*   We acknowledge helpful comments by Ruud Koning and participants at the European Sports Economics Association Conference, Liverpool, 2018 and the 2019 Sports Economics Workshop, University College Cork.
1.   As at 2019/20, the English Football League included three teams from Wales: Cardiff City, Newport County and Swansea City.
2.   During our sample period, overrounds fell considerably from around 12 per cent to 5 per cent or even lower due to increased competition in UK betting markets, including the arrival of a betting exchange, Betfair, offering very low commission (Flepp et al., 2017).
3.   ITV's switch to Champions League coverage on Wednesdays in 2009 displaced its most-viewed soap opera, *Coronation Street*, and many of its fans complained about the resulting change in programme schedule.
4.   From 2019/20, as an innovation for British football broadcasting, each Premier League game will be available for broadcast on Amazon Prime via a red button facility, similar to current provision of Bundesliga 1 games in Germany. The impacts of this innovation on attendances, in all tiers, merit future research (Rumsby, 2017).
5.   The most recent domestic rights deal between the Football League and Sky TV covers 2019/20 to 2023/24 and is worth £120m per season, up from £90m per season in 2015/16 to 2018/19. Overseas rights are negotiated separately. Live streaming via Sky platforms or club websites is an explicit component of the domestic deal (McCaskill, 2018).
6.   In each season, the three teams relegated from the Premier League to Tier 2 (Championship) each receive a 'parachute payment' out of the current domestic broadcast rights deal that is designed to compensate these teams for revenue losses from

demotion to the lower tier. These parachute payments last for three seasons (Wilson et al., 2018).

7. Without solidarity payments, promoted clubs might be so weak on arrival in a higher tier that their games would deliver predictable outcomes and would be dull to watch, hence deterring fans, broadcasters and sponsors.

8. Both the Premier League and the Football League offer 'parachute payments' to compensate clubs for relegation into lower tiers. These payments are ostensibly to help relegated clubs readjust to competition in lower tiers which will necessarily bring lower revenues both from broadcasting and from reduced matchday sources. However, these parachute payments can be criticised for 'subsidising failure' (Wilson et al., 2018).

REFERENCES

Allan, G., and Roy, G. (2008). Does television crowd out spectators? New evidence from the Scottish premier league. *Journal of Sports Economics*, *9*, 592–605.

Allan, S. (2004). Satellite television and football attendance: The not so super effect. *Applied Economics Letters*, *11*, 123–125.

Baimbridge, M., Cameron, S., and Dawson, P. (1996). Satellite television and the demand for football: A whole new ball game? *Scottish Journal of Political Economy*, *43*, 317–333.

Baimbridge, M., Cameron, S., and Dawson, P. (1995). Satellite broadcasting and match attendance: The case of rugby league. *Applied Economics Letters*, *2*, 343–346.

Baker, A. (2018). The EFL enters a new digital age with domestic live streaming – but what does it mean for attendances? *Bristol Post*, August 20. Retrieved from https://www.bristolpost.co.uk/sport/football/football-news/efl-ifollow-live-streaming-attendances-1916179.

BBC Sport (2020). Rick Parry: English Football League clubs face '£200m hole' by September. https://www.bbc.co.uk/sport/football/52543735.

Bojke, C. (2008). The impact of post-season playoff systems on the attendance at regular season games. In J. Albert and R. Koning (eds), *Statistical Thinking in Sports*, Boca Raton, FL: Chapman & Hall/CRC. 179–202.

Borland, J., and Lye, J. (1992). Attendance at Australian Rules football: A panel study. *Applied Economics*, *24*, 1053–1058.

Borland, J., and Macdonald, R. (2003). Demand for sport. *Oxford Review of Economic Policy*, *19*, 476–502.

Buraimo, B. (2008). Stadium attendance and television audience demand in English league football. *Managerial and Decision Economics*, *29*, 513–523.

Buraimo, B., Forrest, D., and Simmons, R. (2009). Insights for clubs from modelling attendance in football. *Journal of the Operational Research Society*, *60*, 147–155.

Buraimo, B., and Simmons, R. (2008). Do sports fans really value uncertainty of outcome? Evidence from the English Premier League. *International Journal of Sport Finance*, *3*, 146–155.

Buraimo, B., and Simmons, R. (2009). A tale of two audiences: Spectators, television viewers and outcome uncertainty in Spanish football. *Journal of Economics and Business*, *61*, 326–338.

Buraimo, B., Simmons, R., and Szymanski, S. (2006). English football. *Journal of Sports Economics*, *7*, 29–46.

Buraimo, B., Tena, J. D., and Diego de la Piedra, J. (2018). Attendance demand in a developing football market: The case of the Peruvian first division. *European Sport Management Quarterly*, *18*, 671–686.

Carmichael, F., Millington, J., and Simmons, R. (1999). Elasticity of demand for rugby league attendance and the impact of BSkyB. *Applied Economics Letters*, *6*, 797–800.

Coates, D., Humphreys, B., and Zhou, L. (2014). Reference-dependent preferences, loss aversion and live game attendance. *Economic Inquiry*, *52*, 959–972.

Conn, D. (2018). Championship clubs feel the strain as financial gap to Premier League grows. *Guardian*, 7 June. Retrieved from https://www.theguardian.com/football/2018/jun/07/championship-financial-gap-premier-league-annual-accounts.

Cox, A. (2012). Live broadcasting, gate revenue and football club performance: Some evidence. *International Journal of the Economics of Business*, *19*, 75–98.

Cox, A. (2018). Spectator demand, uncertainty of results and public interest: Evidence from the English Premier League. *Journal of Sports Economics*, *19*, 3–30.

Czarnitzki, D., and Stadtmann, G. (2002). Uncertainty of outcome versus reputation: Empirical evidence for the first German football division. *Empirical Economics*, *27*, 101–112.

Flepp, R., Nüesch, S., and Franck, E. (2017). The liquidity advantage of the quote-driven market: Evidence from the betting industry. *Quarterly Review of Economics and Finance*, *64*, 306–317.

Forrest, D., and Simmons, R. (2006). New issues in attendance demand: The case of the English Football League. *Journal of Sports Economics*, *7*, 247–266.

Forrest, D., Simmons, R., and Szymanski, S. (2004). Broadcasting, attendance and the inefficiency of cartels. *Review of Industrial Organization*, *24*, 243–265.

García, J., and Rodríguez, P. (2002). The determinants of football match attendance revisited: Empirical evidence from the Spanish football league. *Journal of Sports Economics*, *3*, 18–38.

Humphreys, B., and Zhou, L. (2015). The Louis-Schmelling paradox and the league standing effect reconsidered. *Journal of Sports Economics*, *16*, 835–852.

Hunter, J. (2018). Sunderland's TV income drops 98 per cent following back-to-back relegations. *Chronicle Live*, April 24. Retrieved from https://www.chroniclelive.co.uk/sport/football/football-news/sunderlands-tv-income-drops-98-14565282.

Kringstad, N., Solberg, H., and Jakobsen, T. (2018). Does live broadcasting reduce stadium attendance? The case of Norwegian football. *Sport, Business and Management: An International Journal*, *8*, 67–81.

Martins, A., and Cro, S. (2018). The demand for football in Portugal: New insights on outcome uncertainty. *Journal of Sports Economics*, *19*, 473–497.

McCaskill, S. (2018). EFL iFollow streams every single midweek Championship game for the first time. *Forbes*, August 21. Retrieved from https://www.forbes.com/sites/stevemccaskill/2018/08/21/efl-ifollow-streams-every-single-midweek-championship-game/#17bc6b4f32cf.

Noll, R. (2007). Broadcasting and team sports. *Scottish Journal of Political Economy*, *54*, 400–431.

Peel, D., and Thomas, D. (1992). The demand for football: Some evidence of outcome uncertainty. *Empirical Economics*, *17*, 323–331.

Rumsby, B. (2017). EFL clubs able to live stream midweek matches from 2019 following £600m TV deal but Premier League unlikely to follow. *Telegraph*,

September 12. Retrieved from https://www.telegraph.co.uk/football/2017/09/12/football-league-clubs-able-live-stream-midweek-matches-fans/.

Storm, R., Nielsen, C., and Jakobsen, T. (2018). The complex challenge of spectator demand: Attendance drivers in the Danish men's handball league. *European Sport Management Quarterly, 18*, 652–670.

Sung, H., and Mills, B. (2018). Estimation of game-level attendance in major league soccer: Outcome uncertainty and absolute quality considerations. *Sport Management Review, 21*, 517–532.

Szymanski, S. (2017). Entry into exit: Insolvency in English professional football. *Scottish Journal of Political Economy, 64*, 419–444.

Wallrafen, T., Deutscher, C., and Pawlowski, T. (2020). The impact of live broadcasting on stadium attendance reconsidered: Some evidence from 3rd division football in Germany. *European Sport Management Quarterly.* doi:10.1080/1618 4742.2020.1828967.

Wallrafen, T., Pawlowski, T., and Deutscher, C. (2019). Substitution in sports: The case of lower division football attendance. *Journal of Sports Economics, 20*, 319–343.

Wilson, R., Ramchandari, G., and Plumley, D. (2018). Parachute payments in English football: Softening the landing or distorting the balance? *Journal of Global Sport Management, 3*, 351–368.

11. Mega-events and tourism: the case of the 2014 World Cup in Brazil and the 2016 Rio Summer Olympic Games

Robert Baade, Robert Baumann and Victor Matheson

INTRODUCTION

This chapter examines tourist arrivals in Brazil during mega-sporting events, updating Baumann and Matheson (2018) to include an examination of the 2016 Summer Olympics in Rio de Janeiro. In order to justify the costs of hosting major sporting events, it is often claimed that these events attract large numbers of wealthy foreign visitors and can be engines of economic growth after the event. The 2014 FIFA (Fédération Internationale de Football Association) World Cup and 2016 Summer Olympics were no exception. Both of these events took place in Brazil. Leading up to the World Cup, the Brazilian Ministry of Sports forecast that the event would be worth no less than $70 billion to the Brazilian economy and would attract 600,000 tourists to Brazil (Rapoza, 2011). Such claims were probably necessary to justify the extraordinary expense to host the event. The Ministry of Sports reported that stadium construction costs alone totaled $3.6 billion (Manfred, 2014). FIFA concedes that the overall cost of the event was $15 billion, though the organization contributed $2 billion towards operational costs (FIFA, 2017).

Similarly, the 2016 Summer Olympics were an expensive affair that promised a large economic windfall, at least in part as a result of a deluge of tourists. According to Prada (2016),

> at least 500,000 foreign visitors arrived in Brazil to attend the Olympics in Rio de Janeiro, the government said on Friday, citing recent immigration figures that met a forecast made well before the Games. According to data compiled by federal police at immigration points and released to Reuters by the tourism ministry, a total of 572,961 foreigners entered Brazil between Jul. 1 and Aug. 15.

The total impact of the Olympic Games on the Brazilian economy was estimated to be as high as $51 billion, while the cost of the event, at $14.4 billion, was similar to that of the World Cup two years earlier (De Nicola, 2009). This chapter proposes using Brazilian government tourism data to estimate the economic impact of these two tournaments on Brazil's economy.

BACKGROUND

The need to accurately measure the economic impact of sports mega-events has assumed greater importance in the past several decades. In an age where economic inequality has become more apparent and oppressive, government budgets properly receive greater scrutiny to ensure the allocation of public funds do not exacerbate social inequities. As noted in the introduction, event expenses have escalated and, predictably, interest in hosting has diminished. The International Olympic Committee (IOC) and FIFA have responded through moderating demands and refocusing their charters (IOC, 2020). Certain groups disproportionately benefit from hosting, and they continue to spearhead efforts to attract hallmark events. Claims of financial windfalls to the social whole remain central to those efforts. Numerous economists – such as Baade and Matheson (2004, 2016) and Zimbalist (2015) – have debunked the assertion that mega-event economic benefits eclipse the economic costs. Undeterred, hosting advocates for sports mega-events continue to claim that cost-benefit analysis provides a rationale if benefits are more comprehensively defined to include all manner of legacies (Gratton and Preuss, 2008). Tourist legacies from the event represent an important touchstone for the revamped and expanded benefits strategy.

Scholars have been evaluating the immediate and long-term economic impact of mega-events on tourism for decades. The results vary; but, with few exceptions, the economic impact has been negligible. On the positive side of the continuum, Kang and Perdue (1994) concluded that the 1998 Summer Olympic Games in Seoul, South Korea, created a tourist legacy valued at $1.3 billion. According to Kang and Perdue, the tourism impact realized was greatest the year after the games and eroded thereafter. On the other extreme, Teigland (1999) opined that the tourism impact from the 1994 Winter Olympic Games in Lillehammer, Norway, failed to meet expectations. In fact, 40 percent of the full-service hotels built to accommodate the Games went bankrupt. Allmers and Maennig (2009) estimated that the impact on tourism from two European-hosted World Cups (France 1998 and Germany 2006) failed to contribute much, if anything, to the event hosts. More specifically, they could not identify any economic effect on tourism for the 1998 World Cup, and, in fact, noted that France had 925,000 fewer tourists in June of 1998 compared to June 1997. Allmers and Maennig estimated 700,000 additional overnight stays and $900 million in incremental tourist income for the 2006 World Cup in Germany. However, they opined that fewer than 100,000 of those tourists staying in hotels were visiting Germany for the World Cup.

More recent studies generally draw similar conclusions regarding the absence of a tourism effect attributable to sports mega-events. Baade and Matheson (2016) found that the number of international tourists to the UK fell from 6,568,000 in July and August 2011 to 6,174,000 during the 2012 Olympic Games. Similarly, compared to August 2007, Beijing, China, experienced a reduction of 30 percent in international visitors and a 39 percent reduction in hotel occupancy during the 2008 Summer Olympic Games. One recent analysis noted an important noteworthy exception regarding a tourism legacy inspired by a hallmark event. Zimbalist (2015) observed that the 1992 Summer Olympic Games helped "put Barcelona on the map." Following the Games, Barcelona became the 9th most popular European tourist destination in 2010, compared to 13th in 1990.

Fourie and Santana-Gallego (2011) use a gravity model of annual bilateral tourism for 200 countries between 1995 and 2006 to study the tourism impact of major international sports mega-events. On average, an international mega-event is associated with an increase in tourist arrivals by roughly 8 percent in the year of the event, but the results vary widely. The Summer Olympics, FIFA World Cup, and Cricket World Cup had the largest positive impacts on tourism, while the Winter Olympics and Rugby World Cup were associated with reductions in annual tourist numbers.

More closely related to the study here are two papers by Du Plessis and Maennig (2011) and Peeters et al. (2014) examining monthly tourist arrivals in South Africa during the 2010 FIFA World Cup. Both studies find that the country experienced an increase in tourism during the months of the tournament; but the net increase in tourist arrivals (40,000–80,000 in Du Plessis and Maennig and 220,000 in Peeters et al.) was a fraction of that predicted by tournament organizers.

This chapter proposes to add to the scholarship by including the mega-event experience in South America using monthly foreign tourist data for Brazil between 2003 and 2019.

DATA

The Brazilian Ministério do Turismo releases monthly arrival data into Brazil and several of its states in its Anuário Estatístico (Annual Statistics). In addition, arrival data are available in aggregate and for most countries of origin. The sample frame is January 2003 to December 2019. In comparison, the sample frame in Baumann and Matheson (2018) ends in December 2015, which is prior to the 2016 Summer Olympics. One complication is that this project seeks to understand the economic impact of the 2014 FIFA World Cup and 2016 Summer Olympics, but uses foreign arrivals rather than spending data. However, measurement error is greatly reduced as data collection only involves counting the number of arrivals rather than adding up all expenditures. In addition, expenditure data are notoriously difficult to capture, particularly for large and developing countries like Brazil. This is also problematic in economic impact studies, where disentangling local from outsider spending is vital to identifying the net effect of an event.

Table 11.1 summarizes foreign arrivals into Brazil and the state of Rio de Janeiro, which is the administrative unit that contains the city of the same name. Brazilian state-level data are the smallest geographic area with monthly arrival data, but fortunately the city of Rio de Janeiro dominates its state in population and economic importance.

Table 11.1 underscores the importance of foreign travel to Brazil, which attracts an average of nearly 500,000 foreign visitors each month. The two countries with the highest average visitation to Brazil are Argentina and the United States. We also present summary statistics for Europe, which

Table 11.1　Mean arrivals into Brazil and state of Rio de Janeiro

	Arrivals into Brazil	Arrivals into state of Rio de Janeiro
Total	466,383 (168,964)	90,008 (33,444)
From Argentina	129,187 (110,728)	20,027 (13,906)
From Europe	140,017 (35,930)	34,417 (11,395)
From the United States	52,172 (12,743)	14,106 (5,245)

Note: Standard deviations in parentheses.

sends roughly the same number of tourists to Brazil as Argentina. Taken together, these three sources represent nearly 70 percent of all foreign visits to Brazil. Table 11.1 also illustrates an important feature of Brazilian state-level data from the Anuário Estatístico, where foreign visitation is counted at the state of entry. For example, Argentine visitation to Rio de Janeiro is likely understated since it does not include those that traveled to Rio by automobile and were instead counted at the state of entry.

Figure 11.1 illustrates monthly arrivals in Brazil for a subset of the data that begins in January 2010. Prior to this cutoff, total arrivals into Brazil have similar seasonal patterns and annual peaks and valleys that can be seen from 2010 and 2013 in Figure 11.1. Seasonality is an important feature of tourism data, and Brazil's summer months (December, January, and February) typically attract between two and three times as many foreign visitors compared to its winter. Because of its location in the southern hemisphere, Brazil is an intriguing location to study the impact of the FIFA World Cup and Summer Olympics as both events happen when foreign tourism is typically low.

Figure 11.1 illustrates the impact of the 2014 FIFA World Cup on foreign visitation. The summer prior to the event (December 2013 to February 2014) has low peak, indicating some time-switching behavior where tourists wait for the event rather than visiting the summer prior.

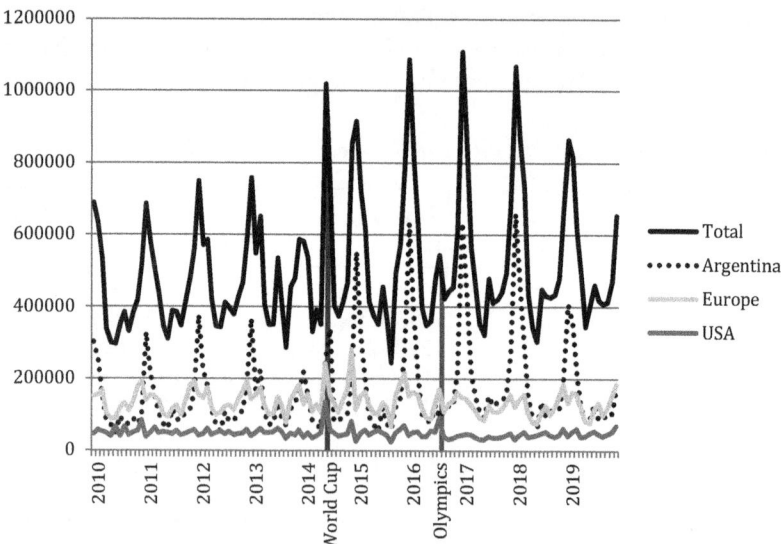

Figure 11.1   Arrivals into Brazil by origin

Foreign tourism during the 2014 FIFA World Cup is the highest up to that point. In addition, the high tourism seasons after this event have larger peaks compared to before 2014, suggesting the FIFA World Cup may have produced long-term tourism benefits. Argentina is a key driver of foreign tourism into Brazil, and the rise in tourism after the 2014 FIFA World Cup largely follows a commensurate increase in Argentine visitation. In comparison to the 2014 FIFA World Cup, foreign tourism during the 2016 Summer Olympics is considerably smaller.

Figure 11.2 presents foreign arrivals into the state of Rio de Janeiro. Recall that foreign tourism data are counted at the Brazilian state of entry, meaning that the data here are (1) predominantly arrivals by air; and (2) likely understate total foreign arrivals into Rio de Janeiro for those entering Brazil by automobile.[1] Nevertheless, we highlight arrivals into Rio de Janeiro because it is home to the Estádio do Maracanã, one of 12 host locations for the 2014 FIFA World Cup. During that event, the Maracanã hosted five matches in June and two matches in July (including the final). By comparison, Rio de Janeiro was the primary host location for the 2016 Summer Olympics, with only a small number of events held outside the city. Despite this concentration of activity, there were fewer foreign arrivals

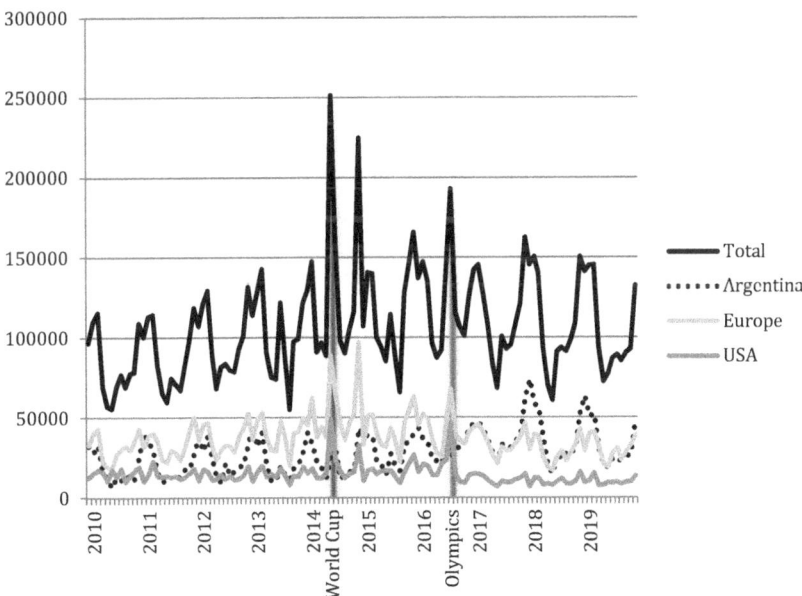

Figure 11.2   Arrivals into state of Rio de Janeiro by origin

into Rio de Janeiro during the 2016 Summer Olympics than the 2014 FIFA World Cup. Similar to the data for the entire country, the seasonal pattern of foreign arrivals into Rio de Janeiro is disrupted in the lead-up to the 2014 FIFA World Cup, and there may be spillover effects of foreign arrivals after the event.

UNIT ROOT TESTING

While Figures 11.1 and 11.2 illustrate an influx of foreign arrivals during the 2014 FIFA World Cup and the 2016 Summer Olympics, this section estimates the net effect of these events by accounting for foreign arrival patterns. Since the arrival data are a time series, it is possible that our samples are not stationary. We employ two standard tests: Augmented Dickey–Fuller using Generalized Least Squares (DF-GLS) (see Dickey and Fuller, 1979, 1981; Elliott et al., 1996) and Phillips–Perron (PP) (Phillips and Perron, 1988). Both methods require specification of the lag structure. We follow the Ng and Perron (1995) protocol, which is a sequential process that searches for the best fit of the lag structure. Starting from a maximum lag amount, it checks the fit of the last lag term. If the fit is poor (typically using a statistical significance test where $\alpha = 0.1$), then the highest lag is eliminated and a new model is estimated with one fewer lag term. This process continues until the highest remaining lag term is statistically significant. We set the maximum lag amount at $floor\left\{12\left[\frac{(T+1)}{100}\right]^{0.25}\right\}$ as suggested by Schwert (1989). Given 204 months of data, this means the Ng–Perron protocol for our data begins at 14 lags (Table 11.2). Finally, both DF-GLS and PP use linear trend terms to account for long-term changes in foreign arrivals, though the conclusions below are not significantly impacted by the decision to include a time trend.

The unit root testing produces mixed results. The DF-GLS testing suggests the data are formed with a unit root process, but the PP results firmly reject this hypothesis. The same conclusions can be drawn from the unit root testing for foreign arrivals into Rio de Janeiro shown in Table 11.3. Though not presented here, unit root testing on the differenced data rejects the existence of a unit root for all foreign arrival variables. For these reasons, the estimations that follow are presented with both differenced and undifferenced data.

Table 11.2   Stationary tests using arrivals into Brazil

	DF-GLS	PP	Number of lags
Total Arrivals	−2.223	−5.820	14
	($p > 0.10$)	($p < 0.001$)	
From Argentina	−1.516	−6.542	14
	($p > 0.10$)	($p < 0.001$)	
From Europe	−2.734	−7.980	11
	($0.05 < p < 0.10$)	($p < 0.001$)	
From the USA	−1.848	−11.58	11
	($p > 0.10$)	($p < 0.001$)	

Note: The null hypothesis in both DF-GLS and PP testing is a unit root.

Table 11.3   Stationary tests using arrivals into state of Rio de Janeiro

	DF-GLS	PP	Number of lags
Total Arrivals	−1.466	−7.322	11
	($p > 0.10$)	($p < 0.001$)	
From Argentina	−1.108	−4.610	12
	($p > 0.10$)	($p = 0.0010$)	
From Europe	−1.254	−8.598	11
	($p > 0.10$)	($p < 0.001$)	
From the USA	−1.932	−10.257	11
	($p > 0.10$)	($p < 0.001$)	

Note: The null hypothesis in both DF-GLS and PP testing is a unit root.

ESTIMATION

In order to estimate the net effect of the 2014 FIFA World Cup and the 2016 Summer Olympics on foreign visitation, we estimate the following model:

$$arrivals_t = \alpha + \beta_1 june2014_t + \beta_2 july2014_t + \beta_3 august2016_t \quad (11.1)$$
$$+ \delta_1 summers\_after\_wc_t + \gamma exchange\_rate_t$$
$$+ \sum^{m} \phi_m m_t + \sum^{y} \varphi_y y_t + \rho_t + \varepsilon_t$$

Least squares estimates Equation (11.1) for each of the six dependent variables represented by *arrivals*: total, Argentinian, European, and American arrivals into Brazil or the state of Rio de Janeiro. Because unit root testing is inconclusive, we also present differenced versions of each arrival type for a total of 16 estimations. We also estimate the model using an ARIMA protocol, but omit these results for brevity as this technique does not substantially change our findings. All aforementioned alternative specifications are available upon request.

We use β_1 and β_2 as estimates of the net effect of the 2014 FIFA World Cup, which ran from June 12 to July 14. Similarly, the estimate of β_3 produces the net effect of the 2016 Summer Olympics, held between August 5 and August 21. We include controls for each Brazilian summer after the 2014 FIFA World Cup in order to isolate additional tourism perhaps stemming from the publicity of Brazil. We also control for exchange rate effects on foreign tourism into Brazil. For total foreign tourism, we use the real broad effective exchange rate. For Argentina, Europe, and the USA, we use Argentine pesos, euros, and American dollars per Brazilian real, respectively.[2] An increase in any of these exchange rates indicates a strengthening real. The coefficients ϕ_m and φ_y control for seasonality and year-specific effects, respectively, and ρ accounts for a time trend in the data. Finally, all estimations use robust standard errors to guard against heteroskedasticity (White, 1980).

Tables 11.4 and 11.5 display least squares estimations for total foreign arrivals and its difference into Brazil. Each specification estimates a net increase of roughly 1 million foreign visitors during the 2014 FIFA World

Table 11.4   Estimation with arrivals into Brazil

	Total	Argentina	Europe	USA
June 2014	720,663	226,258	142,603	86,144
(FIFA World Cup)	($p < 0.001$)	($p < 0.001$)	($p < 0.001$)	($p < 0.001$)
July 2014	331,460	273,375	22,602	11,354
(FIFA World Cup)	($p < 0.001$)	($p < 0.001$)	($p = 0.073$)	($p = 0.010$)
August 2016	126,981	−12,969	49,934	46,401
(Rio Olympics)	($p < 0.001$)	($p = 0.661$)	($p < 0.001$)	($p < 0.001$)
Exchange Rate	−582.0	−11,933	−147,289	−28,412
	($p = 0.502$)	($p = 0.119$)	($p = 0.080$)	($p = 0.203$)
Brazilian Summer	126,981	156,304	2,504	−2,495
after World Cup	($p < 0.001$)	($p < 0.001$)	($p = 0.812$)	($p = 0.496$)
r-squared	0.9261	0.9342	0.7294	0.7043

Note: Though not presented, a time trend and monthly and annual fixed effects are included in each estimation. Full results available on request.

Table 11.5   Estimation with differenced arrivals into Brazil

	Total	Argentina	Europe	USA
June 2014 (FIFA	676,988	192,741	139,974	81,597
World Cup)	($p < 0.001$)	($p < 0.001$)	($p < 0.001$)	($p < 0.001$)
July 2014 (FIFA	290,782	235,588	22,357	7,690
World Cup)	($p < 0.001$)	($p < 0.001$)	($p = 0.015$)	($p = 0.009$)
August 2016 (Rio	82,615	−14,877	36,208	39,171
Olympics)	($p < 0.001$)	($p = 0.078$)	($p < 0.001$)	($p < 0.001$)
Exchange Rate	6,300	24,711	−163,132	1,512
	($p = 0.026$)	($p = 0.265$)	($p = 0.493$)	($p = 0.971$)
Brazilian Summer	111,090	93,859	2,113	−1,170
after World Cup	($p < 0.001$)	($p < 0.001$)	($p = 0.869$)	($p = 0.721$)
r-squared	0.7290	0.6585	0.4370	0.6235

Note: Though not presented, a time trend and monthly and annual fixed effects are included in each estimation. Full results available on request.

Cup. Most of this rise in visitation occurs during June, which corresponds to the opening "group stage" of the event where 32 teams compete. The remaining 30 percent of the net increase in visitation occurs in July, or roughly the timing of the 16-team, single elimination "knockout round" that culminates with the championship game (final) on July 14. Argentina, which shares a land border with Brazil and whose national team advanced to the final, comprises over 80 percent of the increase in July foreign visitation in either specification. These results are consistent with Baumann and Matheson (2018).

We also find that net foreign visitation to Brazil increases by between 82,615 and 126,981 during the 2016 Summer Olympics, or roughly 10 percent of the estimated net increase in foreign visitation during the 2014 FIFA World Cup. While Baumann and Matheson (2018) note that as much as one-quarter of the million increase in foreign visitation is attributable to the progress of the Argentine national team, the draw of the FIFA World Cup would still be far larger than the Summer Olympics even without Argentine visitors. In addition, we find that net Argentine visitation drops during the 2016 Summer Olympics by between 12,969 and 14,877, though the former estimate is not statistically significant. This suggests crowding-out behavior, meaning that some Argentines were dissuaded from visiting Brazil during the Olympics, perhaps due to the increased congestion of the event. Crowding-out is a prime reason why economists believe mega-events result in smaller than anticipated impacts on local economies. Even if a mega-event like the World Cup or the Olympics were to attract, say, 600,000 international visitors to Brazil, if a similar number of non-sports fans were dissuaded from visiting the country during that time period, the sporting event would be large in a gross sense but small in a net sense. But economic impact projections that counted only the sports visitors without accounting for the loss of other tourists would overstate the effect of the mega-event on the local economy by wide margins.

The estimations also show that foreign tourism during the Brazilian summers increased after the 2014 FIFA World Cup as each summer has an estimated net increase of about 120,000 visitors. The estimations that are specific to the country of origin show that Argentina is the source for much of this foreign visitation. Note that these are net effects as the estimation also includes a time trend and binary control variables for each year and month in the data set. While the estimation cannot establish a causal link between an event and future tourism, it is possible that the 2014 FIFA World Cup bolstered Brazil's reputation as a tourism destination, particularly in Argentina, long after it concluded. Based on the estimates in this chapter, Brazil experienced between 1.8 and 2 million additional (Brazilian) summer visitors in the period following the 2014 World Cup, nearly all of whom came from Argentina.

There is some evidence in the data that Brazil's post-mega-event tourist boom is dying out. Country-wide monthly international arrivals in January rose rapidly following the World Cup and peaked in January 2017 at just over 1.1 million visitors. Visitor numbers then slipped in both of the next two years, falling to just 863,000 visitors in January 2019, the lowest January total since before the 2014 World Cup. Unfortunately, it is unlikely to be possible to track future changes in tourist numbers in a meaningful way due to the chaos caused by the COVID-19 pandemic, which decimated international travel to Brazil beginning in roughly March 2020. Disentangling post-mega event trends from the disaster of the coronavirus on international travel may prove to be an impossible task moving forward.

Tables 11.6 and 11.7 present estimations for arrivals into the state of Rio de Janeiro. We estimate that net foreign visitation to Rio de Janeiro increased by over 200,000 during the 2014 FIFA World Cup, meaning Rio de Janeiro attracted roughly 20 percent of the net increase in foreign visitors to the entire country. In comparison, net foreign visitation increased by between 61,129 and 92,264 during the 2016 Summer Olympics. Despite Rio de Janeiro serving as the sole host location for the 2016 Summer Olympics and just one of 12 World Cup host cities, we estimate that net visitation to Rio for the 2014 FIFA World Cup to be about three times as large as net visitation during the 2016 Summer Olympics.

As is the case for Brazil as a whole, Rio also experienced a sustained increase in (Brazilian) summer tourism following the World Cup and the

Table 11.6   Estimation with arrivals into Rio de Janeiro

	Total	Argentina	Europe	USA
June 2014	159,153	13,600	49,891	33,526
(FIFA World Cup)	($p < 0.001$)	($p < 0.001$)	($p < 0.001$)	($p < 0.001$)
July 2014	47,633	10,393	16,611	6,739
(FIFA World Cup)	($p < 0.001$)	($p < 0.001$)	($p < 0.001$)	($p < 0.001$)
August 2016	92,264	2,916	31,762	32,046
(Rio Olympics)	($p < 0.001$)	($p = 0.152$)	($p < 0.001$)	($p < 0.001$)
Exchange Rate	93.72	−1,131	73.18	−13,572
	($p = 0.657$)	($p = 0.006$)	($p = 0.997$)	($p = 0.030$)
Brazilian Summer	21,141	10,686	3,595	−16.14
after World Cup	($p = 0.009$)	($p < 0.001$)	($p = 0.362$)	($p = 0.992$)
r-squared	0.8743	0.8919	0.7732	0.7696

Note: Though not presented, a time trend and monthly and annual fixed effects are included in each estimation. Full results available on request.

Table 11.7   Estimation with differenced arrivals into Rio de Janeiro

	Total	Argentina	Europe	USA
June 2014	165,277	15,638	52,203	32,573
(FIFA World Cup)	($p < 0.001$)	($p < 0.001$)	($p < 0.001$)	($p < 0.001$)
July 2014	54,914	13,459	18,378	6,023
(FIFA World Cup)	($p < 0.001$)	($p < 0.001$)	($p < 0.001$)	($p < 0.001$)
August 2016	61,129	−3,104	21,222	27,041
(Rio Olympics)	($p < 0.001$)	($p = 0.007$)	($p < 0.001$)	($p < 0.001$)
Exchange Rate	226.4	−429.1	−15,418	−2,023.3
	($p = 0.743$)	($p = 0.796$)	($p = 0.858$)	($p = 0.898$)
Brazilian Summer	13,634	6,811	3,549	480.4
after World Cup	($p = 0.084$)	($p = 0.005$)	($p = 0.319$)	($p = 0.730$)
r-squared	0.6367	0.6211	0.4874	0.6848

Note: Though not presented, a time trend and monthly and annual fixed effects are included in each estimation. Full results available on request.

Olympics, although on a significantly smaller scale. Over the entire post-World Cup period, summer international arrivals increased by a cumulative figure of 217,000 to 338,000 visitors. Again, as with the country as a whole, the post-World Cup boom dissipated to some extent, with summer visitor numbers to Rio peaking at roughly 225,000 in January 2015, immediately after the World Cup, a figure which has been declining since that date.

Interestingly, the number of visitors arriving from Argentina during the Summer Olympics (both into Brazil as a whole and into Rio specifically) actually fell by a statistically significant amount under one of the estimations. This is clear evidence of the crowding-out effect that has been identified in numerous academic studies as a reason why the economic impact of mega-events is lower than one might expect (Leeds, 2007; Baade et al., 2010). As noted previously, if the crowds and congestion from increased visitors from Europe and North America dissuaded Argentinians from visiting Rio during the Summer Olympics, the cost of lost Argentinian tourist spending must be subtracted from any gains realized from sport fans coming to the city from other regions.

CONCLUSIONS

This chapter analyzed the effect on tourism in Brazil resulting from hosting the 2014 FIFA World Cup and the 2016 Summer Olympic Games. The tourism impact was evaluated at the time of the event and following the event. Regarding the immediate impact on tourism, we conclude that both sports mega-events induced an increase in the number of foreign visitors to Brazil, but that the World Cup increased the number of foreign tourists by more than ten times the number for the Olympics.

In part, this may be attributable to Brazil's location and sports heritage. Soccer (football) has a much deeper tradition in Latin America than most other Olympic sports. Therefore, a Brazilian World Cup is more likely to attract visitors from neighboring countries such as Argentina and Uruguay than the Olympics. In addition, the World Cup was held in 12 cities scattered across the country, meaning that it is less likely that prospective tourists ran up against capacity constraints for tourism facilities such as hotel rooms during the World Cup.

Finally, as noted by Baumann and Matheson (2018), results may also be partially attributable, perhaps to a significant extent, to outcomes on the pitch, particularly as they relate to the performance of Argentina, one of Brazil's neighboring countries. Argentina advanced to the final of the 2014 World Cup, and it has been estimated that approximately 25 percent of the 1 million increase in foreign visitors (give or take 20 percent of that total) resided in Argentina. Still, even abstracting from the success of the Argentinian team, the evidence does support the thesis that the World Cup draws more fans than the Summer Olympic Games by a significant amount.

Our analysis supports the proposition that sports mega-events do provide something of a tourist legacy, although there is some evidence in the case of Brazil that it may have turned out to only be temporary. Annual foreign visitations increased for each of the first three years following the 2014 World Cup. Once again, however, a non-trivial amount of that additional tourism had Argentinian roots. Could it be that Argentinians, at least for a short period of time following their 2014 success, sought to relive their team's relative success? Data indicate that Argentinians traditionally have accounted for a substantial portion of foreign visitors to Brazil.

Our analysis does, however, sound a note of caution. Countries hosting the World Cup should not expect to experience results similar to Brazil's. It could happen, but that outcome may largely depend on the on-field performance of teams from populous and affluent nations bordering the host country. Qatar, are you paying attention?

NOTES

1. Foreign arrivals into the state of Rio de Janeiro may also come by boat, but in 2018 this represented only about 3.5 percent of arrivals into the state, with the rest arriving by plane.
2. European arrivals include countries such as the United Kingdom and Switzerland that do not use the euro as their currency. We test several alternative currency and country collections without any substantial changes in the results. The Brazilian real broad effective exchange rate data are from Bank of International Settlements. The peso-to-dollar exchange rate data are from the Organisation for Economic Co-operation and Development (OECD), and euro-to-dollar and real-to-dollar rates are from the G.5 series provided by the Board of Governors of the US Federal Reserve System.

REFERENCES

Allmers, S., and Maennig, W. 2009. "Economic Impacts of the FIFA Soccer World Cups in France 1998, Germany 2006, and Outlook for South Africa 2010," *Eastern Economic Journal* 35: 500–519.

Baade, R., and Matheson, V. 2004. "The Quest for the Cup: Assessing the Economic Impact of the World Cup," *Regional Studies* 38(4): 343–354.

Baade, R., and Matheson, V. 2016. "Going for the Gold: The Economics of the Olympics," *Journal of Economic Perspectives* 30(2): 201–218.

Baade, R., Baumann, R., and Matheson, V. 2010. "Slippery Slope? Assessing the Economic Impact of the 2002 Winter Olympic Games in Salt Lake City, Utah," *Région et Développement*, 31: 81–91.

Baumann, R., and Matheson, V. 2018. "Mega-Events and Tourism: The Case of Brazil," *Contemporary Economic Policy* 36(2): 292–301.

De Nicola, B. 2009. "Rio 2016: Economic Impact," *Rio Times*, October 13. http://riotimesonline.com/brazil-news/rio-business/rio-2016-economic-impact.

Dickey, D., and Fuller, W. 1979. "Distribution of the Estimators for Autoregressive Time Series with a Unit Root," *Journal of the American Statistical Association* 74: 427–431.

Dickey, D., and Fuller, W. 1981. "Likelihood Ratio Statistics for Autoregressive Time Series with a Unit Root," *Econometrica* 4(9): 1057–1072.

Du Plessis, S., and Maennig, W. 2011. "The 2010 FIFA World Cup High Frequency Data Economics: Effects on International Tourism and Awareness for South Africa," *Development Southern Africa* 28(3): 349–365.

Elliott, G., Rothenberg, T., and Stock, J. 1996. "Efficient Tests for an Autoregressive Unit Root," *Econometrica* 64: 813–836.

FIFA, "FAQ: Setting the Record Straight," http://www.fifa.com/mm/document/tournament/competition/02/36/32/63/faq_en_neutral.pdf, accessed March 16, 2017.

Fourie, J., and Santana-Gallego, M. 2011. "The Impact of Mega-sport Events on Tourist Arrivals," *Tourism Management* 32: 1364–1370.

Gratton, C., and Preuss, H. 2008. "Maximizing Olympic Impacts by Building up Legacies," *International Journal of the History of Sport* 25(14): 1922–1938.

International Olympic Committee (IOC). 2020. "Olympic Agenda 2020," https://www.olympic.org/olympic-agenda-2020, accessed May 31, 2020.

Kang, Y., and Perdue, R. 1994. "Long-Term Impact of a Mega-Event on International Tourism to the Host Country," *Journal of International Consumer Marketing* 6(3–4): 205–225.

Leeds, M. 2007. "Do Good Olympics Make Good Neighbors?" *Contemporary Economic Policy* 26(3): 460–467.

Manfred, T. 2014. "What Brazil's Brand-New $3.6-Billion World Cup Stadiums Look Like," *Business Insider*, June 9.

Ng, S., and Perron, P. 1995. "Unit Root Tests in ARMA Models with Data-Dependent Methods for the Selection of the Truncation Lag," *Journal of the American Statistical Association* 90: 268–281.

Peeters, T., Matheson, V., and Szymanski, S. 2014. "Tourism and the 2010 World Cup: Lessons for Developing Countries," *Journal of African Economies* 23(2): 290–320.

Phillips, P., and Perron, P. 1988. "Testing for Unit Root in Time Series Regression," *Biometrika* 75: 335–346.

Prada, P. 2016. "Brazil Says Foreign Tourism Met Half-Million Forecast for Games," Reuters, August 19, https://www.reuters.com/article/us-olympics-rio-tourism/brazil-says-foreign-tourism-met-half-million-forecast-for-games-idUSKCN10U23F.

Rapoza, K. 2011. "FIFA World Cup Forecast to Add $70 Billion to Brazil's Economy," *Forbes*, July 8.

Schwert, G. 1989. "Tests for Unit Roots: A Monte Carlo Investigation," *Journal of Business and Economic Statistics* 7: 147–160.

Teigland, J. 1999. "Mega-Events and Impacts on Tourism: The Predictions and Realities of the Lillehammer Olympics," *Impact Assessment and Project Appraisal* 17(4): 305–317.

White, H. 1980. "A heteroskedasticity-Consistent Covariance Matrix Estimator and a Direct Test for Heteroscedasticity," *Econometrica* 48: 817–838.

Zimbalist, A. 2015. *Circus Maximus: The Economic Gamble behind Hosting the Olympics and the World Cup*. Washington, DC: Brookings Institution.

12. The 2015 Women's World Cup and Canadian tourism

E. Frank Stephenson

1. INTRODUCTION

There is an extensive literature analyzing the economic benefits derived from hosting sports competitions or other large events. Much of that research finds little evidence of host city or country benefits (Coates and Humphreys 2008), and even events that do seem to benefit host communities generate smaller benefits than claimed by organizers or proponents (Baumann et al. 2009; Heller et al. 2018). Nonetheless, sports boosters and tourism bureaus continue to proclaim that many events have large economic impacts.

In June and July 2015, Canada hosted the seventh FIFA Women's World Cup (WWC). The 24-team tournament ran from June 6 to July 5 and consisted of 52 matches spread across six host cities (Edmonton, Moncton, Montreal, Ottawa, Vancouver, and Winnipeg). The economic effects of the WWC has been the subject of much less research than other international sports events such as the Olympic Games (Baade and Matheson 2016) and the FIFA Men's World Cup (Baade and Matheson 2004; Baumann and Matheson 2018). The notable exception is Coates (2013), which looked at the effect of hosting the WWC on exports and GDP growth on the development of professional women's soccer, and on endorsement deals for female soccer players.

Since the economic benefit of hosing a large event is attracting visitors, recent approaches to studying the effect of major sports events use granular data to examine tourist inflows. One prominent strategy is examining hotel occupancy (Lavoie and Rodríguez 2005; Depken and Stephenson 2018), which has several advantages—including being able to estimate net gains in occupancy to account for any crowding out of non-sports related travelers (Porter 1999). Another strategy is analyzing tourist inflows (Baumann and Matheson 2018) associated with hosting an international event such as the 2014 FIFA World Cup contested in Brazil. This chapter uses both hotel occupancy and tourist entry approaches to examine the tourism effects associated with Canada's hosting of the 2015 WWC.

2. HOTEL OCCUPANCY

Although daily hotel occupancy data has been used in recent studies, such as Depken and Stephenson (2018), daily data are not available for Canadian cities. However, the Ontario Ministry of Heritage, Sport, Tourism, and Culture Industries reports monthly hotel occupancy rates for various jurisdictions in Canada. This section examines the effect of the WWC on hotel occupancy in the six cities hosting WWC matches.

Figures 12.1–12.6 show 2012–2018 hotel occupancy rates for the six host cities. Hotel occupancy in all six cities is highly seasonal; occupancy in the summer months is roughly 25 percentage points higher than in the winter months. Inspecting Figures 12.1–12.6 gives little indication of a large increase in tourism in June and July 2015, the months of the WWC. Occupancy is relatively high in June and July 2015, but it is high in June and July of other years as well.

Turn now to a regression model of hotel occupancy in the six cities:

$$OCCRATE_{it} = \beta_0 + \Omega_t + \beta_1 WWCVAR_{it} + \beta_2 UNEMP_t + \beta_3 EXCHRATE_t + \varepsilon_{it}$$

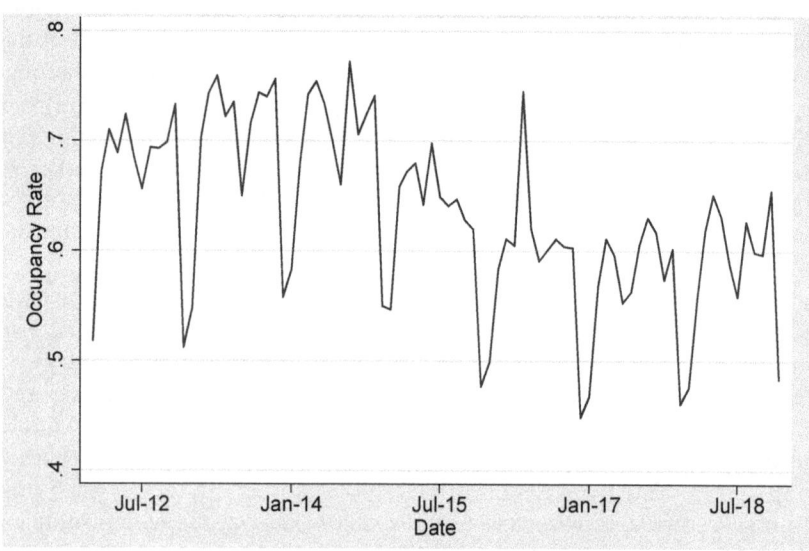

Figure 12.1   Edmonton hotel occupancy rate 2012–2018

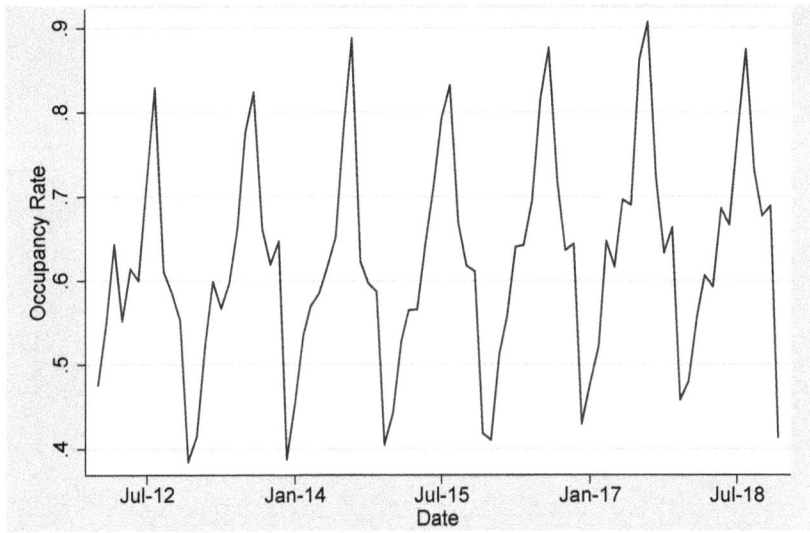

Figure 12.2   Moncton hotel occupancy rate 2012–2018

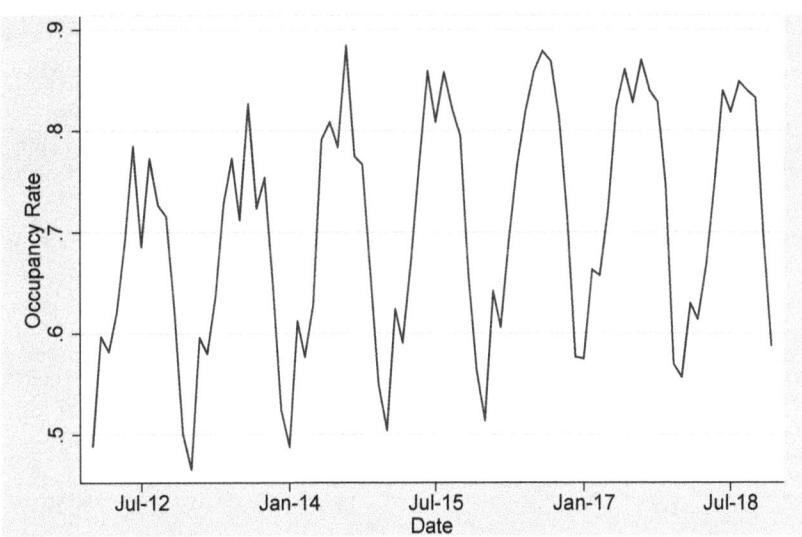

Figure 12.3   Montreal hotel occupancy rate 2012–2018

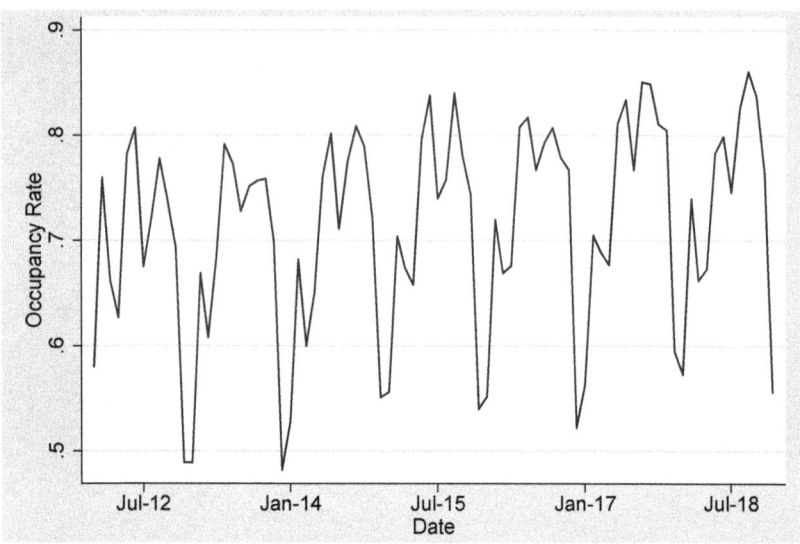

Figure 12.4   Ottawa hotel occupancy rate 2012–2018

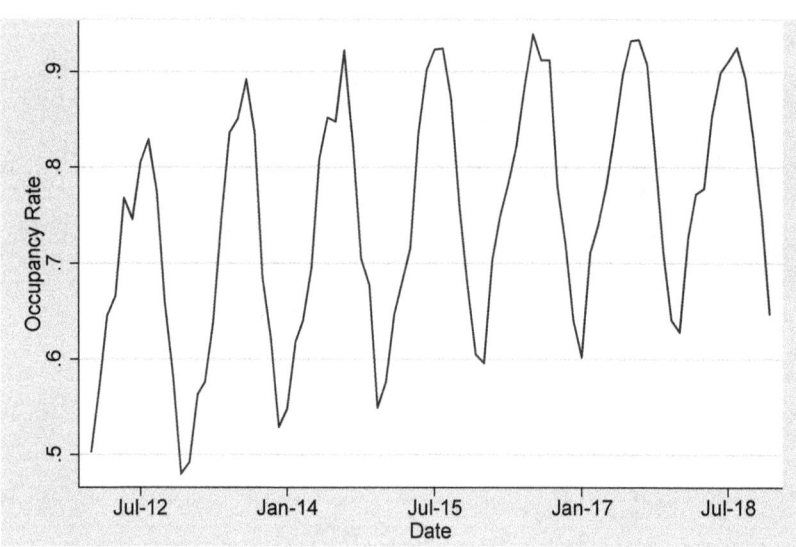

Figure 12.5   Vancouver hotel occupancy rate 2012–2018

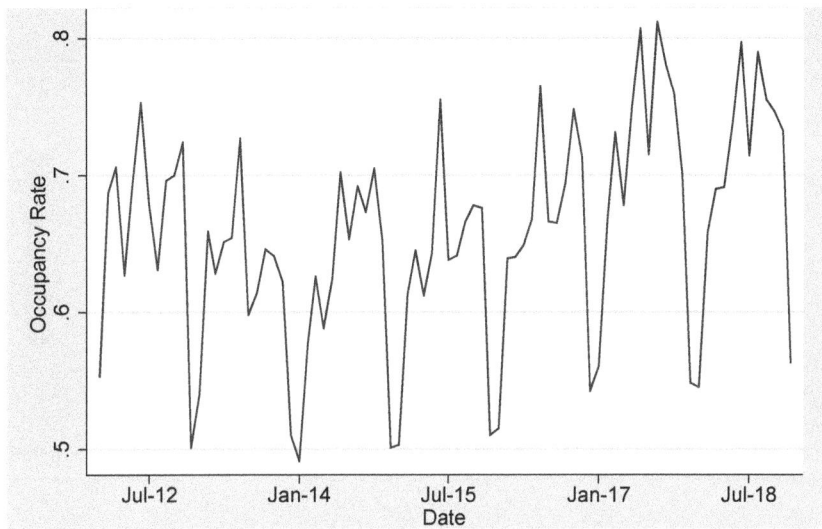

Figure 12.6   Winnipeg hotel occupancy rate 2012–2018

Here the dependent variable is the hotel occupancy rate in host city i in month t ($OCCRATE_{it}$); descriptive statistics are reported in Table 12.1. To control for the seasonal pattern evident in Figures 12.1–12.6, Ω_t is a matrix of month fixed effects; $WWCVAR_{it}$ are the variables of interest in three different specifications. In one specification, $WWCVAR_{it}$ is simply a dummy variable for the months with WWC matches (= 1 for June and July 2015 and 0 otherwise).[1] In the second specification, $WWCVAR_{it}$ is the number of matches played in city i in month t (see Table 12.2). In the group stage of the tournament, many of the matches were played as doubleheaders. For example, on June 6 both Canada vs. China and New Zealand vs. the Netherlands were played in Edmonton's Commonwealth Stadium. Since some matches were played as doubleheaders, the third specification defines $WWCVAR_{it}$ as the number of match days in city i during month t.

The other two variables, the unemployment rate and the exchange rate in a given month, are included to control for macroeconomic effects on tourism; both are expected to be negatively related to hotel occupancy. (The unemployment rate is for all people aged 15 and over and is obtained from the Federal Reserve Bank of St. Louis's FRED data site; the exchange rate index for the Canadian dollar is obtained from the Bank of Canada and takes a value of 100 in 1999.) Including the latter might be especially important because the Canadian dollar had large movements relative to other currencies over the 2012–2018 period. For example, it ranged from

Table 12.1   Descriptive statistics

	Mean	Std. Dev.	Min.	Max.
Occupancy Rate				
Edmonton	0.634	0.080	0.449	0.772
Moncton	0.623	0.125	0.385	0.907
Montreal	0.703	0.115	0.466	0.884
Ottawa	0.714	0.098	0.482	0.861
Vancouver	0.746	0.125	0.480	0.939
Winnipeg	0.659	0.078	0.491	0.812
Unemployment Rate	0.068	0.007	0.052	0.080
Exchange Rate	106.31	10.27	88.86	122.12
Total Intl Visitors (millions)	1.535	0.744	0.662	3.256
US Visitors (millions)	1.074	0.532	0.450	2.307
Other Visitors (millions)	0.462	0.219	0.194	0.989

Table 12.2   Number of matches and match days in each host city

City	June 2015		July 2015	
	Matches	Match Days	Matches	Match Days
Edmonton	9	6	2	2
Moncton	7	5		
Montreal	9	7		
Ottawa	9	6		
Vancouver	8	6	1	1
Winnipeg	7	4		

parity with the US dollar to as low as 1.40 Canadian dollars per US dollar. Lastly, Figure 12.1 shows a large spike in Edmonton's hotel occupancy rate in May 2016. In this month, the city of Fort McMurry, located north of Edmonton, experienced a catastrophic fire, and many residents were evacuated to Edmonton (Austen and Levin 2016), so a dummy variable for the McMurry fire (May 2016 = 1, 0 otherwise) is also included in the Edmonton equation.

Since the errors for the cities are likely to be correlated, the model is estimated as a seemingly unrelated regression (SUR) with 504 observations (84 for each of the six host cities) spanning 2012–2018. Estimation results are reported in Table 12.3, with a separate panel containing estimates from the three different $WWCVAR_{it}$ approaches. Breusch-Pagan tests reject the null that the residuals across cities are uncorrelated. The results are similar for all three specifications of $WWCVAR_{it}$. Edmonton and Moncton have

Table 12.3 *Seemingly unrelated regression estimation results for hotel occupancy 2012–2018*

Variable	Edmonton	Moncton	Montreal	Ottawa	Vancouver	Winnipeg
Panel A						
WWC Dummy	0.0667*	0.0494*	0.0310	0.0282	0.0327	0.0010
	(0.0374)	(0.0291)	(0.0250)	(0.0251)	(0.0245)	(0.0369)
ExchRate	0.0040***	−0.0010***	−0.0030***	−0.0014***	−0.0041***	−0.0001
	(0.0005)	(0.0004)	(0.0003)	(0.0003)	(0.0003)	(0.0005)
UnempRate	0.0179**	−0.0247***	−0.0115*	−0.0198***	−0.0304***	−0.0444***
	(0.0091)	(0.0071)	(0.0061)	(0.0061)	(0.0060)	(0.0090)
McMurryFire	0.0958***					
	(0.0313)					
R^2	0.814	0.954	0.959	0.943	0.967	0.807
Panel B						
WWC Matches	0.0086**	0.0069*	0.0033	0.0029	0.0040	−0.0006
	(0.0040)	(0.0041)	(0.0028)	(0.0028)	(0.0030)	(0.0052)
ExchRate	0.0040***	−0.0010***	−0.0030***	−0.0014***	−0.0041***	−0.0001
	(0.0005)	(0.0004)	(0.0003)	(0.0003)	(0.0003)	(0.0005)
UnempRate	0.0174*	−0.0247***	−0.0115*	−0.0198***	−0.0305***	−0.0443***
	(0.0090)	(0.0071)	(0.0061)	(0.0061)	(0.0060)	(0.0090)
McMurryFire	0.0961***					
	(0.0310)					
R^2	0.817	0.954	0.959	0.943	0.967	0.807

Table 12.3 (continued)

Variable	Edmonton	Moncton	Montreal	Ottawa	Vancouver	Winnipeg
Panel C						
WWC Match Days	0.0131**	0.0096*	0.0042	0.0044	0.0053	−0.0013
	(0.0058)	(0.0058)	(0.0036)	(0.0042)	(0.0040)	(0.0091)
ExchRate	0.0040***	−0.0010***	−0.0030***	−0.0014***	−0.0041***	−0.0001
	(0.0005)	(0.0004)	(0.0003)	(0.0003)	(0.0003)	(0.0005)
UnempRate	0.0171*	−0.0247***	−0.0115*	−0.0198***	−0.0305***	−0.0443***
	(0.0090)	(0.0071)	(0.0061)	(0.0061)	(0.0060)	(0.0090)
McMurryFire	0.0963***					
	(0.0309)					
R^2	0.818	0.954	0.959	0.943	0.967	0.807

Notes: There are 504 observations (84 per city). Parentheses contain standard errors. All models also include month fixed effects. ***, **, and * indicate coefficient estimates different from 0 at the 1%, 5%, and 10% levels, respectively.

relatively large (4.9–6.7 percentage points) and statistically significant increases in hotel occupancy. Montreal, Ottawa, and Vancouver have more modest (roughly 3 percentage points) increases that are not statistically different from zero. No effect is detected for Winnipeg. In all three specifications, the unemployment rate and exchange rate effects are, as expected, negative for five of the six cities, but their estimated effects in Edmonton are positive. The Fort McMurry fire increased Edmonton's hotel occupancy by nearly 10 percentage points in May 2016.

3. TOURIST INFLOWS

This section considers tourist inflows associated with the WWC. Statistics Canada (www.statcan.gc.ca) reports monthly data for total international visitors staying at least one night, along with breakdowns for overnight visitors from the United States and overnight visitors from other countries. This breakdown is useful because one might have expected the WWC to generate a large influx of American fans because the US borders Canada and because the US Women's National Team entered the tournament second in the FIFA rankings (and ended up winning the tournament). Figures 12.7 and 12.8 represent the total number of overnight visitors and the number of overnight visitors from the US. These figures show that overnight tourism to Canada is highly seasonal, with many more visitors in the warmer summer months than the colder winter months. The figures also show no indication of increased overnight tourism overall or specifically from the US.

Turn now to a regression model similar to the model estimated for hotel occupancy. Dickey–Fuller tests reject the presence of a unit root in the overnight visitor data, so the following model is estimated:

$$VISITORS_{it} = \alpha_0 + \Omega_t + \alpha_1 WWCVAR_{it} + \alpha_2 UNEMP_t + \alpha_3 EXCHRATE_t + \mu_{it}$$

As before, t indexes months, but here i indexes each of the three types of overnight visitor (total, US, and other), so $VISITORS_{it}$ is the number of visitors of type i in month t.[2] (Descriptive statistics for the three types of visitor are included in Table 12.1.) As before, month fixed effects (Ω_t) are included to control for systematic differences in tourist inflows across months. $WWCVAR_{it}$ are the variables of interest in two different specifications. In one specification, $WWCVAR_{it}$ is simply a dummy variable for the months with WWC matches (= 1 for June and July 2015, and 0 otherwise),[3] and in the other it is the number of WWC matches played in each month. The latter approach may more accurately capture the arrival of WWC

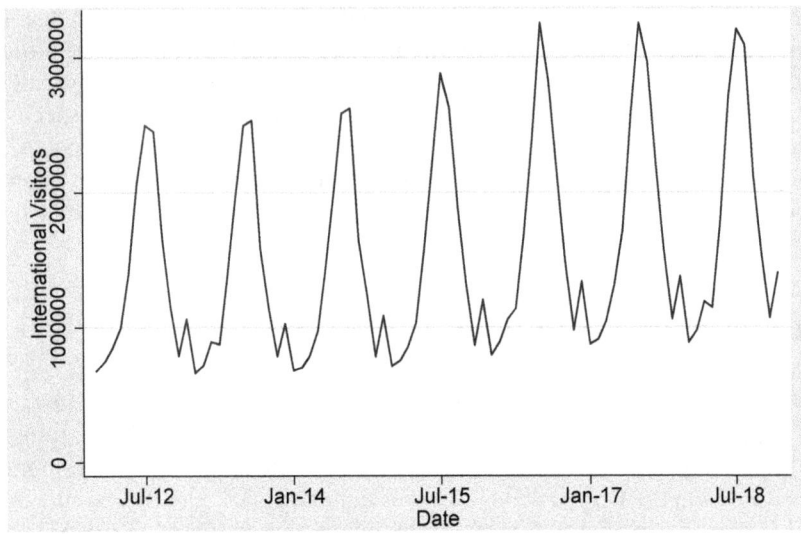

Figure 12.7   Total international overnight visitors 2012–2018

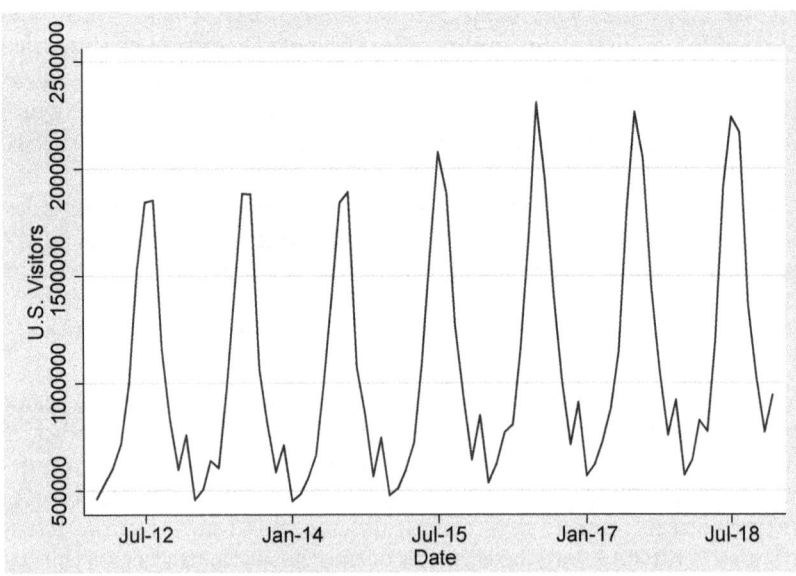

Figure 12.8   Total US overnight visitors 2012–2018

tourists since a much larger number of matches was played in June (49) than in July (3). As before, the unemployment rate and the exchange rate in a given month are included to control for macroeconomic effects on tourism.[4]

Table 12.4 International visitors to Canada and the Women's World Cup

Dependent Variable: All International Visitors		
Variable	(1)	(2)
WWC Dummy	−78,874	
	(71,619)	
WWC Matches		−2313
		(2068)
ExchRate	−10,670***	−10,538***
	(2063)	(2033)
UnempRate	−159,486***	−161,159***
	(34,654)	(34,670)

Dependent Variable: US Visitors		
Variable	(1)	(2)
WWC Dummy	−33,565	
	(47,859)	
WWC Matches		−952
		(1590)
ExchRate	−6221***	−6163***
	(1222)	(1198)
UnempRate	−84,647***	−85,377***
	(20,176)	(20,060)

Dependent Variable: Other Visitors		
Variable	(1)	(2)
WWC Dummy	−49,170	
	(24,649)	
WWC Matches		−1373
		(589)
ExchRate	−4398***	−4313***
	(946)	(939)
UnempRate	−74,314***	−75,397***
	(15,619)	(15,750)

Notes: There are 84 observations (monthly data 2012–2018). Parentheses contain Newey–West corrected standard errors. All models also include month fixed effects. ***, **, and * indicate coefficient estimates different from 0 at the 1%, 5%, and 10% levels, respectively.

Estimation is performed via the Newey–West procedure to control for serial correlation. Results are reported in Table 12.4, with the top panel containing results for total international visitors and the lower two panels reporting separate results for US visitors and other international visitors. The first column reports results obtained with WWCVAR specified as a dummy, and the second column reports results obtained with WWCVAR specified as the number of matches played in a given month. The results are consistent across all six estimations—the WWC is associated with no increase in overnight visitors. As with the hotel occupancy estimations, the exchange rate and unemployment rate are negatively related to the number of international visitors.

4. CONCLUSION

This chapter is the first examination of the hotel occupancy and tourist inflow effects associated with the FIFA Women's World Cup (WWC). The results indicate the tournament was associated with a modest increase in hotel occupancy but no increase in tourist inflows. These findings suggest that any international WWC fans traveling to Canada in 2015 simply supplanted other would-be international visitors, and that the other occupancy increases might have come from Canadian fans traveling to attend matches. Nonetheless, the Canadian Sport Tourism Alliance claims that the WWC tournament supported $493 million in economic activity.[5] However, it also reports that only 50 percent of spectators were out-of-town visitors, so much of the activity it is capturing is simply redirected spending from other local activities. In sum, the WWC generated much fan enjoyment; but, like other large sports events, the evidence that it generates large economic benefits for the host country is very weak.

NOTES

1. Since 49 of the 52 matches were played in June, the model was also estimated with the month dummy taking a value of 1 only for June. The results were similar to those reported below.
2. Estimating the model with the number of visitors in logs rather than levels yields results similar to those reported below.
3. On the premise that many of the fans attending the three matches in early July might have arrived in June, the model was also estimated with the month dummy taking a value of 1 only for June. The results were similar to those reported below.
4. It's not clear a priori that the Canadian unemployment rate should affect international visitation. Presumably some travelers to Canada come for business purposes, and those flows could be related to Canadian macroeconomic conditions. The unemployment rate

is left in the model for consistency with the hotel occupancy estimation, but omitting it has no effect on the results reported below.

5. https://resources.fifa.com/image/upload/canada-2015-economic-impact-assessment-fact-sheet-2730415.pdf?cloudid=pnt3wjce3uqp7nbfznr8.

REFERENCES

Austen, Ian, and Dan Levin. "Evacuated from Canada's wildfires but with nowhere to turn." *New York Times*, May 5, 2016.

Baade, Robert A., and Victor A. Matheson. "The quest for the cup: Assessing the economic impact of the World Cup." *Regional Studies* 38, no. 4 (2004): 343–354.

Baade, Robert A., and Victor A. Matheson. "Going for the gold: The economics of the Olympics." *Journal of Economic Perspectives* 30, no. 2 (2016): 201–218.

Baumann, Robert, and Victor Matheson. "Mega-events and tourism: The case of Brazil." *Contemporary Economic Policy* 36, no. 2 (2018): 292–301.

Baumann, Robert W., Victor A. Matheson, and Chihiro Muroi. "Bowling in Hawaii: Examining the effectiveness of sports-based tourism strategies." *Journal of Sports Economics* 10, no. 1 (2009): 107–123.

Coates, Dennis (2013). "The economic impact of the Women's World Cup," in Leeds, E.M. and Leeds, M.W. (eds), *Handbook on the Economics of Women in Sports*. Cheltenham, UK and Northampton, MA, USA: Edward Elgar Publishing, pp. 365–387.

Coates, Dennis, and Brad R. Humphreys. "Do economists reach a conclusion on subsidies for sports franchises, stadiums, and mega-events?" *Econ Journal Watch* 5, no. 3 (2008): 294–315.

Depken, Craig A., and E. Frank Stephenson. "Hotel demand before, during, and after sports events: Evidence from Charlotte, North Carolina." *Economic Inquiry* 56, no. 3 (2018): 1764–1776.

Heller, Lauren R., Victor A. Matheson, and E. Frank Stephenson. "Unconventional wisdom: Estimating the economic impact of the Democratic and Republican national political conventions." *Papers in Regional Science* 97, no. 4 (2018): 1267–1278.

Lavoie, Marc, and Gabriel Rodríguez. "The economic impact of professional teams on monthly hotel occupancy rates of Canadian cities: A Box-Jenkins approach." *Journal of Sports Economics* 6, no. 3 (2005): 314–324.

Porter, Philip (1999), "Mega-sports events as municipal investments: A critique of impact analysis," in Fizel, J., Gustafson, E., and Hadley, L. (eds), *Sports Economics: Current Research*. Westport, CT: Praeger, pp. 61–74.

13. On the impact of national team tournaments on European professional football leagues[*]

Levi Pérez

1. INTRODUCTION

1.1 Motivation

The coexistence of international and domestic competitions in world football presents interesting trade-offs and potential conflicts that deserve some attention. In particular, the practice of national teams participating in international competitions drawing on players from league clubs may generate impacts on club competitions, which are deprived of their elite players. Of course, the absence of talented players for a significant number of games is a cost presumably anticipated by clubs, but nevertheless one that could affect season planning, game strategies, and perhaps other competition issues. In any case, the overlap of national and club competitions is nowadays a relevant matter for professional football (Murphy, 2000) and an evaluation of the impacts (if any) this type of international competitions may have on professional football leagues can contribute to the debate on this issue between different football governing bodies.

Even though the role of scheduling in tournament settings has been discussed in different types of contest, as far as I know, apart from Longley (2012) and Cairney et al. (2015) – both focusing on hockey – there is almost a complete absence of any literature that examines the effects of competitions overlapping in the case of football.

1.2 A Case Study of AFCON

Specifically, this chapter aims to evaluate the impact the biennial Africa Cup of Nations (AFCON) may have on European professional football when African players leave their clubs for extended periods to compete for their country. The particular interesting issue is that, until recently,

AFCON took place in January, during the European season, and so would be expected to have some externality effect on European professional football leagues.[1]

Certainly, it can be argued that European clubs and leagues are aware of AFCON's schedule and the potential costs of signing African players. However, it is a fact that the migration of African players to Europe has accelerated significantly since the early to mid-1990s (Darby, 2001), and so their presence in European leagues has risen dramatically in recent years, as reported by Darby et al. (2007). By 2000 the number of Africans playing in Europe's 1st and 2nd Division leagues had reached 770 (Ricci, 2000). This can be explained by European leagues realizing that they could increase their total amount of talent, and hence their attractiveness to broadcasters, by signing star players from Africa. Therefore, in Europe, not only the teams but the leagues as well have incentives to compete for African talent.

1.3   The Focus of the Empirical Analysis

In line with Hoehn and Szymanski (1999), this empirical analysis focuses on determining whether elite African players' participation in AFCON might affect leagues' overall competitive balance (CB). Policy implications from findings about AFCON's impact on European leagues' CB can be then drawn according to Groot (2009), whose key concept is the natural level of CB in a sport. Groot claims that lower natural levels of CB justify greater levels of intervention by governing bodies to aid CB. In fact, sports league associations – notably those in the US but also recently UEFA in its communications with the European Commission – have used the argument for maintaining CB to gain special status under antitrust law (Groot, 2009).

2.   A BRIEF LITERATURE REVIEW ON THE RELEVANCE OF COMPETITIVE BALANCE FOR FOOTBALL LEAGUES

Competitive balance has been one of the most studied issues in sports economics over the last decades. The existing literature in the field is vast and spans different sub-areas. However, it shows conflicting predictions concerning the relevance of CB. Notwithstanding, CB has often been seen as a key component of sports leagues. An excessively unbalanced competition might have a negative impact on both demand and fan interest (Kesenne, 2006; Zimbalist, 2003), and may even lead to difficulties for leagues, such as reorganization of top clubs into separate competitions, risk of bankruptcy of poorly performing teams, etc. (Michie and Oughton, 2004).

Previous studies on CB in football reveal important differences in CB across leagues. Some studies detect no significant variation in CB (Feddersen, 2006; Groot, 2008; Koning, 2000; Szymanski, 2001), while others provide evidence of a decline in CB in some leagues (Grossens, 2006; Michie and Oughton, 2004). Many studies analyse the impact of specific factors on CB in football leagues (Buzzacchi et al., 2001; Noll, 2002; Haugen, 2008; Hall et al., 2002; Groot, 2008; Andreff and Bourg, 2006).

Finally, Palomino and Rigotti (2000) consider a multi-period situation in which the demand for sport depends on aggregate talent level, CB and the effort made by teams. However, there are no analyses of changes in CB in domestic leagues that can be attributed to the release of club players to national teams.

3.   DATA AND DESCRIPTIVE ANALYSIS

3.1   European Leagues, AFCON Editions and African Players

The present empirical analysis relies on the "big five" European leagues: the German *Fußball-Bundesliga* (the Bundesliga), the English *Premier League* (EPL), the Spanish *La Liga*, the French *Ligue 1* and the Italian *Serie A*. Evidence from the Portuguese *Primeira Liga* is also considered. Therefore, data and information on clubs and African players from all these leagues have been collected for the following AFCON editions (tournaments): Tunisia 2004, Egypt 2006, Ghana 2008, Angola 2010, Equatorial Guinea and Gabon 2012, South Africa 2013, Equatorial Guinea 2015 and Gabon 2017. The total number of African players in the considered European leagues playing any AFCON edition during the 2004–2017 period was 488. It should be noted that, on average, 90 per cent of national teams participating in any of the eight AFCON editions in the sample called up players from the six European leagues, which included 23–31 per cent of the total number of players in AFCON (mean is 26 per cent).

However, participation in AFCON is not uniform across leagues, and this disparity is particularly evident in some seasons, also indicating substantial variation over time (among seasons). The presence of African players in any AFCON edition during the sample period in the Bundesliga, La Liga, the Primeira Liga and Serie A was quite similar – between one and 16 players, depending on the league and the season, with a mean over the sample period of around eight. Nevertheless, the Premier League and Ligue1 – which account for more than 46 per cent of African

Table 13.1   AFCON players in European leagues, 2004–2017

League	2004	2006	2008	2010	2012	2013	2015	2017
Bundesliga	6	9	12	16	11	4	5	7
EPL	18	22	34	21	13	14	14	22
La Liga	5	5	8	10	3	10	10	10
Ligue 1	48	56	46	37	48	42	48	34
Primeira	1	6	10	9	5	15	12	9
Serie A	3	10	4	7	6	7	9	13
Total	81	108	114	100	86	92	98	95

players playing in the six leagues – show a completely different story. The average per-season number of AFCON players in the EPL is nearly 20, and 49 in the case of Ligue 1. Within a particular league, significant differences among AFCON editions are also observed (Table 13.1). On average, 96.75 of African players participating in any of the analysed AFCON editions came from the six examined European Leagues, representing about 26 per cent of total African players in a particular AFCON edition.

During the sample period, there were 201 teams competing in the leagues, resulting in a total of 1,740 rounds and more than 33,400 games.

3.2   CB Measures

Assuming that the teams that send more players to AFCON are relatively (dis)advantaged, the impact across teams may have potential CB implications on leagues. In order to check this, inter- and intra-seasons CB measures are calculated at the league level, including, as in Pawlowski et al. (2010), a concentration ratio (CR5) and a Herfindahl–Hirschman index (HHI) of CB.

The concentration ration (Equation 13.1) is calculated for the top five clubs (CR5) that regularly play in European competitions as the share of points won by these clubs compared to the entire league. As in Pawlowski et al. (2010), this is weighted by the concentration ratio of a perfectly balanced league:

$$CR5 = \frac{\sum_{i=1}^{N} s_i}{5/N} 100 \qquad (13.1)$$

The Herfindahl–Hirschman index of CB is calculated as the sum of the quadratic share of points won by each club in a league with N teams (Equation 13.2)

$$HHI = \frac{\sum_{i=1}^{N} S_i^2}{1/N} 100 \qquad (13.2)$$

These two measures are computed for each league: at the end of a particular season (2003–04 to 2016–17) – inter-season CB; and on a round-by-round basis – intra-season CB (for all seasons with an AFCON edition). For each of these measures, a decline in CB is reflected by an increase in the corresponding index.

Tables 13.2 and 13.3 show substantial differences among leagues' inter-season CB and intra-season CB.

From the calculations shown in Table 13.2 it seems that those seasons that overlap with AFCON generally exhibit lower CB. So, at first glance, European football seems to be negatively impacted by AFCON in terms of league CB. However, according to Table 13.3, during AFCON the (intra-season) CB of all the considered leagues improves as the two calculated indexes are, on average, lower than in those fixtures that do not overlap with AFCON. To examine these two opposite effects in more depth, a conditional (regression) analysis is performed. This will allow us to check robustness of the briefly outlined insights and to discuss them further.

Table 13.2   Mean inter-season CB measures

	Bundesliga	EPL	La Liga	Ligue 1	Serie A	Primeira
CR5						
All	138.835	145.832	143.520	135.450	145.385	143.592
	(3.655)	(5.714)	(8.261)	(6.656)	(6.566)	(4.408)
AFCON	139.092	147.292	144.495	137.446	146.719	143.827
season	(3.060)	(4.859)	(9.342)	(5.573)	(5.310)	(5.052)
No AFCON	138.495	143.885	142.220	132.788	143.608	143.278
season	(4.625)	(6.624)	(7.191)	(7.539)	(8.122)	(3.819)
HHI						
All	108.869	110.523	109.681	106.997	112.309	110.258
	(1.728)	(2.187)	(3.052)	(1.842)	(2.847)	(2.535)
AFCON	108.838	111.199	110.313	107.447	112.560	110.796
season	(1.227)	(1.870)	(3.558)	(1.406)	(2.362)	(2.798)
No AFCON	108.911	109.621	108.839	106.397	111.974	109.540
season	(2.377)	(2.415)	(2.235)	(2.301)	(3.610)	(2.161)

Note: The standard deviation is shown in parentheses.

Table 13.3　Mean intra-season CB measures

	Bundesliga	EPL	La Liga	Ligue 1	Serie A	Primeira
CR5						
All	148.721	156.011	153.214	145.189	155.158	153.794
	(16.951)	(16.091)	(16.224)	(17.963)	(13.433)	(17.908)
AFCON	143.519	149.250	147.856	137.267	150.893	149.231
fixtures	(4.449)	(3.769)	(6.340)	(5.143)	(5.866)	(8.127)
No AFCON	149.671	157.814	154.615	146.939	156.408	155.056
fixtures	(18.183)	(17.579)	(17.676)	(19.273)	(14.720)	(19.604)
HHI						
All	116.558	118.421	116.704	113.974	120.363	117.892
	(15.293)	(14.887)	(14.348)	(15.257)	(13.614)	(14.608)
AFCON	111.196	112.973	112.138	108.328	115.490	113.607
fixtures	(1.975)	(1.855)	(2.654)	(1.210)	(2.662)	(4.278)
No AFCON	117.537	119.873	117.898	115.221	121.790	119.077
fixtures	(16.427)	(16.432)	(15.849)	(16.709)	(15.127)	(16.161)

Note:　The standard deviation is shown in parentheses.

4.　OVERVIEW OF THE MAIN FINDINGS

The two previously described CB measures are regressed on a set of explanatory variables including, among others, a control for league size, a trend (season) and a dichotomous variable to account for AFCON editions (I). The *AFCON edition* variable is then replaced in the model specification by an indicator of the number of players from a particular league who are called up in AFCON (II). This variable is finally interacted with the corresponding league dummy (III). Estimates for the different model specifications are displayed in Tables 13.4 and 13.5.

As would be expected from the descriptive analysis, results from both models (I) and (II) in Table 13.4 show that (on average) those seasons with AFCON exhibit a lower CB, and that it is negatively impacted by the number of African players drawn to play AFCON. However, this does not happen in all the analysed leagues. AFCON seems to negatively affect the CB of the EPL and Spain's La Liga. The effect is not clear for the Portuguese Primeira Liga; only a statistically significant effect is found when considering the Herfindahl–Hirschman index of CB.

These findings provide initial relative evidence of AFCON impacting European leagues. Notwithstanding, these results must be interpreted with

Table 13.4   Panel data regression (end of season)

Variables	C5(I)	C5(II)	C5(III)	HHI(I)	HHI(II)	HHI(III)
AFCON *edition*	0.016**			0.008**		
AFCON *players*		0.007**			0.003**	
AFCON *players** Bundesliga			−0.010			−0.007
AFCON *players** EPL			0.018**			0.009**
AFCON *players** La Liga			0.018**			0.010**
AFCON *players** Ligue 1			−0.005			−0.002
AFCON *players** Serie A			0.010			0.004
AFCON *players** Primeira			0.012			0.010**
League dummies	YES	YES	NO	YES	YES	NO
Other controls[a]	YES	YES	YES	YES	YES	YES
R^2	0.330	0.340	0.264	0.317	0.323	0.300
N	84	84	84	84	84	84

Notes: Dependent variable is (log of) CB for each considered league at the end of a particular season (2003–04 to 2016–17).
[a] Include *league size* and *trend*; ** means statistically significant at the 5% level.

caution according to the size of estimate coefficients and the way in which CB measures are computed (at the end of a particular season). Intra-season analysis may provide stronger evidence.

Each of the two CB measures (in logs) for each league – now calculated on a round-by-round basis (over a particular season and for all seasons with an AFCON edition) – is regressed on a similar set of covariates but including a dummy variable (*AFCON fixture*) that takes the value 1 for those rounds in a domestic league that are played at the same time as AFCON (I). As previously, models (II) and (III) consider instead the number of African players drawn from the European leagues and its interaction with the leagues' variables, respectively (Table 13.5).

According to the negative sign of the estimate coefficients, it is found that (on average) CB of European leagues increases during AFCON. However, the opposite (sign) and even no effect can be found when looking at particular leagues.

Table 13.5   Panel data regression (round-by-round basis)

Variable	C5(I)	C5(II)	C5(III)	HHI(I)	HHI(II)	HHI(III)
AFCON *fixture*	−0.031**			−0.035**		
AFCON *players*		−0.011**			−0.012**	
AFCON *players* Bundesliga			−0.004			−0.012
AFCON *players* EPL			0.018**			0.013
AFCON *players* La Liga			0.024**			0.012**
AFCON *players* Ligue 1			−0.024**			−0.009
AFCON *players* Serie A			0.001			0.001
AFCON *players* Primeira			−0.003			−0.001
League dummies	YES	YES	NO	YES	YES	NO
Season dummies	YES	YES	YES	YES	YES	YES
Other controls[a]	YES	YES	YES	YES	YES	YES
R^2	0.462	0.460	0.465	0.426	0.423	0.412
N	1740	1740	1740	1740	1740	1740

Notes: Dependent variable is (log of) CB for each considered league on a round-by-round basis (seasons with AFCON editions).
[a] Include *league size* and *trend*; ** means statistically significant at the 5% level.

The observed average increase in intra-season CB could be explained by the concentration of elite African players in top teams whose total talent may converge with that of lower-quality teams during AFCON – making the competition more balanced.

Nevertheless, in Spain's La Liga, the decrease in intra-season CB during AFCON can be understood as most of African players playing for bottom teams, which are even more disadvantaged. When looking at CR5 as a CB measure a similar effect is observed for the EPL.

As mentioned, some of the analysed leagues' CB measures do not appear to be impacted by AFCON. Italian, German and Portuguese teams seem to manage their African players' absence well. As a result, no significant effect of AFCON on intra-season CB is observed for these leagues.

4.1 A Simple Robustness Test

It should be noted, however, that the variable measuring the number of AFCON players in a league could be picking up on some other relationship between AFCON players and league CB that has nothing to do with these players leaving their European teams to play in the AFCON tournament. Therefore, a basic robustness test considered here is to compare CB for each league when the AFCON tournament is and is not taking place. The CB means across seasons are calculated for each league before, after and during AFCON. Then a simple test for difference in means is performed (the test null hypothesis is that there is no difference between the three period means). As shown in Table 13.6 there is a statistically significant difference in CB during the AFCON tournament. The results remain the same when looking at each particular league.

All in all it can be concluded that, in general, European leagues' CB appears to increase during AFCON tournaments, although this impact varies by league.

5. CONCLUDING REMARKS

It has become commonplace for elite professional football players to represent their respective countries in major international competitions. However, no evidence currently exists evaluating the effect of players' absence on domestic leagues outcomes, such as league CB.

This chapter attempts to make an overarching assessment of the impact of national team tournaments on domestic leagues, based on a case study of the biennial Africa Cup of Nations (AFCON).

Table 13.6   Test for difference in CB means

Period	CR5 – mean	CR5 – std. dev.	HHI – mean	HHI – std. dev.
pre-AFCON	161.170	20.798	124.714	19.565
during-AFCON	146.675	7.424	112.410	3.448
post-AFCON	143.617	7.167	110.736	3.201
Prob > F	0.000		0.000	
Bartlett's test (Prob > chi2)	0.000		0.000	

AFCON, the continent's premier national team competition (apart from the FIFA World Cup), which removes top African players from European domestic leagues for as long as six weeks, is unique as it occurs during the European domestic season. This overlap is expected to have caused externality effects on European football leagues.

The results of the present study indicate that European leagues are differentially impacted by AFCON. In general, European leagues exhibit lower CB in those seasons in which AFCON takes place, but intra-season CB seems to increase during AFCON. However, significant differences are observed among leagues (an opposite effect and even no effect are noted in some cases) that can be explained by differential impacts across teams.

If CB has increased by teams with fewer resources being more willing to sign AFCON players, then the overall effect such players in European leagues has been to make these leagues more competitive even if, in some cases, there is a small decline in CB during AFCON tournaments.

The findings here are relevant for the debate about the overlap of national team tournaments with domestic (club) competitions and the release of players to national teams. Whether these outcomes are beneficial or harmful to European football is unclear and beyond the scope of this chapter, but this is a direction for future research.

NOTES

* This chapter is a further development of a research project entitled "The impact of the Africa Cup of Nations on European professional football", which received funding through the UEFA Research Grant Programme (2017/18 edition).
1. Notwithstanding, it should be noted that AFCON 2019 was held from 21 June to 19 July, following the decision of the Confederation of African Football (CAF) Executive Committee in July 2017 to move the tournament from January/February to June/July. It was also expanded from 16 to 24 teams. This shift to the summer months (aligning with the European league season) may reflect recognition of these externalities.

REFERENCES

Andreff, W. and Bourg, J.-F., 2006. Broadcasting rights and competition in European football. In C. Jeanrenaud and S. Kesenne (eds), *The Economics of Sport and the Media* (pp. 37–71). Cheltenham, UK and Northampton, MA, USA: Edward Elgar Publishing.
Buzzacchi, L., Szymanski, S. and Valleti, T., 2001. Static versus dynamic competitive balance: Do teams win more in Europe or in the USA? Economics Group Discussion Paper Series, No. 2001.03. London: Imperial College Management School.

Cairney, J., Joshi, D., Li, Y. and Kwan, M., 2015. The impact of the Olympics on regular season team performance in the National Hockey League. *Journal of Athletic Enhancement*, 4 (doi: 10.4172/2324-9080.1000214).

Darby, P., 2001. The new scramble for Africa: The African football labour migration to Europe. *European Sports History Review*, 3, 217–244.

Darby, P., Akindes, G. and Kirwin, M., 2007. Football academies and the migration of African football labor to Europe. *Journal of Sport and Social Issues*, 31(2), 143–161.

Feddersen, A., 2006. Economic consequences of the UEFA Champions League for national championships: The case of Germany (Hamburg Working Paper Series in Economic Policy, 01/2006). Universität Hamburg, Dep. Wirtschaftswissenschaften.

Groot, L., 2008. *Economics, Uncertainty and European Football: Trends in Competitive Balance*. Cheltenham, UK and Northampton, MA, USA: Edward Elgar Publishing.

Groot, L., 2009. Competitive balance in team sports: The scoring context, referees, and overtime. *Journal of Institutional and Theoretical Economics*, 165(3), 384–400.

Grossens, K., 2006. Competitive balance in European football: Comparison by adapting measures: National measure of seasonal imbalance and top 3. *Rivista di Diritto ed Economia dello Sport*, 2, 77–122.

Hall, S., Szymanski, S. and Zimbalist, A., 2002. Testing causality between team performance and payroll: The case of major league baseball and English soccer. *Journal of Sports Economics*, 3, 149–168.

Haugen, K., 2008. Point score systems and competitive imbalance in professional soccer. *Journal of Sports Economics*, 9, 191–210.

Hoehn, T. and Szymanski, S., 1999. The Americanization of European Football. *Economic Policy*, 14, 204–240.

Kesenne, S. 2006. The win maximization model reconsidered: Flexible talent supply and efficiency wages. *Journal of Sports Economics*, 7, 416–427.

Koning, R., 2000. Balance in competition in Dutch soccer. *The Statistician*, 49, 419–431.

Longley, N., 2012. The impact of international competitions on competitive balance in domestic leagues: The case of the National Hockey League's participation in the Winter Olympics. *International Journal of Sport Finance*, 7, 249.

Michie, J. and Oughton, C., 2004. Competitive balance in football: Trends and effects. (Research Paper 2004 No. 2). London: University of London, Football Governance Research Centre.

Murphy, P., 2000. Club or country: The struggle for supremacy in world football: Patrick Murphy interviews Graham Kelly, the ex-chief executive of the Football Association. Singer & Friedlander Football Review 1999–00 Season.

Noll, R., 2002. The economics of promotion and relegation in sports leagues: The case of English football. *Journal of Sports Economics*, 3, 169–203.

Palomino, F. and Rigotti, L., 2000. Competitive balance vs. incentives to win: A theoretical analysis of revenue sharing. Mimeo, Tilburg University.

Pawlowski, T., Breuer, C. and Hovemann, A., 2010. Top clubs' performance and the competitive situation in European domestic football competitions. *Journal of Sports Economics*, 11, 186–202.

Ricci, F., 2000. *African Football: Yearbook 2000*. Rome: ProSports.

Szymanski, S., 2001. Income inequality, competitive balance and the attractiveness of team sports: Some evidence and a natural experiment from English soccer. *Economic Journal*, 111, F69–F84.

Zimbalist, A., 2003. Reply: Competitive balance conundrums: Response to Fort and Maxcy's comment. *Journal of Sports Economics*, 4, 161–163.

14. The age-performance profile of professional and recreational marathon runners

Bernd Frick

MOTIVATION AND RESEARCH QUESTION

The relationship between age and productivity/performance has for decades been a matter of policy concern. However, given the massive demographic changes that most industrialized societies are confronted with over the next decades (United Nations 2013), this question needs to be addressed again, for example to design adequate pension policies because "policies on aging should take into account physical deterioration rates" (Fair 1994: 117).

While early studies (e.g. Breen and Spaeth 1960; Dennis 1956; Meltzer 1949; Zuckerman 1967) have used rather small samples of either blue-collar workers or researchers to identify the age-performance gradient, more recent studies are based on large samples with detailed information on homogeneous groups of workers such as American farmers (Tauer 1995), Belgian, Canadian, and Dutch manufacturing workers (Cataldi et al. 2011; Dostie 2011; Lallemand and Rycx 2009; van Ours and Stoeldraijer 2011), and German automobile workers (Börsch-Supan and Weiss 2016). Moreover, particular groups of either artists (e.g. British novelists [Crozier 1999] and American contemporary painters [Galenson and Weinberg 2000]) or American physicists and earth scientists (Levin and Stephan 1991), psychologists (Horner et al. 1986), chemists, geologists, mathematicians, and sociologists (Cole 1979), and economists (Oster and Hamermesh 1998) as well as Australian judges (Smyth and Bhattacharya 2003) have been studied to identify an occupation-specific age–performance relationship.[1]

Recently, an increasing number of studies have used sports data to identify physical deterioration rates. These include chess (Bertoni et al. 2015; Fair 2007), auto racing (Castelluci et al. 2011), swimming (Bongard et al. 2007; Rubin et al. 2013), rowing (Baker et al. 2010), cycling (Ransdell et al. 2009), weightlifting (Huebner et al. 2019), triathlon (Sowell and Mounts 2005), baseball (Fair 2008) and, in particular, long-distance running

(Connick et al. 2015; Fair 1994; Fair and Kaplan 2018; Filippin and van Ours 2015; Hunter et al. 2011; Lara et al. 2014; Lepers and Cattagni 2012; Leyk et al. 2010; Lehto 2016; van Ours 2009). However, none of these latter studies combined data on recreational and elite runners on the one hand, and data on recreational runners from different continents on the other. Thus, my analysis extends the available literature insofar as it is based on 6 million observations from Germany and the US over a ten-year period, and 5,000 male and female elite runners over a period of nearly 50 years.

DATA

In this study, I use three rather large data sets to identify the age-performance profile of recreational as well as elite marathon runners. The first data set includes the finish times of 264,647 German men completing 662,144 marathons and 77,630 German women completing 169,587 marathons (yielding a total sample of 831,731 finishes) in the years 2002–2013.[2] The second data set includes 5,000,405 marathon finishes by mostly American runners in the years 1996–2013 and was initially used by Allen et al. (2017) to analyze bunching of finishing times at reference points (e.g. a four-hour marathon).[3] The third data set includes the top 200 marathon performances by male and female runners in each year from 1973 (the first in which women were officially allowed to compete in a marathon) to 2019 (compiled from www.arrs.run and www. worldathletics.org). Thus, the data set consists of 18,800 observations (47 consecutive years with 200 observations per year for male and female athletes).

Using the first two data sets, I estimate the following OLS model:[4]

$$FT = \beta_0 + \beta_1 \Sigma AGD + \beta_1 \Sigma RYD + \varepsilon \qquad (14.1)$$

where

FT: Finish time (in minutes)
AGD: Vector of age group dummies ($M/F\,19,\ M/F\,20,\ M/F\,30,\dots,M/F\,75$)
RYD: Vector of race-year dummies.

Using the third data set, I estimate the following fixed effects model:

$$FT_{ij} = \beta_0 + \beta_1 AGE_{ij} + \beta_2 AGE_{ij}^2 + \beta_3 \Sigma YD + \varepsilon \qquad (14.2)$$

where

FT_{ij}:   Finish time of runner i in year j
AGE_{ij}:   Athlete's age in respective year (plus squared term)
YD: Vector of year dummies (1973 ... 2019).

It appears from Table 14.1 that German women aged 17 to 19 are on average about 2 minutes slower than women in the reference age group (50–54). Women aged 20 to 29 are, in turn, 8 minutes faster and women aged 30 to 34 are nearly 12 minutes faster than those aged 50 to 54. The fastest times are delivered by women aged 35 to 39, who cross the finish line more than 12 minutes earlier than those in the reference group. With increasing age, finish times get slower: women aged 55 to 59 are, on average, 7 minutes slower than those in the reference group, and those aged 60 to 64 nearly 14 minutes slower. A similar picture emerges for German men: Runners aged 17 to 19 are on average about 3 minutes slower than those in the reference group (50–54 years) and those aged 35 to 39 are the fastest age group. Up to the age of 65 to 69, the physical performance of men deteriorates at the same speed as that of women. Apart from the difference between age group 30–34 and age group 35–39 (11.95 vs. 12.25 minutes), all remaining time differences are statistically significant. Thus, the findings suggest that men and women get faster until their late 40s, when their performance starts to deteriorate. Moreover, young women seem to improve their performance faster than young men, while older women seem to slow down faster than older men.

A similar picture emerges in the sample of (predominantly) American runners (Table 14.2). Women as well as men aged 17 to 19 are about 3 minutes slower than those in the respective reference group (again 50–54). Contrary to Germany, women aged 20 to 29 are particularly fast and outperform those in the reference group by more than 24 minutes. Among men, however, peak performances are observed again among those aged 35 to 39. In the US sample, all time differences between adjacent age groups (e.g. women aged 30–34 and women aged 35–39) are significantly different from each other.

Comparing the age-performance profiles of German and US women (Figure 14.1), it appears that, among American women, the effect of age on performance is much stronger than among German women. Compared to the reference age group (50–54), American women improve their performance much more at younger ages and slow down much more than German women at older ages. Thus, the age-performance profile has a more pronounced u-shape among American women.

Table 14.1 *Impact of age on the performance of German recreational marathon runners*

Dependent Variable	Finish Time	
Gender	Women	Men
Age Group 17–19	2.24**	3.29***
	(1.357)	(0.697)
Age Group 20–29	−8.13***	−6.08***
	(0.360)	(0.192)
Age Group 30–34	−11.95***	−9.32***
	(0.357)	(0.185)
Age Group 35–39	−12.25***	−10.01***
	(0.336)	(0.168)
Age Group 40–44	−9.96***	−8.57***
	(0.320)	(0.161)
Age Group 45–49	−5.99***	−5.74***
	(0.332)	(0.168)
Age Group 50–54	Reference Group	
Age Group 55–59	7.39***	6.28***
	(0.507)	(0.231)
Age Group 60–64	13.60***	14.32***
	(0.728)	(0.294)
Age Group 65–69	21.27***	23.87***
	(1.161)	(0.397)
Age Group 70–74	44.66***	37.34***
	(2.131)	(0.756)
Age Group 75–79	–	56.34***
		(1.863)
Year-Race Dummies	Included	
Constant	311.42***	249.62***
	(34.48)	(9.770)
N of observations	169,587	662,144
Adjusted R2*100	12.3	11.0

Notes: Standard errors in parentheses. $^*p < 0.10$, $^{**}p < 0.05$, $^{***}p < 0.01$.
Here and in Table 14.2 the year-race dummies control for differences in course and weather conditions. The coefficients are not reported here due to space constraints but are available on request.

*Table 14.2   Impact of age on the performance of US recreational
marathon runners*

Dependent Variable	Finish Time	
Gender	Women	Men
Age Group 17–19	−3.02***	2.69***
	(0.526)	(0.364)
Age Group 20–29	−24.33***	−12.22***
	(0.168)	(0.109)
Age Group 30–34	−23.07***	−12.70***
	(0.167)	(0.106)
Age Group 35–39	−22.74***	−13.08***
	(0.169)	(0.106)
Age Group 40–44	−19.48***	−12.15***
	(0.171)	(0.105)
Age Group 45–49	−11.23***	−7.59***
	(0.180)	(0.110)
Age Group 50–54	Reference Group	
Age Group 55–59	10.95***	10.30***
	(0.252)	(0.138)
Age Group 60–64	21.87***	22.01***
	(0.349)	(0.172)
Age Group 65–69	33.21***	37.33***
	(0.576)	(0.253)
Age Group 70–74	47.03***	55.64***
	(1.113)	(0.409)
Age Group 75–79	66.91***	74.77***
	(2.386)	(0.802)
Year-Race Dummies	Included	
Constant	274.48***	245.72***
	(5.170)	(2.878)
N of observations	1,830,064	3,148,261
*Adjusted R2*100*	24.1	19.6

Notes: Standard errors in parentheses. * $p < 0.10$, ** $p < 0.05$, *** $p < 0.01$.

Again, a similar picture emerges when comparing American and German men (Figure 14.2). While American men aged 20 to 29 are 12 minutes faster than those in the reference cohort, the respective difference for German runners is only 6 minutes. American men aged 65 to 69 are

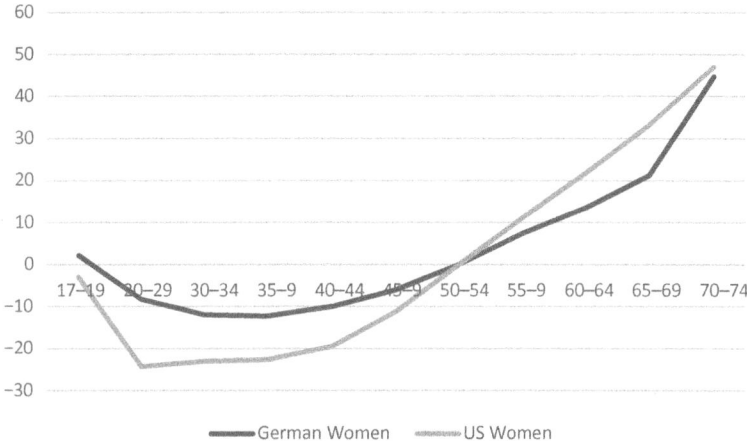

Figure 14.1 Age-performance profiles of female German und US marathon runners

about 37 minutes slower than those aged 50 to 54. This is exactly the time difference between Germans aged 54 and 59 and 70 to 74. In the higher age groups, this "five-year advantage" of German over American runners remains constant. Since the percentage shares of runners in the age groups 65–69, 70–74 and 75–79 are identical in the German and the US sample (at 1.3, 0.4 and 0.1 percent, respectively), selection effects are unlikely to drive the results. Together with the comparable finding for women, this suggests that older Germans are physically fitter than equally old Americans.

ROBUSTNESS CHECKS

Excluding "elite" and "(very) ambitious" runners from the two samples leaves the findings completely unaffected. Who are "elite" and "(very) ambitious" runners? First, I consider women faster than 2:45:00 and men faster than 2:30:00 as belonging to the "marathon elite" (in Germany in 2013 only 0.06 percent of male as well as female runners belonged in that category). Second, as "(very) ambitious", I consider women breaking 3:00:00 (0.34 percent in 2013) and 3:15 (1.48 percent in 2013). The respective figures for men (here the thresholds in 2013 are 2:45 and 3:00) are 0.55 percent and 3.36 percent, respectively. Thus, my results – which are available on request – are not driven by a small minority of exceptionally talented, motivated and well-trained elite athletes.

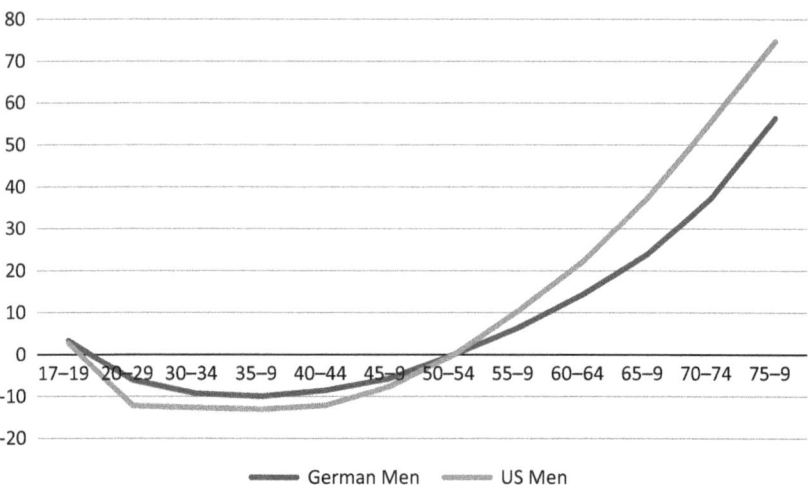

Figure 14.2   Age-performance profiles of male German und US marathon runners

Looking at the age-performance profile of elite runners (Table 14.3), a completely different picture emerges. First, and not surprisingly, elite runners are significantly younger than recreational athletes (29 vs. 37 years among women and 29 vs. 41 years among men).[5]

Second, elite runners deliver their best performance at the age of 30 (women) and 29 (men). Since elite runners typically end their careers in their late 30s, their age-performance profile is much flatter than that of recreational runners (Figure 14.3). This, too, is not surprising because the coefficient of variation of finish times for the male as well as female elite runners is very small (1.73 among the Top 200 women and 1.18 among the Top 200 men in 2019) compared to that of recreational runners (19.22 among American women and 20.81 among American men in 2013). Thus, an elite runner – male or female – will disappear from the annual Top 200 quickly as soon as his/her performance declines only marginally.[6]

CONCLUSION AND IMPLICATIONS

Summarizing, it appears that recreational marathon runners are able to stabilize their physical fitness for quite some time. Even 65- to 69-year-old athletes are, on average, able to finish a 42.195 km race in about 5.5 hours (women) or 4.5 hours (men). While this result was to be expected, the large

Table 14.3   Impact of age on the performance of elite marathon runners

Dependent Variable	Finish Time	
Gender	Women	Men
Age	-1.021^{***}	-0.415^{***}
	(0.1998)	(0.1023)
Age^2	0.0169^{***}	0.0071^{***}
	(0.0031)	(0.0015)
Year Dummies	Included	
Constant	213.6^{***}	142.1^{***}
	(3.205)	(1.349)
Number of observations	9,253	9,374
Number of athletes	2,253	2,884
Observations per athlete	1–43	1–31
R2 within	43.1	16.2
R2 between	93.9	85.9
R2 overall	88.8	73.0

Notes: Standard errors (clustered at athlete id) in parentheses. $^{*}p < 0.10$, $^{**}p < 0.05$, $^{***}p < 0.01$.
The coefficients of the year dummies are not displayed here to save space but are available on request.

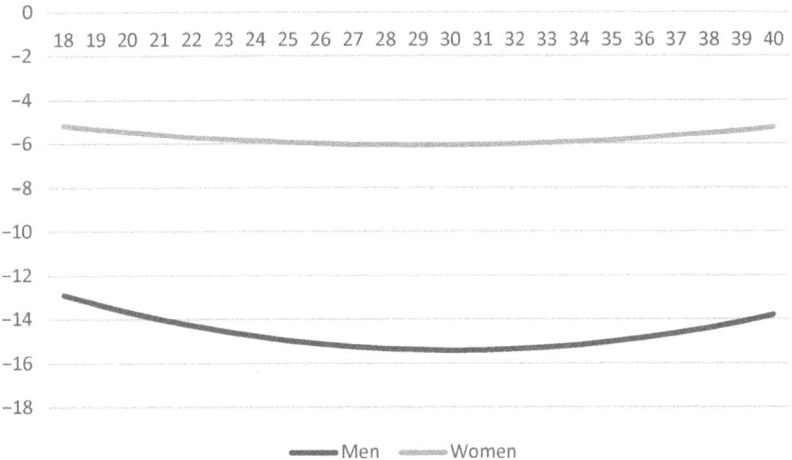

Figure 14.3   Age-performance profiles of female and male elite runners

differences in the performance of older German and US runners are rather surprising, suggesting that the former are in better shape than the latter.[7] Irrespective of these differences, it is likely "that societies have been too pessimistic about losses from aging for individuals who stay healthy and fit. Societies may have passed laws dealing with old people under incorrect assumptions" (Fair 1994: 117).

Future research clearly needs to address various selection effects that likely reinforce each other. Since the US data does not include the runners' names, it is not possible to control for unobserved heterogeneity via fixed effects estimations. However, although the German sample does include names, it is difficult to adequately control for sample attrition. It may well be that the fitter persons continue to run even at an advanced age, while those with more injuries and a lower level of fitness stop running at an earlier age. Thus, even fixed effects estimates may be biased and either over- or underestimate the impact of age on (running) performance.

NOTES

1. Furthermore, a number of meta-analyses (McEvoy and Cascio 1989; Ng and Feldman 2008; Skirbekk 2004) have been published over the years, demonstrating not only the progress that has been made but also that many of the results presented in the literature contradict each other and are, therefore, difficult to reconcile.
2. The data was until recently available at www.marathon-bestenliste.de. However, due to changes in data protection legislation, the provider has removed it from the internet. The data is now available at www.marathon-ergebnis.de.
3. I am grateful to George Wu – one of the authors of the paper – for sharing their data.
4. The major drawback of the German data is that it does not include the year of birth but only the age group of each individual. The advantage, on the other hand, is that it includes the names of the runners and, therefore, allows controlling for unobserved heterogeneity. The results of fixed effects estimations (which are available on request) are, however, virtually identical with the ones presented here.
5. The US sample includes the year of birth of each runner and allows, therefore, calculation of the exact age. Given the distribution of the runners across the age cohorts, it appears that German runners are significantly older than US runners. While 27 (women) and 16 (men) percent of the US sample are 20 to 29 years old, the respective shares in the German sample are only 12 (women) and 10 (men) percent. On the other hand, around 40 percent of the German runners (both male and female) but only 25 (women) and 30 (men) percent of the US sample are between 40 and 49 years old.
6. Frick (2011a, 2011b) demonstrates the development of the closeness (e.g. the level of competitiveness) of long- and ultra-distance running events over nearly four decades (1973 to 2009).
7. Since the percentage of Germans and Americans running at least one marathon a year is nearly identical, this result is not due to a selection effect.

REFERENCES

Allen, E.J., P.M. Dechow, D.G. Pope and G. Wu (2017): Reference-Dependent Preferences: Evidence from Marathon Runners. *Management Science*, 63, 1657–1672.
Baker, A.B. and Y.Q. Tang (2010): Aging Performance for Masters Records in Athletics, Swimming, Rowing, Cycling, Triathlon, and Weightlifting. *Experimental Aging Research*, 36, 453–477.
Bertoni, M., G. Brunello and L. Rocco (2015): Selection and the Age-Productivity Profile: Evidence from Chess Players. *Journal of Economic Behavior and Organization*, 110, 45–58.
Bongard, V., A.Y. McDermott, G.E. Dallal and E.J. Schaefer (2007): Effects of Age and Gender on Physical Performance. *Age*, 29, 77–85.
Börsch-Supan, A. and M. Weiss (2016): Productivity and Age: Evidence from Work Teams at the Assembly Line. *Journal of the Economics of Ageing*, 7, 30–43.
Breen, L.Z. and J.L. Spaeth (1960): Age and Productivity among Workers in Four Chicago Companies. *Journal of Gerontology*, 15, 68–70.
Castellucci, F., M. Padula and G. Pica (2011): The Age Productivity Gradient: Evidence from a Sample of F1 Drivers. *Labour Economics*, 18, 464–473.
Cataldi, A., S. Kampelmann and F. Rycx (2011): Productivity-Wage Gaps Among Age Groups: Does the ICT Environment Matter? *De Economist*, 159, 193–221.
Cole, S. (1979): Age and Scientific Performance. *American Journal of Sociology*, 84, 958–977.
Connick, M.J., E.M. Beckman and S.M. Tweedy (2015): Relative Age Affects Marathon Performance in Male and Female Athletes. *Journal of Sports Science and Medicine*, 14, 669–674.
Crozier, W.R. (1999): Age and Individual Differences in Artistic Productivity: Trends within a Sample of British Novelists. *Creativity Research Journal*, 12, 197–204.
Dennis, W. (1956): Age and Productivity among Scientists. *Science*, 123, 724–725.
Dostie, B. (2011): Wages, Productivity and Aging. *De Economist*, 159, 139–158.
Fair, R.C. (1994): How Fast Do Old Men Slow Down? *Review of Economics and Statistics*, 76, 103–118.
Fair, R.C. (2007): Estimated Age Effects in Athletic Events and Chess. *Experimental Aging Research*, 33, 37–57.
Fair, R.C. (2008): Estimated Age Effects in Baseball. *Journal of Quantitative Analysis in Sports*, 4(1), Article 1.
Fair, R.C. and E.H. Kaplan (2018): Estimating Age Effects in Running Events. *Review of Economics and Statistics*, 100, 704–711.
Filippin, A. and J.C. van Ours (2015): Positive Assortative Matching: Evidence from Sports Data. *Industrial Relations*, 54, 401–421.
Frick, B. (2011a): Gender Differences in Competitive Orientations: Empirical Evidence from Ultra-Marathon Running. *Journal of Sports Economics*, 12, 317–340.
Frick, B. (2011b): Gender Differences in Competitiveness: Empirical Evidence from Professional Distance Running. *Labour Economics*, 18, 389–398.
Galenson, D.W. and B.A. Weinberg (2000): Age and the Quality of Work: The Case of Modern American Painters. *Journal of Political Economy*, 108, 761–777.

Horner, K.L., J.P. Rushton and P.A. Vernon (1986): Relation between Aging and Research Productivity of Academic Psychologists. *Psychology and Aging*, 1, 319–324.

Huebner, M., D. Peltzer and A. Perperoglou (2019): Age-associated Performance Decline and Sex Differences in Olympic Weightlifting. *Medicine and Science in Sports and Exercise*, 51, 2302–2308.

Hunter, S.K., A.A. Stevens, K. Maggenis, K.W. Skelton and M. Fauth (2011): Is There a Sex Difference in the Age of Elite Marathon Runners? *Medicine and Science in Sports and Exercise*, 43, 656–664.

Lallemand, T. and F. Rycx (2009): Are Older Workers Harmful for Firm Productivity? *De Economist*, 157, 273–292.

Lara, B., J.J. Salinero and J. Del Coso (2014): The Relationship between Age and Running Time in Elite Marathoners is U-Shaped. *Age*, 36, 1003–1008.

Lehto, N. (2016): Effects of Age on Marathon Finishing Time among Male Amateur Runners in Stockholm Marathon 1979–2014. *Journal of Sport and Health Science*, 5, 349–354.

Lepers, R. and T. Cattagni (2012): Do Older Athletes Reach Limits in their Performance during Marathon Running? *Age*, 34, 773–781.

Levin, S.G. and P.E. Stephan (1991): Research Productivity over the Life Cycle: Evidence for Academic Scientists. *American Economic Review*, 81, 114–132.

Leyk, D., T. Rüther, M. Wunderlich, A. Sievert, D. Eßfeld, A. Witzki, O. Erley, G. Küchmeister, C. Piekarski and H. Löllgen (2010): Physical Performance in Middle Age and Old Age: Good News for Our Sedentary and Aging Society. *Deutsches Ärzteblatt International*, 107, 809–816.

McEvoy, G.M. and W.F. Cascio (1989): Cumulative Evidence of the Relationship between Employee Age and Job Performance. *Journal of Applied Psychology*, 74, 11–17.

Meltzer, B.N. (1949): The Productivity of Social Scientists. *American Journal of Sociology*, 55, 25–29.

Ng, T.W.H. and D.C. Feldman (2008): The Relationship of Age to Ten Dimensions of Job Performance. *Journal of Applied Psychology*, 93, 392–423.

Oster, S.M. and D.S. Hamermesh (1998): Aging and Productivity among Economists. *Review of Economics and Statistics*, 80, 154–156.

Ransdell, L.B., J. Vener and J. Huberty (2009): Masters Athletes: An Analysis of Running, Swimming and Cycling Performance by Age and Gender. *Journal of Exercise Science and Fitness*, 7, 61–73.

Rubin, R.T., S. Lin, A. Curtis, D. Auerbach and C. Win (2013): Declines in Swimming Performance with Age: A Longitudinal Study of Masters Swimming Champions. *Open Access Journal of Sports Medicine*, 4, 63–70.

Skirbekk, V. (2004): Age and Individual Productivity: A Literature Survey. *Vienna Yearbook of Population Research*, 2, 133–153.

Smyth, R. and M. Bhattacharya (2003): How Fast Do Old Judges Slow Down? A Life Cycle Study of Age and Productivity in the Federal Court of Australia. *International Review of Law and Economics*, 23, 141–164.

Sowell, C.B. and W.S. Mounts (2005): Ability, Age, and Performance: Conclusions from the Ironman Triathlon World Championship. *Journal of Sports Economics*, 6, 78–97.

Tauer, L. (1995): Age and Farmer Productivity. *Review of Agricultural Economics*, 17, 63–69.

United Nations (2013): *World Population Ageing 2013*. New York: UN Department of Economics and Social Affairs, Population Division.

Van Ours, J.C. (2009): Will You Still Need Me – When I'm 64? *De Economist*, 157, 441–460.

Van Ours, J.C. and L. Stoeldraijer (2011): Age, Wage and Productivity in Dutch Manufacturing. *De Economist*, 159, 113–137.

Zuckerman, H. (1967): Nobel Laureates in Science: Patters of Productivity, Collaboration, and Authorship. *American Sociological Review*, 32, 391–403.

15. Dimensions of sports participation: evidence from Mexico

Jaume García and María José Suárez[*]

1. INTRODUCTION

The World Health Organization has developed global recommendations for physical activity to prevent non-communicable diseases (WHO, 2010). In the case of adults, the WHO states that they should do at least 150 minutes of moderate-intensity aerobic physical activity per week, 75 minutes of vigorous-intensity physical activity, or a combination of both. Physical activity should be done in bouts of at least ten minutes. Also, muscle-strengthening activities are recommended at least twice a week. These recommendations highlight the different dimensions of physical activity: frequency, duration, type and intensity.

There are plenty of studies worldwide on the analysis of correlates of exercise or sports, although most of them focus on developed countries. Rhodes et al. (2017) survey the physical activity research, and point out that physical activity can be characterised by the FITT principles (Frequency, Intensity, Time and Type). However, not many studies have addressed the multidimensional nature of physical activity. Researchers usually pay attention to one or two dimensions, for example: the decision to participate; the total amount of time allocated; the number of times; the type of sport; and, to a lesser extent, the intensity of practice.

The aim of this chapter is to study the correlates of different dimensions of sports practice to check whether the conclusions are sensitive to the dimension considered. In particular, we analyse participation, time, frequency and intensity. The results may shed light on some of the differences in results found in the sports economics literature.

The empirical analysis is based on the Mexican National Consumer Confidence Survey (*Encuesta Nacional sobre Confianza del Consumidor*, ENCO). This database has the advantage of providing a range of information on weekly sports practice. This allows us to distinguish the following dimensions of sports: participation; total time allocated to sports per week; number of days per week of sports practice; and intensity of participation.

We focus the analysis on adults, and pool the data collected in November 2015, 2016 and 2017 in order to enlarge the sample size.

Apart from the specific information of the survey, Mexico is an interesting country for this analysis because most empirical studies use data from Europe or North America. Moreover, Mexico is among the Latin American countries with the highest obesity rates, and this incidence has been increasing in the last decades. According to WHO figures, the obesity rate in Mexico, measured as the percentage of the population with a body mass index (BMI) greater than or equal to 30 kg/m^2, has risen steadily from 19.1 per cent in 2000 to 28.4 per cent in 2016. This is more than double the world average in 2016 (13.2 per cent).[1] As the main cause of obesity is the imbalance between diet and physical activity, the study of the determinants of sports practice is important for the design of public policies aimed at fostering physical activity among the general population to increase quality of life and reduce health expenditures from obesity-related diseases.

The main contributions of this work are to expand our knowledge about the sensitivity of the results to the choice of the physical activity measure, a topic that has been little explored in the literature, and to analyse the determinants of physical activity in Mexico, a country that has received little attention in the sports economics literature. The chapter proceeds as follows. Section 2 offers an overview of the economics literature on sports participation. Section 3 describes the main characteristics of our database and the econometric models to be applied. Section 4 presents and discusses the main results. Section 5 summarizes the main conclusions.

2.   BACKGROUND

The study of the determinants of sports practice of populations has received increasing attention in sports economics, especially in developed countries. The objective of this section is to underline the heterogeneous definitions of physical activity in this literature and the empirical approaches that have been applied. We do not intend to make an exhaustive review of the different econometric methods, but offer some examples of the different types of analyses, in particular in the sports economics field.

There is a recent review by Rhodes et al. (2017) about the international research on physical activity. The authors offer an overview of physical activity levels in the world and survey the literature on the health impact of physical activity, as well as the correlates and determinants of sports practice and the interventions to promote physical activity.

Rhodes et al. (2017) consider four dimensions of physical activity: frequency, intensity, time and type; but there is an earlier stage – participation, which refers to the decision to do physical activity. This has been widely analysed in the empirical literature, either alone or jointly with some other dimensions. Given the binary nature of the variable, logit and probit models are the most used econometric specifications to determine the covariates associated with the probability of doing physical activity. This is the case of Downward et al. (2011), who estimate probit models for sports participation in Spain, including as participants those who play sports less than once a month. Rodríguez et al. (2013) study physical activity in Mexico, taking the previous week as reference, and specify a probit model too. Farrell and Shields (2002) define participation as having done sports in the past four weeks and estimate random-effects probit models using an English sample. Downward (2007) defines participation similarly to Farrell and Shields (2002), but they apply a logit model to UK data. Logit has also been used by Scheerder et al. (2005) to analyse the correlates of sports participation in Flanders (Belgium), defining participation on a yearly basis, and by Breuer et al. (2011) to study weekly sports participation in Germany.

Regarding time, the definition of this variable depends on the information available in the database: minutes a day, minutes/hours per week, among others. There is also a wide variety in the econometric specifications adopted, depending basically on the modelling of the relationship between participation and time as a single decision or as two separate decisions, which may or may not be correlated, and on assumptions made about the reasons for not participating. García et al. (2011) apply a Heckman approach to estimate the relative demand of time allocated to sports on a specific day using Spanish data. Humphreys and Ruseski (2006, 2007, 2009, 2011) and Ruseski et al. (2011) study the time allocated per week to do sports in USA, applying Tobit, Heckman or two-part models. Rodríguez et al. (2013) estimate hours allocated in the previous week by the Mexican population to exercise or sports, applying OLS. Eberth and Smith (2010) and Dawson and Downward (2011) analyse time spent on sports in the UK over a four-week period. The former specify a sample selection model, whereas the latter use OLS and count data models. Humphreys and Ruseski (2015) consider minutes doing sports in last three months using Canadian data and specifying a double-hurdle model; and Thibaut et al. (2017) study hours of sports practice over a year in Belgium by estimating a Tobit model.

There are also several economic analyses on the frequency of sports practice. Muñiz et al. (2014) study the number of times that individuals played sports in the previous four weeks using a Spanish database and applying count data models. Borgers et al. (2016) consider frequency – defined as the number of times per week – with data from Belgium and specify log-linear regression models. In other cases, frequency is defined as an ordered variable with different categories, from never to several times a week, and ordered probit or zero-inflated ordered probit are estimated. Examples of this approach are the papers by Downward et al. (2011, 2014) for Spain and EU members, respectively. However, Deelen et al. (2018) analyse Dutch data, focusing on sports participants (the lowest category of the dependent variable is 1–3 times a month) and applying ordinal regression models.

Intensity refers to the degree of effort made, which is usually measured using Metabolic Equivalent Tasks (METS) – the ratio of the exercise metabolic rate and the resting metabolic rate. Few economic studies analyse this dimension of physical activity. Meltzer and Jena (2010) estimate intensity of sports practice by US population, defining it as a continuous variable (METS). There is also one study for Spain by Garrues et al. (2017) in which intensity is defined as an ordered dependent variable from the METS.

Turning to the type of physical activity, heterogeneous definitions have been used, depending on whether they include only sports (e.g. Breuer and Wicker, 2008) or take into account other kinds of physical activity, such as walking or gardening (e.g. Scheerder et al., 2005; Rodríguez et al., 2013). Another interesting classification is whether to consider recreational physical activity or the total amount of physical activity done (Garrues et al., 2017). Most researchers focus on physical activity or sports done in leisure time; but physical activity can also be performed in other life domains – for example, walking or cycling for commuting, or as part of main daily activities (at work, around the house, etc.). Finally, there are also many studies that analyse specific sports in separate ways (e.g. Muñiz et al., 2014) or sports groups with common characteristics (Humphreys and Ruseski, 2007; García et al., 2016).

Among the works discussed above, it is worth highlighting those by Meltzer and Jena (2010), Dawson and Downward (2011) and Borgers et al. (2016). The contributions of these three papers are in line with the objective of this chapter, that is, to make a comparative analysis of the correlates of different dimensions of physical activity. Meltzer and Jena (2010) analyse participation, hours, intensity and energy expenditure, which is the product of intensity and duration. They use a database from the USA, and find that participation and intensity clearly decrease with age while the effect of this variable is not so relevant when explaining time, or even has a positive effect for the elderly when the dependent variable is measured in logs. Another difference in results is in the effect of marital status, which is only significant in time equations. Afro-American and white people exercise less intensively than Hispanics, but they allocate more time to physical activity and, in the case of white people, they are also more likely to participate than Hispanics.

Dawson and Downward (2011) estimate the number of minutes, hours and days of sports participation by the UK population, applying several econometric specifications. The results corresponding to hours and minutes are similar; but, when comparing hours with days, there are some dissimilarities that vary depending on the specification. Borgers et al. (2016) use a sample of parents with school-aged children from Flanders, and estimate separate log-linear regressions of number of times per week, total time per week and average duration of a training session. According to their results, education decreases the time per training session but does not significantly affect the other two measures. Moreover, there are no significant gender differences in the number of times per week, but women spend less time per training session and per week than men.

Summing up, the economic analysis of sports practice is very heterogeneous, and those papers that jointly analyse different dimensions of physical activity show that some conclusions may be sensitive to the definition of the dependent variable.

3.   DATA AND SPECIFICATIONS

The data used in the present study stem from Mexico's National Consumer Confidence Survey (*Encuesta Nacional sobre Confianza del Consumidor*, ENCO). This survey is a rotating panel conducted every month as a result of collaboration between Mexico's Central Bank and the National Institute of Statistics and Geography. Each year, several questions about sports practised are added to the November questionnaire through the Sports Practice and Physical Exercise Module (*Módulo de Práctica Deportiva y Ejercicio Físico*, MOPRADEF). This data set gathers information about several dimensions of physical activity. There are questions about whether an individual does sports or not, how many days in the last week, how many minutes per day and the intensity of practice (moderate versus vigorous). Therefore, we can analyse the correlates of different measures of sports practice and examine the importance of the definition of the dependent variable on the results.

There are four variables under study, which correspond to four of the dimensions discussed in the previous section: participation, time, frequency and intensity. All of them refer to the week prior to the survey. Participation is a dummy equal to one if the person did physical activity or sports in the previous week. Time is defined as the number of minutes allocated to physical activity, and is computed as the product of the number of days times minutes per day. Frequency is measured as the number of days the individual played sports in the past week. Finally, intensity is a binary variable equal to one if the individual did vigorous-intensity physical activity in the previous week and zero if the intensity was moderate.

We pooled the data from November 2015–2017 to increase the sample size, and selected a random subsample of all households to prevent anyone in the sample from appearing more than once. Moreover, we restricted the analysis to adults (18 years of age or older). The final sample size is 4299 observations, of which 1734 do sports (about 40 per cent).

Table 15.1 provides the descriptive statistics of time, frequency and intensity of practice for the subsample of participants. The average frequency of participation is over three days in the previous week, and the total time devoted to sports or physical activity is about 3.5 hours on average. Regarding intensity, around a fifth of participants do vigorous exercise.

The explanatory factors included in our models to determine the four dimensions of physical activity are personal and family characteristics, and economic variables. In particular, covariates are the following: male (a binary variable equal to one for men); age (in years); married (a dummy variable equal to one if the person is married or cohabiting); number of children in the household under 12 years of age; education (three dummies for secondary, upper secondary and higher education, respectively); individual net weekly earnings (for those with missing values in own earnings, a predicted value is imputed from the estimation of an earnings equation); and net weekly earnings of other household members. Table 15.2 provides summary statistics of all variables for the total sample and for the subsample of sports participants. The proportion of men is higher among participants. Moreover, people who do sports are younger and more educated, and both their personal earnings and other family income are higher on average. Finally, the percentage of married people and the average number of children in the subsample of participants are slightly below the corresponding figures for the total sample.

Turning to the econometric specifications, time, frequency and intensity are only observed for sports participants. The estimation of these three equations should be understood as the estimation of the second equation of a two-part model, following an approach similar to García and Suárez (2020) when analysing physical activity among children.[2] This means that

Table 15.1 Physical activity variables for the subsample of participants

	Mean	Standard deviation
Time (minutes per week)	211.84	172.10
Frequency (days per week)	3.66	1.83
Intensity (1 = vigorous)	0.21	0.41

Table 15.2   Descriptive statistics of covariates

	Total sample		Sports participants	
	Mean	St. Dev.	Mean	St. Dev.
Male	0.4343	0.4957	0.5081	0.5001
Age	43.2694	16.3495	41.3893	15.8363
Married	0.5736	0.4946	0.5444	0.4982
#Children < 12	0.6297	0.9168	0.5634	0.8815
Education				
Secondary	0.2468	0.4312	0.2059	0.4045
Upper secondary	0.1819	0.3858	0.1926	0.3945
Higher	0.3478	0.4763	0.4435	0.4969
Worker	0.6367	0.4810	0.6332	0.4821
Weekly earnings/1000	1.0645	1.3981	1.2174	1.7203
Other household income/1000	1.3494	1.8286	1.4770	2.1627

the population of reference is that of sports participants, implying that we do not care about modelling the potential different sources for the zeros corresponding to people not practising physical activity (corner solutions, infrequency or non-potential participants). Consequently, there are no sample selection problems, which makes sense because Heckman's model was introduced to deal with an observability (missing data) problem, as it happens with the estimation of a wage equation, and not as a way of dealing with a significant proportion of zeros for the dependent variable. In this context, we are not interested in estimating an equation of time, or frequency or intensity which applies for the whole population, as in the typical case of estimating a wage equation.[3] In the first part of the two-part model, the probability of sports participation is estimated; and the second part consists of the estimation of the time, frequency or intensity of practice using the subsample of sports participants.

Given that participation and intensity of practice are binary variables, we have opted for probit models against the logit model, although they are usually very similar models in practice. In these discrete choice models the unobserved index (the latent variable), interpreted as the increment in individual welfare, is assumed to depend linearly on a vector of variables X, and it also has a random component that follows a standard normal distribution in the case of the probit model. Therefore, the probability of the dependent variable (d) being equal to one is given by:

$$\Pr\left(d_i = 1\right) = \Phi(X_i'\beta) \tag{15.1}$$

where Φ stands for the standard normal cdf, β is the vector of coefficients to be estimated and the subscript i refers to the individual.

The variable time is measured as the number of minutes the individual performed sports in the past week. Thus, it is a continuous variable that takes positive values for all participants. This is why it is modelled as a normal random variable truncated at zero.[4] Therefore, the contribution to the likelihood function of each observation is the density of y given $y>0$ and is specified as:

$$f(y_i/Z_i, y_i > 0) = \frac{\phi[(y_i - z_i'\delta)/\sigma]/\sigma}{\Phi(z_i'\delta/\sigma)}, \quad y_i > 0 \qquad (15.2)$$

where ϕ stands for the standard normal density function, δ is the vector of coefficients to be estimated, σ is the standard deviation of the random component and y is the dependent variable.

Frequency is measured as the number of days that the individual did exercise or sports in the previous week. Since it is a count variable, in this case we specify a truncated Poisson model with a lower limit in zero and an upper limit in eight, i.e. the zeros are modelled in the first part of the equation of participation. The Poisson probability mass function for this particular case is as follows:

$$f(y_i/Z_i, y_i > 0) = \frac{e^{-\mu_i}\mu_i^{y_i}}{y_i! \Pr(0 < y_i < 8)}, \quad y_i = 1, 2, 3 \ldots 7 \qquad (15.3)$$

where μ is the mean and variance of y and it is assumed to depend on a vector of variables Z:

$$\mu_i = e^{z_i\delta} \qquad (15.4)$$

We have chosen the Poisson model against the negative binomial models because the evidence in Table 15.1 shows that there seems to be no overdispersion problems in our frequency variable, which could not be captured by a Poisson model (the mean is 3.66 and the sample variance 3.34). In some cases a more flexible structure is introduced using an ordered model instead of a count data model, as in García and Suárez (2020).

All these models are estimated by maximum likelihood. The covariates included in the participation equation are gender, age, marital status, children, education, labour status, and own and other household income, whereas in the second stage estimates of time, days and intensity, all the mentioned variables are included – except educational level, which is assumed to determine preferences for sports participation but not other dimensions of sports. However, it is worth noticing that education may have an indirect effect on time, frequency and intensity, through its influence on earnings.

4.   RESULTS

In this section we present and discuss the results of the estimates. Table 15.3 provides information about the four models estimated for each of the four dimensions considered: participation (probit), time (truncated regression), frequency (truncated Poisson) and intensity (probit). The table shows the coefficients and the marginal effects of each covariate on the probability of doing sports, as well as the effect on the conditional and the unconditional expected values of time, frequency or intensity, depending on the model. The marginal effects reported in Table 15.3 correspond to the average of the marginal effects for each individual in the sample. Notice that we have imposed some ad hoc constraints, like the education dummies not being explanatory variables in the equation of the second part of the two-part model.

Regarding the decision to do sports, the results are in line with previous literature,[5] in particular with Rodríguez et al. (2013), who analyse physical activity in Mexico. All the variables included, except the dummy for secondary education, have a significant effect. The probability of practising physical activity is higher among males, young and more educated individuals, whereas being married and having children under 12 living in the household reduce the likelihood of participation. Workers are also less likely to engage in physical activity, but both own and other household earnings increase participation. The factors with the greatest impact on the probability of sports practice are higher education compared to primary school or lower, gender and labour status, which change the probability by more than 10 percentage points.

The time allocated to physical activity is only determined by age and family characteristics. All of these have a negative impact, except for other household earnings, which increases the number of minutes engaged in physical activity. Married people who are sports participants do 30 minutes less physical activity than single or divorced individuals, and an additional child reduces the amount of time allocated by participants by 15 minutes. Regarding days of practice, males, workers, and young and married people engage in sports fewer days a week, and other household earnings have a positive impact on the number of days. Gender and labour status are the factors with the greatest effects on the expected number of days

Table 15.3 Coefficients and marginal effects

	1st stage		2nd stage	
	Participation	Time	Frequency	Intensity
Male				
β	0.334***	3.298	−0.127***	0.437***
∂Pr(y>0)/∂x_j	0.1242	26.2646	0.3199	0.1135
∂E(y)/∂x_j		0.9056	−0.3309	0.1135
∂E(y|y>0)/∂x_j				
Age				
β	−0.006***	−3.125***	0.005***	−0.028***
∂Pr(y>0)/∂x_j	−0.0024	−0.8490	−0.0034	−0.0071
∂E(y)/∂x_j		−0.8577	0.0132	−0.0071
∂E(y|y>0)/∂x_j				
Married				
β	−0.070*	−101.771***	−0.063*	−0.042
∂Pr(y>0)/∂x_j	−0.0259	−17.0927	−0.1627	−0.109
∂E(y)/∂x_j		−28.1605	−0.1649	−0.109
∂E(y|y>0)/∂x_j				
#Children <12				
β	−0.081***	−55.784***	−0.028	−0.024
∂Pr(y>0)/∂x_j	−0.0296	−12.5061	−0.1387	−0.0062
∂E(y)/∂x_j		−15.3094	−0.0736	−0.0062
∂E(y|y>0)/∂x_j				
Secondary ed.				
β	0.102			–
∂Pr(y>0)/∂x_j	0.0361	7.5429	0.1333	
∂E(y)/∂x_j				
∂E(y|y>0)/∂x_j				

Table 15.3 (continued)

		1st stage		2nd stage	
		Participation	Time	Frequency	Intensity
Upper sec. ed.	β	0.264***	–	–	–
	$\partial \mathrm{Pr}(y>0)/\partial x_j$	0.0963	20.0745	0.3555	
	$\partial E(y)/\partial x_j$				
	$\partial E(y/y>0)/\partial x_j$				
Higher ed.	β	0.469***	–	–	–
	$\partial \mathrm{Pr}(y>0)/\partial x_j$	0.1753	36.5019	0.6479	
	$\partial E(y)/\partial x_j$				
	$\partial E(y/y>0)/\partial x_j$				
Worker	β	-0.324***	-33.107	-0.141***	0.224**
	$\partial \mathrm{Pr}(y>0)/\partial x_j$	-0.1183	-28.7806	-0.5985	0.0563
	$\partial E(y)/\partial x_j$		-9.1636	-0.3728	0.0563
	$\partial E(y/y>0)/\partial x_j$				
Weekly earnings	β	0.067***	-5.635	-0.010	-0.003
	$\partial \mathrm{Pr}(y>0)/\partial x_j$	0.0245	4.4602	0.0798	-0.0009
	$\partial E(y)/\partial x_j$		-1.5464	-0.0263	-0.0009
	$\partial E(y/y>0)/\partial x_j$				
Other household income	β	0.024**	11.894**	0.014*	0.015
	$\partial \mathrm{Pr}(y>0)/\partial x_j$	0.0088	3.1879	0.0468	0.0039
	$\partial E(y)/\partial x_j$		3.2643	0.0356	0.0039
	$\partial E(y/y>0)/\partial x_j$				
N		4299	1734	1734	1734

Note: *** p < 0.01, ** p < 0.05, * p < 0.10.

conditioned to participation. Finally, playing sports with vigorous intensity is more likely among males, young people and workers, with gender being the variable with the highest marginal effect: men are 11 percentage points more likely to do intense exercise than women.

The results show some interesting differences between dimensions of physical activity. Males are more likely to participate, and with higher frequency and intensity, than females; but the total time allocated by them is not significantly different from that of women. The research by Humphreys and Ruseski (2009) also reveals a different effect of gender on participation and time, although in a different direction.

Age reduces the probability of doing sports, the intensity and the number of minutes allocated. However, it increases the frequency of participation, so that older people engage in sports for less time but on more days. Meltzer and Jena (2010) also obtain differences in the influence of age depending on the explained variable, but they do not study days of practice.

Being married does not significantly affect the intensity of practice, but it reduces participation, frequency and time; and children only have a negative effect on the likelihood of participation and on the minutes devoted to this activity. The results for being married are similar to those obtained by García et al. (2011) when they estimated a structural two-equation model (participation and hours) using a sample selection model. In addition, the probability of participation and the number of days are lower among workers, but they are more likely to do intense exercise. This result is in line with the hypothesis raised by Meltzer and Jena (2010) – that a higher opportunity cost of time may increase intensity of physical activity to substitute quantity by effort. Regarding economic variables, own earnings only determine participation, whereas other family earnings also have a positive influence on time and frequency.

5. CONCLUSIONS

The main objective of this chapter is to carry out a comparative analysis of the correlates of sports practice across four dimensions: participation, time, frequency and intensity. Although there is a lot of research on general sports participation and some common conclusions can be drawn, the literature is quite heterogeneous, making it difficult to compare results.

We study the probability of participation, the number of minutes and the number of days a week allocated to sports practice, as well as the degree of intensity (moderate or vigorous). In the empirical specification, we assume a two-part model: this includes one equation that explains the probability of practising physical activity for the whole population; and a second equation (time, frequency or intensity) whose population of reference is that of physical activity participants not the overall population.

The methodologies applied vary according to the nature of the dependent variables. A probit model has been specified to study the probability of participation and the probability of doing vigorous-intensity physical activity. Regarding time and frequency, a truncated linear regression model and a truncated Poisson model have been estimated for the subsample of participants, respectively.

The database used is a Mexican survey: the National Consumer Confidence Survey (*Encuesta Nacional sobre Confianza del Consumidor*), corresponding to the waves 2015–2017. The results show relevant disparities in the effect of some variables across dimensions. When comparing minutes versus days, men practise sports on fewer days, but the total time allocated does not differ from that of women. The same happens with labour status. Young people spend more time on sports, but they concentrate the activity on fewer days. Although men are more involved in sports, they do not spend more time on this activity than women. The probability of participation and the number of days allocated are lower among workers, perhaps due to time restrictions, but they do more intense exercise.

Regarding policy recommendations, if the aim of policy makers is to promote participation in sports, the measures should focus on women, workers and people with low educational levels because these are the factors with the greatest negative impact on the probability of sports participation. If the objective is to increase the amount of time engaged in sports, then measures to reconcile work and family life should be implemented, as well as others focused on older people. Finally, if the goal is to increase the intensity of sports practice, the target groups should be women, older people and non-workers.

One of the limitations of our study is that the database does not offer information about some covariates often considered in the literature, such as sports facilities. The availability of facilities or areas to practise sports near the home or the workplace may be a relevant factor. It would also be interesting to carry out this analysis with data from other countries to check whether the patterns are the same. Finally, another extension of this study would be to check the robustness of the conclusions against alternative econometric specifications.

NOTES

*   Jaume García and María José Suárez wish to acknowledge financial support from projects ECO2017-83668-R and ECO2017-86402-C2-1-R, respectively.

1. These figures were retrieved from the WHO web page: https://www.who.int/data/gho/data/indicators/indicator-details/GHO/prevalence-of-obesity-among-adults-bmi-=-30-(crude-estimate)-(-).
2. Note that, in the case of the intensity equation, we have two independent probit models. This is what is sometimes referred in the literature as a sequential model.
3. See Madden (2008) for a comparison of two-part models and sample selection models.
4. Other alternatives for the distribution of the dependent variable could be, for instance, the lognormal or the exponential distributions.
5. See Cabane and Lechner (2015) for a review.

REFERENCES

Borgers, J., Breedveld, K., Tiessen-Raaphorst, A., Thibaut, E., Vandermeerschen, H., Vos, S. and Scheerder, J. (2016). A study on the frequency of participation and time spent on sport in different organisational settings. *European Sport Management Quarterly*, 16(5), 635–654.
Breuer, C., Hallmann, K. and Wicker, P. (2011). Determinants of sport participation in different sports. *Managing Leisure*, 16, 269–286.
Breuer, C. and Wicker, P. (2008). Demographic and economic factors influencing inclusion in the German sport system: A microanalysis of the years 1985 to 2005. *European Journal of Sport and Society*, 5(1), 33–42.
Cabane, C. and Lechner, M. (2015). Physical activity of adults: A survey of correlates, determinants and effects. *Journal of Economics and Statistics*, 235(4–5), 367–402.
Dawson, P. and Downward, P. (2011). Participation, spectatorship and media coverage in sport: Some initial insights. In Andreff, W. (ed.), *Contemporary Issues in Sports Economics: Participation and Professional Team Sports*. Cheltenham, UK and Northampton, MA, USA: Edward Elgar Publishing, pp. 15–42.
Deelen, I., Ettema, D. and Kamphius, C. (2018). Time-use and environmental determinants of dropout from organized youth football and tennis. *BMC Public Health*, 18, 1022.
Downward, P. (2007). Exploring the economic choice to participate in sport: Results from the 2002 General Household Survey. *International Review of Applied Economics*, 21(5), 633–653.
Downward, P., Lera-López, F. and Rasciute, S. (2011). The zero-inflated ordered probit approach to modelling sports participation. *Economic Modelling*, 28(6), 2469–2477.
Downward, P., Lera-López, F. and Rasciute, S. (2014). The correlates of sports participation in Europe. *European Journal of Sport Science*, 14(6), 592–602.
Eberth, B. and Smith, M.D. (2010). Modelling the participation decision and duration of sporting activity in Scotland. *Economic Modelling*, 27(4), 822–834.
Farrell, L. and Shields, M.A. (2002). Investigating the economic and demographic determinants of sporting participation in England. *Journal of the Royal Statistical Society, Series A*, 165(2), 335–348.
García, J. and Suárez, M.J. (2020). Organised and non-organised after-school physical activity among children in Spain: The role of school related variables. *European Sport Management Quarterly*, 20(2), 171–188.

García, J., Lera-López, F. and Suárez, M.J. (2011). Estimation of a structural model of the determinants of the time spent on physical activity and sport: Evidence for Spain. *Journal of Sports Economics*, 12(5), 515–537.

García, J., Muñiz, C., Rodríguez, P. and Suárez, M.J. (2016). Comparative analysis of sports practice by types of activities. *International Journal of Sport Finance*, 11(4), 327–348.

Garrues, M.A., Lera-López, F. and Suárez, M.J. (2017). The correlates of physical activity among the population aged 50–70 years. *Retos*, 31, 181–187.

Humphreys, B.R. and Ruseski, J.E. (2006). *Economic determinants of participation in physical activity and sport*. IASE Working Paper No. 06–13.

Humphreys, B.R. and Ruseski, J.E. (2007). Participating in physical activity and government spending on parks and recreation. *Contemporary Economic Policy*, 25(4), 538–552.

Humphreys, B.R. and Ruseski, J.E. (2009). *The economics of participation and time spent in physical activity*. Working Paper No. 2009–09, Department of Economics, University of Alberta.

Humphreys, B.R. and Ruseski, J.E. (2011). An economic analysis of participation and time spent in physical activity. *B.E. Journal of Economic Analysis and Policy*, 11(1), article 47.

Humphreys, B.R. and Ruseski, J.E. (2015). The economic choice of participation and time spent in physical activity and sport in Canada. *International Journal of Sport Finance*, 10(2), 138–159.

Madden, D. (2008). Sample selection versus two-part models revisited: The case of female smoking and drinking. *Journal Health Economics*, 27(2), 300–307.

Meltzer, D.O. and Jena, A.B. (2010). The economics of intense exercise. *Journal of Health Economics*, 29(3), 347–352.

Muñiz, C., Rodríguez, P. and Suárez, M.J. (2014). Sports and cultural habits by gender: An application using count-data models. *Economic Modelling*, 36, 288–297.

Rhodes, R.E., Janssen, I., Bredin, S.S.D., Warburton, D.E.R. and Bauman, A. (2017). Physical activity: Health impact, prevalence, correlates and interventions. *Psychology and Health*, 32(8), 942–975.

Rodríguez, R.C., Salazar, J.J. and Cruz, A.A. (2013). Determinantes de la actividad física en Mexico. *Estudios Sociales*, 21(41), 186–209.

Ruseski, J.E., Humphreys, B.R., Hallmann, K. and Breuer, C. (2011). Family structure, time constraints, and sport participation. *European Review of Aging and Physical Activity*, 8, 57–66.

Scheerder, J., Vanreusel, B. and Taks, M. (2005). Stratification patterns of active sport involvement among adults. *International Review for the Sociology of Sport*, 40(2), 139–162.

Thibaut, E., Eakins, J., Vos, S. and Scheerder, J. (2017). Time and money expenditure in sports participation: The role of income in consuming the most practiced sports activities in Flanders. *Sport Management Review*, 20(5), 455–467.

World Health Organization. (2010). Global recommendations on physical activity for health. Retrieved from: https://www.who.int/dietphysicalactivity/publications/9789241599979/en/.

16. Exploring the role of sport as physical activity for health promotion in Europe

Paul Downward, Pamela Wicker and Simona Rasciute

1. INTRODUCTION

According to the World Health Organization, non-communicable diseases (NCDs) include cardiovascular diseases such as heart attacks and strokes, cancers, chronic respiratory diseases like chronic obstructive pulmonary disease and asthma, and diabetes (WHO 2018). They increasingly account for premature mortality globally and in Europe (Vandenberghe and Albrecht 2020; WHO 2018). Physical inactivity is a major cause of NCDs (Blair 2009; Kohl et al. 2012), and reduction of inactivity levels is now a general policy objective. Health-enhancing physical activity (HEPA) is identified as a relevant policy target (Foster 2000; Rütten et al. 2013). For adults aged 18–64, these guidelines recommend 'at least 150 minutes of moderate-intensity aerobic physical activity throughout the week or ... at least 75 minutes of vigorous-intensity aerobic physical activity throughout the week or an equivalent combination of moderate- and vigorous-intensity activity' (WHO 2011, p. 1).

Public policy emphasis on such health targets has meant that sport policy agencies have changed their traditional objective of promoting sport for its own sake to seeking to contribute to health through promoting physical activity (Bull et al. 2015; Eime et al. 2015) at both country-specific (Department for Culture Media and Sport 2015; Sport England 2016) and Europe-wide levels (European Commission 2019; Kornbeck 2013). Leaving aside the reasons why this has come to be the case, there is a clear logic to considering the role of sport as part of physical activity. For example, sport can be defined as: "all forms of physical activity which, through casual or organised participation, aim at expressing or improving physical fitness and mental well-being, forming social relationships or obtaining results in competition at all levels (Council of Europe 2001, Article 2, 1a). Moreover,

The term "physical activity" should not be mistaken with "exercise". Exercise, is a subcategory of physical activity that is planned, structured, repetitive, and purposeful in the sense that the improvement or maintenance of one or more components of physical fitness is the objective. Physical activity includes exercise as well as other activities which involve bodily movement and are done as part of playing, working, active transportation, house chores and recreational activities. (WHO n.d., para 3)

It is clear sport and physical activity are closely related as exercise and recreational activities. However, the evidence for the scale of impact of sport on health through increased physical activity levels is not clear. The literature recognises its potential based on claims of the ubiquity of the practice of sport across Europe and because it is a source of enjoyment for participants (Henderson 2009). The purpose of this chapter, therefore, is to explore the extent of sport participation across Europe relative to other forms of physical activity and walking, and to assess the role of sport in contributing to health through HEPA levels.

The chapter proceeds as follows. In the next section the theoretical frameworks that have been used to explore sport participation and physical activity are presented. Though there is some congruence between these, the literature review also identifies that empirical work on sports participation and physical activity has been relatively distinct. Section 3 outlines the methods used in the research. Section 4 presents the results, and a discussion of their implications concludes the chapter.

2. LITERATURE REVIEW

Theoretical research on sports participation in economics and management has developed from both the income–leisure trade-off model and the time allocation model of Becker (1965) (Downward and Muniz 2019). The former can be identified as a special case of the latter; and, at their core of these contributions is the idea that individuals allocate time and other resources to activities that yield individual well-being – i.e. utility (Downward et al. 2009). In the physical activity and health literature other theoretical perspectives have been adopted, drawing upon psychology through self-determination theory (Fortier et al. 2012) and the theory of planned behaviour (Beville et al. 2014) as well as more descriptive ecological frameworks that indicate that multilevel variables might influence physical activity in various domains (Bauman et al. 2012). The domains are captured in the SLOTH model (Cawley 2004, p. 118), where 'S represents time spent sleeping, L time at leisure, O time devoted to occupation (paid work), T time in transportation, and H time spent in home production (unpaid work)'. The focus on time and utility maximisation in this model indicates the congruence between sports economics and management researchers and those working in physical activity and health, as illustrated, for example, in Humphreys and Ruseski (2015).

The sport economic and management empirical literature focussing on the impacts of sport *per se* on health draws on large-scale observational data and tends to assess the impact on subjective measures of health. Analysis has been undertaken across a range of countries, such as Germany (Lechner 2009) and the UK (Downward et al. 2016). Typically, the literature identifies positive effects on health, though they might vary by sport (Oja et al. 2015).

Large-scale observational data analysis has been undertaken for the impact of physical activity generally and distinctly from sport on subjective health. For example, studies on Canadian (Humphreys et al. 2014) and Spanish data (Lera-López et al. 2017) find that physical activity, and particularly leisure-time physical activity, improves subjective health. The general physical activity literature also tends to have a broader evidence base than the sport economic and management participation literature. The former draws upon a variety of designs, including randomised controlled trials of interventions as well as observational studies and large-scale analysis of correlates, and also often focuses on specific health issues (Warburton et al. 2006). Consequently, large volumes of evidence show that physical activity can improve respiration and cardiovascular function (Sofi et al. 2008), reduce the incidence of cancer (Warburton et al. 2007) and type II diabetes (Gill and Cooper 2008), and improve depression and mental illness (Chalder et al. 2012).

Two main gaps exist in the literature. The first is that there is little evaluation of the relative contributions of sport and other physical activity to health. The comparative research across Europe is limited to descriptive incidences of engagement in sport and physical activity (Khan et al. 2012). The second is that analyses exploring the contributions of sport and physical activity to recommended HEPA guidelines do not disentangle their respective roles and look at sport only in one country (Downward and Rasciute 2015), or physical activity in specific countries (Bergman et al. 2008; Coombes et al. 2010).

The contribution of the current chapter therefore is threefold. The first is to provide Europe-wide rather than country-specific insight. The second is to examine the relative contributions of sport, other physical activity and walking to HEPA levels. The third is to provide insight into HEPA as an inherently ordered magnitude through an ordered estimator, recognising the underlying increasing duration and intensity of activity constituting HEPA thresholds. This is not the case in the literature cited above (Bergman et al. 2008; Coombes et al. 2010).

3.   METHODS

Data Source

Data are drawn from the latest Eurobarometer 88.4 (2017) wave that measures sport and physical activity in 28 EU countries. The Eurobarometer is based on multi-stage, random sampling to produce country-level representative samples. The overall sample is 28,031 respondents. After data cleaning, coding, and removal of missing values across the variables and respondents younger than 18 years and older than 64, a sample size of 15,902 observations remained.

Variables

HEPA levels

The Eurobarometer asks a series of questions about sport and physical activity. The sport questions investigate sport and exercise, meaning 'any form of physical activity which you do in a sport context or sport-related setting, such as swimming, training in a fitness centre or a sport club, running in the park'. Other physical activity is then investigated by questions about engagement in physical activity outside sport, such as 'cycling from one place to another, dancing, gardening, etc.' For both sport and physical activity, the number of weekly engagements is identified as well as the number of minutes that the activity is undertaken at a vigorous or a moderate level of intensity on these days. Additionally, respondents are asked similar questions connected with walking for at least ten minutes at a time.

Based on the responses to these questions, an ordered HEPA threshold variable (*WHO Threshold*) is calculated based on converting all minutes of activity into moderate minutes and identifying whether: an individual in an EU country does not undertake any physical activity; whether they undertake some physical activity, but of a level that is less than that recommended; and whether they undertake any physical activity that exceeds the recommended level (WHO 2011).

Covariates

Based on the variables used to calculate HEPA levels, binary covariates are created that identify whether an individual undertakes sport only or undertakes other physical activity only; that they walk only or that they undertake sport and physical activity (other than walking); or that they undertake walking with sport and physical activity.

Confounding variables
To control for confounding influences on the amount of sport and physical activity undertaken, the respondent's gender, age (and its squared term to allow for non-linear impacts), marital status and household composition – including the number of individuals living in the respondent's household – are included in the analysis. Economic influences on physical activity are controlled for by including the respondent's difficulty paying bills, as well as the type of community they live in. Such factors are widely recognised as influencing sport and physical activity (Downward et al. 2014). Table 16.1 provides a definition of each variable and relevant descriptive statistics.

Empirical Analysis

To model the relative influence of sport, other physical activity and walking on HEPA levels, a cross-sectional ordered probit regression analysis is conducted. The variable *WHO Threshold* is regressed on a set of covariates that measure the individual's sole engagement in sport, other physical activity or walking, as well as combinations of these. Key confounding variables identified from the literature are included in the analysis. As the coefficients from ordered probit regressions at best indicate the direction of association between covariates and the highest ordered category of the dependent variable, marginal effects are reported. Analysis is undertaken on the whole sample as well as for males and females separately as the literature indicates distinct patterns in sport and physical activity by gender (Downward and Rasciute 2015, 2016).

4.   RESULTS

Tables 16.1 and 16.2 provide important context for the regression analysis. The mean values of the sport and physical activity variables indicate the sample proportions associated with this activity. The data indicate that sport by itself is a small contributor to overall physical activity. Only 3 per cent of the population undertake sport as a sole form of physical activity, and only 21 per cent of the population take part in sport and other physical activity, but not walking. Moreover, physical activity other than walking is also undertaken by only 10 per cent of the population. The results show that the main source of physical activity is walking only, which is the case for 53 per cent of the population and when walking

Table 16.1   Variable definitions and descriptive statistics (n = 15,902)

Variable	Description	Mean	SD	Min.	Max.
WHO Threshold	Category of activity (3=above threshold, i.e. >150 mins; 2=below threshold, i.e. >0 mins <150mins; 1=no exercise, i.e. 0 mins)	2.44	0.62	1	3
age	Age in years	45.01	12.08	18	64
agesq	Age squared	2,171.31	1,065.10	324	4,096
sex	Gender (1=male; 0=female)	0.45	0.50	0	1
Sportonly	Only undertook sport in the last week (1=yes)	0.03	0.17	0	1
PAonly	Only undertook physical activity in the last week (1=yes)	0.10	0.31	0	1
SpPA	Undertook sport and physical activity in the last week (1=yes)	0.21	0.41	0	1
Walkonly	Only walked at least 10 minutes in the last week (1=yes)	0.53	0.50	0	1
Walkother	Walked as above and undertook other activities (1=yes)	0.32	0.47	0	1
educage	Age finished full-time education	19.88	4.67	2	62
volunteer	Engage in voluntary work for sport (1=yes)	0.07	0.25	0	1
empself	Current occupation: Self-employed (1=yes)	0.11	0.31	0	1
empwc	Current occupation: White collar (1=yes)	0.34	0.47	0	1
empman	Current occupation: Manual work (1=yes)	0.31	0.46	0	1

Table 16.1   (continued)

Variable	Description	Mean	SD	Min.	Max.
emphk	Current occupation: Housekeeper (1=yes)	0.06	0.24	0	1
empretire	Current occupation: Retired (1=yes)	0.11	0.31	0	1
empue	Current occupation: Unemployed (1=yes) (reference)	0.08	0.28	0	1
couple	In a couple (1=yes)	0.72	0.45	0	1
kidsu10	Number of children under 10 years old in household	0.38	0.77	0	20
kids1014	Number of children between 10 and 14 in household	0.21	0.56	0	14
classlower	Self-ranked class: Lower (1=yes) (reference)	0.27	0.44	0	1
classmiddle	Self-ranked class: Middle (1=yes)	0.73	0.45	0	1
classupper	Self-ranked class: Upper (1=yes)	0.01	0.08	0	1
intnetusedy	Daily internet use (1=yes)	0.82	0.39	0	1
rurvillage	Lives in a rural area or village (1=yes) (reference)	0.29	0.45	0	1
townsmall	Lives in a small town (1⁻yes)	0.43	0.50	0	1
townlarge	Lives in a large town (1=yes)	0.28	0.45	0	1
billsdiffmost	Difficulty paying bills most of the time (1=yes) (reference)	0.10	0.30	0	1
billsdiffsometime	Sometimes difficulty paying bills (1=yes)	0.29	0.45	0	1
billsdiffnever	Never difficulty paying bills (1=yes)	0.61	0.49	0	1

is combined with sport and/or physical activity. This is the case with 32 per cent of the population. This makes it clear that walking as a non-organised form of physical activity is greatly important for health outcomes (Khan et al. 2012).

Table 16.2 indicates the relative HEPA levels across the countries in the study. The table reveals considerable heterogeneity across Europe, supporting previous research that people in Northern, Scandinavian and Baltic states exhibit greater physical activity than in Southern Europe (van Tuyckom and Scheerder 2010). This heterogeneity is controlled for in the ordered probit regressions in two ways. The first is to cluster the standard errors of the regression across countries. The second is to include country fixed effects and make use of robust errors. These two versions of the regression analysis respectively control for the variability of HEPA levels according to the country, or control for differences in HEPA levels whilst also controlling for the general heteroscedasticity that will be implied across the countries. Given that the HEPA levels are ordinal, the first specification is the preferred one, but the second acts as a robustness check on the analysis.

Table 16.3 provides the regression results, and reveals that each of the sport and physical activity variables is significant and positive, indicating that they contribute to HEPA levels. However, as noted above, the magnitude of the relationships needs to be identified from the marginal effects, which are presented in Table 16.4. The marginal effects reveal that each of the forms of sport and physical activity contribute to meeting the HEPA levels at the expense of not doing so. This means that these combinations of sport and physical activity *can* shift individuals from doing no exercise, or less than recommended HEPA levels, to meeting HEPA levels. The results also show, moreover, that each of the effects is quite similar and close to 50 per cent, except for walking when undertaken along with other activities, which is less. There is also some marginal evidence that the effects of undertaking sport or physical activity only are larger for males, whereas undertaking sport and physical activity or walking only is larger for females. Such results are consistent with the prevalence of male versus female participation in sport (Downward and Rasciute 2015). Nonetheless, the overriding result is that there is a greater chance that walking has a much greater impact on population HEPA levels. This is because of its greater prevalence across Europe, and its encouragement is just as likely to improve HEPA levels compared to other activities such as sport.

Table 16.2   Activity levels across EU countries (%)

Country	No exercise	Below threshold	Above threshold	*n*
Sweden	0.69	23.50	75.81	434
Estonia	0.63	29.11	70.25	474
Finland	5.24	25.71	69.05	420
Luxembourg	1.91	29.94	68.15	314
Latvia	1.34	31.54	67.11	596
Netherlands	2.29	32.22	65.49	568
Denmark	2.61	31.96	65.43	460
Slovenia	3.33	34.17	62.50	600
Germany	2.51	36.60	60.89	836
Belgium	4.01	36.79	59.20	598
Czech Republic	4.41	38.68	56.91	680
Austria	8.23	36.80	54.97	644
Slovakia	11.69	34.93	53.37	667
Lithuania	5.71	42.10	52.19	525
Great Britain and NI	5.66	42.27	52.07	724
France	4.77	45.49	49.74	587
Hungary	6.66	44.58	48.76	646
Ireland	6.70	46.57	46.73	612
Croatia	8.44	44.92	46.64	699
Spain	2.95	51.15	45.90	610
Poland	10.26	45.91	43.83	575
Bulgaria	6.08	55.07	38.85	592
Cyprus	20.54	42.64	36.82	258
Romania	10.17	56.15	33.69	659
Greece	6.95	60.17	32.88	590
Italy	17.75	50.65	31.60	614
Portugal	14.44	57.90	27.66	658
Malta	23.66	56.87	19.47	262
28 EU countries	6.76	42.03	51.21	15,902

Note: Percentage of respondents in countries sorted in descending order by Above threshold and then by Below threshold.

5.   DISCUSSION

The above results are significant in two main ways. For the first time they explore the potential importance of sport to contributing to health policy outcomes, which is something that sports organisations and other policy makers increasingly advocate. The results suggest that whilst undertaking

Table 16.3 Ordered probit regression estimates on WHO Threshold

	(1) All	(1) Males	(1) Females	(2) All	(2) Males	(2) Females
age	-0.0179*	-0.0231**	-0.0138	-0.0136*	-0.0226*	-0.00757
	(-2.56)	(-2.60)	(-1.67)	(-1.99)	(-2.23)	(-0.81)
agesq	0.000172*	0.000189	0.000152	0.000107	0.000171	0.0000653
	(2.13)	(1.86)	(1.62)	(1.35)	(1.46)	(0.60)
sex	0.149***	N/A	N/A	0.159***	N/A	N/A
	(6.33)			(7.57)		
Sportonly	1.520***	1.624***	1.382***	1.577***	1.697***	1.432***
	(17.33)	(15.02)	(8.26)	(18.45)	(14.35)	(11.35)
PAonly	1.593***	1.647***	1.519***	1.526***	1.593***	1.441***
	(12.76)	(12.65)	(9.10)	(20.44)	(16.02)	(12.59)
SpPA	1.913***	1.863***	1.927***	1.851***	1.833***	1.833***
	(16.84)	(17.60)	(10.93)	(24.43)	(18.18)	(15.81)
Walkonly	1.640***	1.630***	1.645***	1.609***	1.614***	1.604***
	(19.58)	(19.15)	(14.67)	(38.08)	(26.76)	(27.23)
Walkother	0.361***	0.339***	0.409***	0.367***	0.339***	0.423***
	(5.11)	(4.42)	(4.12)	(5.88)	(4.19)	(4.29)
educage	0.0208***	0.0170***	0.0244***	0.0131***	0.00929*	0.0168***
	(6.94)	(3.71)	(7.38)	(4.84)	(2.27)	(4.60)
volunteer	0.584***	0.639***	0.510***	0.502***	0.559***	0.434***
	(10.97)	(11.93)	(6.33)	(9.80)	(8.19)	(5.55)
empself	0.138*	0.153*	0.112	0.221***	0.242***	0.185**
	(2.34)	(2.47)	(1.31)	(4.56)	(3.39)	(2.72)
empwc	0.0543	0.0548	0.0420	0.104**	0.114	0.0768
	(0.93)	(0.74)	(0.60)	(2.62)	(1.81)	(1.49)
empman	0.114*	0.116*	0.0974	0.140***	0.167**	0.100*
	(2.07)	(2.16)	(1.30)	(3.72)	(2.85)	(2.02)

	(1)	(2)	(3)	(4)	(5)	(6)
emphk	-0.0203	0.181	-0.0236	0.0488	0.195	0.0413
	(-0.35)	(1.18)	(-0.33)	(0.97)	(1.09)	(0.70)
empretire	-0.0344	-0.0276	-0.0390	-0.0502	-0.0214	-0.0854
	(-0.64)	(-0.43)	(-0.62)	(-1.07)	(-0.31)	(-1.34)
couple	-0.0169	0.0675	-0.0674*	0.0288	0.119**	-0.0321
	(-0.66)	(1.79)	(-2.06)	(1.23)	(3.26)	(-1.03)
kidsu10	-0.000564	-0.00686	0.00678	-0.0223	-0.0266	-0.0152
	(-0.04)	(-0.31)	(0.37)	(-1.56)	(-1.11)	(-0.83)
kids1014	0.00836	0.0150	0.00269	-0.00198	0.0148	-0.0124
	(0.39)	(0.45)	(0.13)	(-0.10)	(0.46)	(-0.50)
classmiddle	0.109**	0.0320	0.170***	0.147***	0.0840*	0.198***
	(2.82)	(0.52)	(3.90)	(6.00)	(2.27)	(6.02)
classupper	0.137	0.218	0.0369	0.225	0.308	0.115
	(1.38)	(1.09)	(0.25)	(1.74)	(1.65)	(0.63)
intnetusedy	0.137***	0.143*	0.136***	0.0905**	0.106*	0.0823*
	(3.60)	(2.20)	(4.84)	(3.21)	(2.51)	(2.15)
townsmall	-0.0613	-0.0673	-0.0580	-0.0887***	-0.106**	-0.0754*
	(-1.71)	(-1.46)	(-1.43)	(-3.54)	(-2.79)	(-2.25)
townlarge	-0.118**	-0.116*	-0.122**	-0.118***	-0.122**	-0.113**
	(-2.67)	(-2.06)	(-2.70)	(-4.31)	(-2.94)	(-3.08)
billsdiffsome	0.0931**	0.150**	0.0514	0.0736*	0.136*	0.0195
	(2.63)	(3.19)	(0.98)	(2.12)	(2.54)	(0.42)
billsdiffnever	0.272***	0.319***	0.243***	0.167***	0.218***	0.125**
	(6.27)	(5.91)	(4.03)	(4.70)	(3.99)	(2.64)
Country effects	No	No	No	Yes	Yes	Yes
n	15,902	7,132	8,770	15,902	7,132	8,770

Notes: *t*-statistics in parentheses; * $p < 0.05$; ** $p < 0.01$; *** $p < 0.001$; (1) clustered standard errors on country; (2) robust standard errors and country fixed effects.

Table 16.4 Marginal effects

	(1) All	(1) Male	(1) Female	(2) All	(2) Male	(2) Female
Sportonly						
No activity	-0.130***	-0.139***	-0.118***	-0.131***	-0.142***	-0.119***
	(-14.52)	(-14.26)	(-7.86)	(-18.47)	(-14.25)	(-11.45)
Below WHO Threshold	-0.367***	-0.377***	-0.341***	-0.371***	-0.383***	-0.343***
	(-19.19)	(-14.42)	(-8.96)	(-18.51)	(-14.51)	(-11.31)
Exceeds WHO Threshold	0.497***	0.517***	0.459***	0.503***	0.525***	0.462***
	(-19.06)	(-15.07)	(-8.86)	(-18.72)	(-14.68)	(-11.44)
PAonly						
No activity	-0.136***	-0.141***	-0.130***	-0.127***	-0.133***	-0.120***
	(-11.60)	(-11.28)	(-9.02)	(-20.52)	(-15.93)	(-12.72)
Below WHO Threshold	-0.385***	-0.382***	-0.375***	-0.359***	-0.360***	-0.345***
	(-14.05)	(-13.58)	(-9.69)	(-20.51)	(-16.21)	(-12.55)
Exceeds WHO Threshold	0.521***	0.524***	0.504***	0.486***	0.493***	0.465***
	(-13.88)	(-13.31)	(-9.82)	(-20.82)	(-16.48)	(-12.72)
SpPA						
No activity	-0.164***	-0.160***	-0.164***	-0.154***	-0.153***	-0.152***
	(-13.53)	(-13.19)	(-10.43)	(-24.19)	(-17.83)	(-15.81)
Below WHO Threshold	-0.462***	-0.433***	-0.475***	-0.436***	-0.414***	-0.439***
	(-20.28)	(-20.61)	(-12.21)	(-24.98)	(-18.74)	(-16.01)
Exceeds WHO Threshold	0.626***	0.593***	0.640***	0.590***	0.567***	0.591***
	(-19.14)	(-18.77)	(-12.27)	(-25.32)	(-19.00)	(-16.23)

	(1)	(2)	(3)	(4)	(5)	(6)
Walkonly						
No activity	−0.140***	−0.140***	−0.140***	−0.134***	−0.135***	−0.133***
	(−13.56)	(−13.37)	(−11.95)	(−38.09)	(−26.12)	(−27.88)
Below WHO Threshold	−0.396***	−0.379***	−0.406***	−0.379***	−0.364***	−0.384***
	(−25.73)	(−21.80)	(−18.03)	(−39.11)	(−27.92)	(−27.54)
Exceeds WHO Threshold	0.536***	0.519***	0.546***	0.513***	0.499***	0.518***
	(−22.11)	(−19.56)	(−17.20)	(−41.08)	(−29.18)	(−29.10)
Walkother						
No activity	−0.0309***	−0.0291***	−0.0349***	−0.0306***	−0.0283***	−0.0351***
	(−4.80)	(−4.28)	(−3.87)	(−5.87)	(−4.18)	(−4.27)
Below WHO Threshold	−0.0872***	−0.0788***	−0.101***	−0.0864***	−0.0766***	−0.101***
	(−5.33)	(−4.51)	(−4.24)	(−5.91)	(−4.21)	(−4.30)
Exceeds WHO Threshold	0.118***	0.108***	0.136***	0.117***	0.105***	0.137***
	(−5.21)	(−4.46)	(−4.16)	(−5.90)	(−4.21)	(−4.3)
n	15,902	7,132	8,770	15,902	7,132	8,770

Notes: t-statistics in parentheses; * $p < 0.05$; ** $p < 0.01$; *** $p < 0.001$; (1) clustered standard errors on country; (2) robust standard errors and country fixed effects.

sport can contribute to HEPA levels with the same marginal contribution as other forms of physical activity, the limited overall participation in sport *per se* across Europe suggests that focussing on sport to achieve HEPA levels would not be an efficient endeavour. Consistent with the literature, the results of this chapter suggest that focussing on other forms of physical activity, such as walking, would be more efficient and also likely more effective (Khan et al. 2012). In the latter regard, whilst the research has not addressed the ease of seeking behavioural change with respect to each of the forms of physical activity, existing theoretical explanations suggest that the time and other costs of participation in an activity are likely to be inversely related to the extent of that activity being undertaken (Downward and Rasciute 2010; Humphreys and Ruseski 2015). This means that it will be easier to encourage walking than sport.

The results also suggest that, to the extent that sport might contribute to the health agenda, this is more likely to be the case if it is transformed from its traditional format and is linked to a wider, more active lifestyle. In this regard sport undertaken with other physical activity and walking offers a potentially comparable impact on HEPA levels as walking only. The converse of this analysis is that sport organisations need to recognise that they are essentially marginal potential contributors to health policy outcomes. Seeking to be engaged in health policy is thus likely to require a more substantial change to their activities and operations than simply allying existing activities to that policy.

REFERENCES

Bauman, A.E., Reis, R.S., Sallis, J.F., Wells, J.C., Loos, R.J., and Martin, B.W., Lancet Physical Activity Series Working Group (2012) Correlates of physical activity: Why are some people physically active and others not? *Lancet* 380(9838): 258–271.

Becker, G.S. (1965) A theory of the allocation of time. *Economic Journal* 75(299): 493–517.

Bergman, P., Grjibovski, A.M., Hagströmer, M., Bauman, A., and Sjöström, M. (2008) Adherence to physical activity recommendations and the influence of socio-demographic correlates: A population-based cross-sectional study. *BMC Public Health* 8: 1–9. https://doi.org/10.1186/1471-2458-8-367.

Beville, J.M., Umstattd Meyer, M.R., Usdan, S.L, Turner, L.W., Jackson, J.C., and Lian, B.E. (2014) Gender differences in college leisure time physical activity: Application of the theory of planned behavior and integrated behavioral model. *Journal of American College Health* 62(3): 173–184.

Blair, S.N. (2009) Physical inactivity: The biggest public health problem of the 21st century. *British Journal of Sports Medicine* 43: 1–2.

Bull, F., Milton, K., and Kahlmeier, S. et al. (2015) Turning the tide: National policy approaches to increasing physical activity in seven European countries.

British Journal of Sports Medicine 49: 749–756. https://doi:10.1136/bjsports-2013-093200.

Cawley, J. (2004) An economic framework for understanding physical activity and eating behaviors. *American Journal of Preventive Medicine* 27(3): 117–125.

Chalder, M., Wiles, N.J., and Campbell. J. et al. (2012) Facilitated physical activity as a treatment for depressed adults: Randomised controlled trial. *BMJ* 344: e2758. https://doi.org/10.1136/bmj.e2758.

Coombes, E., Jones, A.P., and Hillsdon, M. (2010) The relationship of physical activity and overweight to objectively measured green space accessibility and use. *Social Science and Medicine* 70: 816–822. https://doi.org/10.1016/j.socscimed.2009.11.020.

Council of Europe (2001) Recommendation No. R (92) 13 Rev of the Committee of Ministers to member states on the Revised European Sports Charter. https://rm.coe.int/16804c9dbb. Accessed 13 May 2020.

Department for Culture, Media and Sport (2015) Sporting Future: A new strategy for an active nation. https://www.gov.uk/government/uploads/system/uploads/attachment_data/file/486622/Sporting_Future_ACCESSIBLE.pdf. Accessed 13 December 2019.

Downward, P., Dawson, A., and Dejonghe, T. (2009) *Sports Economics: Theory, Evidence and Policy*. London: Routledge.

Downward, P., Dawson, P., and Mills, T.C. (2016) Sports participation as an investment in (subjective) health: A time series analysis of the life course. *Journal of Public Health* 38: e504–e510. https://doi.org/10.1093/pubmed/fdv164.

Downward, P., Lera-López, F., and Rasciute, S. (2014) The correlates of sports participation in Europe. *European Journal of Sport Science* 14: 592–602. https://doi.org/10.1080/17461391.2014.880191.

Downward, P., and Muniz, C. (2019) Sports participation, in Downward, P., Frick, B., Humphreys, B.R., Pawlowski, T., Ruseski, J.E., and Soebbing, B.P. (eds). *The SAGE Handbook of Sports Economics*. London: Sage.

Downward, P., and Rasciute, S. (2010) The relative demands for sports and leisure in England. *European Sport Management Quarterly* 10: 189–214. https://doi.org/10.1080/16184740903552037.

Downward, P., and Rasciute, S. (2015) Exploring the covariates of sport participation for health: An analysis of males and females in England. *Journal of Sports Sciences* 33: 67–76. https://doi.org/10.1080/02640414.2014.924056.

Downward, P., and Rasciute, S. (2016) 'No man is an island entire of itself': The hidden effect of peers on physical activity. *Social Science and Medicine* 169: 149–156. https://doi.org/10.1016/j.socscimed.2016.09.038.

Eime, R.M., Sawyer, N., Harvey, J.T., Casey, M.M., Westerbeek, H., and Payne, W.R. (2015) Integrating public health and sport management: Sport participation trends 2001–2010. *Sport Management Review* 18: 207–217. https://doi.org/10.1016/j.smr.2014.05.004.

European Commission (2019) Sport in the European Union. https://ec.europa.eu/assets/eac/sport/library/documents/eu-sport-factsheet_en.pdf. Accessed 13 December 2019.

Fortier, M.S., Duda, J.L., Guerin, E., Teixeira, P.J. (2012) Promoting physical activity: Development and testing of self-determination theory-based interventions. *International Journal of Behavioral Nutrition and Physical Activity* 9(1): 20.

Foster, C, (2000) *Guidelines for Health-Enhancing Physical Activity Promotion Programmes*. Tampere: UKK Institute for Health Promotion Research.

Gill, J.M.R., and Cooper, A.R. (2008) Physical activity and prevention of type 2 diabetes mellitus. *Sports Medicine* 38: 807–824.

Henderson, K.A. (2009) A paradox of sport management and physical activity interventions. *Sport Management Review* 12: 57–65. https://doi.org/10.1016/j. smr.2008.12.004.

Humphreys, B.R., McLeod, L., and Ruseski, J.E. (2014) Physical activity and health outcomes: Evidence from Canada. *Health Economics* 23: 33–54. https:// doi.org/10.1002/hec.2900.

Humphreys, B.R., and Ruseski, J.E. (2015) The economic choice of participation and time spent in physical activity and sport in Canada. *International Journal of Sport Finance* 10: 138–159.

Khan, K.M., Thompson, A.M., and Blair, S.N. et al. (2012) Sport and exercise as contributors to the health of nations. *Lancet* 380: 59–64. https://doi.org/10.1016/ S0140-6736(12)60865-4.

Kohl, H.W., Craig, C.L., and Lambert, E.V. et al. (2012) The pandemic of physical inactivity: Global action for public health. *Lancet* 380: 294–305. https://doi. org/10.1016/S0140-6736(12)60898-8.

Kornbeck, J. (2013) The European Union, sport policy and health-enhancing physical activity (HEPA): The case of exercise by prescription. *Deutsche Zeitschrift für Sportmedizin* 64: 157–161. https://doi.org/10.5960/dzsm.2012.072.

Lechner, M. (2009) Long-run labour market and health effects of individual sports activities. *Journal of Health Economics* 28: 839–854. https://doi.org/10.1016/j. jhealeco.2009.05.003.

Lera-López, F., Ollo-López, A., and Sánchez-Santos, J.M. (2017) How does physical activity make you feel better? The mediational role of perceived health. *Applied Research in Quality of Life* 12: 511–531. https://doi.org/10.1007/ s11482-016-9473-8.

Oja, P., Titze, S., and Kokko, S. et al. (2015) Health benefits of different sport disciplines for adults: Systematic review of observational and intervention studies with meta-analysis. *British Journal of Sports Medicine* 49: 434–440. https://doi. org/10.1136/bjsports-2014-093885.

Rütten, A., Abu-Omar, K., Gelius, P., and Schow, D. (2013) Physical inactivity as a policy problem: Applying a concept from policy analysis to a public health issue. *Health Research Policy and Systems* 11: 1–9. https://doi. org/10.1186/1478-4505-11-9.

Sofi, F., Capalbo, A., Cesari, F., Abbate, R., and Gensini, G.F. (2008) Physical activity during leisure time and primary prevention of coronary heart disease: An updated meta-analysis of cohort studies. *European Journal of Cardiovascular Prevention and Rehabilitation* 15: 247–257. https://doi.org/10.1097/HJR.0b013e3282f232ac.

Sport England (2016) *Towards an Active Nation: Strategy 2016–2021.* https:// www.sportengland.org/media/10629/sport-england-towards-an-active-nation.pdf. Accessed 13 December 2019.

Vandenberghe, D., and Albrecht. J. (2020) The financial burden of non-communicable diseases in the European Union: A systematic review. *European Journal of Public Health* 30: 833–839. https://doi.org/10.1093/eurpub/ ckz073.

van Tuyckom, C., and Scheerder, J. (2010) Sport for all? Insight into stratification and compensation mechanisms of sporting activity in the 27 European Union member states. *Sport, Education and Society* 15: 495–512. https://doi.org/10.108 0/13573322.2010.514746.

Warburton, D.E., Nicol, C.W., and Bredin, S.S. (2006) Health benefits of physical activity: The evidence. *CMAJ* 174: 801–809. https://doi.org/10.1503/cmaj.051351.

Warburton, D.E.R., Katzmarzyk, P.T., Rhodes, R.E., and Shephard, R.J. (2007) Evidence-informed physical activity guidelines for Canadian adults. *Applied Physiology, Nutrition, and Metabolism* 32: S16–S68. https://doi.org/10.1139/H07-123.

WHO (n.d.) Global strategy on diet, physical activity and health. https://www.who.int/dietphysicalactivity/pa/en. Accessed 14 May 2020.

WHO (2011) Global recommendations on physical activity for health. http://www.who.int/dietphysicalactivity/physical-activity-recommendations-18-64years.pdf?ua=1. Accessed 13 December 2019.

WHO (2018) Noncommunicable diseases. https://www.who.int/en/news-room/fact-sheets/detail/noncommunicable-diseases. Accessed 13 December 2019.

17. Labour market restrictions in English professional team sports

Peter J. Sloane

It is traditionally argued that some control over the ability to recruit players is necessary to protect against the possibility that richer clubs will become too strong relative to smaller clubs, and thus threaten uncertainty of outcome. But another argument is that competitive bidding in the market for players will increase wage costs and lead to financial instability. We assume that the objective of clubs is to maximise playing success rather than profit maximisation, though this will not influence the underlying case for salary capping. Each league is assumed to be open rather than closed (though closed leagues have been discussed in some English sports), so that clubs may be promoted to a higher division or relegated to a lower one. Hence, some financial transfers from the top clubs may be required to protect clubs in lower divisions from harmful financial losses or against the adverse consequences of relegation. In this chapter we focus on the four major team sports in England, namely football, cricket and the two rugby codes – union and league. It is noteworthy that different approaches have been adopted in these sports, reflecting their different circumstances and different financial strengths and sizes.

THEORETICAL CONSIDERATIONS IN SALARY CAPPING

Salary capping is longer established in North America than in Europe. Thus, the National Basketball Association (NBA) established a cap in 1976 and the US National Football League (NFL) in 1994. The former has a soft cap (which allows exceptions for certain categories of player) and a luxury tax, which transfers income from clubs exceeding a certain level of expenditure on players and transfers it to clubs below the limit. The attempt to introduce a salary cap in basketball led to a players' strike in 1994/95. The owners then proposed a luxury tax, which was agreed in 1997 with a tax rate of 35 per cent on payrolls exceeding $51 million.

In contrast, the NFL has a hard cap (which means equal wage bills for each team without exceptions) and a hard floor (which aims to prevent teams from pocketing the transfers from richer clubs) at 64 per cent of gross revenues, which was reduced to 63 per cent in 1995 and 62 per cent in 1997. The NHL abandoned the salary cap which existed in its early days, but then restored it after the 2004/05 lockout in the form of a hard cap, but without luxury taxes or exemptions. Baseball has a luxury tax, which is effectively a salary cap as there are penalties for exceeding certain thresholds. In North America the imposition of salary caps is frequently a cause of industrial conflict.

The schemes adopted in North America are as below. The parties agree upon defined gross revenues (DGR) for sharing purposes and what share (S) will go to the players. In a league of n teams the following determines the cap on team spending on talent C:

$$C = (1/n) \times S \times DGR \ t-1 \qquad (17.1)$$

It is assumed that owners will only introduce a salary cap that lowers the wage bill. If all clubs end up spending the same amount on players and have equally capable management teams, each club would have roughly the same playing strengths and would end up with 50 per cent winning percentages. However, the effect of the salary cap is to move clubs from their profit-maximising positions where the marginal returns to winning equal the marginal costs for each club. This is why a salary minimum is required as well as a salary maximum. There is also an economic incentive to cheat.

Fort and Quirk (1995) conclude that such a salary cap is the only cross-subsidisation scheme that can achieve the financial viability of small market teams, as well as achieving a greater degree of competitive balance in a league, when there is a maximum amount that clubs are allowed to spend on players in a season. However, there are important organisational differences between North America and Europe, as Dietl et al. (2011) note. In the former only the owners have votes and negotiate collective bargaining agreements with player unions. In the latter national and international governing bodies are involved, and in many countries a majority of football clubs are owned by the members; therefore, while profit maximisation may operate in North America, this is less likely in Europe, where maximising winning percentages fits the facts more. It follows that salary capping will be much more complex in Europe given shareholder diversity. The only workable solution in European football, given the wide dispersion in revenues among clubs, seems to be a percentage of revenue cap – though in cricket and the two rugby codes absolute salary caps have prevailed.

In North America the amount of the cap is the same for every club, so the cap is absolute rather than relative. An alternative to this which has partially been adopted in European football is that there is a maximum wage/turnover ratio, so that there is a maximum amount each team can spend on player salaries, which is different for each team depending on its turnover. This is a relative rather than absolute measure, and is likely to worsen competitive balance in both profit and win maximum cases, as the big clubs have larger turnovers than small clubs and thus are less constrained. It will, however, tend to reduce financial instability.

SALARY CAPS IN ENGLAND

Different sports will have narrower or wider distributions of income among clubs, as well as different numbers of clubs, and this will inform about what policies are appropriate for each sport. Here, we limit consideration to the four major team sports in England. Thus, football has 92 clubs split over four divisions. The Premier League of 20 clubs has a separate management structure from the Football League, which is responsible for 72 clubs split across three divisions. Below these is an elaborate pyramid structure of leagues. In Rugby Union the Gallagher Premiership has 12 clubs, as has the lower Green King IPA Championship. Below these are three national leagues, each with 16 clubs, together with a pyramid of lower leagues, following the example of football. In Rugby League, which is more restricted geographically and mainly located in the North of England, there are 12 clubs in the Betfred Super League, and 14 clubs in each of the Championship and League 1. In County Cricket the 18 counties were split in 2003 into two divisions of eight and ten counties respectively, with promotion and relegation between them. These differences reflect the relative financial strength of the four sports and their ability to access TV income, which has become increasingly important over time. An open system has the advantage of giving teams a greater incentive to improve team quality than is the case with a closed league in order to achieve promotion or avoid relegation. The system of promotion and relegation also allows the location of teams to reflect better the level of demand, albeit imperfectly, without the need for the relocation of existing member clubs (Andreff, 2019). However, when a team in a larger market is demoted and replaced by a team in a smaller market this will likely impose some financial cost on teams in the higher division (see Noll, 2002). The historical background is summarised in Box 17.1.

Unlike many other team sports, rugby split into two codes in 1885 after a dispute over broken time payments whereby players were compensated

---

BOX 17.1   BACKGROUND TO WAGE CONTROLS

The simplest form of control is to impose maximum limits on individual player salaries. Thus, in the English Football League (EFL) a maximum wage was established in 1901, initially £4 per week, and this was only removed in 1961 when it had risen to £20 per week – not very different from the industrial average prevailing at the time. Eventually the players' union was successful in negotiating its abolition. The only other example of a maximum wage appears to be in the first division of the German Bundesliga, where both a minimum and maximum salary, together with a maximum transfer fee, were introduced in 1962, before being abandoned in 1972 (see Frick, 2010). Competition from rival leagues would likely have made such restrictions impossible to maintain, even without the presence of players' unions. Club-wide salary caps allow for more flexibility in terms of payments to individual players and have been introduced into both rugby codes and County Cricket.

---

for loss of working time in their main employment – with Union remaining amateur and League becoming professional, though League clubs were mainly restricted to the North of England. The codes developed different rules, the major one being that Union consists of 15 players per team as opposed to 13 in League. In 1995 Union belatedly adopted professionalism, with a league structure of its own replacing the previous system of friendly games between individual clubs. The Six Nations league – consisting of England, Wales, Ireland, Scotland, France and Italy – has traditionally been of more importance than the club games, with much larger crowds and television coverage; and this may have stunted the development of club competitions. A salary cap was introduced into Premiership Rugby Union in 1999 with the explicit objective of ensuring the financial viability of all 12 clubs in the top division and to provide for a competitive league. The cap is monitored by a Salary Cap Manager, and each September all clubs are required to detail their spending during the previous salary cap year. The level of the cap has been adjusted over time and in 2017/18 was set at £7 million per club, though clubs can nominate two players whom they wish to be excluded from the salary cap arrangements. Further, financial credits are given for players under the age of 24 who joined the club before their 18th birthday and for the replacement of players who have been out of action through injury for 12 weeks or more.

The maximum penalty for the infringement of rules is a very severe deduction of 35 points. Despite this, suspected breaches of the regulations are not uncommon. Thus, in 2019 a leading club, Saracens, was investigated concerning an arrangement whereby certain players were operating businesses under the auspices of the club owner and received additional income through this mechanism. Despite the fact that no deliberate deception was held to have been committed, the club was found to have breached the salary cap in each of the previous three seasons and received the maximum 35 points deduction and a fine of £5.3 million. Subsequently, rival clubs have requested that Premiership players should also declare their earnings to the league, so that they can also be held accountable for any breaches of the salary cap.

While a degree of flexibility in the arrangements gives clubs scope for creative accounting, being caught out can not only have serious consequences for transgressor clubs, but also the deduction of points threatens the integrity of the league. In December 2019 Premiership Rugby announced that a salary cap review would be undertaken by Lord Myners, a former City minister. He was to examine whether opportunities existed for greater monitoring and investigatory powers, and whether enhanced resources were required. He was also to consider how salary caps were implemented in different sports around the world.

The English Rugby Football League was reformed in 1995 with the introduction of the Super League and a change in the timing of the competition to the summer months when the weather is better and there is less competition from football. This was done at the behest of Sky TV. A salary cap was introduced in 1997, and further reforms in 2015 saw a return to 12 clubs – initially with a closed league structure but including a team from France as well as a London club. There is no system of automatic promotion and relegation between the five tiers that now exist, although teams have moved between them in the past. From the 2015 season promotion and relegation were reintroduced in a revised format including end-of-season play-offs. The new structure for 2019 guarantees one up and one down in the case of the Super League. The salary cap was fixed at £2 million, much lower than the financially stronger Rugby Union. A sum of £900,000 per annum was given to each club from the proceeds of the £87 million TV contract to be earned over five years. (In comparison, Premiership Rugby Union signed a £152 million four-year TV deal with BT Sport in 2012.) As with rugby union, a number of breaches of the salary cap limit have been reported, with the normal penalty being the deduction of two points (see Plumley et al., 2016).

Cricket has features that set it apart from other team sports. There is an important distinction between county and test cricket. A select number of test cricketers (currently ten in number) are paid under central contracts according to a fixed scale, but with provision for bonus payments related to performance. There are also a number of test cricketers on incremental contracts, mostly paid on county salaries, but again with some provision for bonus payments. Eligibility for County Cricket is based on birth and residential rules, which limits player mobility. No cricketer may play for more than one county during the same season. A cricketer born in one county and resident in another is free to choose for which of these counties he wishes to play. In addition, up to 2008 two overseas players were allowed to play for each county, but after this date it was ruled that only one could do so. There is a salary cap of £2 million for each county per season, but in practice this exceeds by a substantial amount the actual expenditure on players.

County championship games take place over four days. Though the long duration is not attractive to spectators, few of whom are drawn to attend, it is seen as necessary to prepare players for international test cricket, which takes place over five days. A review of the financial health of the game carried out in 1997 (see Plumley et al., 2019) found that there were a number of strategic weaknesses, including an over-reliance on annual grants from the governing England and Wales Cricket Board (ECB) – the recipient of test gate receipts and TV income, both of which are substantial but dependent on players selected from the counties. Without this income the county clubs would be insolvent (see Shibli and Wilkinson-Riddle, 1997). The introduction of one-day cricket, which is much more popular with spectators, has improved the financial environment both at county and international level. Further, in 2003 short-duration 20-over (T20) matches were introduced, with sell-out crowds not uncommon. Following a delay from 2020 due to the Covid-19 pandemic, The Hundred – a city-based, franchised 100-ball tournament – is due to be introduced in 2021. This involves eight new teams, and follows a similar arrangement to that in India, which has proved successful there and has been copied in a number of other countries. Each team is made up of 15 players, of which a maximum of three can be overseas players. Players are signed using a draft system common in the other franchise leagues. The draft is based on seven salary bands ranging from £30,000 to £150,000, and teams can pick two players from each band. A player will take no further part in the draft if not picked in his allocated salary level. The difference from the North American player draft system is that established players are involved and competitive bidding is not permissible. TV income has also increased as a result of these developments. The latest TV agreements with Sky and the BBC will provide broadcasting revenue of £1.1 billion over a five-year period from 2020 to 2024.This will allow the 18 first-class counties each to be paid £1.3 million per annum in total. Such product market development has enabled cricket to arrest decline and offer a promising future.

The most extensive labour market controls are to be found in football, where qualification for European competitions for the top six or seven clubs in the Premier League promises major increases in income as well as potential glory for the winners. This is buttressed by TV contracts that dwarf those in the other sports. Promotion from the Championship to the Premier League can increase income by as much as £180 million per annum for each promoted club. This encourages clubs to overspend in the pursuit of promotion if left to their own devices; and there are similar incentives for clubs pursuing a place in the top six of the Premier League in order to gain entry into European competitions. The UEFA Financial Fair Play (FFP) regulations aim to restrict clubs which have qualified for entry into their competitions to acceptable annual losses of 30 million euros over a three-year period, which cannot be covered by subsidies from their owners. Clubs are required to submit detailed information about their finances to enable effective monitoring to take place. Certain investments are excluded from the break-even calculations. These exclusions include investments in club stadia, training facilities, infrastructure and youth development.

Possible sanctions include fines, the withholding of prize money, points deductions, a refusal to register a number of players otherwise allowable in the roster for UEFA competitions and ultimately disqualification from UEFA competitions. Thus, Moscow Dynamo was banned from the Champions League for one season for failing to meet the break-even requirements. Paris Saint-Germain (PSG) and Manchester City also fell foul of the rules concerning their receipt of income from parties who were considered not to be independent of their owners. In the former case the Qatar Tourism Authority (QTA) agreed to pay the club between 700 and 1.125 billion euros over five years depending on tournament performance. Under FFP what mattered was whether the QTA was 'a related party', which in turn meant the club could count only a market value for the contract under FFP rules. UEFA regarded the QTA as a related party because the owner of PSG, Qatar Sports Investments, was majority owned by the Qatar Ministry of Finance. Further, it was suggested that the contract was substantially over-valued in the accounts. PSG subsequently agreed to limit spending and reduce losses as the price for accepting a fine and avoiding greater sanctions.

Manchester City faced similar issues in relation to a three and a half year sponsorship contract with Aabar (a state-controlled investment fund in Abu Dhabi), Etihad Airlines and Elisalat (a telecoms company). After its emails were hacked and articles appeared in German newspaper *Der Spiegel*, UEFA threatened to exclude the club from participation in the Champions League. The club appealed to the European Court of Sports Arbitration (CAS), but this was rejected on the basis that the matter was still under consideration and UEFA had not yet completed its investigations. UEFA subsequently banned the club from participation in the Champions League over the next two seasons and imposed a fine of 50 million euros – harsher than any previous sanction. Manchester City then appealed to CAS that no evidence had yet been produced that the rules had, indeed, been infringed, and CAS found in favour of the club. The fine was also reduced to 30 million euros, the remaining fine being imposed because of the club's failure to co-operate with UEFA's investigation. These examples show that policing FFP is a complex issue.

Peeters and Szymanski (2014) note that the break-even rule could be construed as a means to raise profitability by controlling wage inflation, and therefore as an anti-competitive vertical restraint under European Union (EU) competition law. UEFA argues, however, that the system of club licensing has had a major impact on clubs in Europe, with 100 out of 548 applications rejected. Some 51 million euros has been withheld under FFP regulations; nine clubs were sanctioned in 2013/14, and 15 in 2014/15. UEFA regards club licensing into which FFP was incorporated in 2010 as a great success. Now over 1500 clubs in Europe undergo club licensing on an annual basis, and 51 of UEFA's 54 member associations apply such rules to domestic competitions. Whereas in 2011 net losses of 1.7 billion euros were reported by European clubs, in the following five years or so this had fallen by two-thirds.

England has no formal club licensing system, but extensive rules apply domestically covering both financial and non-financial matters. UEFA's FFP regulations are only relevant to those clubs qualifying for European competitions. Presumably with this in mind the English Premier League has introduced its own FFP regulations which allow the 20 member clubs only a £4 million increase in the wage bill per season and permitted losses of £105 million over a three-year period. The compatibility of these twin arrangements remains to be determined. In addition, the Football League has its own regulations for its 72 member clubs. In this case permitted losses are £5 million per annum. Leagues 1 and 2 have limits on total player wages as a proportion of each club's turnover – 60 per cent in the case of Division 1 and 55 per cent in the case of Division 2. Questions arise when clubs are promoted or relegated between divisions as the financial restrictions will change.

A number of clubs have exploited a loophole in the EFL rules by selling their own stadium and leasing it back. Thus Derby County reported a pre-tax profit of £14.6 million in 2019/20 when losses in excess of the break-even requirement would have put the club in breach of these requirements without the sale and leaseback arrangements for the ground. What was relevant was whether the asset on the club's books was fairly valued at £41 million. Aston Villa, Sheffield Wednesday and Reading have used similar devices. Middlesbrough have threatened to sue the league for an alleged failure to enforce its own rules. In the previous season Birmingham City were docked nine points after recording total losses of £48.8 million for

2015/16 to 2017/18, almost £10 million over the £39 million limit. Bolton and Bury are the latest clubs to go into voluntary liquidation, and were each deducted 12 points. There were doubts about their ability to fulfil their fixtures. Eventually Bolton were reprieved through a take-over, but Bury were expelled from League 1. Macclesfield Town in League 2 failed to pay player wages, leading to a player strike and a refusal to fulfil their fixtures. This was eventually resolved, but the club was docked six points. The club was subsequently expelled from the league. This shows that even with strict rules many clubs find it difficult to remain financially viable, especially in the lower leagues.

The Premier League already provides subsidies to teams in the lower divisions. Each Championship club receives £2.3 million per season, Division 1 clubs £360,000 and Division 2 clubs £240,000. There is also a system of parachute payments for relegated clubs. Since the 2016/17 season each club has received a 55 per cent share of broadcasting revenue in the first year after relegation, 45 per cent in the following year and 20 per cent in the third year. Clubs relegated after a single season in the Premier League receive 55 per cent, followed by 40 per cent over two seasons, with the third payment eliminated. The Premier League also committed itself to invest at least £1 billion to improve facilities down the football pyramid over the three years of the 2016/17 TV contracts.

The challenges facing promoted clubs may be no less onerous than those facing relegated clubs. Goddard (2014) points out that no fewer than 12 out of the 30 clubs promoted from the Championship to the Premier League between seasons 1998/99 and 2007/08 were immediately relegated after one season. Gaining promotion often involves an increase in expenditure greater than the increase in revenue during the year after which promotion was achieved. In the reverse situation, only six out of the 30 relegated teams bounced straight back into the Premier League. Frequently revenues fall more steeply than costs for relegated teams – due to the fact, at least in some cases, that contracts entered into on promotion lack appropriate escape clauses when relegation occurs. A recent investigation by Deloitte and Vysyble (as reported in Tucker, 2019) found that, despite new profit and sustainability rules introduced by the English Football League in 2016/17, many Championship clubs recorded significant losses over one or two seasons in an attempt to gain promotion to the Premier League. Over 50 per cent of the clubs were spending more on wages than their total revenues. Championship sides made a total loss of £307 million in 2017/18, and a number of clubs are likely to breach the £39 million limit allowed over three seasons. This contrasts markedly with the Premier League, where most clubs are now profitable. The coronavirus has imposed new strains on all clubs, and the UK Government has asked the Premier League to provide financial assistance to all Football League clubs to ensure their survival.

CONCLUSIONS

All four major professional team sports leagues in England analysed in this chapter have measures in place to reduce the degree of open competition in the market for players, in the belief that this will help avoid financial ruin from an arms race to hire the best players. Both rugby codes have conventional salary caps, which also helps achieve competitive balance. In these cases international club competitions do not play such a significant role as in football, where the Champions League and the Europa League are major revenue earners. Setting a cap as in the two rugby codes would make it more difficult for the top British clubs to compete with the major clubs in other European countries.

In football UEFA has claimed that Financial Fair Play rules have improved financial performance throughout Europe, and there is some evidence for this; but it is difficult to separate out the effects of FFP from the effects of the dramatic increase in TV revenues. There is, however, a problem in enforcement as there are many ways to compensate players besides their regular salary, and cartel cheating appears to be a common phenomenon. The optimal form of salary capping may vary according to the nature of the league, and this is reflected in the diversity of arrangements in the four sports considered in this chapter. Even within football different arrangements apply to different divisions in the league, reflecting the wide spread of earnings capacity within the four divisions. This points to the difficulty of achieving competitive balance in open leagues when clubs are of very different sizes in terms of wealth-creating capacity. It may take time for a promoted club to achieve financial balance, and relegation may occur before such balance is achieved. There is a need for all four team sports to review their policies for salary capping, and perhaps consider the introduction of luxury taxes in order to protect the integrity of their competitions. This is even more pressing as a result of the coronavirus epidemic.

REFERENCES

Andreff, W., Origins and Developments of Sports Systems, in Downward, P., Frick, B., Humphreys, B., Pawlowski, T., Ruseski, J. and Soebbing, B. (eds), *The Sage Handbook of Sports Economics*, London: Sage, 2019, pp. 8–17.

Dietl, H., Franck, E., Lang, M. and Rathke, A., Organisational Differences between US Major Leagues and European Leagues: Implications for Salary Caps, IASE Working Paper 11–05, March 2011.

Fort, R. and Quirk, J., Cross-subsidization, Incentives and Outcomes in Professional Team Sports Leagues, *Journal of Economic Literature*, 33(3), 1995, 1265–1299.

Frick, B., The Football Players' Labor Market: Recent Developments, in Devecioglu, S. (ed.), *Football Economics*, IESE Business School, Barcelona, September, 2010.

Goddard, J., The Promotion and Relegation System, in Goddard, J. and Sloane, P. (eds), *Handbook on the Economics of Professional Football*, Cheltenham, UK and Northampton, MA, USA: Edward Elgar Publishing, 2014, pp. 23–40.

Noll, R., The Economics of Promotion and Relegation in Sports Leagues: The Case of English Football, *Journal of Sports Economics*, 3(2), 2002, 169–203.

Peeters, T. and Szymanski, S., Financial Fair Play in European Football, *Economic Policy*, 79(78) 2014, 343–390.

Plumley, D., Wilson, R. and Barrett, D., Staring into the Abyss? The State of UK Rugby's Super League, *Managing Leisure*, 20(6), 2016, 293–310.

Plumley, D., Wilson, R., Millar, R. and Shibli, S., Howzat? The Financial Health of English Cricket: Not Out, Yet, *International Journal of Financial Studies*, 7(1), 2019, 1–17.

Shibli, S. and Wilkinson-Riddle, G., The Financial Health of English Cricket: An Analysis Based upon the 1995 Annual Reports and Annual Statement of the 18 First Class Counties, *Journal of Applied Accounting Research* (4), 1997, 1–37.

Tucker, M. 'Championship Bubble Waiting to Burst' with Clubs Posting Record Losses in Premier League 'Gamble', BBC Radio 5 Live Investigations Unit, 12 December 2019.

18. Red cards: (mis)carriage of justice?

Ruud H. Koning and Lara van Steen

1. INTRODUCTION

Recent research has shown considerable variation in the way referees enforce the rules of professional sporting contests. Dawson et al. (2007) show inconsistency of refereeing standards in English soccer. Even after conditioning on team and match specific variables, they find significant fixed referee effects. Garicano et al. (2005) show that professional soccer referees tend to add more stoppage time in case the home team benefits from that extra time, and that they shorten close games when the home team is ahead. In American basketball, more personal fouls are awarded against players when the referees are from an opposite race (Price and Wolfers, 2010). Judges tend to assess female gymnasts who perform later in a final better than earlier ones, even though the order of performance is randomized (Joustra et al., 2021). Buraimo et al. (2010) show that in the English Premier League (EPL) and German Bundesliga home teams are treated more favorably in that they receive fewer yellow and red cards. Even though sporting rules are supposed to be identical for all participants, they are not enforced identically for all participants.

In this chapter, we add to this literature by examining specifically the direct red card in professional soccer. When a player is shown a red card in soccer, he has to leave the field, and his team is one man short for the remainder of the game.[1] In this sense, it is an irreversible decision in soccer matches. Ridder et al. (1994) show that the team left with 11 players has a higher scoring intensity, both if playing at home and when it plays away. Hence, a team is put at a significant disadvantage when a player is sent off. In the judicial process that follows a direct (straight) red card, the decision is sometimes reversed: the player receives no punishment, and the card is dismissed (revoked or rescinded). In other words, the red card should not have been given, and the team has unjustifiably suffered from being one player short. In this chapter, we assess determinants of a direct red card, possible determinants of dismissal of a red card, and the consequences of these dismissals. Are lower-ranked teams more likely to receive red cards that are eventually rescinded? During the sample period that we cover, the Video Assistant Referee (VAR) was introduced. As a consequence, one would expect any bias to have disappeared and dismissals of direct red cards to have decreased.

The chapter is arranged as follows. In the next section, we discuss the institutional setting. Data are presented in Section 3, and empirical results in Section 4. We end with conclusions in Section 5.

2.   INSTITUTIONAL SETTING

According to the International Football Association Board, in a match the referee is authorized to take disciplinary action from the moment players, substitutes and team officials enter the field of play up to when they leave the field of play (IFAB, 2016). Disciplinary action may be caused by either cautionable or sending-off offences, and the action is communicated by a yellow or a red card, respectively.

> A player is cautioned if guilty of: delaying the restart of play, dissent by word or action, entering, re-entering or deliberately leaving the field of play without the referee's permission, failing to respect the required distance when play is restarted with a corner kick, free kick or throw-in, persistent infringement of the Laws of the Game (no specific number or pattern of infringements constitutes "persistent"), and unsporting behaviour. (IFAB, 2016, p. 85)

Two yellow cards in one match results in a sending-off right after the second yellow card has been given. The punishment is automatically that the player is banned for one match.

> A player, substitute or substituted player who commits any of the following offences is sent off: denying the opposing team a goal or an obvious goal-scoring opportunity by deliberately handling the ball (except a goalkeeper within their penalty area), denying an obvious goal-scoring opportunity to an opponent moving towards the opponents' goal by an offence punishable by a free kick (unless as outlined below), serious foul play, spitting at an opponent or any other person, violent conduct, using offensive, insulting or abusive language and/or gestures, receiving a second caution in the same match.
>
> A player, substitute or substituted player who has been sent off must leave the vicinity of the field of play and the technical area. (IFAB, 2016, pp. 86–87)

During the period of our dataset (2010/11–2019/20) there were no major changes to the laws of the game relating to cautioning or sending-off.

If a red card is shown, the player is immediately sent off the field. After the match, the referee notes the incident on the online match form. This goes to the prosecutor of the football association, who can propose a settlement or send the procedure immediately to the disciplinary committee. In the latter case, or if the player rejects the proposed settlement, the disciplinary committee considers the case. They again propose a settlement that the player and the prosecutor consider. If no agreement is reached, the case goes to the committee of appeals for a final decision. This decision is binding and may or may not be stricter than the initial settlement proposed by either the prosecutor or the disciplinary committee. The conclusion in each of these scenarios is that the player is suspended for a certain number of matches, or that the red card is rescinded. In the latter case, the player has been sent off mistakenly and his team wrongly played with a man short for the remainder of the match.

Recently, the Video Assistant Referee (VAR) has been introduced in the top Dutch league, the Eredivisie. During a match, the referee and VAR are in direct communication. When an incident happens, the VAR can advise the referee or the referee can ask the VAR for input, but in either case the referee makes a final decision. The VAR can intervene in a limited number of situations, but only where there is clear error. These cases are: whether or not a goal has been scored preceded by an offence (for example, handball or offside); whether or not a penalty kick should be given; whether or not a direct red card should be given; and if a player's identity is mistaken when giving either a red or a yellow card. Advice from the VAR can be to reconsider a decision via on-field review; pitch-side monitors allow the referee to watch a specific situation from different angles, and hence make a better-informed decision.

The VAR's debut in the Eredivisie was on 21 September 2016 during the KNVB cup final between Ajax and Willem II. It immediately proved its worth as the match referee decided to give a red card instead of a yellow card after consulting the VAR. From the 2018/19 season onwards, the VAR has been used in all Eredivisie matches.

3. DATA

We compiled a dataset of all red cards given in the Dutch top league during the 2010/11–2019/20 seasons, and collected information on whether or not the card was eventually dismissed.[2] This dataset was extended with match-specific information such as winning odds of the home team, ranking of both teams at the start of the game, etc. However, we do not have within-match information (except for the time and match score when a direct red card or second yellow card was shown). Also, we do not know the referee in the matches where no player is sent off.

All seasons have 306 matches, except for 2019/20, which was suspended after 184 matches, and not resumed, due to the coronavirus pandemic. To incorporate this season, we express all quantities as rates, so the total number of events divided by the number of matches. The development of the incidence of direct red cards and double yellow cards are shown in Figure 18.1. In 2010/11, 46 direct red cards were given, corresponding to a rate of 0.15 per match. Over time, this fell to 0.072 direct red cards per match in the 2018/18 season. As of 2018/19, the referees have been supported by the VAR. The first complete VAR season had a total of 44 direct red cards (0.14 per match), which in the last partial season available decreased again to an average of 0.12 per match.

The incidence of double yellow cards does not show such a marked decrease over time. The average is 0.085 per match in 2010/11 and decreased slightly to 0.069 in 2019/20. There was no increase in the rate in 2018/19 since the VAR can only intervene in the case of a yellow card given to the wrong player. However, the VAR cannot advise the referee to caution a player if the referee has not done so. It is possible that some cautions missed by the referee have resulted in a direct red card after a VAR intervention, whereas the referee would have given a yellow card had he seen the foul well enough himself.

The fraction of dismissed direct red cards varies from 21 percent in 2012/13, when 10 out of 48 were dismissed, to 4.1 percent in 2011/12

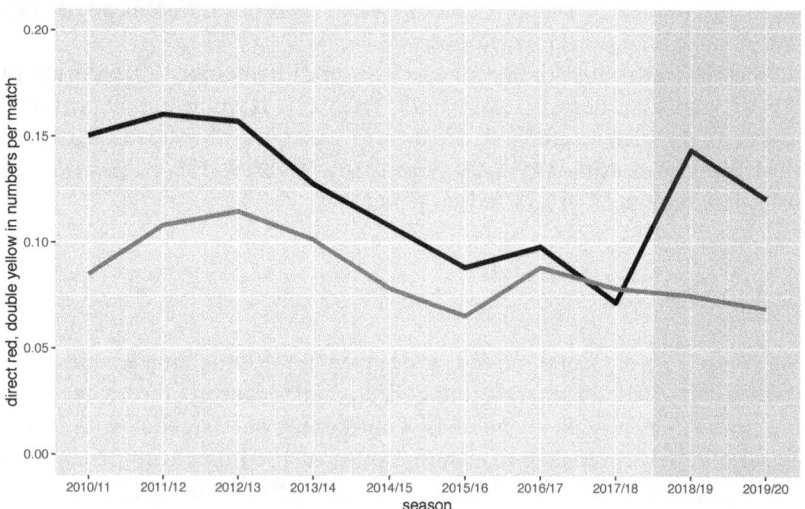

Figure 18.1   Incidence of red cards by season (black line: direct red, grey line: double yellow)

Table 18.1   Incidence of cards and dismissals by period

	No VAR	VAR	*p*-value
Double yellow	0.090	0.072	0.225
Direct red	0.120	0.134	0.420
Dismissals	0.122	0.083	0.467

(only 2 out of 49). After the introduction of the VAR, dismissal rates were 9.1 percent in 2018/19 and 7.1 percent in 2019/20.

The rates of direct red cards and double yellow cards by time period (no VAR vs. VAR) are given in Table 18.1. The bottom row gives the rate of dismissals per red card. The last column gives *p*-values of tests of equality of proportions, which clearly suggest that the incidence of double yellow and direct red cards and dismissals of direct red cards are similar in the periods without and with the VAR.

4.   EMPIRICAL RESULTS

First, we model the incidence of dismissals in a match. As discussed in Section 2, a player can be sent off either by receiving a second caution (a second yellow card) or by receiving a direct red card. In the first model, the dependent variable is whether or not one or more players in a team are sent off. In the empirical analysis, we take a match played by a certain team as the unit of observation. So, each match results in two observations. To allow for possible dependence between these two observations, we cluster them in the calculation of the standard errors.

Based on the literature, we use the following as explanatory variables for the incidence of dismissals. First, a dummy indicates whether or not the team is playing at home. It is well known that there is a significant home advantage in soccer, so it is important to allow for that. A second variable is the team's position in the rankings at the moment the match is played. Lower-ranked teams have less quality, and therefore may resort to illegal means when trying to make up for this lack of quality. The third variable is the probability of winning, as derived from bookmaker odds. It is important to take this variable into account as home advantage (if any) may also indicate that the home team is more likely to play offensively. Since denying an opponent a clear goal-scoring opportunity is punishable by a red card, players of the underdog team (usually the away team) are more likely to be sent off. However, variation in home and away win probabilities allows us to separate home advantage from this quality effect: not all home teams are favorite in a given match. Finally, we measure outcome uncertainty by the absolute value of the difference between the probabilities of a home win and an away win. Note that the scale is inverted: the value for a match with an equally likely home and away winner has value 0; if the match is very uneven the value is positive and higher. Matches that are closely contended may be more likely to result in aggressive play and players being sent off.

Summarizing, we expect a negative effect for the home variable, a positive sign for position (a large position value means the team is low in the ranking), a negative value for a team's win probability, and a negative value for the effect of our measure of outcome uncertainty. Because of the significant season-to-season variation in the incidence of dismissals (see Figure 18.1), we also include season dummies.

First, we discuss the estimation results for the model of any sending-off in a match (Table 18.2), so that includes cases due to a second yellow card and a direct red card. The results consist of a column using all observations and two columns for the periods without and with VAR (no VAR and VAR) respectively. Considering all observations, the probability of a player being sent off is significantly lower if the match is played at home. That probability also depends negatively on the team's *ex ante* win probability in that match and on the uncertainty of outcome. All these effects are significantly different from 0 ($\alpha = 0.05$); team position has no effect. In other words, in the 2010/11–2019/20 period a team was more likely to have a player sent off if it is playing away, it is the underdog, and if the match is even. Finally, the estimated season effects follow the pattern shown in Figure 18.1.

Once we distinguish between the no-VAR period and the VAR period the picture changes. Interestingly, the home effect is significant in the period without VAR, but it is no longer statistically significant once the VAR has been introduced. Since we control for team quality by including the team's position and win probability as covariates, we interpret this as a 'true' home bias that is not confounded by a different style of play when playing at home (usually, more offensively). This home advantage ceases to exist once the VAR is introduced. The VAR is not physically in the stadium but at the headquarters of the national football association, and hence not subject to crowd pressure, unlike the referee.

Next, we estimate a model to explain the probability of a direct red card, with results shown in Table 18.3. We use the same set of covariates as before, and a consistent picture emerges. First of all, there is no home advantage. Depending on the other covariates, a home team is no more or less likely to receive a direct red card, and this is found both in the complete sample and when we distinguish between the no-VAR and the VAR period.

Table 18.2 *Logit models to explain probability of dismissal during a game (clustered standard errors)*

	All (1)	No VAR (2)	VAR (3)
home	−0.305***	−0.279**	−0.386
	(0.101)	(0.112)	(0.241)
position	−0.0004	−0.002	0.005
	(0.011)	(0.012)	(0.027)
pwin	−1.238***	−1.355***	−0.827
	(0.304)	(0.346)	(0.694)
uo	−0.486**	−0.380	−0.878**
	(0.205)	(0.232)	(0.426)
season 2011–2012	0.115	0.112	
	(0.189)	(0.188)	
season 2012–2013	0.125	0.126	
	(0.192)	(0.193)	
season 2013–2014	−0.130	−0.127	
	(0.199)	(0.200)	
season 2014–2015	−0.216	−0.211	
	(0.202)	(0.201)	
season 2015–2016	−0.491**	−0.484**	
	(0.212)	(0.212)	
season 2016–2017	−0.250	−0.247	
	(0.203)	(0.202)	
season 2017–2018	−0.495**	−0.493**	
	(0.210)	(0.212)	
season 2018–2019	−0.143		
	(0.196)		
season 2019–2020	−0.224		−0.089
	(0.221)		(0.222)
Constant	−1.326***	−1.314***	−1.501***
	(0.243)	(0.266)	(0.505)
Observations	5,876	4,820	1,056
Log Likelihood	−1,834.071	−1,510.476	−322.724
Akaike Inf. Crit.	3,696.143	3,044.953	657.449

Note: * $p < 0.1$; ** $p < 0.05$; *** $p < 0.01$.

As before, a team's current ranking does not influence the likelihood of a red card. Then, favorites (teams with a high win probability) are in all three models less likely to receive a direct red card. This again shows the importance of distinguishing a home effect from a quality effect, as also discussed extensively in Buraimo et al. (2010). Also, matches that have

Table 18.3   Logit models to explain probability of direct red card during a game (clustered standard errors)

	All (1)	No VAR (2)	VAR (3)
home	−0.124	−0.126	−0.110
	(0.124)	(0.140)	(0.282)
position	−0.008	−0.006	−0.025
	(0.014)	(0.015)	(0.035)
pwin	−1.438***	−1.392***	−1.695**
	(0.382)	(0.432)	(0.864)
uo	−0.676**	−0.509*	−1.307***
	(0.264)	(0.308)	(0.496)
season 2011–2012	0.023	0.018	
	(0.234)	(0.235)	
season 2012–2013	0.090	0.091	
	(0.232)	(0.233)	
season 2013–2014	−0.253	−0.250	
	(0.250)	(0.250)	
season 2014–2015	−0.330	−0.323	
	(0.257)	(0.254)	
season 2015–2016	−0.634**	−0.625**	
	(0.270)	(0.267)	
season 2016–2017	−0.422*	−0.418*	
	(0.253)	(0.252)	
season 2017–2018	−0.791***	−0.788***	
	(0.286)	(0.284)	
season 2018–2019	−0.108		
	(0.239)		
season 2019–2020	−0.251		−0.155
	(0.278)		(0.279)
Constant	−1.656***	−1.755***	−1.307**
	(0.300)	(0.326)	(0.630)
Observations	5,876	4,820	1,056
Log Likelihood	−1,286.427	−1,046.629	−238.939
Akaike Inf. Crit.	2,600.855	2,117.259	489.878

Note: * $p < 0.1$; ** $p < 0.05$; *** $p < 0.01$.

lower uncertainty of outcome have a lower incidence of direct red cards. One could argue that crowd pressure could influence the referee to being more lenient towards teams playing at home, and that the introduction of the VAR has mitigated this effect. However, from our estimates it is clear that there is no home advantage in the period without the VAR in the first place. We conclude that direct red cards are more likely if a team is expected to play defensively (low win probability) and if both teams are evenly matched (small difference in win probability).

Now that we have seen that the incidence of direct red cards varies systematically with win probability and uncertainty of outcome, we continue by looking at the potential dismissal of a direct red card. Since disciplinary actions are taken by the referee, Figure 18.2 shows the total number of direct red cards given by the 15 referees appearing most frequently in our dataset.

As noted earlier, we do not know the referee for every match in the dataset. The fact that Kevin Blom has shown 38 direct red cards may be due to his tendency to issue direct red cards or to him officiating in many more matches than the other referees in Figure 18.2. However, 16 percent of his direct red cards were dismissed, and that number can be compared to Bas Nijhuis having 7 percent of his red cards dismissed (2 out of 29) and Pol van Boekel having none dismissed (0 out of 26). Clearly, there is a lot of variation in dismissal rates by referees; and, indeed, the distribution of dismissals conditionally on the number of red cards given by each referee

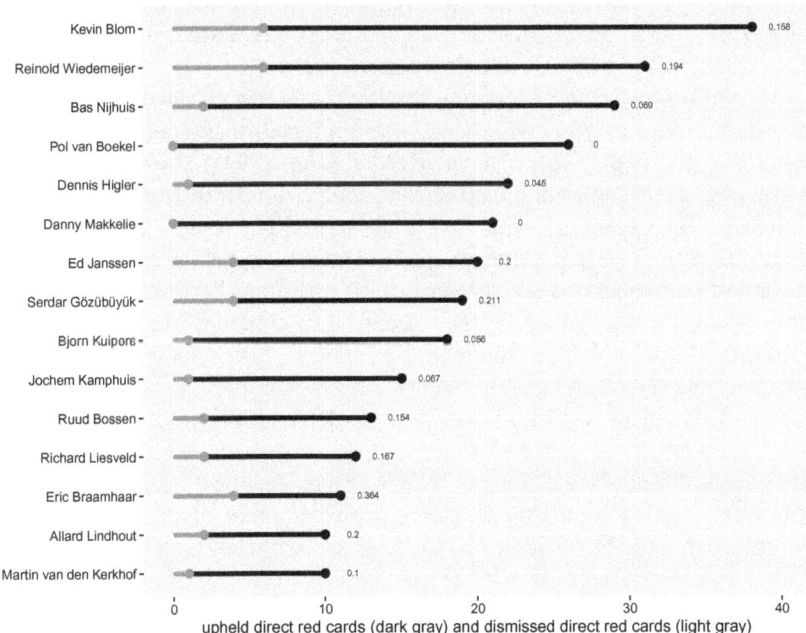

Figure 18.2   Number of upheld (dark gray) and dismissed red cards (light gray) by referee (fraction of dismissals at line ends)

is not compatible with the assumption that the probability of a card being dismissed is equal for all referees.

However, part of this variation may be due to observable covariates. Referees are not allocated randomly to matches. To see whether any observable factors determine dismissal, we use the same covariates as earlier: home advantage, team position, win probability, and uncertainty of outcome. To these we also add the time the red card was given. Referees and players become more tired during the match and may become more prone to errors. Moreover, we include disappointment at the time of the card, measured by the difference between the *ex ante* expected number of points and the actual number of points at that moment. This variable would be positive if a team is expected to win but behind in the actual score. Disappointed players may lose control and be more emotional. Direct red cards due to violent conduct or verbal abuse may be easier to determine unambiguously than those due to dangerous play.

We estimate both a logit model with these six covariates and a conditional logit model where we allow for referee-specific fixed individual effects (Chamberlain, 1980). The estimation results are shown in Table 18.4. From these results, it is clear that none of the covariates bear any significant relation to the probability of dismissal. We therefore conclude that variation in the likelihood of dismissal is due to referee-specific individual heterogeneity rather than observable match characteristics.

It requires a stretch of the imagination to determine the effect of direct red cards that are rescinded. Clearly, the affected teams may be short of points at the end of the season. Ridder et al. (1994) show that a team with 11 players remaining on the field has a significantly higher scoring intensity: the expected number of goals scored per minute increases by a factor of 2.00 for home teams and 1.56 for away teams. In other words, the team left with ten players is at a serious disadvantage because they concede more goals on average; and if the red card is rescinded during the judiciary process, it is possible that that team may have lost the match because of an error by the referee. The team may finish lower in the final rankings, with due consequences regarding distribution of television proceeds, qualification for lucrative European tournaments, relegation, etc. The effect of dismissed red cards is not negligible. We calculate the amount of noise in the final ranking by taking the score at the moment of the red card that would eventually be dismissed as the final score of that match. Clearly, this is not a realistic assumption if the card was given early in the match, but we maintain this assumption here. Also, we ignore dynamics during a season: teams may put in more effort if they face relegation.

As a descriptive measure of the consequences of rescinded red cards, we calculated the number of teams that would have changed position in

Table 18.4   Logit models to explain probability of dismissal of direct red card

	Logit	Conditional logit
home	−0.590	−0.576
	(0.449)	(0.476)
position	0.017	−0.008
	(0.041)	(0.045)
pwin	0.021	−0.367
	(1.341)	(1.423)
ou	0.459	−0.053
	(0.807)	(0.872)
disappointment	−0.112	−0.179
	(0.225)	(0.254)
time card	−0.009	−0.009
	(0.007)	(0.007)
Constant	−1.709*	
	(0.901)	
Observations	356	356
Log Likelihood	−122.839	−81.916
Akaike Inf. Crit.	259.678	

Note: * $p < 0.1$; ** $p < 0.05$; *** $p < 0.01$.

the final ranking. On average, between three and four teams change position each season, with a minimum of zero teams in some seasons and a maximum of 11 in 2012/13. The final ranking in that season was evidently tainted by dismissed red cards. In both 2010/11 and 2011/12 teams in 16th position in the final ranking had to play promotion/relegation matches post-season. In both cases the teams would have finished 15th (with no post-season playoffs) had the score at their dismissed direct red cards been the final score of those matches.

5.   CONCLUSION

This chapter has looked at the determinants of direct red cards in soccer. We have shown that the rate of red cards per match has not changed since the introduction of the Video Assistant Referee (VAR). The probability of a referee giving a red card was shown to depend significantly on win probability and uncertainty of outcome. An underdog team or a team playing an opponent with similar win probability is more likely to receive a direct red card. Direct red cards can be appealed against, and an appeal may lead to the card being rescinded. However the probability of a successful appeal was shown to vary according to the referee who initially gave the direct red card, but not with observable covariates. At an aggregate level, the likelihood of overturning a direct red card has not changed with the introduction of the VAR. Finally, we have shown that under restrictive assumptions incorrect direct red cards do have an effect on final league ranking, with possible consequences for the distribution of television receipts, qualification for European tournaments, and promotion/relegation.

NOTES

1. For simplicity, and in accordance with the empirical analysis below, we take players to be males. Of course, red cards are an equally important sanction in women's soccer.
2. An earlier version of the dataset was compiled by honors students Marlijn Botter and Melissa Spijkers.

REFERENCES

Buraimo, B., D. Forrest, and R. Simmons (2010). The 12th man?: Refereeing bias in English and German soccer. *Journal of the Royal Statistical Society, Series A, 173*(2), 431–449.

Chamberlain, G.A. (1980). Analysis of covariance with qualitative data. *Review of Economic Studies, 47*(146), 225–238.

Dawson, P., S. Dobson, J. Goddard, and J. Wilson (2007). Are football referees really biased and inconsistent? Evidence on the incidence of disciplinary sanctions in the English Premier League. *Journal of the Royal Statistical Society, Series A, 170*, 231–250.

Garicano, L., I. Palacios-Huerta, and C. Prendergast (2005). Favoritism under social pressure. *Review of Economics and Statistics, 87*(2), 208–216.

IFAB (2016). Laws of the game 2016/17. Technical report, International Football Association Board, Zurich.

Joustra, S.J., R.H. Koning, and A. Krumer (2021). Order effects in elite gymnastics. *De Economist, 169*, 21–35.

Price, J., and J. Wolfers (2010). Racial discrimination among NBA referees. *Quarterly Journal of Economics, 125*(4), 1859–1887.

Ridder, G., J.S. Cramer, and P. Hopstaken (1994). Down to ten: Estimating the effect of a red card in soccer. *Journal of the American Statistical Association, 89*, 1124–1127.

19. "Form is temporary, class is permanent": an English Premier League analysis

Stefan Szymanski and Guy Wilkinson

1. INTRODUCTION

The outcome of a contest depends on the relative resources brought to bear in the contest by each side. This observation is the mainstay of the economic theory of contests (see e.g. Corchón (2007) and Van Long (2015)). This theory has a natural application to sporting contests such as Association football (see e.g. Szymanski (2003)). It is now fairly uncontroversial to argue that team resources in football can be measured by wage payments (e.g. Peeters and Szymanski (2014)) or public estimates of player transfer values, which are closely correlated with salaries (Szymanski (2013)). That is because there is a well-developed market for players, with many buyers and sellers who are well informed about player abilities (because players perform often and in public), and hence most of the problems typically associated with asymmetric information in labour markets are absent.

"Form is temporary, class is permanent" is a sporting cliché, sometimes attributed to the legendary Liverpool manager of the 1960s and 1970s, Bill Shankly. In our context, "class" may be thought of as the perceived ability of a player, which determines the salary agreed under contract. Without questioning the truth of the cliché, "form", broadly defined, also plays a role in determining the outcome of a sporting contest. In this chapter we examine various ways of defining form, which may contribute to the outcome of football matches. Specifically, we define a narrow version of form as the outcome of the previous five games played by each team. In addition we define team "sharpness" as the number of consecutive games played by each player in the last five games, and team "cohesion" as the number of players who have appeared as starters in the previous five games. While these factors are largely under the control of the coach, we consider two factors over which they have less control. One is the distance to be travelled by the visiting team, which is completely beyond the control of the team. The other is the amount of rest time of the starting players since the previous game (up to a maximum of 77 days – one week for each starter). While the coach has some control over this, through selection, scheduling constraints are externally imposed.

We examine three ways in which our measures of class and form might influence outcomes. First, we consider the "aggregate result", meaning the total goals scored, or the whether the outcome was decisive (i.e. not a draw). Second, we consider the "home team result" – the outcome of the game for the home team (win, draw, lose). Finally, we consider "surprise" – meaning the extent to which *ex ante* probabilities (measured by betting odds) differ from the actual outcome (Van Ours and Van Tuijl (2016)).[1] Temporary factors such as those described above would be the ones most likely to contribute surprises. We find that only relative team value (class) significantly affects the aggregate result, while the home team result is significantly influenced by both class and form factors.

2. LITERATURE

Studies of the determinants of match outcomes in football have largely focused on the estimation either of production functions (for a survey see Jamil (2019)) or prediction models focused on the possibility of outperforming bookmaker odds (for a survey see Vaughan Williams (2009)). From the perspective of economic analysis, both of these are problematic.

Treating sports team performance as a production function depending on labour and capital inputs misses the fundamental context of the game – neither team can produce anything without the input of its opponent. Studies have not treated opponents as inputs, and it's not clear a priori how such an analysis would be conducted. Statistical models designed for the purposes of prediction rather than analysis lack a behavioural foundation. Typically results are modelled contingent on past results, so winning leads to more winning and losing leads to more losing. Such models can frequently match the accuracy of bookmaker odds, but lack economic content.

Szymanski and Smith (1997) modelled league performance as a contest, and used financial data on English clubs to identify the relationship between resources (wage spending) and contest success (league position). They also controlled for the number of different players appearing for each team in each season, a proxy for injury effects. Peeters and Szymanski (2014) extended this to a game-by-game analysis, also using data on financial resources, but had no information on individual players. Szymanski and Wilkinson (2016) used data on individual player transfer values to identify the contribution of each individual player to team success. In this chapter we use that same dataset, using player values to control for player quality ("class", if you will).

Numerous studies have argued that team structure, i.e. the way in which the team is composed, plays a role in outcomes. Such studies have examined the proposition that salary inequality undermines team effectiveness, although the results vary widely: some find that inequality leads to a higher team winning percentage, while others find the opposite (see Cyrenne (2018) for a review of the literature). As far as we are aware, the measures of sharpness and cohesion, which we discuss in the next section, have not been experimented with in the previous literature. On the issue of rest, however, there is a substantial literature.

Soccer is a sport with both physically and mentally demanding components. Top-class players on average travel 11km during each match, varying by player and team position (Bangsbo (1994); Reilly (1997)). Players perform around 1350 individual activities, inclusive of 69 high-speed runs and 109 moderate-speed runs (Mohr et al., (2003)). In addition to these runs, other energy-demanding activities include accelerating, dribbling, tackling, jumping and turning (Bangsbo, (1994)). Conceptually, rest times should matter as players will need time to recover from their physical exertions.

The role of fatigue in sports has mostly been researched from outside the perspective of economics, but some research exists that looks not just at rest but at related factors that may affect performance. Looking at the National Basketball Association (NBA) over a 19-year period, Ashman et al (2010) find that the home team performs poorly when playing the second of two back-to-back games and where the visiting team had one or two days' rest. This effect is greater when the home team had travelled easterly across time zones between games. Entine and Small (2008) show that lack of rest for the road (away) team is an important, although not dominant, factor in determining NBA home-court advantage. Differences in rest and travel between teams can also contribute to home advantage. Carmichael and Thomas (2005) find evidence for home advantage in the English Premier League (EPL), suggesting team selection for home and away games as a contributing factor. Neville and Holder (1999) provide evidence to suggest that travel factors contribute in part to home advantage provided the journey crosses several time zones. In countries where the travel distance is not so large, crowd factors appeared to be the main cause of home advantage rather than travel distance. Some papers analyse the relationship between team performance in soccer and the distance travelled to an away game. Oberhofer et al. (2010) show that team performance declines the further the distance to the away venue. In the US National Football League (NFL), Nichols (2014) finds that teams are more likely to lose if they are travelling a longer distance, especially when crossing at least one time zone from east to west. This is supported by Nutting and Price (2017), who similarly find that teams win more often in the NBA when playing to the east of their home time zones and less often when playing to the west during the 1991–2002 seasons. This relationship existed for these seasons' day games rather than the more frequent night games, and the relationship disappeared in the 2002–2013 seasons.

Krumer and Lechner (2018) investigate whether midweek games give an advantage to teams in the German Bundesliga. They find that home teams perform far worse in midweek matches than in weekend matches, such that the home advantage completely disappears for midweek games. Since mid-week matches are allocated unevenly among teams, the schedule favours teams with fewer home games midweek. The authors hypothesize that home teams perform worse for midweek games due to lower attendance and the perception that these home games are less important. Importantly, they rule out the hypothesis that the midweek effect is a result of teams being more tired because they have less rest time. Rohde and Breuer (2017) find that football clubs reduce effort if intra-season objectives have been met in the German Bundesliga, if UEFA Champions League (UCL) knock-out rounds have been clinched, or if important UCL games follow within the next five days of a Bundesliga match. Football managers engage in strategic behaviour, they argue, motivated by financial incentives and team fitness concerns.

Scoppa (2015) investigated the role of fatigue in matches played by national teams in all tournaments of the FIFA World Cup and UEFA European Championship, finding that, under the current structure of these international tournaments, there are no relevant effects of different days of rest on team performance.

3.   DATA

In this chapter we analyse data for Premier League teams for the 21 seasons 1992/93–2012/13. The main variables considered in our analysis are:

1.   Team ability ("class"): we use a Transfer Price Index (TPI).[2] The data includes information on teams and their players who participated in each individual game over the 21 seasons, giving a total 2557 players in 8226 individual matches (with 90,486 separate player appearances)

contested by 45 unique Premier League football teams. A transfer fee value requires a transfer to have occurred, while 28.3 per cent of appearances were by "homegrown" players for whom a fee had never been paid. We normalized the value of a player in any given season by the average rate of annual transfer fee price inflation, and then we assumed that homegrown players had the median value of a transferred player in that season. Thus we are able to construct a TPI index for each team in each game.

2. Form: for this we take the total number of points won (3 for a win, 1 for a draw) in the previous five games of the season.
3. Distance travelled by the visiting team: based on the distance between clubs.[3]
4. Cohesion: the number of unique players in the last five games (ranging from 11 to 55) then normalized by dividing through by 11.
5. Sharpness: the combined total of the last five games each member of the starting XI also started. This ranges from 0 (no players played in any of the previous five games) to 55 (all 11 players started in all of the last five games).
6. Rest: in order to construct a measure of rest periods we had to take account of games played outside of the Premier League, including 1250 European Cup (Champions League, Europa League, and their previous incarnations), 1380 League Cup, and 1469 FA Cup fixtures. The Total Rest Period (TRP) counts the total number of days each starting player on the team had rested before the current game (up to a maximum of 77 days), while the Total Opponent Rest Period (TORP) captures this measure for the opposing team.

Table 19.1 presents summary statistics of team characteristics over three partitions of the dataset. The TPI mean value for teams is higher on average for teams having just played a midweek game, which is consistent with the fact that better teams play more often midweek. This is heavily influenced by many midweek games being played in European competitions. Therefore, the average rest time for these teams is approximately ten days lower than their opponents'. While this may appear a large difference, it translates to just under one less day of rest per starting player. The goal difference for home teams averages at 0.4 goals per game. This increases to 0.6 when selecting for home teams who have played midweek. When playing away from home the average goal difference decreases to 0.3 goals per game, which may be a factor of both home advantage and team rest. Measures of team sharpness, cohesion and player rotation appear broadly consistent throughout, suggesting no drastic rotation strategies adopted by teams playing midweek games. The average net change in TPI value for

Table 19.1   Descriptive statistics of team characteristics

Variable	All League Games (N = 8226)	Weekend League Games after Home Team Midweek Games (N = 2438)	Weekend League Games after Away Team Midweek Games (N = 2419)
TPI of home team (£m)	68.3 (53.2)	80.5 (61.1)	67.8 (53.3)
TPI of away team (£m)	67.9 (52.8)	67.0 (53.0)	79.0 (58.9)
Rest time for home team (days)	62.5 (16.0)	49.6 (10.0)	59.4 (15.3)
Rest time for away team (days)	62.7 (15.9)	59.8 (15.3)	50.0 (10.1)
Goal difference (home team)	0.4 (1.7)	0.6 (1.7)	0.3 (1.8)
Home team sharpness	37.4 (10.9)	38.1 (8.5)	38.4 (9.0)
Away team sharpness	37.1 (10.9)	38.5 (8.8)	37.8 (9.0)
Home team cohesion	1.4 (0.2)	1.5 (0.2)	1.4 (0.2)
Away team cohesion	1.4 (0.2)	1.4 (0.2)	1.5 (0.2)
Number of home team players changed from last game	2.1 (1.8)	2.7 (2.3)	2.3 (2.0)
Number of away team players changed from last game	2.2 (1.8)	2.3 (2.1)	2.7 (2.3)
Net TPI of home team players changed from last game (£m)	0.9 (11.3)	2.0 (14.7)	1.4 (11.5)
Net TPI of away team players changed from last game (£m)	0.2 (11.6)	1.0 (12.2)	1.4 (15.4)

Note: Standard deviation reported in parentheses.

home teams is higher than for away teams as home teams usually field their strongest side to make the most of a their home advantage. After playing a midweek game we find that teams will rotate in a slightly stronger team for a home weekend game than if they are the away team.

4.   RESULTS

In our empirical results we were interested in three questions. First, how are the total goals scored and the result of a game affected by our variables? Second, how was the result (win, draw, lose for the home team) affected by our variables? Third, to the extent that a result was unexpected (a surprise), to what extent was it affected by our variables?

4.1 Total Goals and Result (Draw/No Draw)

By "result" in this context we mean a game that does not end in a draw. Table 19.2 reports our regression estimates. As can be seen, very few variables register any statistical significance, and the overall explanatory power is low. The one factor that appears to influence the total number of goals in a game is the absolute value of TPI differences – in other words, the more unbalanced the teams in terms of class, the more goals will be scored. This perhaps helps explain why the uncertainty of outcome hypothesis, which asserts that demand is increasing in the product of win probabilities for each team, is so seldom supported in the data (see Szymanski and Winfree (2018) for a recent review). Perhaps not surprisingly, this difference also makes it more likely that the game will end in a result rather than a draw. The probability of a result is increasing in the distance travelled by the visiting team and the difference in form of the two teams. Notably, the only variables in the result regressions that are significant are those that relate to differences, not absolute values.

4.2 Home Team Result (Win, Draw, Loss) and Goal Difference

We now consider the outcome of the game from the perspective of the home team (Table 19.3). What matters for the result of each game is not the absolute resources of each team, but the team resources relative to its rival. Distance once again plays a very significant role: if the visiting team had a long way to travel this favours the home team, a result that has previously been remarked upon in the literature. Likewise, the squad values as measured by the TPI have nearly equal and opposite signs. The more "class", the more likely the team is to win; and, once again, this result is well established in the literature. Likewise, the home team's form enters positively and the away team's negatively.

Cohesion, which measures the extent to which the team composition changes from game to game, is not significant. However, sharpness, meaning the extent to which the starting XI had appeared in the previous five games, is highly significant. Clearly, cohesion and sharpness are related concepts; but the former largely represents the cohesion of the team as a whole, while the sharpness measure focuses on individuals.

The rest variable is ambiguous. For most specifications it is significant for the home team but not the visiting team. More rest for the home team appears to improve performance, but this effect diminishes (the squared term is negative). This makes sense since too much rest reduces match sharpness.

Table 19.2   Total results: goals and decisiveness (i.e. game not drawn)

Dependent variable	Total goals OLS	Total goals OLS	Result logit	Result logit
Distance between home and away team ground	0.0102 (0.0185)	0.0113 (0.0194)	0.0546** (0.0242)	0.0681*** (0.0262)
Sum of teams' TPI values (log £m)	0.0648 (0.0417)	0.0923 (0.075)	0.140** (0.0547)	0.083 (0.101)
Absolute difference of teams' TPI values (log £m)	0.171*** (0.0321)	0.116*** (0.0388)	0.171*** (0.0427)	0.174*** (0.0528)
Sum of home and away team form	−0.00343 (0.00487)	−0.00585 (0.00501)	−0.00165 (0.00635)	−0.00404 (0.00665)
Absolute difference of home and away team form	−0.00619 (0.00716)	−0.00808 (0.00718)	0.0202** (0.00974)	0.0206** (0.00992)
Sum of home and away team cohesion	0.0793 (0.0646)	0.0882 (0.0661)	0.147* (0.0859)	0.118 (0.0894)
Absolute difference of home and away team cohesion	−0.0051 (0.15)	−0.0374 (0.15)	−0.0323 (0.201)	−0.0215 (0.203)
Sum of home and away team sharpness	0.000184 (0.00101)	0.000109 (0.00102)	−0.000383 (0.00135)	−0.000114 (0.00137)
Absolute difference of home and away team sharpness	−0.000865 (0.00437)	−0.000464 (0.00442)	0.00999* (0.00605)	0.00957 (0.0061)
Sum of home and away team rest	0.000891 (0.000708)	0.00119* (0.000716)	−0.000107 (0.000939)	−6.42E−06 (0.000953)
Absolute difference of home and away team rest	0.00195 (0.00168)	0.00187 (0.00168)	0.000991 (0.00226)	0.000788 (0.00229)
/cut			12.502** (1.001)	1.435 (1.939)
Constant	0.937 (0.758)	0.526 (1.43)		
Observations	8,057	8,057	8,057	8,057
Home and away team fixed effects	No	Yes	No	Yes
R-squared	0.006	0.024		

Note: Robust standard errors in parentheses; *** $p < 0.01$, ** $p < 0.05$, * $p < 0.1$.

Table 19.3   Home team result (win, lose or draw) and goal difference

Dependent variable	Result logit	Result logit	Goal difference OLS	Goal difference OLS
Distance between home and away team ground	0.0867*** (0.0204)	0.0802*** (0.0222)	0.0712*** (0.0169)	0.0631*** (0.0177)
TPI of home team (log £m)	0.528*** (0.0332)	0.403*** (0.0654)	0.514*** (0.0273)	0.337*** (0.052)
TPI of away team (log £m)	−0.528*** (0.0344)	−0.361*** (0.065)	−0.495*** (0.0275)	−0.364*** (0.0524)
Home team form	0.0427*** (0.00756)	0.0207*** (0.00795)	0.0409*** (0.00634)	0.0189*** (0.00654)
Away team form	−0.0376*** (0.00767)	−0.0131 (0.00814)	−0.0371*** (0.00641)	−0.0165** (0.00663)
Home team cohesion	0.256* (0.147)	0.0362 (0.152)	0.239** (0.122)	0.0547 (0.123)
Away team cohesion	−0.067 (0.149)	0.0854 (0.154)	−0.0615 (0.122)	0.0566 (0.123)
Home team sharpness	0.0165*** (0.00419)	0.0191*** (0.00428)	0.0115*** (0.00346)	0.0142*** (0.00345)
Away team sharpness	−0.0158*** (0.00427)	−0.0184*** (0.00434)	−0.00937*** (0.00346)	−0.0120*** (0.00344)
Home team rest (days)	0.0364*** (0.0141)	0.0305** (0.0146)	0.0219* (0.0116)	0.0165 (0.0116)
Home team rest (days) squared	−0.000317*** (0.00012)	−0.000256** (0.000124)	−0.000196** (9.94E−05)	−0.000142 (9.93E−05)
Away team rest (days)	−0.0119 (0.014)	−0.00815 (0.0145)	−0.00924 (0.0118)	−0.00623 (0.0118)
Away team rest (days) squared	0.000108 (0.000119)	6.41E−05 (0.000124)	8.65E−05 (0.000101)	5.30E−05 (0.000101)
/cut1	0.318 (0.889)	0.996 (1.705)		
/cut2	1.584* (0.889)	2.293 (1.705)		
Constant			−0.957 (0.739)	−0.0345 (1.349)
Observations	8,057	8,057	8,057	8,057
Home and away team fixed effects	No	Yes	No	Yes
R-squared			0.141	0.173

Note: Robust standard errors in parentheses; *** $p < 0.01$, ** $p < 0.05$, * $p < 0.1$.

4.3 Surprise

We can use the form variable to derive simple measure of the "surprise" associated with a result. We can define the probability of home win as the ratio homeform/(homeform + awayform), and therefore the surprise is the difference between the outcome and the probability, where the outcome = 1 if a home win, 0.5 if a draw and 0 if a home defeat.

Table 19.4 reports a regression of surprise on our variables of interest. A positive coefficient indicates a surprise in favour of the home team, and a negative value means a surprise that favoured the visiting team. Longer distances travelled by the visiting team favour the home team, while the quality of each team, as measured by the TPI, is positively associated with a favourable surprise for that team. Form is negatively associated with the success of each team, suggesting there is some regression to the mean. Once again cohesion does not appear significant; however, sharpness is highly significant and once again rest increases the chance of a surprise, but only insofar as the rest relates to the home team.

5. CONCLUSION

In this chapter we have attempted to quantify the contributions of "class" and "form" to the performance of English Premier League results. We assume that we can proxy class by the transfer value of a player, while form is represented by a variety of measures which include the recent results of the teams, the cohesion and sharpness of the teams, the amount of rest they had and the distance the visiting team had to travel.

We examine three issues: the contribution of these variables to (1) the overall result – goals scored and whether the game produced a winner; (2) the success of the home team in the game; and (3) the extent to which the game generated a surprise based on recent results.

We find that the only factor that seems to influence the overall result significantly is the relative TPI values of the two teams – our measure of "class". When it comes to the result viewed by the home team, all the variables except cohesion play a significant role, and have the expected signs. These variables also tend to explain surprises, although the coefficients are generally smaller and less likely to be statistically significant.

There are a number of ways this research could be extended. The availability of transfer market data, which can be shown to correlate closely with audited wage payments from clubs, means that this exercise could be conducted for a number of different leagues. It would also be possible to develop a model in which each variable was weighted by the value of

Table 19.4   Regression of surprise results

Dependent variable	Surprise OLS	Surprise OLS
Distance between home and	0.0171***	0.0150***
away team ground	(0.00425)	(0.00447)
TPI of home team (log £m)	0.110***	0.0826***
	(0.00672)	(0.0129)
TPI of away team (log £m)	−0.110***	−0.0733***
	(0.00672)	(0.0129)
Home team form	−0.0249***	−0.0298***
	(0.00154)	(0.0016)
Away team form	0.0243***	0.0297***
	(0.00159)	(0.00165)
Home team cohesion	0.0604**	0.0146
	(0.0299)	(0.0303)
Away team cohesion	−0.0252	0.0078
	(0.0304)	(0.0307)
Home team sharpness	0.00318***	0.00367***
	(0.000844)	(0.000842)
Away team sharpness	−0.00296***	−0.00347***
	(0.00085)	(0.000844)
Home team rest (days)	0.00767***	0.00638**
	(0.00291)	(0.00293)
Home team rest (days) squared	−6.63e−05***	−5.33e−05**
	(2.49E−05)	(2.50E−05)
Away team rest (days)	−0.00273	−0.00189
	(0.00292)	(0.00293)
Away team rest (days) squared	2.44E−05	1.51E−05
	(2.49E−05)	(2.50E−05)
Constant	−0.168	−0.334
	(0.184)	(0.34)
Observations	8,057	8,057
Home and away team fixed effects	no	yes
R-squared	0.088	0.119

Note: Robust standard errors in parentheses; *** $p < 0.01$, ** $p < 0.05$, * $p < 0.1$.

the player concerned so that, for example, the rest time of a star player is more valuable than the rest time of a journeyman. Ultimately, it might be possible to construct an index of player volatility, where volatility in performance could be accounted for by factors related to form, and their share in the ability measure quantified.

NOTES

1. Previous studies have found that surprise is an important factor in determining demand for attendance at football matches.
2. The TPI index was compiled by Graeme Riley, a football statistician. We are grateful to him for allowing us to use his data.
3. Data kindly supplied by Professor Tunde Buraimo.

REFERENCES

Ashman, T., Bowman, R.A., and Lambrinos, J. (2010). The role of fatigue in NBA wagering markets: The surprising "home disadvantage situation". *Journal of Sports Economics*, 11(6), 602–613.

Bangsbo, J. (1994). The physiology of soccer: With special reference to intense intermittent exercise. *Acta Physiologica Scandinavica. Supplementum*, 619, 1–155.

Carmichael, F., and Thomas, D. (2005). Home-field effect and team performance: Evidence from English premiership football. *Journal of Sports Economics*, 6(3), 264–281.

Corchón, L.C. (2007). The theory of contests: A survey. *Review of Economic Design*, 11(2), 69–100.

Cyrenne, P. (2018). Salary inequality, team success, league policies, and the superstar effect. *Contemporary Economic Policy*, 36(1), 200–214.

Entine, O.A., and Small, D.S. (2008). The role of rest in the NBA home-court advantage. *Journal of Quantitative Analysis in Sports*, 4(2), 1–9.

Jamil, M. (2019). Team production and efficiency in sports. In Downward, P., Frick, B., Humphreys, B., Pawlowski, T., Ruseski, J., and Soebbing, B. (eds), *The SAGE Handbook of Sports Economics*. London: Sage, 210–218.

Krumer, A., and Lechner, M. (2018). Midweek effect on performance: Evidence from the German soccer Bundesliga. *Economic Inquiry*, 56(1), 193–207.

Mohr, M., Krustrup, P., and Bangsbo, J. (2003). Match performance of high-standard soccer players with special reference to development of fatigue. *Journal of Sports Sciences*, 21(7), 519–528.

Neville, A.M., and Holder, R.L. (1999). Home advantage in sport. *Sports Medicine*, 28(4), 221–236.

Nichols, M.W. (2014). The impact of visiting team travel on game outcome and biases in NFL betting markets. *Journal of Sports Economics*, 15(1), 78–96.

Nutting, A.W., and Price, J. (2017). Time zones, game start times, and team performance: Evidence from the NBA. *Journal of Sports Economics*, 18(5), 471–478.

Oberhofer, H., Philippovich, T., and Winner, H. (2010). Distance matters in away games: Evidence from the German football league. *Journal of Economic Psychology*, 31(2), 200–211.

Peeters, T., and Szymanski, S. (2014). Financial fair play in European football. *Economic Policy*, 29(78), 343–390.

Reilly, T. (1997). Energetics of high-intensity exercise (soccer) with particular reference to fatigue. *Journal of Sports Sciences*, 15(3), 257–263.

Rohde, M. and Breuer, C. (2017). Financial incentives and strategic behavior in European professional football: A match day analysis of starting squads in the

German Bundesliga and UEFA competitions. *International Journal of Sport Finance*, 12(2), 160–182.

Scoppa, V. (2015). Fatigue and team performance in soccer: Evidence from the FIFA World Cup and the UEFA European Championship. *Journal of Sports Economics*, 16(5), 482–507.

Szymanski, S. (2003). The economic design of sporting contests. *Journal of Economic Literature*, 41(4), 1137–1187.

Szymanski, S. (2013). Wages, transfers and the variation of team performance in the English Premier League. In Rodríguez, P., Kesenne, S., and García, J. (eds), *The Econometrics of Sport*. Cheltenham, UK and Northampton, MA, USA: Edward Elgar Publishing, 53–62.

Szymanski, S., and Smith, R. (1997). The English football industry: Profit, performance and industrial structure. *International Review of Applied Economics*, 11(1), 135–153.

Szymanski, S., and Wilkinson, G. (2016). Testing the O-ring theory using data from the English Premier League. *Research in Economics*, 70(3), 468–481.

Szymanski, S., and Winfree, J. (2018). On the optimal realignment of a contest: The case of college football. *Economic Inquiry*, 56(1), 483–496.

Van Long, N. (2015). The theory of contests: A unified model and review of the literature. In Congleton, R.D., and Hillman, A.L. (eds), *Companion to the Political Economy of Rent Seeking*. Cheltenham, UK and Northampton, MA, USA: Edward Elgar Publishing, 19–52.

Van Ours, J.C., and Van Tuijl, M.A. (2016). In-season head-coach dismissals and the performance of professional football teams. *Economic Inquiry*, 54(1), 591–604.

Vaughan Williams, L. (2009). *Information Efficiency in Financial and Betting Markets*. Cambridge: Cambridge University Press.

20. Peer enforcement in teams: evidence from high-skill professional workers with repeated interactions

Brad R. Humphreys and Jie Yang

INTRODUCTION

Firms often organize employees into teams. Economists posit that firms organize workers into teams to take advantage of complementarities, increasing the productivity and output of teams beyond that of individual workers. Organizing workers into teams also generates problems. Holmstrom (1982) showed that groups of workers with inter-related productive inputs generate a moral hazard problem in the form of an incentive for some team members to supply less effort, or shirk. Successful teams exploit complementarities and reduce the incentive for individual workers to shirk.

The incentive to shirk in teams can be mitigated in several ways. Che and Yoo (2001) analyzed incentives in teams when the team members repeatedly interact and observe the behavior of others. Their model shows that compensation schemes rewarding an employee when co-workers perform well, and punishing when co-workers perform poorly, have desirable properties under repeated teammate interaction. Ishida (2006) generalizes this model to address relative, not absolute, compensation and generates similar predictions. The key feature in these models is the existence of sanctions imposed by team members for past behavior that can reduce shirking.

We develop evidence from the field that incentives like those described in the model developed by Che and Yoo (2001) exist. Mas and Moretti (2009), Ichino and Maggi (2000), Chan et al. (2014), and Bäker and Mechtel (2019) develop evidence of peer interaction in teams using data from cashiers in a national supermarket chain, an Italian bank, cosmetic sales in a department store in China, and a laboratory experiment respectively. Mas and Moretti focus on peer interaction and productivity; Ichino and Maggi focus on the incidence of shirking. Depken and Haglund (2011) also develop evidence of peer effects in team sports, although this evidence is based on observed productivity, not earnings of team members.

We analyze performance and earnings of members of a high-skill, high-salary team that interacts repeatedly – offensive linemen in the US National Football League (NFL). Offensive line play in the NFL is complex and highly inter-related. We find that, after controlling for unobservable worker-specific heterogeneity, experience, and other personal and team-specific characteristics, a specific observable effort signal generated by teammates reduces the salaries of offensive linemen but has no effect on teammates' salaries, providing an optimal, low powered sanctioning mechanism for individual workers. This result supports predictions from the model developed by Che and Yoo (2001).

MOTIVATION AND CONTEXT

Che and Yoo (2001) developed a model of team behavior that includes long-term interaction among team members; the model features an infinitely repeated game in which team members observe the effort of other workers on the team and decide how much effort to supply in each period. Ishida (2006) extended this model to the case where only relative performance analysis takes place. Each worker's strategy is a function that maps all possible past effort decisions into a probability distribution over current effort decisions by team members.

In this model a firm hires two identical workers to repeatedly perform a specific project or task. Each worker makes a binary effort decision k to either supply effort ("work," $k = 1$) or not supply effort ("shirk," $k = 0$) in each period. Effort requires a cost e, but shirking entails no effort-related cost. The key feature of the model is that the workers experience close interaction in each period, so they perfectly observe all effort decisions. The model includes mutual monitoring, an important feature of any team-based work arrangement. The workers interact only through their effort decisions in this model; they cannot exchange side payments. The model predicts that effort decisions generate self-enforcing incentives that take the form of punishing other team members by shirking.

Firms do not observe individual effort decisions made by workers in this model. Instead, firms receive a binary signal, x_i, that is either good ($x_i = 1$) or bad ($x_i = 0$). This imperfect signal about the workers' effort decision reflects both the individual's effort and a random environmental shock that affects both workers. This common environmental shock is either favorable or unfavorable, and the probability of a favorable common shock is σ. In an alternative version of the model, the firm receives a single imperfect signal that is the result of the team effort and the environmental shock instead of a signal for each team member. The predictions of the model do not depend critically on the nature of this signal.

The team production arrangement is open-ended and terminates with probability $1 - \delta$ at the end of each period, so δ indicates how long teams remain together. The workers always have incentive to shirk since effort is costly but shirking is not easily observed given the imperfect effort signal.

The firm wants to induce workers to supply positive effort in each period because the outcome when both workers provide positive effort is more valuable than other outcomes. The firm's problem is to motivate both workers to provide positive effort in every period at minimum cost using some wage scheme. Specifically, the wages cannot be negative and depend on the verifiable signals received by the firm. Clearly, an important feature of the wage scheme designed by the firm in this context is how an individual's compensation relates to the performance of other team members.

Two possible wage schemes exist in this setting: a wage scheme based on relative performance evaluation (RPE) under which a worker is penalized when other team members perform well and rewarded when other team members perform poorly; and a wage scheme based on joint performance evaluation (JPE) under which a worker is rewarded when other team members perform well and penalized when other team members perform poorly.

Tournament theory represents a special form of RPE; under RPE, the worker perceived to perform the best, based on the signals received, earns the highest compensation, the second best the second highest, and so on. RPE wage schemes appear to be ineffective when workers interact closely with each other, perhaps because it leads to competition among team members, especially when workers can sabotage others in the competition (Lazear, 1989).

JPE wage schemes overcome these problems in settings where workers interact repeatedly by reducing the negative aspects of competition while providing team members with a mechanism to deter shirking. Under JPE, a worker can shirk in order to punish another team member because the other team member's compensation will be reduced by this action. Che and Yoo (2001) show that the firm can make a larger profit under JPE than under RPE when workers repeatedly interact because the total cost of the wage scheme is lower under JPE than RPE.

Che and Yoo (2001) demonstrate that JPE wage schemes are optimal relative to RPE wage schemes in settings where workers on a team interact repeatedly, no matter how long workers remain in teams. RPE wage schemes are more likely to be optimal as the probability of favorable common shocks increases. JPE wages schemes have another important property in this model: the explicit incentives, those that affect wages directly, must be relatively low powered for shirking to be a credible pun-ishment strategy. In other words, for shirking to be deterred, the deterrence mechanism must affect the other worker more than the worker who seeks to deter shirking; the effect must be asymmetric.

The presence of JPE or RPE wage schemes in a team can be empirically investigated. Given data on the earnings of individual workers who are organized into teams and interact repeatedly in production, and proxy variables for positive or negative effort signals received by firms, under RPE wage schemes, a larger number of negative signals from other workers on the team would be associated with higher earnings by a given worker, and a larger number of positive signals from other workers would be asso-ciated with lower earnings for a given worker. Under JPE wage schemes, a larger number of negative effort signals from other workers represent peer sanctions. In addition, the model developed by Che and Yoo (2001) predicts that JPE wage schemes would be more likely to be observed in a setting where the teams are relatively long-lived and where the probability of common positive shocks to team members is relatively low.

One setting where JPE wage schemes might be present is among offensive linemen in professional leagues like the NFL. Che and Yoo (2001) identify three characteristics of a team in the context of their model: (1) frequent and consistent interaction over a long period of time; (2) autonomy to make independent decisions on assignments and problem solving; and (3) encouragement to monitor and motivate each other.

Offensive linemen must work together closely in a highly coordinated way. Assignments for individual linemen on each play are highly inter-related and complex. NFL teams attempt to reduce turnover in personnel on the offensive line; and, since NFL players only gain free agency after three years of experience in the league, offensive linemen often play together for a number of seasons. During the game, the offensive line makes its own play calls at the line of scrimmage after the quarterback calls the play in the huddle, suggesting that the offensive line has some independent decision-making power.

On an NFL team the offensive line typically contains five team members. The center plays in the middle of the line and snaps the football, handing or throwing it between his legs to the quarterback to initiate each play. Next to the center are the right and left guard, and outside the guards are the right and left tackle. Offensive linemen cannot touch the ball in most circumstances; the goal of this team is to provide open space for other players advancing the ball by running and to protect the quarterback when he passes the ball.

The primary activity performed by offensive linemen, "blocking," involves physical interaction with defensive players; a large body of rules specify exactly how an offensive lineman can legally touch a defensive player, and specify illegal forms of interaction that, if detected by an official, will result in a penalty. Offensive linemen also must, by rule, remain absolutely still until the center snaps the ball to the quarterback and cannot run forward on passing plays.

In the context of effort supply, we interpret penalties committed by offensive linemen as a signal of shirking. Seven officials monitor play in NFL games. Three of these officials monitor offensive linemen for rule violations as these players are subject to a large number of rules that proscribe specific activities.

Two common penalties committed by offensive linemen are false starts and holding. A false start occurs when an offensive lineman moves before the center has snapped the ball to the quarterback, and results in a 5-yard penalty. Holding occurs when an offensive lineman (or other offensive player) grabs or tackles a defensive player in a way prohibited by the rules, and results in a 10-yard penalty. When an offensive lineman commits holding, he supplies less effort than he would do if no penalty was committed. A false start is a mental error, but can also be interpreted as supplying less effort – in this case effort to remember the signal for the snap of the ball.

In the model developed by Che and Yoo (2001), firms receive a signal that reflects both effort supplied by workers and a common random shock. NFL teams receive signals about the effort supplied by offensive linemen during games. Clearly, NFL players could engage in a number of forms of shirking. In addition to penalties, giving up sacks is a second possible type of shirking. On a passing play, the offensive line attempts to keep defensive players from tackling the quarterback before he can throw the ball.

A sack occurs when a defensive player tackles the quarterback in the backfield before he can throw the ball. This results in a loss of yardage, a bad outcome for the offense. We interpret a sack allowed by an offensive lineman as a signal of shirking. Implicitly, if an offensive lineman had supplied more effort, a sack could have been avoided on a play. Unlike penalties, which are monitored by the officials, coaches and other workers must monitor offensive linemen on passing plays to determine the amount of effort supplied.

Since the effort signal includes a random component, shirking can be masked by ability, random events, or the presence of a relatively strong opponent. Shirking frequently occurs when a player faces an evenly matched or stronger opponent (a negative shock) since shirking would be easily observed when facing a weaker opponent (a positive shock). In practice, shirking may be identified by a coach after reviewing game video, which is costly and inefficient. Shirking cannot be easily determined during a game, when coaches must make personnel decisions based on the game situation and specific player match-ups. Also, some sacks can't be awarded to specific players even after video review. But offensive linemen on the field during the game have better information about effort supply. Because of repeated interactions, they know more than anyone else about their colleagues' effort supply. So, mutual monitoring and punishment would be an efficient and less costly way to deter shirking during games.

We empirically analyze the relationship between these two effort signals and the salaries earned by these players. Again, we assume that penalties committed and sacks allowed can be interpreted as signals of effort supplied by offensive linemen. Since we observe both signals received by the firm and the salaries of the team members, this information can be exploited to determine if a JPE wage scheme exists for these high-skilled workers. Again, under JPE wage schemes, workers are penalized for poor performance by teammates, a mechanism through which workers, over the course of repeated interaction, punish other workers for supplying lower levels of effort. If penalties committed or sacks allowed by team-mates reduces the compensation of offensive linemen, then outcomes in this setting are consistent with JPE wage schemes, supporting the model developed by Che and Yoo (2001).

DATA DESCRIPTION

Our data include information about the performance and earnings of NFL offensive linemen, and their NFL teams, over the 2000 to 2009 regular seasons. Our basic unit of observation is an individual NFL offensive lineman over a season. Offensive line play is highly inter-related. Unlike many other positions on an NFL team, the offensive linemen must cooperate and work as a unit in order to perform well. The data set we construct contains five types of information about offensive linemen: (1) individual performance data for each season; (2) player characteristics; (3) salary; (4) financial data for NFL teams; and (5) NFL team offensive performance.

The data were collected from a number of sources. The player performance and characteristics data are from several sports data websites, including the official NFL website, Stats Incorporated's fee-based STATSPASS database, and www.pro-football-reference.com; the salary data are from the *USA Today* NFL Salary database; the team-specific financial data are from the estimates published in *Forbes* magazine and on their website; and the teams' offensive performance data are generated from data on www.pro-football-reference.com. The data set contains 2,652 player-year observations including data for 688 unique players over the

Table 20.1   Summary statistics

Variable	Mean	Std. Dev.	Min.	Max.
Real Salary (millions)	1.87	1.89	0.089	14.20
Position: Center	0.17	0.38	0	1
Position: Guard	0.21	0.41	0	1
Position: Tackle	0.27	0.45	0	1
Multiple Position Player	0.35	0.47	0	1
Height (inches)	76.4	1.63	72	81
Weight (pounds)	310	20.2	228	375
Years' Experience	5.75	3.32	1	20
Overall Draft Selection	137	97	1	277
Undrafted Player	0.21	0.41	0	1
Games Started	10.1	6.45	0	16
Yards per Penalty	6.02	3.31	0	15
Yards per Sack	5.28	3.22	0	22
Teammates' Yards per Penalty	7.18	0.77	4.93	10
Teammates' Yards per Sack	6.41	0.94	3	10.37

2000 to 2009 seasons.[1] Summary statistics for the player characteristics and salary variables are shown in Table 20.1.

NFL player compensation consists of guaranteed pay in the form of a "signing bonus," an annual "base salary" paid to players who remain on the team's roster, and performance-based pay that depends on team performance and the number of plays each player participated in over the course of a season.[2] Neckermann et al. (2014) analyze such bonus pay in a different setting. See Salaga et al. (2014) for a general discussion of player investment decisions in professional sports leagues. Our measure of salary is the "cap value" accounted for by each player on the offensive line.

The NFL regulates the fraction of total revenues that can be paid to players. While this is called a "salary cap," a more accurate description is a ceiling and floor on total payroll. The NFL "salary cap" does not regulate or limit the amount that can be paid to any player; it places a lower and upper limit on the total payroll for players on each team as a fraction of specific revenues. Most salaries in the NFL are not guaranteed, and players under contract for multiple years can be released at any time.

The "cap value" is the compensation paid to each player that counts toward total team payroll; it includes base salary, a prorated portion of the signing bonus, and incentive bonuses. The cap value reflects the total compensation of the player in a season, including performance bonuses that depend on the number of plays participated in per season. Cap value can vary depending on the number of plays an individual participates in, so coaches can affect this salary by keeping players on the sideline. Cap value is the standard salary measure in the NFL and was used by Berri and Simmons (2009), Simmons and Berri (2009), Berri et al. (2011), and Keefer (2013). The average salary in the sample is $1.87 million per season. The salary variable exhibits high variability and a long right tail.

In American football, there are three offensive line positions: center, guard, and tackle. In our data, some players are identified as generic offensive linemen and not as playing a specific position. Players identified as generic offensive linemen either played multiple positions on the offensive line or information about their specific position is not available. The latter case happens in the early years of our data. We create four indicator variables to identify linemen playing these four positions.

From Table 20.1, about one-third (35 percent) of the players are identified as generic offensive linemen in the sample. Notice that creating dummy variables in this way has a limitation: We do not differentiate between left tackle and right tackle. NFL teams often treat left tackles and right tackles differently. A left tackle is often paid more because he protects the quarterback's "blind side"; since most NFL quarterbacks are right-handed, a defensive player approaching the quarterback from his left cannot be easily seen.

Size is an important characteristic for offensive linemen. We collected data on the players' height in inches and weight, which ranges from 228 to 375 pounds (103–170 kilograms). The offensive linemen in the sample have a large weight range; the difference between the maximum and minimum weight is 147 pounds. However, weight may not be a good indicator of characteristics that affect performance in this setting.

Like other North American professional sports leagues, the NFL conducts an annual reverse-order entry draft to allocate incoming players to teams. In this sample period, the NFL entry draft contained seven rounds. *Overall Draft Selection* is the position where each player was selected. Hendricks et al. (2003) show that draft order is an important measure of the value of a player in the NFL. If a player was not drafted, teams expected that he might not be good enough to make an NFL roster. For undrafted players, we assign 277 to their pick number.[3] We also incorporate an indicator variable, *Undrafted*, equal to one if the player was not drafted, together with *Overall Draft Selection*, to capture the effect of not being drafted on salaries; 20 percent of the players in the sample were undrafted.

Better players should start in more games in a season, and receive higher salaries. The variable *Games Started* equals the number of games started by each player in the sample. The average offensive lineman in the sample started ten games per season. *Years' Experience* measures the number of years played in the NFL. For players who entered the NFL through the entry draft, experience is based on the draft year. For players who were not drafted, experience is based on the first year they entered the league.

The variables of interest are the player effort signals. Stats Incorporated's STATSPASS database contains information about the performance of individual offensive linemen in the NFL. This includes information about the number of penalties committed by each offensive lineman, the number of sacks given up by each offensive lineman, and the yards lost associated with each of these effort signals.

For each player, we divide *penalty yards* by *penalties committed* to estimate *Yards per Penalty*. Average yards per penalty committed reflect both the rate at which penalties are committed and how much the team is punished for the penalties. For example, if two players have the same total penalty yards, say 15, three 5-yard penalties (average 5) may be less harmful to the team than one 15-yard penalty (average 15). The second reason to use average yards per penalty is that reserves play fewer downs than starters, and so could have fewer penalties and fewer penalty yards. But a reserve player's average yards per penalty may not be small.

The same problem also applies to sacks allowed and sack yards. Thus we also calculate *Yards per Sack* from *sacks allowed* and *sack yards*. Moreover, since offensive line play is highly inter-related, we incorporate other offensive linemen's performance variables into the model. Those variables are *Teammates' Yards per Penalty* and *Teammates' Yards per Sack* in Table 20.1.

Manski (1993) pointed out a problem that occurs when a researcher observes the distribution of behavior in a population and tries to determine the extent to which this behavior influences the behavior of individuals in this population – the "reflection" problem. We avoid this issue by explaining variation in the salary of an individual offensive lineman using variables that reflect the behavior of all other members of the offensive line excluding that individual. *Teammates' Yards per Penalty* and *Teammates' Yards per Sack* only reflect the behavior of other teammates, and differ for each individual in the sample.

The average offensive lineman in the sample committed 3.29 penalties per season. Only in about 17 percent of the player-seasons did a lineman not commit a penalty. However, many of those penalty-free player-seasons were by little-used reserves. Among players who started eight or more games, only about 4 percent of the player-seasons were penalty-free. The maximum number of penalties committed in the sample was 17. The average yards per penalty in the sample was just over 6.

The average offensive lineman in the sample allowed just under three sacks over the course of a season. In about 18 percent of the player-seasons the player did not give up a sack. Again, this is sensitive to the number of games started. Among players who started at least eight games in a season, the average number of sacks allowed was four, and only 3 percent of the player-seasons in the sample were seasons with no sacks given up. The average yards per sack given up in the sample was just over 5.

EMPIRICAL ANALYSIS

We analyze longitudinal data on the performance of NFL offensive line-men over ten seasons. We observe individual performance and salary for the same offensive linemen over multiple seasons, so our data constitute an unbalanced panel. Controlling for unobservable heterogeneity – in the form of ability, desire, and other intangible characteristics – represents an important econometric issue in this setting.

Researchers typically consider two types of estimators when analyzing panel data with unobservable heterogeneity: fixed effects (FE) and random effects (RE) estimators. Mundlak (1978) points out that the RE estima-tor assumes all explanatory variables are exogenous and uncorrelated with unobservable individual effects, while the FE estimator assumes all explanatory variables are endogenous and correlated with the unobserv-able individual effects. In the case where some explanatory variables are exogenous and uncorrelated with unobservable individual effects and other explanatory variables are endogenous and correlated, neither the FE nor the RE estimator works well. We likely face a situation where some, but not all, of the observable variables are correlated with unobservable individual characteristics. Kahn (1993) discusses this problem and the merits of these two estimators in the context of empirical research on earnings in profes-sional sport.

Hausman and Taylor (1981) proposed an estimator appropriate for the case where some of explanatory variables are correlated with unobservable individual effects and others are not. This estimator is based on an instru-mental variables (IV) approach. The instruments are constructed using the strictly exogenous variables between and within variations. This estimator is called the Hausman–Taylor or HT estimator (Baltagi et al., 2003). Buraimo et al. (2008) applied the HT estimator to data from professional sport; Dixit and Pal (2010) used it to analyze group incentives.

In general, the estimator developed by Hausman and Taylor (1981) takes the form

$$y_{it} = X_{it}\beta + Z_i\alpha + d_i + u_{it} \tag{20.1}$$

where the subscript i identifies the cross-sectional unit ($i = 1, 2, ..., N$) and the subscript t identifies the time periods ($t = 1, 2, ..., T$). In this context, the cross-sectional units are players and the time periods seasons.

X_{it} is a vector of time-varying explanatory variables and Z_i is a vector of time-invariant explanatory variables; d_i and u_{it} are unobservable random variables that affect the dependent variable y_{it}; d_i is assumed to be *i.i.d* $(0, \sigma^2_d)$ and u_{it} is *i.i.d* $(0, \sigma^2_u)$. Both are independent of each other and among themselves; d_i is the unobservable individual effect. In this setting, d_i captures a player's skill, ability, motivation, or "coachability" that cannot be reflected in performance statistics and other unobservable factors that affect the performance of offensive linemen in the NFL, including but not limited to the will to win, morale, leadership, and other intangibles. Both X and Z can be split into two sets of variables, i.e. $X = [X_1, X_2]$ and $Z = [Z_1, Z_2]$. X_1 and Z_1 are exogenous and uncorrelated with both d_i and u_{it}; X_2 and Z_2 are endogenous and correlated with d_i only.

Again, neither the RE nor the FE estimator applies in this setting. The RE estimator, which is basically GLS applied to Equation (20.1), ignoring the endogeneity of X_2 and Z_2, will yield consistent but biased parameter estimates, while the FE estimator, or mean-differencing the explanatory variables in Equation (20.1), eliminates the individual effect d_i as well as the time-invariant variables Z_i, and hence cannot yield estimates of the vector α, though it can yield consistent estimates of β. The HT estimator resolves this problem.

Hausman and Taylor (1981) develop a variant of the standard IV estimator. It first premultiplies Equation (20.1) by $\Omega^{-1/2}$, where Ω is the covariance matrix of error term $d_i + u_{it}$. After the transformation, it uses a standard two-stage least squares IV (2sls) approach with instruments $[Q, X_1, Z_1]$, where Q is for demeaning the variable, specifically $Q y_{it} = y_{it} - \bar{y}_i$. Therefore, the Hausman–Taylor estimator is basically equivalent to perform 2sls using $[\tilde{X}, \bar{X}1, Z_1]$ as instruments. Intuitively, $\tilde{X}$ can be the instrument for X_2 and $\bar{X}1$ is for Z_2. The advantage of the HT estimator is that all the instruments are derived from within the model: $\tilde{X}$ is the matrix of the deviation of X (both X_1 and X_2) from its associated mean; $\bar{X}1$ is the mean of the exogenous time-varying variables. These are the standard within and between components of the FE and RE estimators.

Another important issue associated with the HT estimator is the identification condition for the model. As pointed out by Baltagi et al. (2003), if the number of exogenous time-varying variables X_1 is greater than or equal to the endogenous time-invariant variables Z_2, the model is identified and the HT estimator is more efficient than the FE estimator. If the condition fails, the model is under-identified and the HT estimator cannot outperform FE and the coefficient on Z, α, cannot be estimated.

The specific form of the HT estimator in this case is:

$$\ln salary_{it} = X_{1it}\beta_1 + X_{2it}\beta_2 + Z_{1i}\alpha_1 + Z_{2i}\alpha_2 + d_i + u_{it} \qquad (20.2)$$

where X_{1it} is a vector of $n \times k_1$ exogenous, time-varying explanatory variables that are assumed to be uncorrelated with d_i; X_{2it} is a vector of $n \times k_2$ endogenous, time-varying variables that are assumed to be correlated with d_i; Z_{1i} is a vector of $n \times l_1$ exogenous, time-invariant explanatory variables that are not correlated with d_i; Z_{2i} is a vector of $n \times l_2$ endogenous, time-invariant variables that are correlated with d_i; and d_i is a player-specific effect. The model is identified when $k_1 \geq l_2$. Note that X_{1it} contains variables identifying the NFL team that each lineman played for over the sample period, capturing unobservable heterogeneity across NFL teams. It is time-varying because some players change NFL teams in the sample period. Unobservable NFL team-specific heterogeneity may arise from various sources, such as organizational culture, managerial style, owner and coach preferences, and factors related to the city where the team plays.

Again, we have an unbalanced panel; the cross-sectional unit is an individual NFL offensive lineman. The dependent variable is the natural logarithm of each player's real salary in each season. The model contains 43 variables classified in four categories (exogenous time-varying, endogenous time-varying, exogenous time-invariant, and endogenous time-invariant).

The vector of exogenous time-varying variables contains 34 variables, including 32 NFL team dummy variables *Years' Experience* and its square, *Years' Experience*^{2}, which together measure the effect of experience. All these variables are assumed to be independent of the unobservable individual characteristics. It is unlikely that unobservable individual characteristics (for example ability, will to win or competitive drive) influence the player's NFL team or experience.

Though a talented player is expected to play longer in the league, many talented NFL players retire early because of injury. The typical NFL career is short, normally less than ten years. Some less-talented players may stay in the league for a relatively long time as long as they stay healthy. We include *Years' Experience* and *Years' Experience*^{2} in the model; we expect a positive coefficient on *Years' Experience* and a negative coefficient on the squared term.

The vector of endogenous time-varying variables includes six variables: an indicator variable identifying linemen who played multiple positions over the course of the season; the number of games started in the season; and four variables reflecting the effort signals received by the team – yards per penalty, yards per sack allowed, teammates' yards per penalty, and teammates' yards per sack allowed.

Linemen who played multiple positions are likely to be reserves filling in occasionally at many positions, perhaps because they lack the ability to start at a position full time. We expect the coefficient on this variable to be negative. Better players should start in more games in a season, so *Games Started* should have a positive coefficient.

Again, effort signals received about individual players (yards per penalty and yards per sack) reflect both effort decisions and a common shock experienced by all offensive linemen on a team. Penalty yards and sack yards reflect shirking by a player, so those variables are expected to have negative coefficients, based on standard efficiency wage theory. The signals received about other players' effort (teammates' yards per penalty and teammates' yards per sack) are motivated by the model of repeated interaction among workers on a team developed by Che and Yoo (2001) and discussed above. The estimated parameters on these variables will indicate the presence of JPE wage schemes, if negative, and RPE wage schemes, if positive.

The performance variables are all likely to be correlated with the unobservable individual effect. For example, if a player works very hard in both practice and games, he will probably perform well in games and the good performance would in turn affect his desire to win and/or other unobservable factors.

The only exogenous time-invariant variable is *Height*, which is constant over time. Height should be unrelated to ability or other unobservable individual characteristics in this setting. Height may be a basic physical qualification to become an offensive lineman; but, conditional on becoming a lineman, we can't say taller players are superior to shorter players, and the players themselves would not believe that being a few inches taller would bring them some advantage over other players. Unobservable individual heterogeneity should be uncorrelated with height.

Among offensive linemen, generally speaking, tackles are tallest, then guards, and centers are often the shortest players. NFL teams usually pay tackles, especially left tackles, more than other linemen. Taller players earn higher salaries, and we tentatively expect a positive coefficient on *Height*. In our data about 25 percent of players switch positions over their careers; height and position are not highly correlated.

The two endogenous time-invariant variables are *Undrafted* and *Overall Draft Selection*. These two variables, especially the second one, are indicators of players' ability and have significant effects on salary. Moreover, since draft order reflects NFL teams' assessment of individual ability, this variable is likely correlated with unobservable individual characteristics.

A player who is believed to have greater ability and potential will be selected earlier in the draft. Those factors will in turn influence attitude toward the game and effort. Since a smaller draft number means a better player, we expect *Overall Draft Selection* will have a negative coefficient. But for *Undrafted*, the sign could be either negative or positive because the effect of being undrafted is captured by both these variables. If the sign is positive for *Undrafted*, the coefficient on *Overall Draft Selection* plus the coefficient on *Undrafted* should be negative, in which case undrafted players earn less than the last drafted player.

In our model, $k_1 = 34$ and $l_2 = 2$; even after omitting one team indicator variable, k_1 is still much larger than l_2. Therefore, our model is identified.

RESULTS AND DISCUSSION

The parameter estimates, standard errors, and p-values obtained from the HT estimator applied to Equation (20.2) are shown in Table 20.2. We do not report the parameter estimates from the 31 team indicator variables since their effects are not of primary interest. These results are available by request from the authors.

The relationship between experience and salary takes the standard hump-shaped form, first increasing as human capital accumulates and then decreasing as it depreciates. Declining physical ability and the cumulative effect of injury and physical wear-and-tear also contribute to the decline in earnings as experience increases in this setting. As expected, linemen who play multiple positions earn less than those who play a single position, even holding games started constant. This effect may also reflect returns to specialization among offensive linemen in the NFL. Starting linemen earn a significant premium over reserves who start no games, or perhaps only a few games, per season.

The main variables of interest in the HT regression model are the two effort signals: committing penalties and allowing sacks. Again, the salary variable includes signing bonus, base salary, and performance-related pay that varies systematically with the number of plays participated in over the course of a season. Effort signals can affect salary if coaches make substitutions based on these signals over the course of a game, generating differences in the number of plays each player participates in over the course of a season.

The results exhibit an asymmetric pattern that supports the idea that a JPE wage scheme exists in this setting. One effort signal, giving up sacks, affects the salary of teammates. Each additional yard per sack given up by teammates reduces the earnings of an offensive lineman by about

Table 20.2 Hausman–Taylor regression results, NFL offensive linemen 2000–2009

Dependent Variable: Log(Real Salary)	Coefficient	Std. Err.	p-value
Variable Type: Time-Varying Exogenous			
Years' Experience	0.481	0.015	<0.001
Years' Experience^2	−0.024	0.001	<0.001
Variable Type: Time-Varying Endogenous			
Multiple Position Player	−0.158	0.046	0.001
Games Started	0.017	0.003	<0.001
Yards per Penalty	−0.010	0.004	0.014
Yards per Sack	−0.001	0.004	0.841
Teammates' Yards per Penalty	0.015	0.015	0.333
Teammates' Yards per Sack	−0.025	0.013	0.045
Variable Type: Time-Invariant Exogenous			
Height	0.154	0.059	0.009
Variable Type: Time-Invariant Endogenous			
Overall Draft Selection	−0.004	0.002	0.007
Undrafted	−0.017	0.504	0.972
Observations	2297		
Individuals	611		

2.5 percent. However, yards per sack given up by an offensive lineman do not reduce his own earnings. This pattern suggests that a low powered mechanism exists through which offensive linemen can punish teammates for shirking.

In the repeated interaction that takes place on an NFL offensive line over a season, if teammates observe another lineman shirking, they can punish him by giving up sacks without reducing their own salary, providing a low power mechanism for enforcing a sub-game perfect equilibrium in which these workers supply effort in each period, just as the model developed by Che and Yoo (2001) predicts.

Note that sacks have less impact on salary than offensive holding, a penalty that might be committed to avoid a sack; offensive holding results in a 10-yard penalty, while the average sack in the 2002–2009 NFL seasons resulted in a 6.37-yard loss (median 7-yard loss). This result is consistent with the use of JPE wage schemes based on sacks allowed among teams of workers on the offensive line.

The other effort signal, penalties committed, does not appear to be a viable mechanism to punish other workers who shirk. The yards per penalty committed by other teammates does not affect the earnings of individual linemen. However, the larger the yards per penalty committed, the lower that lineman's salary, other things equal. Unlike sacks allowed, the commission of penalties is monitored by an independent party. Each additional yard of penalties committed reduces the earnings of a lineman by 1 percent. This result can be motivated by the model developed by Kvaløy and Olsen (2012), which includes indispensable human capital in teams. Alternatively, standard efficiency wage models, or principal–agent models with firm monitoring, can also motivate this result.

The results indicate that a salary premium to height exists in this setting. Taller offensive linemen earn more than their shorter teammates, other factors constant. The premium to height is substantial, about 15 percent per inch. The premium could be due to higher productivity among taller linemen. Persico et al. (2004) find a wage premium to height in the general population and attribute this to events in early adulthood. Schultz (2002) finds a wage premium to height and attributes it to human capital accumulation. These two explanations could also hold in this population.

The results also show that linemen drafted higher in the entry draft earn a higher salary, even years after being drafted and controlling for experience. This persistence of draft position in salaries was also documented by Hendricks et al. (2003) in the NFL. Note that 65 percent of the variation in the dependent variable can be attributed to unobservable player-specific heterogeneity captured by the random effects term in Equation (20.1).

ROBUSTNESS CHECKS

Table 20.2 contains results for a single model specification. The HT estimator can be sensitive to the specification of the time-varying endogenous and exogenous variables. No reliable, commonly used tests exist to provide guidance about which variables belong in which category in the HT estimator. We performed a number of robustness checks on the results reported in Table 20.2. The results, specifically the sign and significance of the effort signal variables, were not sensitive to these changes to the model.

We added a series of indicator variables for each season in the sample to capture any unobservable heterogeneity in offensive line play that would affect compensation, sacks allowed and penalties committed. These factors could include changes to the specific rules about what offensive linemen can and cannot do, and any changes in the enforcement of the existing rules that might vary systematically across seasons. The inclusion of this vector of indicators to the time-varying exogenous variable list had no effect on the parameter estimates of interest. We also added an indicator variable for changes in the head coach of the team; this also had no effect on the results.

Equation (20.1) does not control for systematic variation in the salaries of offensive linemen across positions on the line. If sorting by ability takes place – say the most talented linemen become tackles or the smartest linemen become centers – then this needs to be controlled for in the regression model. We included a vector of variables identifying the specific position played by the linemen in our sample, both as a time-varying exogenous and a time-varying endogenous variable. The inclusion of these indicator variables had no effect on the results. Similarly, changing the indicator variable for a lineman who played multiple positions from time-varying endogenous to time-varying exogenous had no effect on the results.

We also added *BMI* (body mass index) to the model as a time-varying endogenous variable. Although height does not change, weight does. *BMI* could affect agility, or other factors that affect the play of a lineman. Adding *BMI* and BMI^2 had no effect on the results.

The relationship between sacks allowed and the salary of offensive linemen could be affected by some confounding factors like the tendency of the team's offense to pass, the overall efficiency of the team's offense, or some other characteristic of the offense that affects the team's overall success. The results reported in Table 20.2 were robust to the inclusion of a variety of variables like the fraction of plays that were passes, yards per pass, the fraction of passes completed, and first down efficiency to the list of time-varying endogenous variables.

Differences in team financial conditions might systematically change the impact of effort signals on player salaries. For example, teams with lower revenues might punish players with many negative shirking signals more than teams with higher revenues. The results reported in Table 20.2 were robust to the inclusion of a variety of variables reflecting the revenues earned by teams and the fraction of the team's revenues paid to players.

We also estimated a fixed effect model version of Equation (20.1); the results were similar to the Hausman–Taylor results in Table 20.2 for the effort signal variables. Note that the three time-invariant variables *Height*, *OverallDraftSelection*, and *Undrafted* were omitted due to collinearity. As mentioned in the empirical approach section, the FE estimator can yield consistent estimates of time-varying variables by eliminating the individual effect and time-invariant variables.

EVIDENCE FROM PLAY-BY-PLAY DATA

The regression results in the previous section suggest that giving up a quarterback sack represents a low powered effort signal in a joint performance evaluation wage scheme. In order to give up a quarterback sack, a form of shirking, to be a low powered signal it must be possible for NFL offensive linemen to send such signals at points in the game where the game outcome will not be too adversely affected. For example, sending such a signal when the player's team is about to score a touchdown to tie or go ahead would not be low powered since it could lead to the team losing a winnable game. Also, not all sacks allowed are shirking-related signals; in some cases, sacks are unavoidable consequences of the game situation and personnel.

In order to assess the viability of allowing sacks as a shirking-related signal in a JPE wage scheme, we analyzed outcome data at the individual play level for all regular season games in the 2002 through 2009 seasons.[4] The sample contains information about 305,483 individual plays. We removed kickoffs, field goal attempts, punts, extra point attempts, and two-point conversion attempts as these plays could not result in a quarterback sack. We identified plays resulting in a quarterback sack, and the number of yards lost, from the remaining plays. A sack was defined as a play in which the quarterback was tackled at or behind the line of scrimmage. Plays where the quarterback advanced the ball for positive yardage were not identified as sacks: 10,394 of these 305,484 plays resulted in a quarterback sack for an average frequency of 3.4 sacks per 100 plays.

The average sack resulted in a loss of 6.37 yards; the longest sack in the sample resulted in a loss of 38 yards.[5] Unfortunately, we cannot link specific offensive linemen to a sack in this data set. Only the season-level data set analyzed in the previous section links specific offensive linemen to quarterback sacks allowed. This data source does contain information on the exact game conditions in terms of time, field position, down and distance, and score for each play during the NFL season. We identify games and game situations where giving up a quarterback sack would not have a large impact on the game outcome or season outcome for teams. In these situations, giving up a quarterback sack would have a low cost to the team in terms of the effect of this signal on the game or season outcome, a low powered signal.

We identified five different situations in which a quarterback sack might not affect game or season outcome: games early in the season; games with large point spreads where one team is much stronger than the other team; plays during games where one team has a large lead; plays late in games where one team has a large lead; and games where one of the teams has been eliminated from playoff contention. Sacks during these games, or plays during games with these conditions, could be considered low powered signals.

Table 20.3 summarizes the frequency and losses for quarterback sacks in each of these low and high power game situations. The first two columns are for high power game situations and the second two columns are for low power game situations. The first case is games early and later in the season. We divided games into the first four games of the season (games 1–4) and the last 12 games of the season (5–16). Games early in the season may be less important than games later in the season. From the top panel of Table 20.3, 228,480 plays took place in games 5–16 in this sample and 77,003 plays took place in games 1–4. The frequency of sacks allowed was identical in these two periods, 3.4 per 100 plays. The average loss on each sack was similar. There were 7,756 sacks in games 5–16 and 2,638 sacks in games 1–4 in these seasons.

The second low power setting is plays when one team has a large lead over the other team. We define a large lead as one of 14 points or more. From the second panel in Table 20.3, of the 305,483 plays analyzed, 60,875 (just under 20 percent), took place when one team had a 14-point lead or

Table 20.3   Sack statistics for low and high power game situations

	Mean	Number	Mean	Number
	Games 5–16		*Games 1–4*	
Sack frequency	0.034	228,480	0.034	77,003
Yards lost per sack	−6.39	7,756	−6.34	2,638
	Score difference ≤13		*Score difference ≥14*	
Sack frequency	0.033	244,608	0.037	60,875
Yards lost per sack	−6.34	8,170	−6.52	2,224
	Score difference ≤13, 4th Q		*Score difference ≥14, 4th Q*	
Sack frequency	0.036	54,916	0.037	27,749
Yards lost per sack	−6.30	1,952	−6.71	1,035
	Point spread ≤9		*Point spread ≥10*	
Sack frequency	0.034	259,200	0.034	46,283
Yards lost per sack	−6.37	87,98	−6.42	15,96
	Teams with ≤9 losses		*Teams with ≥10 losses*	
Sack frequency	0.034	268,810	0.034	36,673
Yards lost per sack	−6.38	9,132	−6.35	1,262

larger. The sack frequency was slightly higher when one team had a large lead, and the average sack resulted in a slightly larger loss, 6.52 yards, compared to the average loss during closer game situations.

A substantial number of sacks took place during these low powered game situations, providing offensive linemen with ample opportunities to send low powered effort signals. The third panel summarized sacks in the fourth quarter when one team has a large lead. This should be an even more low powered situation since little time remains in the game for the losing team to stage a comeback. The 27,749 plays run in this condition represents 9 percent of the plays in the sample. Again, the sack frequency is higher and the average sack results in a larger loss in this relatively low powered situation.

The fourth low powered setting analyzed involves games where one team is much stronger than the other. Since the weaker team is less likely to win a game, games with a large point spread could represent a low powered setting since the stronger team is much more likely to win the game no matter how many sacks are given up. We obtained data on the closing point spread for all NFL regular season games over the 2002–2009 seasons. We defined games where one team is perceived as much stronger than the other as games when one team was favored by ten or more points. This occurred in about 15 percent of the games played in this period. The rate of sack frequency was the same in games with a heavy favorite and games with no favored team or games with a smaller point spread. The average loss per sack was similar in the two groups of games.

Finally, games involving a team with no chance of making the playoffs could be low powered settings since one of the teams has less incentive to win the game. During the sample period, no team with more than nine losses qualified for the NFL post-season, so we split the sample into a subsample of games involving at least one team with ten or more losses and a subsample of games with no teams with ten or more losses. Games played by one or more teams with ten or more losses always occur late in the 16-game NFL season. From the bottom panel in Table 20.3, the sack frequency and average loss per sack were very similar in these two groups of games: 1,262 of the 10,394 sacks in the sample took place in games where one or more teams had ten or more losses. From Table 20.3, NFL offensive linemen have substantial opportunities to send low powered effort signals by allowing a quarterback sack over the course of an NFL season. Thousands of quarterback sacks take place in games, or game settings, where a quarterback sack is unlikely to have a large impact on the game or season outcome for the team.

CONCLUSIONS

Che and Yoo (2001) and Ishida (2006) developed models that describe the optimal incentives in a setting where a team of workers repeatedly interact in producing a specific type of output. These models conclude that when workers on a team interact repeatedly, firms have an incentive to use joint performance evaluation (JPE) wage schemes as they result in lower incentive costs when workers can monitor the effort decisions made by other team members and use a low powered punishment mechanism to deter other team members from shirking.

Offensive line play in the NFL contains a number of institutional characteristics that closely resemble the setting for the models developed by Che and Yoo (2001) and Ishida (2006). These workers interact repeatedly, can monitor each other, often motivate each other, and have significant autonomy to carry out their tasks during the course of a game; in addition, relative performance evaluation occurs in this setting. We collected data on two plausible effort signals that teams receive from offensive linemen: penalties committed, which can reflect shirking and are monitored by a group of independent agents, the officials in NFL games; and sacks allowed, which are monitored only by the players and coaches of the team.

We find that sack yards allowed by other linemen on the team significantly reduce the earnings of offensive linemen, but sack yards given up by each lineman does not reduce his own earnings, other things equal. These results are consistent with the presence of a low power punishment mechanism through which a group of team members can punish another team member who shirks during their repeated workplace interaction. The results are also consistent with the presence of JPE wage schemes in this setting. Both are features of the models developed by Che and Yoo (2001) and Ishida (2006), so the results here suggest that these models explain observed outcomes in the performance and earnings of NFL offensive linemen.

These results also extend the growing literature of the importance of peer effects in sport. Depken (2000) found evidence supporting peer effects in Major League Baseball. Guryan et al. (2009) found no evidence of peer effects in professional golf, based on a setting that includes random assignment of teammates. Depken and Haglund (2011) found evidence of peer effects in foot races. This analysis uses a novel setting, offensive line play in the NFL, which exploits the repeated nature of productive interaction in teams and which generates plausible observable effort signals. Both these features are unique to the literature on peer effects in teams.

Finally, the presence of JPE wage schemes and viable weak-powered enforcement mechanisms have important implications for research on the payroll–success relationship in professional sports. Many models in this literature assume that higher payrolls lead to increased production of wins; see, for example, the model developed by Fort and Quirk (1995). Che and Yoo (2001) show that JPE wage schemes generate incentives at a lower cost than relative performance evaluation (RPE) incentive schemes. If JPE wage incentive schemes are widespread in professional sports, then the relationship between total payroll and team success may not be as well-behaved or strong as many existing models of team production in sport assume, especially if some teams use JPE wage schemes and others use RPE schemes.

NOTES

1. Our data end in 2009 because that marks the end of our (quite expensive) access to the STATSPASS database, the source of the player-specific performance data. No significant changes in compensation or offensive line play have occurred in the NFL since this time.
2. Beginning in the 2002 season, NFL players qualified for performance-based compensation based on playing time. All players qualify for this performance-based pay. The largest bonus was $42,048 in 2002 and increased to $299,465 in 2012.
3. The largest draft number for drafted players in the sample is 276.
4. These data come from http://www.advancedfootballanalytics.com/2010/04/play-by-play-data.html.
5. Philadelphia quarterback Donovan McNabb versus the Oakland Raiders on 18 October 2009 in the second quarter when trailing by seven points.

REFERENCES

Bäker, A. and Mechtel, M. 2019. The impact of peer presence on cheating. *Economic Inquiry*, 57(2): 792–812.

Baltagi, B., Bresson, G., and Pirotte, A. 2003. Fixed effects, random effects or Hausman–Taylor? A pretest estimator. *Economics Letters*, 79(3): 361–369.

Berri, D.J. and Simmons, R. 2009. Race and the evaluation of signal callers in the National Football League. *Journal of Sports Economics*, 10(1): 23–43.

Berri, D.J., Simmons, R., Van Gilder, J., and O'Neill, L. 2011. What does it mean to find the face of the franchise? Physical attractiveness and the evaluation of athletic performance. *Economics Letters*, 111(3): 200–202.

Buraimo, B., Forrest, D., and Simmons, R. 2008. Insights for clubs from modelling match attendance in football. *Journal of the Operational Research Society*, 60(2): 147–155.

Chan, T.Y., Li, J., and Pierce, L. 2014. Compensation and peer effects in competing sales teams. *Management Science*, 60(8): 1965–1984.

Che, Y. and Yoo, S. 2001. Optimal incentives for teams. *American Economic Review*, 91(3): 525–541.

Depken, C.A. 2000. Wage disparity and team productivity: Evidence from major league baseball. *Economics Letters*, 67(1): 87–92.

Depken, C.A. and Haglund, L. 2011. Peer effects in team sports: Empirical evidence from NCAA relay teams. *Journal of Sports Economics*, 12(1): 3–19.

Dixit, K. and Pal, R. 2010. The impact of group incentives on performance of small firms: Hausman–Taylor estimates. *Managerial and Decision Economics*, 31(6): 403–414.

Fort, R. and Quirk, J. 1995. Cross-subsidization, incentives, and outcomes in professional team sports leagues. *Journal of Economic Literature*, 33(3): 1265–1299.

Guryan, J., Kroft, K., and Notowidigdo, M. 2009. Peer effects in the workplace: Evidence from random groupings in professional golf tournaments. *American Economic Journal: Applied Economics*, 1(4): 34–68.

Hausman, J.A. and Taylor, W.E. 1981. Panel data and unobservable individual effects. *Econometrica*, 49(6): 1377–1398.

Hendricks, W., DeBrock, L., and Koenker, R. 2003. Uncertainty, hiring, and subsequent performance: The NFL draft. *Journal of Labor Economics*, 21(4): 857–886.

Holmstrom, B. 1982. Moral hazard in teams. *Bell Journal of Economics*, 13(2): 324–340.

Ichino, A. and Maggi, G. 2000. Work environment and individual background: Explaining regional shirking differentials in a large Italian firm. *Quarterly Journal of Economics*, 115(3): 1057–1090.

Ishida, J. 2006. Team incentives under relative performance evaluation. *Journal of Economics and Management Strategy*, 15(1): 187–206.

Kahn, L. 1993. Free agency, long-term contracts and compensation in major league baseball: Estimates from panel data. *Review of Economics and Statistics*, 75(1): 157–164.

Keefer, Q. 2013. Compensation discrimination for defensive players: Applying quantile regression to the National Football League market for linebackers. *Journal of Sports Economics*, 14(1): 23–44.

Kvaløy, O. and Olsen, T.E. 2012. The rise of individual performance pay. *Journal of Economics and Management Strategy*, 21(2): 493–518.

Lazear, E.P. 1989. Pay equality and industrial politics. *Journal of Political Economy*, 97(3): 561–580.

Manski, C.F. 1993. Identification of endogenous social effects: The reflection problem. *Review of Economic Studies*, 60(3): 531–542.

Mas, A. and Moretti, E. 2009. Peers at work. *American Economic Review*, 99(1): 112–145.

Mundlak, Y. 1978. On the pooling of time series and cross section data. *Econometrica*, 46(1): 69–85.

Neckermann, S., Cueni, R., and Frey, B.S. 2014. Awards at work. *Labour Economics*, 31: 205–217.

Persico, N., Postlewaite, A., and Silverman, D. 2004. The effect of adolescent experience on labor market outcomes: The case of height. *Journal of Political Economy*, 112(5): 1019–1053.

Salaga, S., Ostfield, A., and Winfree, J.A. 2014. Revenue sharing with heterogeneous investments in sports leagues: Share media, not stadiums. *Review of Industrial Organization*, 45(1): 1–19.

Schultz, T. 2002. Wage gains associated with height as a form of health human capital. *American Economic Review*, 92(2): 349–353.

Simmons, R. and Berri, D. 2009. Gains from specialization and free agency: The story from the gridiron. *Review of Industrial Organization*, 34(1): 81–98.

21. Competing against the same team: does the length of time between the games matter? Evidence from the UEFA Champions League*

Alex Krumer

1. INTRODUCTION

There are many examples in professional sports in which two teams compete several times against each other over a short period of time.[1] This structure raises many questions, including: Does the winner of the first match have a higher win probability in the second match? Does the length of time between these matches have an effect on win probabilities? Does it matter whether the winner of the first match was the underdog or the favorite? These questions are mostly asked by sports fans, journalists and coaches. However, repeated games may be of much broader interest among economists, psychologists and others. This is because repeated interactions occur very often in many areas of life, such as politics, the labor market, tenders, etc. Therefore, insights obtained from sports competitions may also be useful in other domains.

In this study, I take advantage of real-life contests between professionals with large monetary rewards, where each pair of contestants competes against each other twice. However, some pairs compete twice in a row in two consecutive matches, whereas other pairs compete against each other for the second time after a longer period of time. Moreover, the allocation of pairs into treatment groups (playing the return match after a short period of time) and control groups (playing the return match after a long period of time) was determined via explicit randomization, which simplifies credible causal inference (Manski, 1995).

More specifically, I study the group stage of the European Champions League tournament organized by UEFA (the Union of European Football Associations), the sport's governing body in Europe. This is the most prestigious soccer tournament among clubs in Europe. According to UEFA, in the 2016/17 season, more than 1.3 billion Euros were shared among the clubs in the Champions League.[2] The group stage takes the form of a double round-robin tournament. Each group consists of four teams, and each team plays against the other teams at home and away. Therefore, each pair plays two games, and every team plays six matches (rounds).

What makes this structure suitable for studying the effect of length of time between the first and second match is that the teams that play against each other in Round 1 *always* compete for a second time in Round 5; teams that play against each other in Round 2 *always* meet again in Round 6; and, finally, teams that play against each other in Round 3 *always* compete for the second time in Round 4 (see Table 21.1). We can see that the only consecutive rounds that involve the same pair of teams are Rounds 3 and 4. Therefore, if there is an effect of the gap between the matches that involve the same teams, the results of the matches in Round 4 should differ from the results in the other matches.

Indeed, based on 1,961 matches covering the seasons 1995/96 to 2015/16, I find that a stronger team (the favorite) with regard to UEFA rankings achieves significantly fewer points in the 4th round than in any other round.[3] The estimated negative effect is about 0.20 points. Furthermore, in pairs in which the favorite did not win in the first leg (in Rounds 1–3), which may be considered a successful result for the underdog, the favorite achieved significantly fewer points in Round 4 compared to Rounds 5 and 6. The effect is approximately 0.30 points, which is about 25 percent of the standard deviation of the number of points per match a favorite achieves in the first three games. In contrast, no significant effect of Round 4 was found in pairs in which the favorite won the first leg (in Rounds 1–3).

Table 21.1   Schedule of sequential matches in the UEFA Champions League

Round 1	Team 1 – Team 2
	Team 3 – Team 4
Round 2	Team 2 – Team 3
	Team 4 – Team 1
Round 3	**Team 4 – Team 2**
	Team 1 – Team 3
Round 4	**Team 2 – Team 4**
	Team 3 – Team 1
Round 5	Team 2 – Team 1
	Team 4 – Team 3
Round 6	Team 3 – Team 2
	Team 1 – Team 4

I also find evidence that, in general, it is much more difficult to win two matches against the same opponent (both favorite and obviously underdog). However, as already noted, the findings suggest that successful result for the underdog team in the first game provides it with a better chance against a given favorite, but only if the next game between the teams takes place after a shorter period of time. The difference between the effects of previous success of underdog and favorite may stem from the fact that the underdog's success in the first leg was less expected. Therefore, it is possible that this unexpected success provided the underdog with additional confidence that turned into momentum in the next match. However, a win for the favorite is a much more expected result, and so is less likely to affect its performance in the following games.

The results of this study are in line with the literature on the relationship between confidence and performance. In his seminal paper, Bandura (1977) hypothesized that there was a positive relationship between self-confidence and performance. Hoff and Stiglitz (2010) showed that "Confidence, based on a person's perception ... of his empirical frequency of past success, affects the probability of success ... in future attempts, in ways that may be beyond his conscious control" (p. 11). Moreover, being more likely to succeed again after a successful action seems to be an evolutionary feature that goes beyond just humans: this effect was observed among insects (Adamo and Hoy, 1995), rats (van de Poll et al., 1982), and birds (Drummond and Canales, 1998).[4]

In addition, this chapter relates to the hot-hand literature that also deals with the effect of previous success on performance. The seminal paper by Gilovich et al. (1985), who coined the term "hot-hand fallacy," followed by many other works, argued that hot streaks in the performance of basketball players are most likely due to random variation, and are only a cognitive illusion and a general misconception of chance.[5] However, by using statistical measures with superior identifying power over previous studies, several more recent papers have shown that the hot-hand phenomenon is not a fallacy (Yaari and Eisenmann, 2011; Bocskocsky et al., 2014; Miller and Sanjurjo, 2014, 2018).

This hot-hand effect over different periods of time was also discovered in other settings. For example, Rosenqvist and Skans (2015) showed that golfers who succeeded marginally in one tournament performed better in the following tournament, which typically took place about one week later, than players who just marginally failed. Similarly, Jetter and Walker (2015) found that an additional win in ten recent tennis matches increased the likelihood of winning the next match. In their study, in about half of the observations the previous ten matches occurred within 12 weeks for men and 16 weeks for women. Unlike two previous papers that investigated the effect of success over longer periods of time, more recently Cohen-Zada et al. (2017) and Page and Coates (2017) studied the performance of contestants who competed very shortly after a previous success. Based on judo competitions, Cohen-Zada et al. found that in men's bronze medal fights a winner of the previous fight had a higher probability of winning against a loser of the previous fight. Similarly, based on tennis matches, Page and Coates showed that, among men, a winner of a closely fought tiebreak in the first set was more likely to win the second set. By varying the duration from a previous success, the findings of the current chapter suggest that the hot hand becomes colder with time.

Finally, this study is also applicable to the literature on the effects of schedule in tournaments. For example, it has been shown theoretically (Krumer et al., 2017) and confirmed empirically (Krumer and Lechner, 2017) that the probability of winning depends on the schedule in a single round-robin tournament. In another paper, Page and Page (2007) showed that there is advantage of playing in the second home leg game in soccer European tournaments. Krumer (2013) explained this result theoretically, assuming that the winner of a first stage has a psychological advantage in the second stage. More recently, Krumer and Lechner (2018) found a significantly reduced home advantage in midweek matches of the German soccer Bundesliga. Following the same line, Goller and Krumer (2020) showed that underdog teams have a reduced home advantage on non-usual weekdays in the top four European leagues. In the same spirit, Krumer (2020) found that underdog teams have a reduced home advantage in games that start at 21:00 CET in the group stage of the UEFA Europa League. The current study emphasizes an additional feature related to tournament schedule, namely the length of time between games involving the same teams.

The remainder of the chapter is organized as follows. The description of the natural experiment is presented in Section 2. The data are described in Section 3. In Section 4, I describe the estimation strategy. Section 5 presents the results. Finally, Section 6 offers concluding remarks.

2.   DESCRIPTION OF THE SETTINGS

The UEFA Champions League is the largest soccer club tournament in Europe that is organized as multi-stage contest. First there are several qualifying rounds for the right to compete in the group stage. The winners of the group stage then advance to the elimination rounds and compete until the final.[6] Of interest here is the group stage. Over the years the number of groups in the competition has varied. However, each group has always been composed of four teams and organized as a double round-robin tournament, with teams playing each other over two legs, home and away.[7] Thus each team plays six matches.

One possible allocation of matches is described in Table 21.1. The usual break between rounds is two weeks, during which teams also compete in domestic competitions.[8] The identity of the teams that play home or away matches can differ from the ones presented in Table 21.1, but teams that played against each other in Round 1 *always* meet for the second time in Round 5. Teams that played each other in Round 2 *always* meet for the second time in Round 6. Finally, teams that played against each other in Round 3 *always* meet for the second time in Round 4. We can see that the only consecutive rounds that involve the same pair of teams are Rounds 3 and 4.

The composition of the groups is determined by a draw; however this is not fully randomized since it is based on a seeding system, meaning that the top clubs cannot play each other in the group stage. The seeding is based on UEFA's coefficients for the clubs and countries. More specifically, club coefficients are determined by the sum of all points won in the previous five years, plus 20 percent of the association coefficient over the same period.[9] There are several additional restrictions during the draw. For example, teams from the same country cannot play each other in the same group, and teams from the same city do not play at home in the same round. In addition, UEFA's emergency panel recently ruled that Ukrainian and Russian clubs would not be drawn against each other "until further notice" due to the political unrest between the countries. Finally, Belarussian, Kazakh and Russian teams do not play at home in the last round, which takes place in December, due to cold weather.

It is important to note that the allocation of *pairs* in different rounds is random. Nevertheless, in Section 4, I will show that the various restrictions do not affect the order of the matches by demonstrating that there are no differences between the characteristics of the teams allocated to different rounds.

3. DATA AND DESCRIPTIVE RESULTS

3.1 Dataset

The data were collected on all UEFA Champions League group matches from the 1995/96 to the 2015/16 seasons. Five matches that were delayed or abandoned due to weather, violence or political reasons were eliminated. In addition, 48 matches in Groups E, F, G and H in the 2001/02 Champions League season were eliminated because the order of these matches was changed due to the terror attacks on September 11, 2001. In addition, I removed two matches between teams with the same UEFA coefficients since it was not possible to determine the identity of the favorite and the underdog in this pair (see the Appendix for the full list). Eliminating these problematic fixtures left a total of 1,961 matches.

All data were downloaded from the official UEFA website (www.uefa.com). For every match, information was available regarding: the identity of the home and away teams; the round in which the match took place; the number of goals scored by each team; each team's number of points before the respective match; and whether a team had already qualified for the next stage or had lost any theoretical chance to do so. Finally, I obtained all team coefficients according to their UEFA rankings.[10] These coefficients are used as a proxy of the teams' abilities as they determine their seeding position in the draw. Since these coefficients increase every season, I standardized them for each season, so they take into account the within-season variation. For each match, the favorite is defined as the team with the higher standardized coefficient and the underdog as the team with the lower standardized coefficient.

3.2 Variables and Descriptive Statistics

To estimate the possible effects of the scheduling of the match I used the number of points obtained by the favorite as the outcome variable. Note that a winning team gets three points and a losing team zero points. In case of a draw each team gets one point. Not surprisingly, Table 21.2 shows that in general favorites achieve more points per match than underdogs. However, in Round 4, the favorite has the lowest number of points, while the underdog is obviously the highest scorer among all the rounds. In addition, we can also see that up to the 5th round each team has a theoretical chance of qualifying for the next stage, and no team has yet ensured qualification.

4. ESTIMATION STRATEGY

I estimate the impact of competing against the same opponent as soon as possible. As already described, Round 4 is the only round in which two teams compete against each other for the second consecutive time. In addition, as described in Section 2, the composition of the groups is determined by a draw, albeit one that is not fully randomized. Therefore, in Table 21.3, I tested whether the teams' pre-treatment characteristics differed between the rounds. I compared only the first half of the group stage,

Table 21.2 Descriptive statistics

Variable	Round 1 (N = 327)	Round 2 (N = 327)	Round 3 (N = 327)	Round 4 (N = 328)	Round 5 (N = 326)	Round 6 (N = 326)
Favorite's points	1.875	1.920	1.872	1.634	1.721	1.687
	(1.270)	(1.284)	(1.316)	(1.309)	(1.314)	(1.303)
Underdog's points	0.875	0.865	0.936	1.104	1.040	1.052
	(1.167)	(1.193)	(1.245)	(1.254)	(1.251)	(1.238)
Favorite's standardized coeff.	0.713	0.726	0.707	0.709	0.708	0.729
	(0.802)	(0.791)	(0.795)	(0.794)	(0.802)	(0.791)
Underdog's standardized coeff.	−0.638	−0.647	−0.639	−0.636	−0.641	−0.647
	(0.663)	(0.648)	(0.673)	(0.675)	(0.662)	(0.649)
Favorite's home advantage	0.480	0.513	0.514	0.485	0.521	0.488
	(0.500)	(0.500)	(0.501)	(0.501)	(0.500)	(0.501)
Favorite's aggregate points	0	1.676	3.226	5.101	6.570	8.307
	(0)	(1.324)	(1.943)	(2.432)	(3.010)	(3.366)
Underdog's aggregate points	0	1.064	2.312	3.241	4.503	5.540
	(0)	(1.238)	(1.916)	(2.384)	(2.750)	(3.200)
Favorite already qualified	0	0	0	0	0.058	0.436
	(0)	(0)	(0)	(0)	(0.235)	(0.497)
Underdog already qualified	0	0	0	0	0.021	0.126
	(0)	(0)	(0)	(0)	(0.145)	(0.332)
Favorite already lost chance	0	0	0	0	0.018	0.071
	(0)	(0)	(0)	(0)	(0.135)	(0.256)
Underdog already lost chance	0	0	0	0	0.024	0.224
	(0)	(0)	(0)	(0)	(0.155)	(0.418)

Note: Standard deviations are reported in brackets.

namely Rounds 1–3, because the second half consisted of the same pairs.[11] More specifically, for each round I present the results of the linear univariate regression of each characteristic as a dependent variable on a dummy variable representing the respective round. The coefficient represents the difference in means for each round relative to other rounds with regard to the respective characteristic. Clustered standard errors at the group level are shown in brackets. We can see that none of the teams' pre-treatment characteristics differed between the rounds. In addition, I also conducted the Wald test of joint difference in means for each characteristic. It was obtained from a linear regression without intercept of each characteristic as a dependent variable on three dummies representing each of the rounds. In these regressions the standard errors were clustered at the group level as well. This test also revealed that the teams' standardized coefficients and the home advantage status did not differ significantly across different rounds. Taken together, the results presented in Table 21.3 allow us to conclude that the allocation of pairs among different rounds is indeed random.

Nevertheless, it is important to note that it is still possible that some draw restrictions described in Section 2 might create a systematic

Table 21.3   Pre-treatment characteristics

Variable	Round 1	Round 2	Round 3	Wald test (p-val)
Favorite's standardized coeff.	−0.004	0.016	−0.012	0.754
	(0.024)	(0.022)	(0.023)	
Underdog's standardized coeff.	0.005	−0.008	0.003	0.937
	(0.024)	(0.022)	(0.023)	
Difference in standardized coeff.	−0.009	0.024	−0.015	0.858
	(0.047)	(0.044)	(0.046)	
Favorite's home advantage	−0.033	0.017	0.017	0.670
	(0.040)	(0.042)	(0.030)	

Notes: For each round the result of the linear univariate regression of each characteristic as a dependent variable on a dummy representing the respective round is presented.
The coefficient represents the difference in means for each round relative to other rounds with regard to the respective characteristic.
Clustered standard errors at the group level are reported in brackets.
In the last column, the p-value is reported for the Wald test of joint difference in means for each characteristic obtained from a linear regression without intercept of each characteristic as a dependent variable on three dummies representing each of the rounds with clustered standard errors at the group level.
*, **, *** denote significance at the 10%, 5%, 1% levels.

difference. Although none of the above-mentioned restrictions affect the allocation of pairs among different rounds, the restriction according to which the Belarussian, Kazakh and Russian clubs do not host the last match in December is a systematic one. A potential concern of this systematic restriction is that for some reason it might also systematically affect other characteristics. In addition, longer flights and different time zones may be reasons for higher fatigue compared to groups comprising teams from Central and Western Europe only. Therefore, failing to control for this unobserved heterogeneity between the groups may bias the results. Consequently, I use group fixed effects as part of the identification strategy. This allows controlling for all the features of the specific group that were common for all the teams in a group.

Using a fixed effects model, our specification takes the following form:

$$Points_{fugr} = \alpha_1 \cdot R4_{fug} + \alpha_2 \cdot Q_{fugr} + \alpha_3 \cdot X_{fugr} + \alpha_4 \cdot Z_{fugr} + \delta_g + \varepsilon_{fugr} \quad (21.1)$$

where $Points_{fugr}$ is the number of points of favorite f in the match against underdog u of group g in round r; $R4_{fug}$ is a dummy variable with the value of one if the respective match takes place in Round 4 and zero otherwise; Q_{fugr} is the set of qualification status controls, namely dummies of whether a favorite and an underdog have already qualified or have no chance of qualifying for the next stage; X_{fugr} is the set of basic controls that includes the teams' standardized coefficients and home advantage of a favorite; and Z_{fugr} is the aggregate number of points of the favorite and the underdog before the respective match. Note that Q_{fugr} and Z_{fugr} are not determined randomly, as can be seen in Table 21.2. Finally, δ_g is the group fixed effects.

5. EMPIRICAL EVIDENCE

5.1 Main Results

Column 1 of Panel A in Table 21.4 presents the results from estimating Equation (21.1) without list of controls and by using group fixed effects, where standard errors clustered at the group level are presented in brackets. The results show that the coefficient of $R4_{fug}$ is negative and significant at the 2.0 percent level. In Columns 2 and 3, I also use qualification status controls and basic controls, respectively. We can see that a favorite achieves on average 0.20 fewer points in Round 4 compared to other rounds, with a significance level of 0.5 percent in both cases. Finally, in Column 4, I add each team's aggregate number of points before the respective match. The results are robust to inclusion of these controls as well.

One possible concern is that, since the dependent variable can only have three values (3, 1, or 0), the use of the linear regression is questionable. Therefore, I also used a Poisson pseudo-maximum likelihood estimator (Poisson-PML), which uses the same first-order conditions that are derived from the Poisson distribution as shown by Santos Silva and Tenreyro (2006). However, Poisson-PML does not require the dependent variable to have a Poisson distribution and is consistent with over-dispersion (i.e. when variance is larger than the mean). The authors showed that the Poisson-PML is robust to different forms of heteroscedasticity and measurement error. Another advantage of the Poisson-PML is that it allows for a large fraction of zeros, as shown by Santos Silva and Tenreyro (2011).[12] Panel B of Table 21.4 presents the results of the average marginal effects of the Poisson-PML regressions, where clustered standard errors at the group level are reported in brackets. We can see that these results are very similar to those of the linear model.

Table 21.4   The effects of competing in the fourth round

	(1)	(2)	(3)	(4)
	Panel A: Linear model			
Round 4	−0.179**	−0.218***	−0.203***	−0.182**
	(0.077)	(0.077)	(0.071)	(0.071)
Observations	1,961	1,961	1,961	1,961
	Panel B: Poisson-PML average marginal effects			
Round 4	−0.186**	−0.224***	−0.209***	−0.186**
	(0.082)	(0.083)	(0.077)	(0.078)
Observations	1,961	1,961	1,961	1,961
Qualification status controls	N	Y	Y	Y
Basic controls	N	N	Y	Y
Aggregate points	N	N	N	Y
Group fixed effects	Y	Y	Y	Y

Notes: The dependent variable is the number of points obtained by the favorite in the respective match.
Qualification status controls include dummies of whether a favorite and/or an underdog has already qualified or had no chance of qualifying for the next stage.
Basic controls include the teams' standardized coefficients and home advantage of a favorite.
Clustered standard errors at the group level are reported in brackets.
*, **, *** denote significance at the 10%, 5%, 1% levels.

5.2 Possible Confidence of the Underdog

A possible explanation of the results presented in Section 5.1 is increased confidence of an underdog team, caused by its earlier success against a given favorite. To test this hypothesis, I collected all the *return* matches (Rounds 4–6) of the pairs in which the underdog did not lose the first leg between the teams (Rounds 1–3). The underdog team might consider not losing against a favorite as a successful result. This may theoretically, and even unconsciously, increase its confidence. In total, there are 434 such return matches. In Panel A of Table 21.5 we can see the distribution of matches between these pairs. Since I selected the pairs in which the underdog did not lose in the first meeting between the teams, obviously the number of points obtained by the favorite is relatively low in the first meeting (Rounds 1–3). It is also interesting to see that in the second meeting of the teams, the favorite obtained a much higher number of points. However, this number is the lowest in Round 4 (1.51) compared to Rounds 5 (1.68) and 6 (1.77).

Next, I conducted a similar analysis presented in Section 5.1. Table 21.6 shows that when a favorite competes in Round 4 after not winning in Round 3, this reduces its number of points compared to competing in Round 5 (after not winning in Round 2) and Round 6 (after not winning in Round 1). The estimated negative effect is approximately 0.3–0.35 points, which is in line with the hypothesis that the shorter the period of time from the previous success of the underdog team in a head-to-head match against a given favorite, the better is the outcome for the underdog (as represented by the favorite's lower number of points).

Table 21.5   Number of points obtained by the favorite in different pairs

Variable	Round 1	Round 5	Round 2	Round 6	Round 3	Round 4
Panel A: Pairs in which the favorite did not win in the first match between the teams						
Favorite's points	0.547	1.680	0.496	1.771	0.438	1.514
	(0.499)	(1.307)	(0.502)	(1.300)	(0.498)	(1.301)
Observations	150	150	141	140	144	144
Panel B: Pairs in which the favorite won in the first match between the teams						
Favorite's points	3	1.756	3	1.624	3	1.728
	(0)	(1.323)	(0)	(1.306)	(0)	(1.311)
Observations	177	176	186	186	183	184

Notes: Round 1 is matched with Round 5; Round 2 is matched with Round 6; and Round 3 is matched with Round 4. Standard deviations are reported in brackets.

Table 21.6   The effect of competing in the fourth round in pairs in which the underdog did not lose in the first half of the tournament

	(1)	(2)	(3)
Panel A: Linear model			
Round 4	−0.268*	−0.298*	−0.319**
	(0.154)	(0.167)	(0.155)
Observations	434	434	434
Panel B: Poisson-PML average marginal effects			
Round 4	−0.281*	−0.309*	−0.357**
	(0.164)	(0.172)	(0.165)
Observations	426	426	426
Qualification status controls	N	Y	Y
Basic controls	N	N	Y
Group fixed effects	Y	Y	Y

Notes: This table presents the results of estimating the data from Rounds 4–6 only, and only in those pairs in which the underdog did not lose in the first match between the teams.
The dependent variable is the number of points obtained by the favorite in the respective match.
The qualification status controls include dummies of whether a favorite and/or an underdog had already qualified or had no chance to qualify for the next stage.
The basic controls include the teams' standardized coefficients and home advantage of a favorite.
Clustered standard errors at the group level are reported in brackets.
*, **, *** denote significance at the 10%, 5%, 1% levels.

It is important to note that I do not include the aggregate number of points before the respective match as an additional control because of the endogenous nature of this variable. This is endogenous because the selection of the data already assumes a relatively higher number of points for the underdog and a relatively lower number of points for the favorite before Round 4, which is the first round of this dataset. It is also endogenous because obtaining a good result in Round 4, which is the variable of interest here, has an effect on the aggregate number of points in the following rounds. Therefore, once we include the previous performance of the teams on the right-hand side of Equation (21.1) and conduct a fixed effects estimation, we will have a bias because the error term includes $\varepsilon_{fugr-1}, \varepsilon_{fugr-2},\ldots$, which is naturally correlated with $R4_{fug}$. Therefore, the inclusion of these endogenous variables will obviously bias the results toward zero.[13]

5.3   Possible (Over)Confidence of the Favorite

In this section we test whether the length of time since the previous meeting between the teams in which the favorite won has an effect on the outcome of the next meeting between these teams. As in the case with the previous success of the underdogs, it is possible that the favorites also perform better the shorter the gap between the matches. However, there is a possibility that favorites may be overconfident, implying that they may overestimate their chances of success and thus harm their performance (e.g., van den Steen, 2004). Similarly to Section 5.2, I collected all the return matches (Rounds 4–6) in which the favorite won the first match between the teams (Rounds 1–3), a total of 546 such matches. In Panel B of Table 21.5 we can see that in the return match a favorite gets fewer points than in the first meeting between the teams. However, we do not see any abnormal outcome in Round 4, where the favorite gained 1.73 points compared to Rounds 5 (1.76 points) and 6 (1.62 points). The lowest number of points of the favorite in Round 6 can be explained by the fact that many matches in this round involve favorites that have already qualified and are therefore less incentivized, allowing weaker teams to have a higher probability of winning (see also Page and Page, 2009).

Our regression analysis, presented in Table 21.7, shows that there is no significant effect of competing in Round 4 compared to Rounds 5 and 6 in terms of the favorite's points. This result suggests that the length of time since the favorite's previous success does not affect the outcome of the future matches between the teams.

One possible explanation of the differences in findings of the effect of length of time between the previous success of the underdog and favorite is that the underdog's success in the first meeting (in Round 3) was less expected than the favorite's success. Therefore, it is possible that this unexpected success gave the underdog additional confidence that turned into momentum in the next match. However, a win by the favorite is a much more expected result which does not turn into increased confidence that may enhance performance in subsequent matches.

6.   CONCLUDING REMARKS

The main motivation of this study is the potential effect of scheduling on the performance of high-profile agents in a real competitive environment. More specifically, I was driven by the question of whether the length of time between the first and the return matches between the same pair of

Table 21.7   *The effect of competing in the fourth round in pairs in which the favorite won in the first half of the tournament*

	(1)	(2)	(3)
Panel A: Linear model			
Round 4	0.128	0.080	0.113
	(0.125)	(0.148)	(0.136)
Observations	546	546	546
Panel B: Poisson-PML average marginal effects			
Round 4	0.133	0.088	0.095
	(0.129)	(0.153)	(0.144)
Observations	532	532	532
Qualification status controls	N	Y	Y
Basic controls	N	N	Y
Group fixed effects	Y	Y	Y

Notes: This table presents the results of estimating the data from Rounds 4–6 only, and only in those pairs in which the favorite won in the first match between the teams.
The dependent variable is the number of points obtained by the favorite in the respective match.
The qualification status controls include dummies of whether a favorite and/or an underdog had already qualified or had no chance to qualify for the next stage.
The basic controls include the teams' standardized coefficients and home advantage of a favorite.
Clustered standard errors at the group level are reported in brackets.

teams affects the outcome of the return match. Based on all matches in the group stage of the UEFA Champions League in the seasons 1995–96 to 2015–16, this study finds that a shorter gap between the two matches favors the underdog team, especially if it did not lose in the first meeting between the teams.

The results of this study provide support for the importance of the self-confidence gained by recent previous successes in a competitive environment and have implications for many different areas. For example, in the labor market, improving self-confidence – which can be done through increased frequency of positive feedback after successful actions – may increase productivity, especially among workers with low self-image. This is also true in fields that involve very complex and ambitious tasks, such as R&D and political campaigns. In these fields, to increase the probability of future success, it is worth setting ambitious goals not too long after a previous success.

Finally, future research could investigate whether this chapter's results are unique to the UEFA Champions League or can be found in other settings as well. Therefore, I call for additional research on schedule effects in general, and on the effect of the length of time between the games that involve the same opponents in particular in other sports tournaments.

NOTES

* This chapter is a substantially revised version of "Memory and Confidence," a presentation at Sports and Consumer Behaviour: XII Gijón Conference on Sports Economics, 1–6 May 2017. I am deeply grateful to Michael Lechner for his generous advice and encouragement throughout this project. I also acknowledge Ignacio Palacios-Huerta, Thomas Epper, Danny Cohen-Zada, Lionel Page, Florian Lindner, Michael Knaus, Simone Balestra, Oliver Guertler and Andreas Steinmayr for helpful comments. The usual disclaimer applies.
1. See for example https://sports.stackexchange.com/questions/5465/have-two-teams-ever-played-each-other-twice-in-the-same-world-cup and https://www.reddit.com/r/nfl/comm ents/3tl4zl/has_a_team_ever_played_the_same_team_two_weeks_in/. Last accessed on 03.11.2018.
2. From http://www.uefa.com/uefachampionsleague/news/newsid=2398575.html. Last accessed on 03.11.2018.
3. Note that a winning team gets three points and a losing team gets zero points. In case of a draw each team gets one point.
4. For additional details see the comprehensive review by Hsu et al. (2006).
5. See Bar-Eli et al. (2006) for additional discussion on the hot-hand phenomenon.
6. See http://www.uefa.com/uefachampionsleague/season=2017/matches/index.html#rd/2 000784/2 for more details on the structure of the tournaments. Last accessed on 03.11.2018.
7. See Moskowitz and Jon Wertheim (2011), who investigated 19 sports leagues in more than 40 countries between 1871 and 2009 and showed that intra-league home advantage "is almost eerily constant through time" (p. 113).
8. The usual gap between Rounds 2 and 3 is three weeks.
9. For additional details see http://www.uefa.com/memberassociations/uefarankings/club/. Last accessed on 03.11.2018.
10. Up to 2004 the coefficients were obtained from http://kassiesa.home.xs4all.nl/bert/uefa/data/method1/. After 2004 they were obtained from http://www.uefa.com/memberas sociations/uefarankings/club/season=2005/index.html. Last accessed on 03.11.2018.
11. Comparing Rounds 4–6 would give the same significant levels.
12. All the estimations were performed via the *ppml* command in Stata. See http://personal. lse.ac.uk/tenreyro/lgw.html for additional information on *ppml* command. Last accessed on 03.11.2018. The results are very similar when using a Poisson regression analysis. These results are available on request.
13. When controlling for the aggregate number of points of the favorite and the underdog, these variables, as well as $R4$, are not significant. The results of these regressions are available on request.

REFERENCES

Adamo, S.A. and Hoy, R.R., 1995. Agonistic behaviour in male and female field crickets, *Gryllus bimaculatus*, and how behavioural context influences its expression. *Animal Behaviour*, 49(6), 1491–1501.

Bandura, A., 1977. Self-efficacy: Toward a unifying theory of behavioral change. *Psychological Review*, 84(2), 191–215.

Bar-Eli, M., Avugos, S. and Raab, M., 2006. Twenty years of "hot hand" research: Review and critique. *Psychology of Sport and Exercise*, 7(6), 525–553.

Bocskocsky, A., Ezekowitz, J. and Stein, C., 2014. Heat check: New evidence on the hot hand in basketball. Mimeo. Available at SSRN: https://ssrn.com/abstract=2481494.

Cohen-Zada, D., Krumer, A. and Shtudiner, Z., 2017. Psychological momentum and gender. *Journal of Economic Behavior and Organization*, 135, 66–81.

Drummond, H. and Canales, C., 1998. Dominance between booby nestlings involves winner and loser effects. *Animal Behaviour*, 55(6), 1669–1676.

Gilovich, T., Vallone, R. and Tversky, A., 1985. The hot hand in basketball: On the misperception of random sequences. *Cognitive Psychology*, 17(3), 295–314.

Goller, D. and Krumer, A., 2020. Let's meet as usual: Do games played on non-frequent days differ? Evidence from top European soccer leagues. *European Journal of Operational Research*, 286(2), 740–754.

Hoff, K. and Stiglitz, J.E., 2010. *Equilibrium Fictions: A Cognitive Approach to Societal Rigidity*. Cambridge, MA: National Bureau of Economic Research.

Hsu, Y., Earley, R.L. and Wolf, L.L., 2006. Modulation of aggressive behaviour by fighting experience: Mechanisms and contest outcomes. *Biological Reviews*, 81(1), 33–74.

Jetter, M. and Walker, J.K., 2015. Game, set, and match: Do women and men perform differently in competitive situations? *Journal of Economic Behavior and Organization*, 119, 96–108.

Krumer, A., 2013. Best-of-two contests with psychological effects. *Theory and Decision*, 75(1), 85–100.

Krumer, A., 2020. Testing the effect of kick-off time in the UEFA Europa League. *European Sport Management Quarterly*, 20(2), 225–238.

Krumer, A. and Lechner, M., 2017. First in first win: Evidence on schedule effects in round-robin tournaments in mega-events. *European Economic Review*, 100, 412–427.

Krumer, A. and Lechner, M., 2018. Midweek effect on soccer performance: Evidence from the German Bundesliga. *Economic Inquiry*, 56(1), 193–207.

Krumer, A., Megidish, R. and Sela, A., 2017. First-mover advantage in round-robin tournaments. *Social Choice and Welfare*, 48(3), 633–658.

Manski, C.F., 1995. *Identification Problems in the Social Sciences*. Cambridge, MA: Harvard University Press.

Miller, J.B. and Sanjurjo, A., 2014. A cold shower for the hot hand fallacy. IGIER Working Paper No. 518. Mimeo. Available at SSRN: https://ssrn.com/abstract=2450479.

Miller, J.B. and Sanjurjo, A., 2018. Surprised by the hot hand fallacy? A truth in the law of small numbers. *Econometrica*, 86(6), 2019–2047.

Moskowitz, T. and Wertheim, L.J., 2011. *Scorecasting: The Hidden Influences Behind How Sports are Played and Games are Won*. New York: Crown Archetype.

Page, L. and Coates, J., 2017. Winner and loser effects in human competitions: Evidence from equally matched tennis players. *Evolution and Human Behavior*, 38(4), 530–535.

Page, L. and Page, K., 2007. The second leg home advantage: Evidence from European football cup competitions. *Journal of Sports Sciences*, 25(14), 1547–1556.

Page, L. and Page, K., 2009. Stakes and motivation in tournaments: Playing when there is nothing to play for but pride. *Economic Analysis and Policy*, 39(3), 455–464.

Rosenqvist, O. and Skans, O.N., 2015. Confidence enhanced performance? The causal effects of success on future performance in professional golf tournaments. *Journal of Economic Behavior and Organization*, 117, 281–295.

Santos Silva, J. and Tenreyro, S., 2006. The log of gravity. *Review of Economics and Statistics*, 88(4), 641–658.

Santos Silva, J. and Tenreyro, S., 2011. Further simulation evidence on the performance of the Poisson pseudo-maximum likelihood estimator. *Economics Letters*, 112(2), 220–222.

Van de Poll, N.E., De Jonge, F., Van Oyen, H.G. and Van Pelt, J., 1982. Aggressive behaviour in rats: Effects of winning or losing on subsequent aggressive interactions. *Behavioural Processes*, 7(2), 143–155.

Van den Steen, E., 2004. Rational overoptimism (and other biases). *American Economic Review*, 94(4), 1141–1151.

Yaari, G. and Eisenmann, S., 2011. The hot (invisible?) hand: Can time sequence patterns of success/failure in sports be modeled as repeated random independent trials? *PloS One*, 6(10), e24532.

APPENDIX: LIST OF MATCHES REMOVED FROM THE SAMPLE

1. Two matches between Dynamo Kyiv and Newcastle United in Rounds 2 and 6 of Group C in season 1997–98. Since both teams had the same coefficients, it was not possible to define favorite and underdog in this pair.
2. Galatasaray v Juventus. Round 5 of Group B in season 1998–99. This match was delayed because of anti-Italian sentiment in Turkey over Italy's refusal to extradite Kurdish rebel leader Abdullah Öcalan. It was played a week later in Istanbul.
3. Manchester United v Girondins Bordeaux. Round 3 of Group B in season 1999–2000. This match started 45 minutes later than officially scheduled because of a serious traffic incident that jammed the roads to the stadium.
4. Galatasaray v Juventus. Round 5 of Group D in season 2003–04. This match was delayed after terrorist attacks in Istanbul, and was played a week later in Dortmund, Germany.
5. Roma v Dynamo Kyiv. Round 1 of Group B in season 2004–05. This match was abandoned at half-time after referee Anders Frisk was hit by an object thrown from the crowd. UEFA awarded Dynamo Kyiv a 3–0 win.
6. Galatasaray v Juventus. Round 6 of Group B in season 2013–14. This match was abandoned after 31 minutes due to snow, and resumed the following day from the point of abandonment.
7. Due to the terror attacks on September 11, 2001, the schedule of Groups E, F, G and H in the 2001–02 Champions League season was changed, and the teams played according to a different order of matches (in total 48 matches).

22. Predicting match outcomes in football by an Ordered Forest estimator

Daniel Goller, Michael C. Knaus, Michael Lechner and Gabriel Okasa*

1. INTRODUCTION

Predicting the outcome of football (i.e. soccer) games based on past information is a non-standard predictive task because of the nature of the game outcome, as well as because of the importance of uncertainty (luck and unobservables). The game outcome consists of the scores of the two teams that are usually either collapsed into a goal-difference or further aggregated to reflect whether the game ended as a win for the home or away team, or as a draw. From a statistical perspective, such outcomes have bounded support and, thus, standard linear modelling can be expected to perform poorly. The large amount of uncertainty in the game outcomes due to just luck or due to game- or team-specific unobservables (e.g. hidden injuries of players, etc.) makes it imperative to use prediction methods that fully exploit the potential of the available information, as well as to uncover the uncertainty of a match outcome. The latter is also relevant when interest is not only in single games but also in a league table at the end of the season. Obviously, such league tables should capture the uncertainty for the single games accumulated over a season to be useful guides on what to expect.

Recently, machine learning methods have shown their power in all sorts of prediction problems,[1] in particular in situations where the relation of the variables capturing the information used to predict with the target of the prediction, i.e. here the outcome of the game, is non-linear. However, so far there has been only little development in gearing these methods explicitly towards the estimation of the probabilities of ordered outcomes, such as score differences and points, or just wins, draws, and losses. Lechner and Okasa (2019) propose adapting classical random forest estimation, which is known to have excellent predictive performance (e.g. Biau and Scornet (2016), Fernández-Delgado et al. (2014)) to the problem of predicting probabilities of ordered categorical outcomes, such as the win-draw-loss problem of a football game. In this chapter, we use their approach to predict game outcomes of the German Bundesliga 1 (BL1) based on more than ten years' data on game outcomes as well as extensive information about teams, their players, and their environment. These predictions are then used to obtain the final season rankings in a way that reflects and shows the magnitude of the inherent uncertainty of football games.

While there are many approaches to predicting football games (e.g. Leitner et al. (2010), Nakamura et al. (2019) and references therein), the use of machine learning methods is still rather rare (e.g. for international championships see Groll, Kneib et al. (2018) and Groll, Ley et al. (2018)). In a recent paper, Baboota and Kaur (2019) used gradient boosting, another machine learning method, to predict the game outcomes of the English Premier League. A major difference of their approach compared to our approach is that their goal was to get the best prediction of a game – i.e. will it be a win, a draw, or a loss – while we are interested in the probabilities of these events occurring. In technical terms, they considered a classification problem, while our problem has the structure of a regression problem. The latter is required if the goal is to use these predictions to predict the final season outcome probabilistically, i.e. to end up with probabilities that a particular team becomes the champion, is relegated or will play in the UEFA Champions League next season.

In the next section, we briefly introduce the machine learning method developed to predict the probabilities of the ordinal outcomes. Section 3 shows how these predicted probabilities are used to obtain the end-of-season results. Section 4 illustrates the empirical application of the methods to German Bundesliga 1 and compares the predictions to other publicly available predictions as well as betting odds. Section 5 concludes. Finally, the Appendix documents the data used for the application.

2.   THE ORDERED FOREST ESTIMATOR

2.1   Random Forests

In the machine learning literature, random forests as developed by Breiman (2001) became a widely used prediction method. The random forest algorithm is based on randomly constructing and combining regression trees (Breiman et al., 1984). In particular, the trees are combined via bootstrap aggregation, so-called bagging, with additional randomness within the tree construction. A single regression tree recursively splits the covariate space into separate regions based on minimizing the sum of squares at each split of the tree. The final prediction for evaluation point x is then the average of the observations falling into the same end-node $L(x)$, the so-called leaf. Regression trees with many splits tend to have low bias but rather high variance due to the path-dependent structure. Bagged trees achieve a variance reduction by averaging many low bias trees. However, as opposed to bagged trees, the random forest decorrelates the trees to lower the variance even further (Hastie et al. 2009). This is achieved within the tree-growing step where, at each split point, only a random subset of covariates is considered. More formally, the random forest algorithm draws a bootstrapped sample b of size N and grows a regression tree $T_b(x)$ by choosing m out of p covariates ($m << p$) at random for the split until the minimum leaf size is reached. The final random forest estimate $RF^B(x)$ is the ensemble of B regression trees as

$$RF^B(x) = \frac{1}{B} \sum_{b=1}^{B} T_b(x) \ \text{with}$$

$$T_b(x) = \frac{1}{\left|\{ i : X_i \in L(x) \}\right|} \sum_{\{i:X_i \in L(x)\}} Y_i$$

(22.1)

where X_i denotes the covariates and Y_i the outcomes. In their recent contributions, Wager and Athey (2018) and Athey, Tibshirani, and Wager (2019) further modify the random forest algorithm and implement the so-called honest splitting rule, which uses different observations for placing the splits and for the estimation. This is important for statistical inference and contributes to the prediction accuracy as it helps reduce the bias of the estimates even further.

2.2   Random Forest Estimation of Ordered Probability Models

Despite the widespread use of random forests as a prediction tool (Athey, 2018), the major targets are either continuous or discrete outcomes, while the estimation of models involving ordered outcomes, as those of a football game, is not well established.[2] However, similar to the standard econometric ordered probability models (see Wooldridge (2010) for an overview), it is desirable to take the ordering nature into account to prevent loss of valuable information. To do so, Lechner and Okasa (2019) develop an Ordered Forest estimator, which explicitly incorporates the ordering information in the outcomes. Due to the underlying random forest algorithm, the estimator can flexibly deal with large-dimensional covariate spaces, while still providing the standard econometric output such as ordered outcome probabilities and marginal effects. Moreover, under certain conditions, statistical inference about the estimated effects is feasible as well. Thus, the Ordered Forest estimator can be regarded as a more flexible alternative to traditional econometric models, such as ordered logit or ordered probit. An extensive discussion of the estimator and the inference procedure as well as a simulation study is provided in Lechner and Okasa (2019).

Consider an ordered outcome variable $Y_i \in \{1,...,M\}$ with ordered categories m. For a sample of size N ($i = 1,...,N$) the estimation of the conditional ordered outcome probabilities evaluated at x, i.e. $P[Y_i = m|X_i = x]$ is based on an estimation of cumulative probabilities given by binary indicators $Y_{m,i} = \underline{1}(Y_i \leq m)$ for $m = 1,...,M-1$. Then a regression random forest is estimated for all $M-1$ binary indicators, obtaining the predictions $\hat{Y}_{m,i} = \hat{P}(Y_{m,i} = 1|X_i = x)$. The prediction for the M-th category is given as $\hat{Y}_{M,i} = 1$ as the cumulative probabilities must sum up to one. Based on the cumulative probabilities, the probabilities for each respective category m for all i are subsequently computed. The probability of the first outcome category is defined as $\hat{P}_{1,i}^{tot} = \hat{Y}_{1,i}$ and stems directly from the random forest estimation as in the case of a binary outcome the estimated conditional mean translates to a valid probability estimate. For the following outcome categories $m = 2,...M$ the algorithm exploits the nature of cumulative probabilities and as such isolates the probability of the m-th category by subtracting the estimated probability of the preceding category as $\hat{P}_{m,i}^{tot} = \hat{Y}_{m,i} - \hat{Y}_{m-1,i}$. If some of the resulting probabilities become negative,[3] these are set to zero, i.e. $\hat{P}_{m,i}^{tot} = 0$ if $\hat{P}_{m,i}^{tot} < 0$. Lastly, it is ensured that the probabilities sum up to one and as such for all outcome categories $m = 1,...M$ the

probabilities are normalized as $\hat{P}_{m,i} = \dfrac{\hat{P}_{m,i}^{tot}}{\sum_{m=1}^{M} \hat{P}_{m,i}^{tot}}$ where the probabilities

$\hat{P}_{m,i}$ correspond to the conditional ordered outcome probabilities, i.e. $\hat{P}_{m,i} = \hat{P}[Y_i = m|X_i = x]$. A graphical illustration of the algorithm is depicted in Figure 22.1.

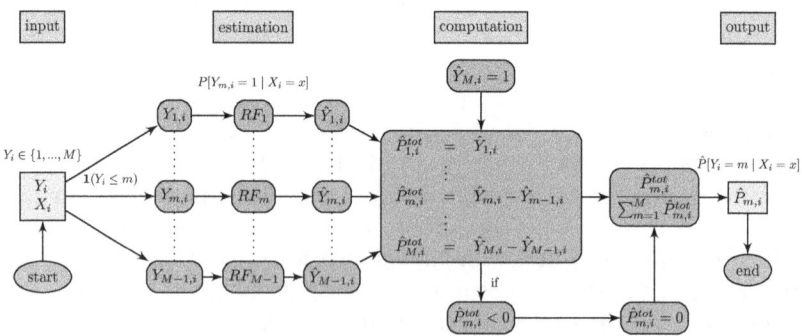

Figure 22.1   *Illustration of the Ordered Forest algorithm*

Note that the above approach makes use of linear combinations of probability estimates from the regression random forest. Hence, if a regression random forest fulfils the conditions needed for the consistency and normality, the Ordered Forest shares these properties too, and thus enables us to conduct statistical inference. Computationally, the Ordered Forest as described above requires the estimation of $M - 1$ regression random forests in the training data. Although this might appear a rather demanding exercise, given the majority of empirical applications feature a limited number of outcome categories and the fast software implementations available, this becomes less of an issue.[4]

3. PREDICTING LEAGUE OUTCOMES: BASIC METHODOLOGY

Once the probability of a win, draw or loss for a particular team has been predicted, such predictions can be aggregated to obtain the final league table. It appears natural to compute the expected points per team per game (3 points for a win, 1 for a draw, 0 for a loss) using the estimated probabilities and add the points over all games, leading to expected end-of-season points for all teams. Ordering the teams according to their expected points in the season leads to the final ranking. In order to capture the uncertainty in game outcomes, we also use an alternative approach. Instead of computing the expected points of a game, we randomly draw a simulated outcome based on the predicted probabilities. Depending on the realization of the random variable, we assign 3, 1 or 0 points to teams, do this for all games, and then add up the points. This process is repeated many times.[5] Finally, the probability of becoming champion, for example, is computed by counting the number of times a team was first in the simulations and dividing this number by the number of simulations. In the same way, all other probabilities of ranking positions of interest can be obtained.

4. AN ILLUSTRATION: THE GERMAN BUNDESLIGA

4.1 The Database

Starting from the 2007/08 season, we collected data on all matches in the German Bundesliga. The season 2018/19 is therefore the 12th year of data in this database, which is continuously updated before every game day. This resulted in 3366 observations before the 2018/19 season's first game day. About 300 variables are used for the predictions, gathered from various sources. In the following, we briefly explain the categories of variables and their sources.

We collect a wide range of player information, team composition and club specifics to approximate team abilities. Various variables are constructed using information about teams, players and coaches from www.transfermarkt.com.[6] Those are, e.g., market values, as well as height and age structure within the team. Since team compositions change before as well as after the first half of the season, this information is updated whenever there are potential changes. The same source is used for the weekly updates of the reported stadium attendance, as well as potential managerial changes. TV revenues are calculated using the allocation key published by the Deutsche Fußball Liga (DFL) for the seasons 2006/07 to 2009/10 and taken from www.fernsehgelder.de for the season 2010/11 onwards.

Other factors influencing team performance may be location related. Thus, data regarding distance and travel time are calculated as shortest routes between the two competing cities from www.google.com/maps. Capacity of the stadiums is taken from www.worldstadiums.com, as well as the respective Wikipedia pages.

Accounting for schedule-related factors constitutes another large part of the database. Information on international association competitions, qualification rounds and friendly matches are collected from www.fifa.com once before the season. The schedules of the European club competitions are taken from www.uefa.com, as well as www.kicker.de. This is updated for teams in the European competitions, i.e. the Champions League and the Europa League, on a regular basis. The Bundesliga schedule is obtained from www.transfermarkt.com and updated as soon as the exact timing is published.

Information regarding the regional economic situation is collected from www.regionalstatistik.de.[7] Previous seasons' game outcomes are constructed using match-specific information from www.football-data.co.uk. Here we collect outcomes of the previous week's matches before every game day. Additionally, we use the same source to account for previous game outcomes using information on the last 1–4 matches of each team.

Finally, we obtain pre-match betting odds from seven major bookmakers: Bet365, Bwin, Interwetten, Ladbrokes, Pinnacle, William Hill and BetVictor from www.football-data.co.uk. Odds are collected on Friday afternoon for the weekend games and Tuesday afternoon for midweek games, and include the odds for a home win, draw and away win.[8] Those are not used in the estimation but to benchmark the predictions against the bookmakers.

4.2   The 2017/18 and 2018/19 Seasons

We started using the Ordered Forest to predict the Bundesliga season 2017/18. The prediction model was estimated with the information in our database before the first match day. This model was then used to predict the expected ranking and the expected points at the end of the season as described in Section 3. Table 22.1 shows the resulting predictions and the comparison to the actual outcomes of the season. Every season produces its positive and negative surprises. For the season 2017/18, VfB Stuttgart performed unexpectedly well, with a predicted rank of 16 and a realized rank of 7. In contrast, 1. FC Köln was predicted to finish in mid-table but finished last and was unexpectedly relegated. Such differences between predicted and actual outcomes are common for football predictions because it is unrealistic to predict all developments and dynamics over a whole season.

To assess the predictive performance of the Ordered Forest, we compare the predictions of Table 22.1 with other predictions of final ranking and

Table 22.1   Comparison of predicted and actual final table of Bundesliga season 2017/18

Team	Rank		Points	
	Predicted	Actual	Predicted	Actual
FC Bayern München	1	1	74.5	84
Borussia Dortmund	2	4	64.7	55
Bayer 04 Leverkusen	3	5	54.1	55
Borussia Mönchengladbach	4	9	52.4	47
Schalke 04	5	2	52.1	63
RB Leipzig	6	6	50.0	53
TSG Hoffenheim	7	3	47.0	55
VfL Wolfsburg	8	16	46.1	33
1. FC Köln	9	18	45.2	22
Hertha BSC Berlin	10	10	43.4	43
Werder Bremen	11	11	40.5	42
FC Augsburg	12	12	40.0	41
Mainz 05	13	14	39.9	36
Eintracht Frankfurt	14	8	39.9	49
SC Freiburg	15	15	39.7	36
VfB Stuttgart	16	7	38.8	51
Hamburger SV	17	17	38.5	31
Hannover 96	18	13	37.0	39

points. To this end, we access 12 predictions from www.bstat.de, which collects forecasts from experts or algorithms before each season.[9]

We consider Spearman's rank correlation coefficient of the actual table and each prediction as performance measure for the ranks and the root mean squared error (RMSE) to assess the accuracy of the predicted points. Table 22.2 shows that the Ordered Forest is outperformed by three alternative predictions in terms of rank correlation. The expert predictions of the newspapers *General-Anzeiger* and *Spiegel Online*, as well as the algorithmic prediction of Goalimpact show larger rank correlations, which indicates that their predictions were closer to the true ranking than the one based on the Ordered Forest. However, in terms of accurately predicting the final points, the Ordered Forest performs best, showing the smallest RMSE of all available forecasts.

Section 3 described that the predictions of the final table produce probabilities for the outcomes of each match as a by-product. These predictions are updated after each match day to incorporate recent developments. In the following, we compare these predictions to the betting odds of the seven bookmakers in our database.

We evaluate the performance by using different betting strategies and calculating the hypothetical returns on investment (ROI) for each. First, we consider a *proportional strategy*. This means that we bet 1 Euro on each match and split it according to the predicted probabilities of the Ordered Forest for each outcome. For example, if the predicted probability of a

Table 22.2   Comparison of predictions for the final table of Bundesliga season 2017/18

	Rank correlation	RMSE
Ordered Forest	0.64	8.9
bundesliga-prognose.de	0.43	16.8
Club Elo	0.62	–
Euro Club Index	0.61	9.0
FiveThirtyEight	0.63	9.9
Fupro.de	0.63	11.5
fussball-manager.com	0.58	16.4
fussballmathe.de	0.63	12.1
General-Anzeiger	0.74	–
Goalimpact	0.71	9.0
kickform.de	0.61	9.4
Spiegel Online	0.75	–
transfermarkt.de	0.60	–

home win is 50 per cent, we bet 50 per cent of our hypothetical money on a home win. To see how we would earn or lose money, consider the cases where the home team actually wins and where the betting odds are 1.9, 2.0 or 2.1. In the first case we lose money because we spend 1€ and receive 1.9*0.5€ = 0.95€. Accordingly, we break even for the second case and earn if the odds are 2.1. In the latter case, the probability that is implied by the betting odds is 1/2.1 = 47.6%. This means our predicted probability of the actual outcome was higher, and we thus realize a ROI of (1.05–1)/1 = 5%. The first three columns of Table 22.3 show the ROI of this strategy for the 2017/18 season, the 2018/19 season up to the eighth match day, and both seasons combined.

The results show negative ROIs of between −3 per cent and −7 per cent for the 2017/18 season.[10] However, after the first eight matches of 2018/19 some ROIs are positive, showing up to 2.9 per cent for Pinnacle.

There are at least two explanations for the mostly negative results. First, the Ordered Forest has no access to short-term developments like injuries or other player-related information. However, this information is most likely reflected in the betting odds. Second, the betting odds include implicit fees as the implied probabilities of the three outcomes sum to more than 100 per cent. To correct for this and to get a "fair" comparison of our probabilities and the probabilities used by the bookmakers, we would need access to their probabilities. However, it is not clear how they distribute their fees over the outcomes (see for discussions e.g., Levitt (2004), Paul

Table 22.3 *Return on investment (%) of different betting strategies in different seasons*

	Odds			Odds net of fees		
	2017/18	2018/19	2017/19	2017/18	2018/19	2017/19
B365	−5.7	0.2	−4.6	−0.8	5.5	0.4
Bwin	−5.9	−0.1	−4.8	−1.0	5.0	0.2
Interwetten	−5.9	−1.1	−5.0	−0.6	4.2	0.3
Ladbrokes	−7.1	−0.7	−5.9	−1.0	5.7	0.3
Pinnacle	−3.3	2.9	−2.1	−1.1	5.6	0.2
William Hill	−6.3	−1.0	−5.3	−0.6	4.9	0.5
BetVictor	−4.9	1.3	−3.7	−1.2	5.2	0.1
Value bet	−6.9	34.5	1.0	–	–	–

Note: Results are based on the probabilities obtained by the Ordered Forest and betting odds provided by www.football-data.co.uk.

and Weinbach (2007, 2008)). For simplicity, we assume that the fees are proportionally distributed over the different outcomes and create odds that are 'net of fees' in the following way. We invert the odds of the three outcomes to get the implied probabilities; we normalize those to sum to 100 per cent, and invert the normalized probabilities again to obtain the net odds. The results in the last three columns of Table 22.3 using these net odds show two things. First, the losses in season 2017/18 are dramatically reduced to about −1 per cent and the returns after the first eight matches of season 2018/19 would be clearly positive, around 5 per cent. Second, the variation of the returns across different bookmakers is much smaller and the hypothetical returns are very similar. This implies that the differences using the unadjusted odds are mostly driven by different fees charged by the bookmakers.

This correction for fees is rather ad hoc. Thus, we implement a second betting strategy that bets only on those outcomes where our estimated probabilities exceed those that are implied by the bookmakers' odds. For example, consider again a predicted probability of a home win of 50 per cent. Even if we knew that this is the true value, we would lose money in the long run if the betting odds are below 2.[11] This could happen because the bookmakers wrongly expect a higher probability of a home win or because of the implicit fee they charge. The so-called *value bet* strategy therefore only bets on outcomes for which the predicted probabilities are larger than the probabilities implied by the odds. If this happens for several bookmakers or outcomes, we bet on the bookmaker–outcome combination with the highest ratio of our predicted probability and the bookmakers' implicit probability. The last row of Table 22.3 shows the ROIs of such a strategy, where we bet 1€ if our predicted probabilities exceed the bookmakers' implicit probabilities. The −6.9 per cent return suggests that the prediction model was not competitive in season 2017/18. However, for the first eight matches of season 2018/19 this strategy would have created a positive return of 34.5 per cent. Note that this is not the result of few lucky bets, but we bet on 71 out of 72 matches.

Section 3 describes how we use the Ordered Forest to obtain probabilities for each rank. Our database comprises no betting odds for specific ranks or competing forecasts to validate these probabilities. However, we illustrate the information obtained and how the predictions evolve during the season in Table 22.4. It aggregates the probabilities for each rank for different aspirations, such as champion (rank 1), qualification for the Champions League (rank 2–4), etc., in the current season at the time of writing, 2018/19. The left part of the table shows the probabilities before the season and the right part the most recent updates after match

Table 22.4   Probabilities (%) of achieving different season goals in Bundesliga season 2018/19

Season goals	Before season start						After match day 8					
	1	2–4	5–6	7–15	16	17–18	1	2–4	5–6	7–15	16	17–18
FC Bayern München	79	18	2				71	28				
Borussia Dortmund	6	47	19	27			21	70	6	3		
RB Leipzig	5	49	17	28			4	56	22	19		
Bayer 04 Leverkusen	4	44	19	32				19	22	55	1	2
Borussia Mönchengladbach	2	27	20	45	2	4	3	60	21	16		
Schalke 04	2	20	18	53	3	4		2	7	73	7	10
TSG Hoffenheim		20	13	55	5	7		9	18	66	3	4
VfB Stuttgart		16	15	57	4	8			6	66	11	17
Hertha BSC Berlin		11	11	61	7	11		18	24	55	1	1
Werder Bremen		8	10	62	7	13		20	27	51		
VfL Wolfsburg		8	10	63	7	11		2	7	72	7	12
FC Augsburg		7	8	62	8	15		3	8	73	7	10
Eintracht Frankfurt		5	8	65	7	15		10	17	67	2	3
Mainz 05		6	5	64	9	16	1	5		72	9	13
Hannover 96		5	8	60	10	18			3	59	11	27
SC Freiburg		4	7	58	10	21			3	64	12	20
Fortuna Düsseldorf		2	4	55	12	28				36	15	48
1. FC Nürnberg		3	5	54	9	29			2	52	13	32

Note: Probabilities below 1 per cent are not shown.

day 8.[12] Table 22.4 shows how taking into account the materialized results so far changes the probabilities over the course of the season. For example, the probability of Borussia Dortmund winning the league increased from 6 per cent before the start of the season to 21 per cent because they were currently four points ahead of Bayern München. In the opposite direction, VfB Stuttgart started as a promising candidate to qualify for the Champions League (16 per cent) or the Europa League (15 per cent). However, the bad season start reduced these chances substantially, and instead more than doubled the probability of finishing in the relegation zone.

5. CONCLUSION

In this chapter, we presented a machine learning based algorithm to predict the season outcome of sports leagues in a probabilistic fashion. As a by-product, we also obtain predictions of particular games in any round of interest. This approach was applied to the 2017/18 season to predict the match and season outcomes of the German Bundesliga 1. The fact that the target of the prediction problem is to estimate the league table at the end of the season limits the number of variables that can be updated during the season as such variables would require their own prediction models. Despite this, when comparing our game predictions to those of the betting firms, which use a much more up-to-date information set, they are surprisingly close and we can even form strategies that outperform them for the current season. In the future, it will be interesting to apply the suggested methods to other leagues and other sports.

NOTES

* We thank Alex Krumer for his invaluable contributions in the earlier stages of the Soccer Analytics project.
1. For a statistical treatment of many of these methods see Hastie et al. (2009) and James et al. (2013).
2. The few exceptions are the works of Hothorn et al. (2006) and Hornung (2020).
3. In practice this is a rather rare case, especially when the forests are estimated with honesty.
4. The R-package "orf" (Lechner and Okasa, 2020) implementing the Ordered Forest estimator can be downloaded from the CRAN repository (R Core Team, 2020). For a GAUSS version see https://www.michael-lechner.eu/statistical-software/.
5. Predictions are dynamic in the sense that the points achieved so far are also part of the covariates. If this variable is not observed (e.g. because we are predicting games for round 34 but so far only 23 rounds have been played), then the unknown points are either substituted by their expectations or their simulated values, depending on the particular method used.
6. We refer the reader to the works of Bryson et al. (2013) and Franck and Nüesch (2012) for a discussion on the reliability of the information generated by this source, as well as how well this approximates teams' abilities.
7. In more detail: for unemployment we take table code 13211-01-03-4; for GDP table code 82111-01-05-4.
8. For the full set of covariates, as well as some descriptive statistics, see the Appendix.
9. The results of SEW Soccer Analytics that are reported there were estimated with an old version of the algorithm based on Lasso prediction while the Ordered Forest was still in the test phase. However, note that all results reported here were obtained by using only the information that was available before the season.
10. Also Baboota and Kaur (2019) find that their method is slightly outperformed by the bookmakers' odds.
11. This means that we would earn 50 per cent of the time less than double our bet, which leads to an expected loss.
12. The most recent results can be found at www.sew.unisg.ch/soccer_analytics.

REFERENCES

Athey, S. (2018). The impact of machine learning on economics. In S. Athey, *The Economics of Artificial Intelligence: An Agenda* (pp. 507–547). Chicago: University of Chicago Press. doi:10.1257/jep.31.2.87.

Athey, S., Tibshirani, J., and Wager, S. (2019). Generalized random forests. *Annals of Statistics*, *47*(2), 1148–1178. doi:10.1214/18-AOS1709.

Baboota, R., and Kaur, H. (2019). Predictive analysis and modelling football results using machine learning approach for English Premier League. *International Journal of Forecasting*, *35*(2), 741–755. doi:10.1016/j.ijforecast.2018.01.003.

Biau, G., and Scornet, E. (2016). A random forest guided tour. *Test*, *25*(2), 197–227. doi:10.1007/s11749-016-0481-7.

Breiman, L. (2001). Random forests. *Machine Learning*, *45*(1), 5–32. doi:10.1023/A:1010933404324.

Breiman, L., Friedman, J.H., Olshen, R.A., and Stone, C.J. (1984). *Classification and Regression Trees*. Boca Raton, FL: Routledge. doi:10.1201/9781315139470.

Bryson, A., Frick, B., and Simmons, R. (2013). The returns to scarce talent: Footedness and player remuneration in European soccer. *Journal of Sports Economics*, *14*(6), 606–628. doi:10.1177/1527002511435118.

Fernández-Delgado, M., Cernadas, E., Barro, S., Amorim, D., and Amorim Fernández-Delgado, D. (2014). Do we need hundreds of classifiers to solve real world classification problems? *Journal of Machine Learning Research*, *15*(1), 3133–3181. doi:10.1016/j.csda.2008.10.033.

Franck, E., and Nüesch, S. (2012). Talent and/or popularity: What does it take to be a superstar? *Economic Inquiry*, *50*(1), 202–216. doi:10.1111/j.1465-7295.2010.00360.x.

Groll, A., Kneib, T., Mayr, A., and Schauberger, G. (2018). On the dependency of soccer scores: A sparse bivariate Poisson model for the UEFA European football championship 2016. *Journal of Quantitative Analysis in Sports*, *14*(2), 65–79. doi:10.1515/jqas-2017-0067.

Groll, A., Ley, C., Schauberger, G., and Van Eetvelde, H. (2018). Prediction of the FIFA World Cup 2018: A random forest approach with an emphasis on estimated team ability parameters. *arXiv preprint arXiv:1806.03208*.

Hastie, T., Tibshirani, R., and Friedman, J. (2009). *The Elements of Statistical Learning. Elements, 1*. New York: Springer. doi:10.1007/b94608.

Hornung, R. (2020). Ordinal forests. *Journal of Classification*, *37*, 4–17. doi:10.1007/s00357-018-9302-x.

Hothorn, T., Hornik, K., and Zeileis, A. (2006). Unbiased recursive partitioning: A conditional inference framework. *Journal of Computational and Graphical Statistics*, *15*(3), 651–674. doi:10.1198/106186006X133933.

James, G., Witten, D., Hastie, T., and Tibshirani, R. (2013). *An Introduction to Statistical Learning: With Applications in R*. New York: Springer.

Lechner, M., and Okasa, G. (2019). Random forest estimation of the ordered choice model. *arXiv preprint arXiv:1907.02436*, 1–75.

Lechner, M., and Okasa, G. (2020). orf: Ordered Random Forests. *R package version 0.1.3*.

Leitner, C., Zeileis, A., and Hornik, K. (2010). Forecasting sports tournaments by ratings of (prob)abilities: A comparison for the EURO 2008. *International Journal of Forecasting*, *26*(3), 471–481. doi:10.1016/j.ijforecast.2009.10.001.

Levitt, S. (2004). Why are gambling markets organised so differently from financial markets? *Economic Journal*, *114*, 223–246. doi:10.1111/j.1468-0297.2004.00207.x.

Nakamura, L., Cerqueira, P., Ramires, T., Pescim, R., Rigby, R., and Stasinopoulos, D. (2019). A new continuous distribution on the unit interval applied to modelling the points ratio of football teams. *Journal of Applied Statistics*, *46*(3), 416–431. doi:10.1080/02664763.2018.1495699.

Paul, R.J., and Weinbach, A.P. (2007). Does Sportsbook.com set pointspreads to maximize profits? Tests of the Levitt model of sportsbook behavior. *Journal of Prediction Markets*, *1*(3), 209–218. doi:10.5750/JPM.V1I3.429.

Paul, R., and Weinbach, A. (2008). Price setting in the nba gambling market: Tests of the Levitt model of sportsbook behavior. *International Journal of Sport Finance*, *3*(3), 1–137.

R Core Team. (2020). R: A language and environment for statistical computing. R Foundation for Statistical Computing. Vienna, Austria. Retrieved from https://www.R-project.org/.

Wager, S., and Athey, S. (2018). Estimation and inference of heterogeneous treatment effects using random forests. *Journal of the American Statistical Association*, *113*(523), 1228–1242. doi:10.1080/01621459.2017.1319839.

Wooldridge, J. (2010). *Econometric Analysis of Cross Section and Panel Data*. Cambridge, MA: MIT Press.

DATA APPENDIX

As mentioned in Section 4.1 we collected player and team characteristics as well as match, schedule, location-related and regional economic information.

The first set of variables is previous seasons' outcomes. We collected the average numbers of shots, shots on target, fouls committed, corners, yellow and red cards, final points and attendance, as well as share of capacity of each team in the previous season. The resulting variables are marked as "home" if they concern the home team, "away" for the away team and "home–away" if the numbers are the difference between the home and the away team.

The database contains several previous game outcomes. We constructed variables with mean points in the last 1–4 matches for each team, as well as the difference between the teams. As an example, *PG points last 3 matches/ home* captures the mean points that the home team earned in the last three matches. Further, there are variables such as *PG points share of total/away*, with the share of all potential points gained by the away team from the start of the season.

Location-related factors are captured with a variable that accounts for the capacity of the home stadium as well as the shortest distance (in km) between the home cities of the competing teams and the travelling time for the shortest route (in minutes).

To capture potential schedule-related effects we created a set of indicators for the season (constructed as 07 = 2007/08, ..., 17 = 2017/18), day of the week (where 1 = Monday, 2 = Tuesday, ..., 7 = Sunday) or round. *Weekend home advantage* indicates whether the home team is playing at home on Friday, Saturday or Sunday.

If there was an international game day involving friendly or qualification matches of the national teams the dummy variable *After International Break* is equal to 1, and 0 otherwise. For matches that were not held according to the schedule the variable *Delayed match* is used. *Short week* denotes one in which there is a midweek match in addition to the usual weekend matches, while *Weekend after midweek round* indicates those weekends separately.

Seasons after a European or World Championship are denoted by the variable *World Cup/European Championship season*, with two separate dummy variables for the two months before and after those events. A season that includes the African Cup of Nations is indicated by *African cup season*, and the specific months in which the cup took place by *African cup months*. Further, *already champion/home–away* and *already relegated/home–away* are 0 if neither (or both) teams are already champion/relegated, 1 if the home team and −1 if the away team. Teams are "already champion" or "already relegated" if no theoretical chance remains that the outcome of the season will be different.

The variables *before/after European match* indicate whether the home/ away team that played the days before has to play another match in a European competition in the following days. *Round * begin/mid/end* indicate the beginning, middle and end of the season, with the respective rounds in brackets.

Teams promoted the preceding year from the second division are for example denoted by the *promoted/away* variable. The variable *market value* carries information on the market values of the teams, as well as values standardized by season. *TV revenue* is the national revenue from sales of the broadcasting rights.

Further, there are variables constructed from information on team composition. Those are the (normalized) Herfindahl–Hirschman index, (d) HHI, which is defined as the sum of squares of the shares of the market value of each player within the team. There are also variables capturing within-team inequality, measured as the ratio of the Top 3 (11) most valuable players to the market value of those ranked 12–14 (12–21). *New coach* is defined as 1 if the team got a new coach after the start of the season.

Team diversity is represented by several age-related variables, such as minimum, maximum or standard deviation of age, and the share of left-footed or two-footed players, as well as variables regarding the height of the players in the squad or the 11 most valuable players.

Moreover, *traditional club* is a selection of clubs with a history, such as Borussia Dortmund or VfB Stuttgart; *yo-yo club* is one that is often relegated and/or promoted; and *other clubs* are those which are neither traditional nor yo-yo clubs.

Finally, two regional economic variables capture the economic situation in the form of the log of GDP per capita in the team's city, as well as unemployment.

Table 22A.1   Descriptive statistics

Variables	Reference	Unit	Mean (Std. dev.)	Update
Previous season (PS) outcomes				
PS shots	home	numerical	14.70 (2.31)	yearly
PS shots difference	home–away	numerical	2.71 (2.90)	yearly
PS shots on target	home	numerical	5.65 (1.50)	yearly
PS shots on target difference	home–away	numerical	1.10 (1.46)	yearly

Table 22A.1 (continued)

Variables	Reference	Unit	Mean (Std. dev.)	Update
PS fouls	home	numerical	15.66 (2.11)	yearly
PS fouls difference	home–away	numerical	−1.23 (2.48)	yearly
PS corners	home	numerical	5.63 (1.08)	yearly
PS corners difference	home–away	numerical	1.23 (1.30)	yearly
PS yellow cards	home	numerical	1.62 (0.36)	yearly
PS yellow cards difference	home–away	numerical	−0.34 (0.50)	yearly
PS red cards	home	numerical	0.07 (0.06)	yearly
PS red cards difference	home–away	numerical	−0.03 (0.10)	yearly
PS points	home	numerical	1.70 (0.43)	yearly
PS points difference	home–away	numerical	0.50 (0.60)	yearly
PS attendance	home	numerical	43837 (15424)	yearly
PS attendance difference	home–away	numerical	1336 (15499)	yearly
PS share of capacity	home	percentage	0.92 (0.08)	yearly
PS share of capacity difference	home–away	percentage	0.001 (0.08)	yearly
Location related				
Public transport time between cities		minutes	197.58 (91.76)	once
Distance between cities		kilometre	373.37 (185.98)	once
Home stadium capacity		discrete	46813 (17550)	match
Previous game (PG) outcomes				
PG points last match	home	numerical	1.18 (1.26)	match
PG points last 2 matches	home	numerical	1.35 (0.92)	match
PG points last 3 matches	home	numerical	1.32 (0.76)	match
PG points last 4 matches	home	numerical	1.36 (0.69)	match
PG points share of total	home	percentage	0.45 (0.19)	match
PG points last match	away	numerical	1.58 (1.31)	match
PG points last 2 matches	away	numerical	1.40 (0.93)	match

Table 22A.1   (continued)

Variables	Reference	Unit	Mean (Std. dev.)	Update
PG points last 3 matches	away	numerical	1.43 (0.79)	match
PG points last 4 matches	away	numerical	1.39 (0.69)	match
PG points share of total	away	percentage	0.46 (0.19)	match
PG points last match difference	home–away	numerical	−0.40 (1.83)	match
PG points last 2 matches difference	home–away	numerical	−0.05 (1.30)	match
PG points last 3 matches difference	home–away	numerical	−0.11 (1.08)	match
PG points last 4 matches difference	home–away	numerical	−0.04 (0.96)	match
PG points share of total difference	home–away	percentage	−0.01 (0.27)	match
Schedule related				
Season id		categorical	12.00 (3.16)	yearly
Weekday		categorical	5.91 (1.00)	match
Weekend home advantage		dummy	0.47	match
Round		categorical	17.50 (9.81)	yearly
After international break		dummy	0.10	match
Delayed match		dummy	0.002	match
Short week		dummy	0.10	match
Weekend after midweek round		dummy	0.05	match
World Cup/European Championship season		dummy	0.45	yearly
African cup season		dummy	0.55	yearly
African cup months		dummy	0.09	yearly
Post-World Cup/ European Championship		dummy	0.08	yearly
Pre-World cup/ European Championship		dummy	0.11	yearly
Already champion difference	home–away	categorical	0.001 (0.10)	match

Table 22A.1   (continued)

Variables	Reference	Unit	Mean (Std. dev.)	Update
Already relegated difference	home–away	categorical	−0.001 (0.07)	match
Before European match	home	dummy	0.10	match
Before European match	away	dummy	0.10	match
After European match	home	dummy	0.10	match
After European match	away	dummy	0.10	match
Round * begin (matches 1–11)		categorical	1.94 (3.33)	yearly
Round * mid (matches 12–22)		categorical	5.50 (8.16)	yearly
Round * end (matches 23–34)		categorical	10.06 (13.78)	yearly
Team characteristics				
Promoted	home	dummy	0.13	yearly
Promoted	away	dummy	0.13	yearly
Promoted difference	home–away	categorical	0 (0.49)	yearly
Market value	home	EURO	112329501 (102768312)	regular
Market value difference	home–away	EURO	22825 (144964414)	regular
Standardized market value	home	–	0 (1.00)	regular
Standardized market value difference	home–away	–	0.0002 (1.45)	regular
Market value share	home, away	ratio	1.60 (1.94)	regular
TV revenue	home	EURO	24216389 (9618865)	yearly
TV revenue difference	home–away	EURO	0 (7764625)	yearly
Market value/TV revenue	home	EURO	4.44 (2.82)	regular
Market value/TV revenue difference	home–away	EURO	0.001 (3.99)	regular
Market value – TV revenue	home	EURO	88113112 (97807758)	regular
Market value – TV revenue difference	home–away	EURO	22825 (139769918)	regular

Table 22A.1   (continued)

Variables	Reference	Unit	Mean (Std. dev.)	Update
HHI	home	ratio	0.06 (0.01)	regular
HHI difference	home–away	ratio	−0.000001 (0.02)	regular
dHHI	home	ratio	0.03 (0.01)	regular
dHHI difference	home–away	ratio	0.000004 (0.01)	regular
Average market value	home	EURO	3757742 (3783521)	regular
Std. dev. market value	home	std. dev.	3607418 (3635022)	regular
Ratio of Top 3 to ranked 12–14 players' market value	home	ratio	3.07 (0.94)	regular
Ratio of Top 11 to ranked 12–21 players' market value	home	ratio	2.99 (0.85)	regular
Average market value difference	home–away	EURO	−49.62 (5301092)	regular
Std. dev. market value difference	home–away		1843 (5126814)	regular
Ratio of Top 3 to ranked 12–14 players' market value difference	home–away	ratio	0.0001 (1.34)	regular
Ratio of Top 11 to ranked 12–21 players' market value difference	home–away	ratio	0.001 (1.21)	regular
New coach	home	dummy	0.18	match
New coach difference	home–away	categorical	0.0003 (0.52)	match
Age mean difference	home–away	numerical	−0.001 (1.21)	regular
Age std. dev. difference	home–away	std. dev.	0.0002 (0.72)	regular
Age 11 most valuable players difference	home–away	numerical	0.001 (1.48)	regular
Age ratio of Top 11 to ranked 12–21 difference	home–away	numerical	0.0002 (0.09)	regular
Age of those above 20 difference	home–away	numerical	0.0003 (1.12)	regular

Table 22A.1 *(continued)*

Variables	Reference	Unit	Mean (Std. dev.)	Update
Minimum age in the squad difference	home–away	categorical	−0.001 (1.20)	regular
Maximum age in the squad difference	home–away	categorical	−0.01 (2.89)	regular
Share left-footed players difference	home–away	percentage	0 (0.08)	regular
Share two-footed players difference	home–away	percentage	0 (0.08)	regular
Share left-footed players among 11 most valuable players difference	home–away	percentage	0 (0.16)	regular
Share two-footed players among 11 most valuable players difference	home–away	percentage	0 (0.12)	regular
Mean height difference	home–away	numerical	0 (1.51)	regular
Std. dev. height difference	home–away	std. dev.	0 (1.03)	regular
Mean height Top 11 difference	home–away	numerical	0 (2.32)	regular
Std. dev. height Top 11 difference	home–away	std. dev.	0 (1.92)	regular
Traditional club	home	categorical	11.69 (13.45)	once
Yo-yo club	home	categorical	6.45 (9.38)	once
Other clubs	home	categorical	1.27 (4.75)	once
Traditional club	away	categorical	11.69 (13.45)	once
Yo-yo club	away	categorical	6.45 (9.38)	once
Other clubs	away	categorical	1.27 (4.75)	once
Regional Economic Indicators				
Log GDP per capita difference	home–away	EURO	0 (0.25)	yearly
Unemployment difference	home–away	percentage	0 (5.15)	yearly

Notes: Standard deviation is reported in parentheses and not reported for dummy variables.
Updates which are indicated as *regular* are updated at least three times each season, i.e. before the season starts and after the transfer window closed in summer and winter, but as soon as there are major changes. Update category *match* points to updates in this variable before each new match day.

Index